CONCEPTS AND UNDERSTANDING
The Educational Research Council
Social Science Program

THE GROWTH OF CIVILIZATION

*Prepared by the Social Science Staff of the
Educational Research Council of America*

ALLYN AND BACON, INC.

Boston   Rockleigh, N.J.   Atlanta   Dallas   San Jose
London   Sydney   Toronto

This book was prepared by the following members of the social science staff of the Educational Research Council of America:

Nancy Bostick, Marilyn McLaughlin, Elaine Wrisley Reed,
Mary Ritley, Judith Wentz, Marlene Zweig

Marie M. Richards, Coordinator K-6   Agnes M. Michnay, Editor in Chief

Directing and Consulting Staff of the Educational Research Council of America Social Science Program

George H. Baird	President and Executive Director, ERCA
Duane J. Mattheis	Associate Director, ERCA
L. Romanos (deceased)	Associate Director, ERCA
Russell Kirk	Director of Social Science Program and Consultant in Philosophy

Consultants

Phillip H. Bacon	Geography
Harold F. Clark	Economics
Raymond English	Political Science
William H. McNeill	World History
James M. McPherson	U.S. History
Ralph H. Ojemann (deceased)	Psychology

This book is dedicated to the memory of Charles Rieley ("Chuck") Armington in the hope that students will develop the individual initiative and active concern for others that marked the life and spirit of Chuck.

As the present edition evolved from early experimental versions and two successive nationally distributed editions, suggestions and feedback came from thousands of teachers, students, and parents in many parts of the United States and in American schools abroad. For these helpful inputs the Educational Research Council of America is most grateful.

Production and Illustration   Bookmakers, Inc.
Cover photos: Color photo   Stock, Boston, Inc./Owen Franken
                  Black and white photo   French Government Tourist Office

Publisher's Staff

Editor	Richard Foster
Design Coordinator	Beverly Fell
Photo Researcher	Mary Ruzila
Preparation Services Coordinator	Martha E. Ballentine
Buyer	Linda Jackson
Cover Designer	L. Christopher Valente
Cover Photo Researcher	Mary Ruzila

© Copyright 1982 by the Educational Research Council of America. All rights reserved. No part of the material protected by this copyright notice may be reproduced or utilized in any form or by any means without written permission from Allyn and Bacon, Inc.

Printed in the United States of America

ISBN 0-205-06795-6

Library of Congress Catalog Card Number 80-69410

1 2 3 4 5 6 7 8 9 90 89 88 87 86 85 84 83 82 81

Contents

Preface	History and Ourselves	1
Chapter 1	Locating Ourselves in Time	5
Chapter 2	Locating Ourselves on the Earth	25
Chapter 3	The Great Leap Forward	39
Chapter 4	Discovering the Earliest Civilization: Sumer	71
Chapter 5	The Civilized Culture of Sumer	89
Chapter 6	The Rise and Fall and Spread of Civilization	121
Chapter 7	Some World Views at the End of Ancient History	149
Chapter 8	The Classical Civilization of Greece	189
Chapter 9	The Roman Republic and Empire	231
Chapter 10	Islam and the Arab Empire	271
Chapter 11	Civilizations of Africa	295
Chapter 12	Civilizations in the New World	325
Chapter 13	Civilizations and Barbarians in Asia in the Middle Ages	343
Chapter 14	The Rise of Latin Christendom	369
Chapter 15	Latin Christendom in the High Middle Ages	389
Chapter 16	The Modern Age Begins	419
Conclusion	Lessons of History	459
Glossary		472
Index		480
Acknowledgments		488

Maps

The Earth's Rotation	9
The Earth's Rotation and Revolution	10
The Moving Shadow of the Earth	13
Daytime and Nighttime If the Earth's Axis Were Not Tilted	14
Meridians of Longitude	16
Standard Time Zones	18
Parallels of Latitude	28
Global Grid	29
Measuring a Circle and Measuring Angles	30
The Earth's Tilt and the Important Latitudes	31
The Earth's Tilt and the Seasons in the Northern Hemisphere	32
Part of the Middle East, a Locator Map	34
Grid Map of Part of the Middle East	35
How Racial Differences Probably Came About	49
The Middle East Showing Mesopotamia	55
Physical Features of Mesopotamia	58
Rainfall of Mesopotamia	60
Sumerian Cities	82
Hammurabi's Empire	127
Three Earliest Civilizations	128
Civilization Spreads to Rain-Watered Lands	137
The Persian Empire in 525 B.C.	140
China in the Sixth Century B.C.	155
Palestine in the Ancient Middle East c. 2000 B.C.	175
The Divided Kingdom, 931 B.C.	180
Some Civilized Cultures c. 500 B.C.–A.D. 100	191
Physical Features of Greece	193

Some Greek City-States, Fifth Century B.C.	209
The Athenian Empire c. 450 B.C.	221
Conquests of Alexander the Great	227
Ancient Italy and Its Physical Features	233
Mediterranean World c. 264 B.C.	246
Empire of Augustus, A.D. 14	257
Palestine at the Time of Jesus	258
The Muslim World Today	273
Annual Rainfall of the Arabian Peninsula	274
The Arab Empire, A.D. 632–732	281
Climate and Vegetation Regions of Africa	297
The Nile Valley in Ancient Times	299
African Kingdoms, A.D. 700–1600	305
Wind Patterns of the Earth	328
The Main Ocean Currents	329
Mayan and Aztec Lands	332
Physical Features of Japan	345
The Steppes of Asia	359
The Mongol Empire in the Time of Kublai Khan (1259–1294)	363
Christendom and Islam c. A.D. 1200	371
Waterways, Mountains, and Some Trading Cities of Western Europe	427
Some Early European Explorations	431
Nation-States of Europe c. 1500, at the Beginning of the Modern Period	440
Important European Colonies and Trading Posts Set Up between 1470 and 1652	445
Religion in Europe after the Reformation (c. 1648)	452

Pronunciation Key

Many words in this book are respelled to help you pronounce them. The pronunciation of each word is shown in brackets just after the word. Two levels of stress are shown. A strong or primary stress is marked with a bold mark (′) as in **abbreviate** [ə brē′ vē āt]. A lighter or secondary stress is marked with a lighter mark (′) as in **abbreviation** [ə brē′ vē ā′ shən]. The key below will help you to read the respellings.

a	hat, cap	i	it, pin	p	paper, cut	v	very, save
ā	age, face	ī	ice, live	r	run, try	w	will, woman
ä	father, far			s	say, yes	y	young, yet
		j	jam, enjoy	sh	she, rush	z	zero, breeze
b	bad, rob	k	kind, seek	t	tell, it	zh	measure, seizure
ch	child, much	l	land, coal	th	thin, both		
d	did, red	m	me, am	ᴛʜ	then, smooth	ə	represents:
		n	no, in				a in about
e	let, best	ng	long, bring	u	cup, butter		e in taken
ē	equal, be			u̇	full, put		i in pencil
ėr	term, learn	o	hot, rock	ü	rule, move		o in lemon
		ō	open, go				u in circus
f	fat, if	ô	order, all				
g	go, bag	oi	oil, voice				
h	he, how	ou	house, out				

The Pronunciation Key is from *Thorndike-Barnhart Intermediate Dictionary* by E. L. Thorndike and Clarence L. Barnhart. Copyright © 1974 by Scott, Foresman and Company. Reprinted by permission.

Notes to Students

This book is about human societies. It tells how early people lived. At first people had to search for food. Then they learned to produce their own food. This change was a great leap forward for human societies. It led to a new way of living called *civilization*.

Social science is knowledge that helps you to understand human societies. It helps you to work out things for yourself. This social science book will help you to find out things for yourself and to use the things you already know. Think about the problems and questions as you read. They are marked ▶, ●, and ★. Here is what the symbols mean:

▶   You should be able to give the right answer. The answer may come from the book. Or it may be something you know quite well.

●   You will have to explain the answer. You may have to discuss it. Some of these questions do not have one "right" answer.

★   You will have to do something extra to find the answer. You may have to look it up. You may have to ask questions at home. You may have to look around in your community.

Over the centuries humans have developed new and better ways of performing the same tasks. In agriculture, for example, mechanized equipment *(above)* has in most parts of the world replaced traditional methods *(below)*. New inventions and technical advances have greatly changed peoples' ways of life.

PREFACE

History and Ourselves

This book tells the story of our ancestors up to about the time that English settlers came to North America in the seventeenth century. All of us who read this book are reading about our families. We are reading about our *roots* in the past. The study of the past is called **history.**

We learn about history through the work of *scholars* [skol′ ərz]. A **scholar** is a learned person—especially a person who knows a great deal about a certain subject. Some scholars know a great deal about history. They are called *historians*. **Historians** learn about the past by studying written records. They write about what they have learned so that others can study the past too.

As we go back in time, we find that we have more and more *relatives*. We share the same ancestors. That is why we can think of all other human beings as our brothers and sisters. The human race is one *species* [spē′ shēz]. A **species** is a group of creatures who are alike. Members of a species are so alike that any female and male can join together to have babies.

For about 50,000 years, all humans have been people like us. We call our species "modern man," or *Homo sapiens.* "Man" in this sense means all humans, male and female. *Homo sapiens* is Latin for "wise human." We call ourselves wise because we can *think.* Because we can think, we can *invent* things. We invented tools. We discovered new ways to get food. We built towns. Thus the ways of human living changed quite fast.

The most important human invention may have been *language.* With language, humans could tell their children about their ideas. So old and new ideas were passed on through the years.

Because we are human, we share the ideas and inventions of our ancestors. We *add* to those ideas and inventions. We build on the work of our ancestors, which is what makes history important.

History tells us how we came to be the way we are. History tells us, too, about problems that humans have had. We still have problems today. And it looks as if we always shall have problems.

What big problems have come up in history again and again? How have humans dealt with those problems? History gives us answers to those questions. Without history, we would be like people who have lost their memories. We would not know about what our ancestors did and learned. We would have to discover for ourselves all the things our ancestors discovered.

Humans have always known a bit of history. Long ago, parents told their children what they remembered about the past. They told **legends**, or stories, that *their* parents had told them. Often, however, they knew very little of the past.

Today we can know much more history than anyone knew in the past. That is because we have scholars who have discovered things that had been forgotten for thousands of years. Some of the things in this book were not known until a few years ago.

We cannot read about *all* history in one book. We can look at some of the most interesting things. In this book, we shall read about the things that seem especially important for us today.

Oral folk tradition has helped to keep alive the legends of long ago. Here an Ivory Coast (Africa) elder relates some tribal legends to village boys.

HISTORY AND OURSELVES 3

CHAPTER 1

Locating Ourselves in Time

At every point in history we need to know where we are in *time*. Are we talking about time 100 years ago or 1,000 years ago or 6,000 years ago? (We will also need to know where we are in *space*. Are we in India or China or the United States or where?)

To locate ourselves in time, we must know how time is measured. Time is measured by the movement of the earth. The earth is our biggest clock!

First, let us read a story about a world where time is not like our time.

Time in a Looking Glass World

This story is from *Through the Looking Glass.* Alice goes through a looking glass, or mirror, into a topsy-turvy world. Alice was used to a world of order. She found the other world strange indeed. Even telling time was changed.

In this story Alice is talking with the White Queen. The Queen wants Alice to be her maid. She offers to pay Alice two pennies a week and to give her jam every *other* day.

An Adventure Through the Looking Glass

Alice couldn't help laughing as she said, "I don't want you to hire *me*—and I don't care for jam."

"It's very good jam," said the Queen.

Well, I don't want any *today,* at any rate."

"You couldn't have it if you *did* want it," the Queen said. "The rule is, jam tomorrow and jam yesterday—but never jam *today*."

"It *must* come sometimes to 'jam today,'" Alice objected.

"No, it can't," said the Queen. "It's jam every *other* day: today isn't any *other* day, you know."

"I don't understand you," said Alice. "It's dreadfully confusing!"

"That's the effect of living backwards," the Queen said kindly: "it always makes one a little giddy at first—"

"Living backwards!" Alice repeated in great astonishment. "I never heard of such a thing!"

"—but there's one great advantage in it—that one's memory works both ways."

"I'm sure *mine* only works one way," Alice remarked. "I can't remember things before they happen."

"It's a poor sort of memory that only works backwards," the Queen remarked.

"What sort of things do *you* remember best?" Alice ventured to ask.

"Oh, things that happen the week after next," the Queen replied in a careless tone. "For instance, now," she went on, sticking a large piece of plaster on her finger as she spoke, "there's the King's Messenger. He's in prison now, being punished: and the trial doesn't even begin till next Wednesday: and of course the crime comes last of all."

"Suppose he never commits the crime?" said Alice.

"That would be all the better, wouldn't it?" the Queen said, as she bound the plaster round her finger with a bit of ribbon.

Alice felt there was no denying *that*. "Of course it would be all the better," she said: "but it wouldn't be all the better his being punished."

"You're wrong *there,* at any rate," said the Queen. "Were *you* ever punished?"

"Only for faults," said Alice.

"And you were all the better for it, I know!" the Queen said triumphantly.

"Yes, but then I *had* done the things I was punished for," said Alice: "that makes all the difference."

In this John Tenniel illustration from Lewis Carroll's *Through the Looking Glass,* Alice carefully brushes and dresses the Queen's hair.

Then Alice remarks to the Queen: "Come, you look rather better now! But really you should have a lady's maid!"

The Queen replies: "I'm sure I'll take *you* with pleasure! Twopence a week, and jam every other day."

The text at the top of page 6 continues the story.

"But if you *hadn't* done them," the Queen said, "that would have been better still; better, and better, and better!" Her voice went higher with each "better," till it got quite to a squeak at last.

Alice was just beginning to say "There's a mistake somewhere—" when the Queen began screaming so loud that she had to leave the sentence unfinished. "Oh, oh, oh!" shouted the Queen, shaking her hand about as if she wanted to shake it off. "My finger's bleeding! Oh, oh, oh, oh!"

Her screams were so exactly like the whistle of a steam engine that Alice had to hold both her hands over her ears.

"What *is* the matter?" she said, as soon as there was a chance of making herself heard. "Have you pricked your finger?"

"I haven't pricked it *yet,*" the Queen said, "but I soon shall—oh, oh, oh!"

"When do you expect to do it?" Alice asked, feeling very much inclined to laugh.

"When I fasten my shawl again," the poor Queen groaned out, "the brooch will come undone directly. Oh, oh!" As she said the words the

LOCATING OURSELVES IN TIME

brooch flew open, and the Queen clutched wildly at it, and tried to clasp it again.

"Take care!" cried Alice. "You're holding it all crooked!" And she caught at the brooch; but it was too late. The pin had slipped, and the Queen had pricked her finger.

"That accounts for the bleeding, you see," she said to Alice with a smile. "Now you understand the way things happen here."

"But why don't you scream *now*?" Alice asked, holding her hands ready to put over her ears again.

"Why, I've done all the screaming already," said the Queen. "What would be the good of having it all over again?"

A ● Why was Alice mixed up? Explain her problem in your own words. Have you ever been mixed up in the same way? When? What happened?

B ● How do things look when you see them in a mirror or a looking glass? After Alice went through the looking glass, what did she learn about time in the topsy-turvy world?

Time and the Earth's Rotation and Revolution

In our real world, time goes forward. It goes forward at a never-changing speed. Sometimes time *seems* to pass quickly. Sometimes it *seems* to pass slowly. But time always goes by at the same speed. That is because our big clock, the earth, never changes its speed.

On most clocks, the hands go around. One hand tells seconds. One tells minutes. One tells the hours.

The earth goes around, too. The earth spins around on its *axis*. The **axis** is an imaginary line through the center of the earth from the North Pole to the South Pole. Another word for "spin" is *rotate*. So we can say that the earth *rotates* on its axis. One complete **rotation** takes 24 hours, or one day. Let us say that the earth has rotated on its axis seven times. Seven rotations make seven days. We call seven days a *week*.

The earth also goes around the sun. We say it *revolves* around the sun. One complete **revolution** takes 365 ¼ days. We call this a *year*.

8   THE GROWTH OF CIVILIZATION

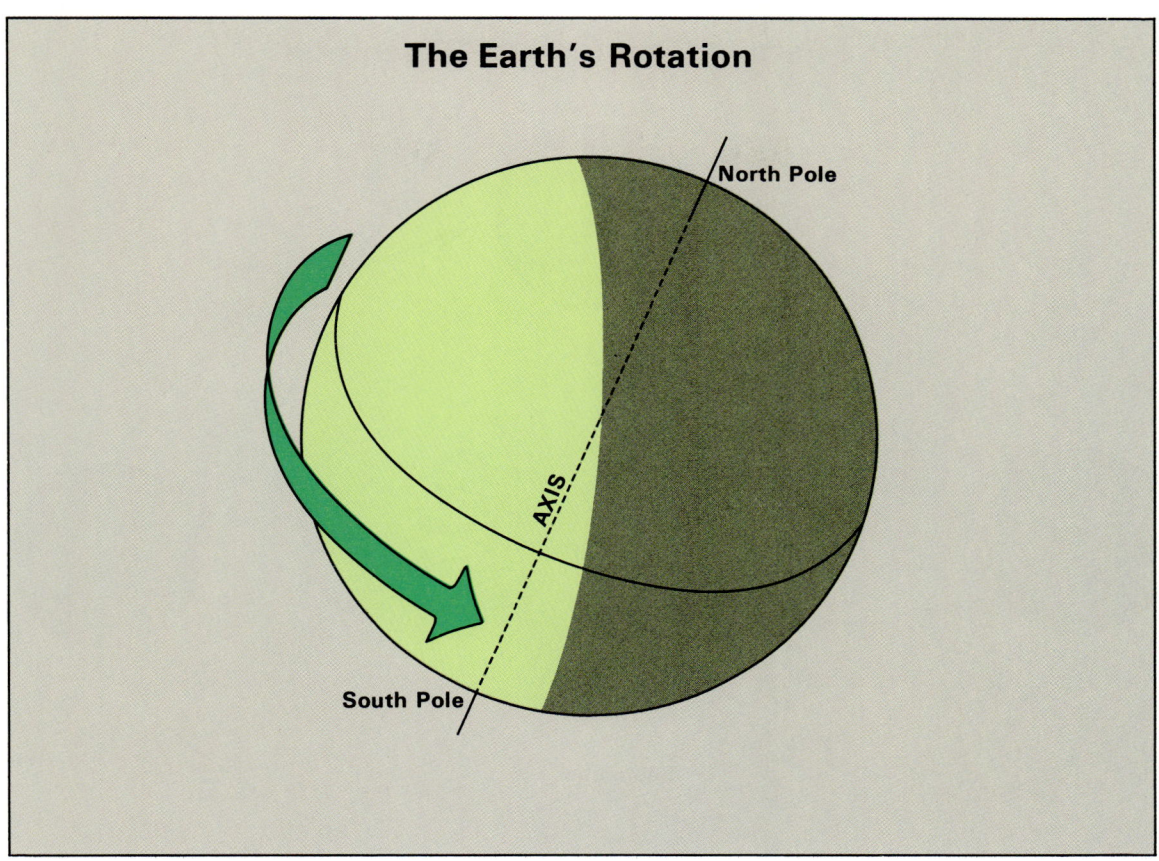

Think of the earth's axis as an imaginary line. The line goes through the earth from the North Pole to the South Pole.

A ▶ Look at the diagram "The Earth's Rotation" above.
1. What is the axis of the earth? What are the ends of the axis?
2. In which direction does the earth rotate—west to east or east to west?
3. How long does one rotation take?
4. How many hours are in a day?

B ▶ Look at the diagram "The Earth's Rotation and Revolution" (page 10).
1. Which arrows show rotation? Which arrows show revolution?
2. How long does a complete revolution take?
3. What causes nighttime and daytime?
4. What causes sunrise and sunset? In which direction does the sun "rise"? In which direction does the sun "set"?

LOCATING OURSELVES IN TIME 9

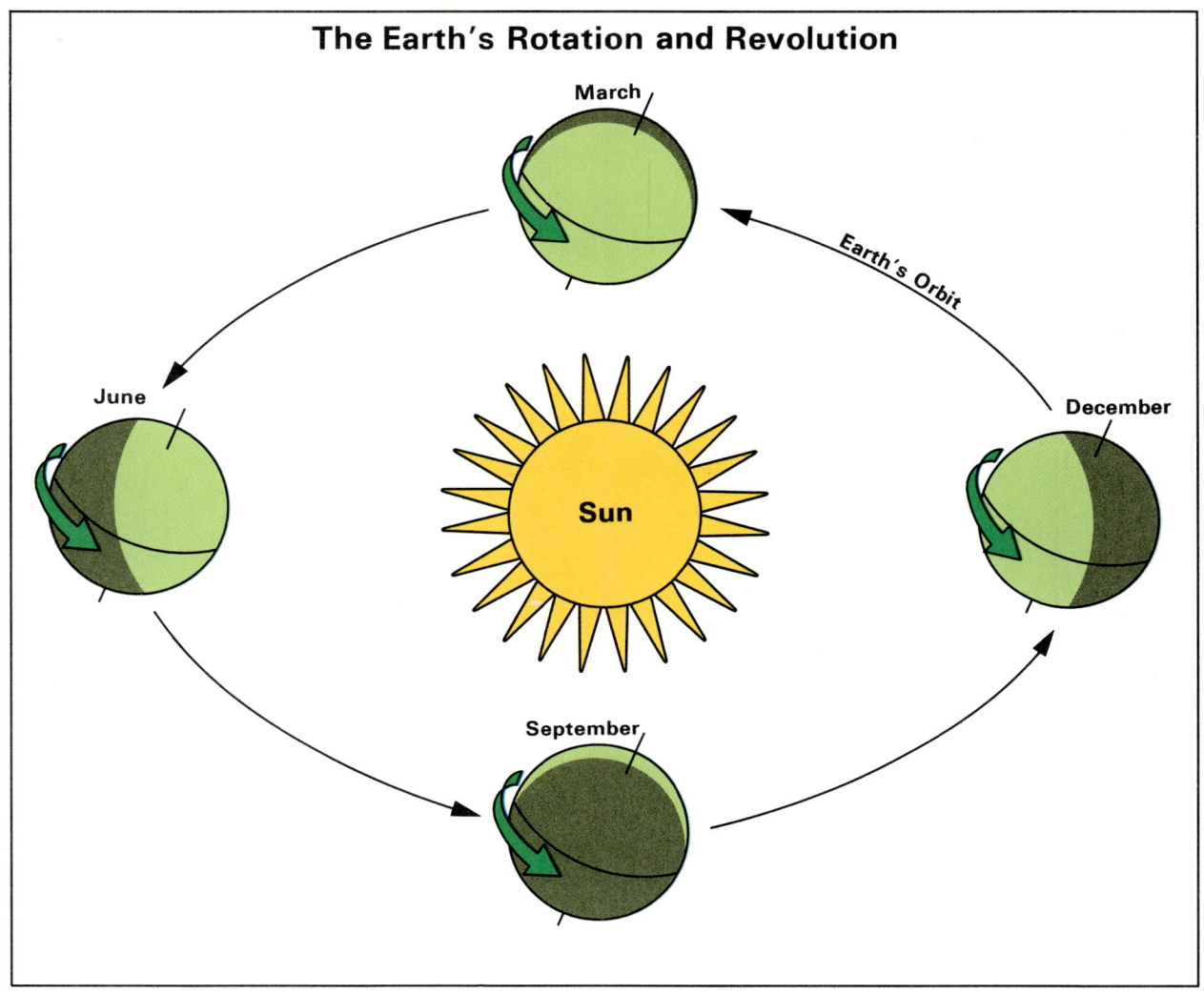

Suppose the earth has revolved around the sun ten times. Ten revolutions equal ten years. We call *ten years* a **decade.** Now suppose the earth has revolved around the sun 100 times. That equals 100 years, and we call *100 years* a **century.** Let us say that the earth has revolved around the sun 1,000 times.. That equals 1,000 years. We call *1,000 years* a **millennium.**

C▶ How many years are there in seven and one-half centuries?
D▶ The plural of millennium is *millennia.* How many years are there in six millennia?
E● *Homo sapiens* has been on the earth for perhaps 50,000 years. How many millennia is that length of time?

10   THE GROWTH OF CIVILIZATION

Using rotation and revolution, humans have worked out time measurements. We divide the day into hours, minutes, and seconds. We divide the year into months, weeks, and days.

Time Measurements

1 rotation	= 1 day (or day and night)
1 revolution	= 365¼ days
	365 days = 1 ordinary year
	366 days = 1 leap year
1 day	= 24 hours
1 hour	= 60 minutes
1 minute	= 60 seconds
1 year	= 12 calendar months or about 52 weeks (or about 365 days)
1 decade	= 10 years
1 century	= 100 years
1 millennium	= 1,000 years

F▶ Look at the box "Time Measurements" above. Make sure you know how days and years are divided. How many years are in a decade? In a century? In a millennium?

G★ What is a *leap year*? Why do we have leap years?

People use watches and clocks to help them keep track of time each day. They use calendars to keep track of days, weeks, months, and years.

H▶ Look at the box "Keeping Track of Time" (page 12).
  1. How many days are there in July? In August? In November?
  2. What month gets an extra day in leap year?
  3. What years will be leap years from 1984 through 1994?

As the earth rotates, the sun seems to rise along different parts of the earth's surface. When the sun is appearing ("rising") at one place, it will be disappearing ("setting") at another place. When the sun is highest in the sky at a place, the time at that place is 12 o'clock *noon.* On the opposite side of the earth, the time is 12 o'clock *midnight.*

LOCATING OURSELVES IN TIME

Keeping Track of Time

The Calendar

The calendar months have different numbers of days. Most of us remember the number of days in each month by remembering an old rhyme:

> Thirty days hath September,
> April, June, and November.
> All the rest have 31,
> Except February alone,
> Which has 28 days clear,
> And 29 in each leap year.

How To Find Leap Years

If the number of the year can be exactly divided by four, it is a leap year. For example. 1988 ÷ 4 = 497. Therefore, 1988 is a leap year. However, if the year is at the *end of a century* (1700, 1800, 1900, or 2000), the number of the year must be divisible evenly by 400. Thus of the four end-of-century years given, only 2000 is a leap year.

▶ Look at the diagram "The Moving Shadow of the Earth" (page 13).
1. Where is the sun?
2. Which side of the earth is in shadow?
3. With your finger, trace the *terminator* on the diagram. What do you think the terminator line is?
4. Point A is a place on the equator. How will the sun look from A? Will it be "setting" or "rising"?
5. Suppose three or four hours pass. Will it be daytime or nighttime at point A? Explain.
6. Now look at point B in the diagram. Is it morning or afternoon at point B?
7. Suppose three or four hours pass. Will it be sunrise or sunset at point B?

---

12   THE GROWTH OF CIVILIZATION

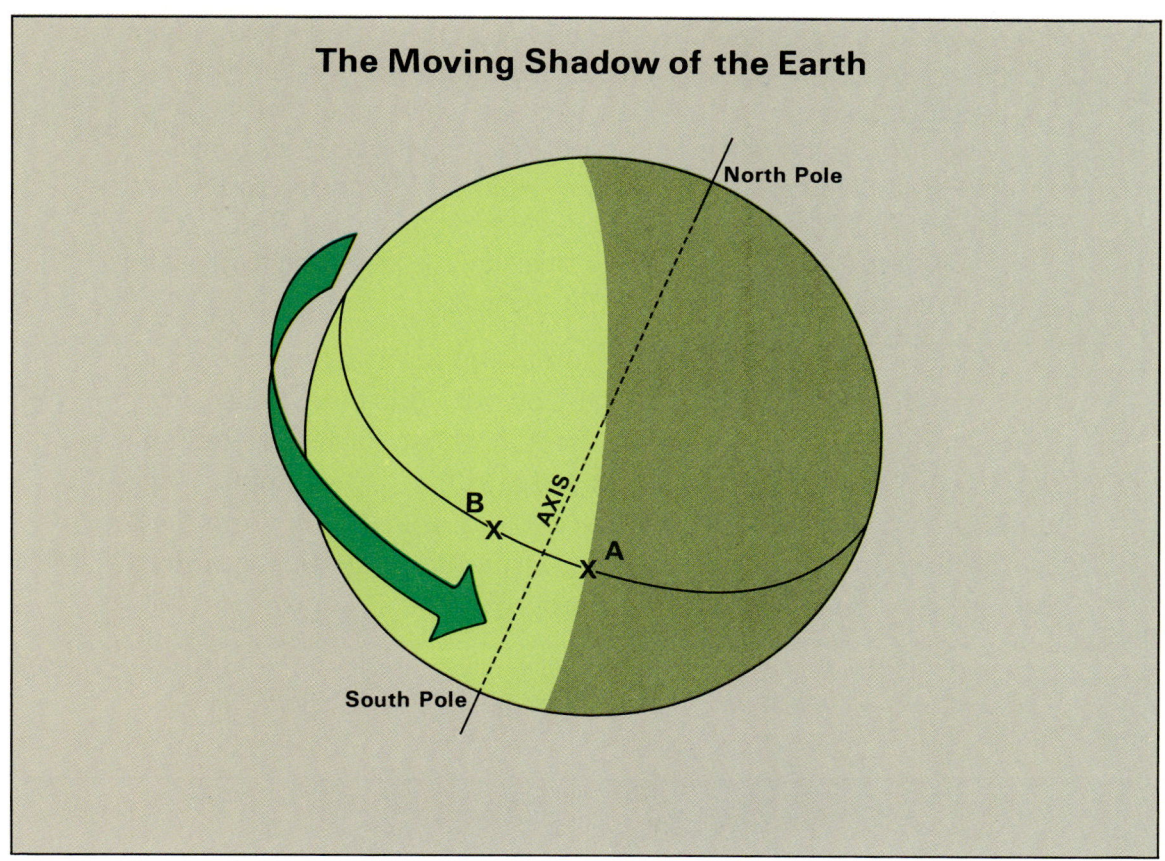

Time and the Earth's Tilt

The earth's **terminator** is the dividing line between light and darkness. Every place along the terminator is having either sunset or sunrise. We might therefore measure time from sunrise at any place on the earth. Long ago that is how people measured time. It would be a good way of measuring time *if the earth's axis were not tilted.* It would work because sunrise and sunset would always be at the same time anywhere along a line drawn through the poles and around the earth. Daytime and nighttime would be equal at every place on the earth. Daytime would be 12 hours. Nighttime would be 12 hours.

But the earth's axis is tilted. It is always tilted at an angle of 23½ degrees (23½°). And it is always tilted in the same direction.

LOCATING OURSELVES IN TIME 13

A ● Look at the diagram "Daytime and Nighttime If the Earth's Axis Were Not Tilted" below. Can you see how daytime and nighttime would always be equal? Can you see why sunset and sunrise would be at the same time every day on all places along lines going through the poles? Would we have *seasons*? Explain.

B ▶ Now look at the diagram "The Earth's Rotation and Revolution" (page 10). Can you see how the tilt of the axis keeps the terminator from following a line through the poles?

Because of the tilt, the position of the terminator changes a bit every day. On only two days each year does the terminator follow a line through the poles. Each of those days is called an *equinox* [e′ kwə noks′]. **Equinox** is Latin for "equal night." On about March 21 and September 22, day and night are equal everywhere in the world. We call March 21 the **spring equinox.** We call September 22 the **autumn equinox.**

C ▶ The positions of the earth at the equinoxes are shown on the diagram on page 10. Find the two positions.

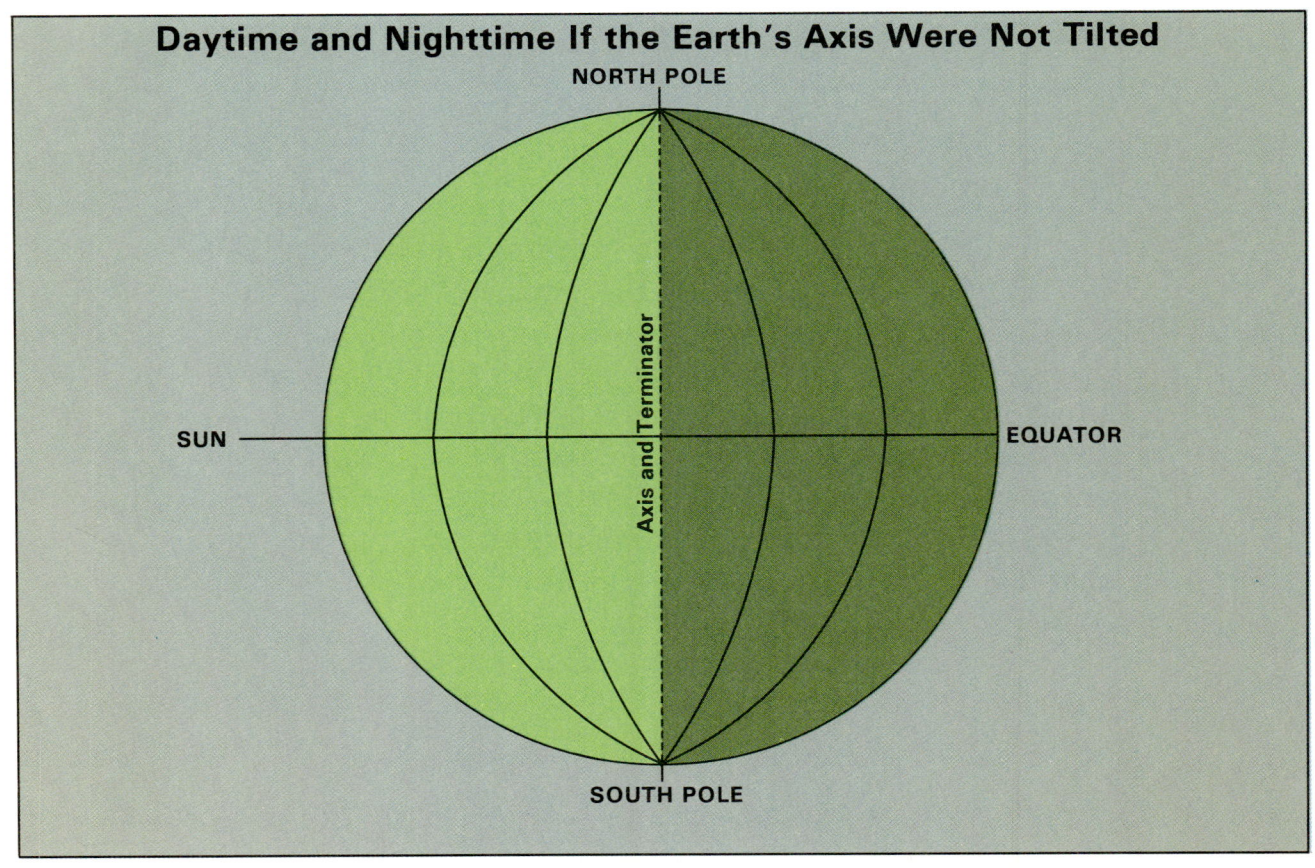

Longitude and Time

The time when the sun appears in the sky changes a bit each day. We cannot set our clocks each day when the sun appears. If we did, our time would soon be as mixed up as it was in *Looking Glass* land.

In order to measure time, we use imaginary lines going through the poles. These lines are called **lines of longitude,** or *meridians of longitude.* **Meridian** is Latin for "midday." *At the equinoxes,* every place along the same meridian has exactly the same time by the sun. The sun is highest at midday along a meridian.

Lines of longitude, or meridians, are measured in degrees. There are 360 degrees of longitude. Degrees of longitude are measured east and west from zero degrees (0°), or the **prime meridian.** Meridians east and west of the prime meridian are numbered up to 180°. There is only one meridian numbered 180°. So longitude 180° east and longitude 180° west are the same meridian.

- A ▶ Look at the diagram "Meridians of Longitude" (page 16). It shows how we number the meridians. Find the prime meridian.
- B ● On a globe find the prime meridian. It was first worked out by astronomers at Greenwich [gren' ich] near London, England. It goes through Greenwich. Trace the prime meridian through the North Pole and the South Pole. What is the number of this meridian on the opposite side of the earth?

All through the year, people along a given meridian can use the same time instead of measuring time from sunrise. Measuring time from sunrise would give every place along the same meridian a different time. That is because the sun rises at different times at the places along the same meridian, except at the equinoxes. At the equinoxes, the sun rises everywhere at about 6 A.M.

- C ★ What do you know about sunrise and sunset at the North and South poles?
- D ★ In many places we do change our clocks one hour in spring. Why? Why is this called *daylight saving*?

LOCATING OURSELVES IN TIME 15

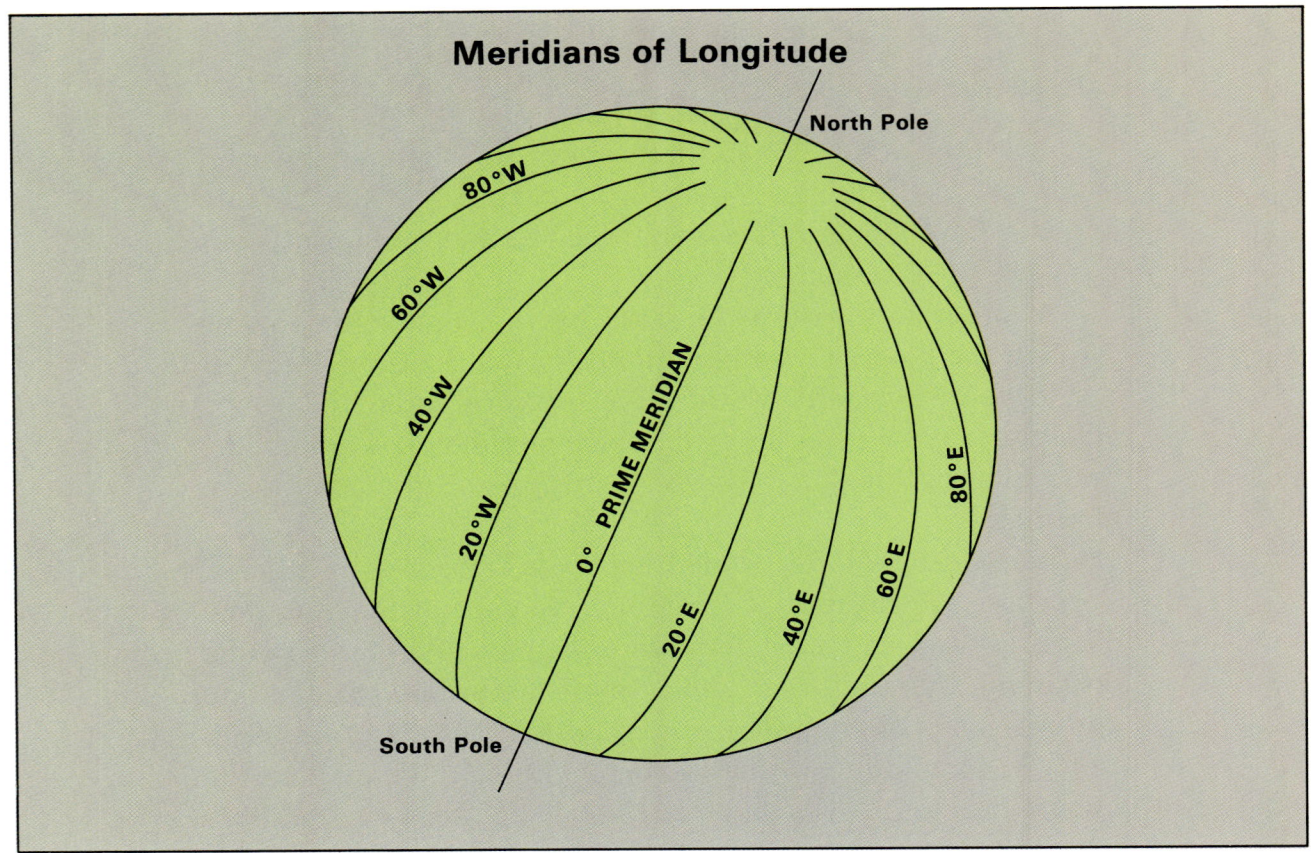

Time Zones

We know that the earth rotates once in 24 hours. This means that once every 24 hours any point on the earth passes through a whole circle. There are 360° in a circle. So every 24 hours the earth rotates 360°.

A ▶ There are 360° of longitude. How many degrees of longitude does the earth rotate in one hour?

B ● How many minutes are in 24 hours? How many minutes of time are equal to each degree of longitude?

It would be too much trouble to change our clocks four minutes whenever we crossed a degree of longitude. So we generally change the time every 15 degrees of longitude. Every 15 degrees of longitude means a change of one hour.

C ★ If you go 15° west, will the time be one hour earlier or one hour later? Explain.

16 THE GROWTH OF CIVILIZATION

Until about 150 years ago, no one could travel more than 160 kilometers (100 miles) in 24 hours. People and messages could not move faster than horses could carry them. Then the train and the telegraph were invented. It became important to know the exact time at places all over the world.

D● Why do fast communication and fast travel make it important to know the exact time everywhere?

E★ Look at a globe or a world map. Find 0°. Now measure roughly 7½° east and 7½° west of 0°. This would be exactly 15° of longitude, and every place between 7½° east and 7½° west would have the same time. Would some countries and even some cities have two different times? Explain.

The people of the world decided to have *time zones*. These **time zones** are roughly equal to 15° of longitude. Some of the lines marking the time zones are bent. Thus small countries can have the same time in their eastern and western parts. Larger countries, such as the United States and Canada, have several time zones. These time zones usually follow the boundaries of states or provinces.

F▶ Look at the map "Standard Time Zones" (page 18). It shows the time anywhere in the world when the time is noon on the prime meridian. When it is noon in London, England, what time is it in New York City? In Los Angeles, California? In Tokyo, Japan?

G● You can use the map to find the time anywhere in the world at any time. For instance, you can see that the time in London is always five hours later than the time in New York City.
1. When it is 5 P.M. in New York City, what is the time in London?
2. When it is 5 P.M. in New York, what is the time in California?

Notice that sometimes the *date* will be different in other places. For example, if it is 11 P.M. on June 21 in New York, it will be 4 A.M. on June 22 in London.

H★ What are the time and date in California when it is 1 A.M. on June 22 in New York?

I★ Space travel has started another problem. Suppose astronauts orbit the earth along the equator. Suppose their spaceship circles the earth in four hours. How many time zones will it pass through?

LOCATING OURSELVES IN TIME   17

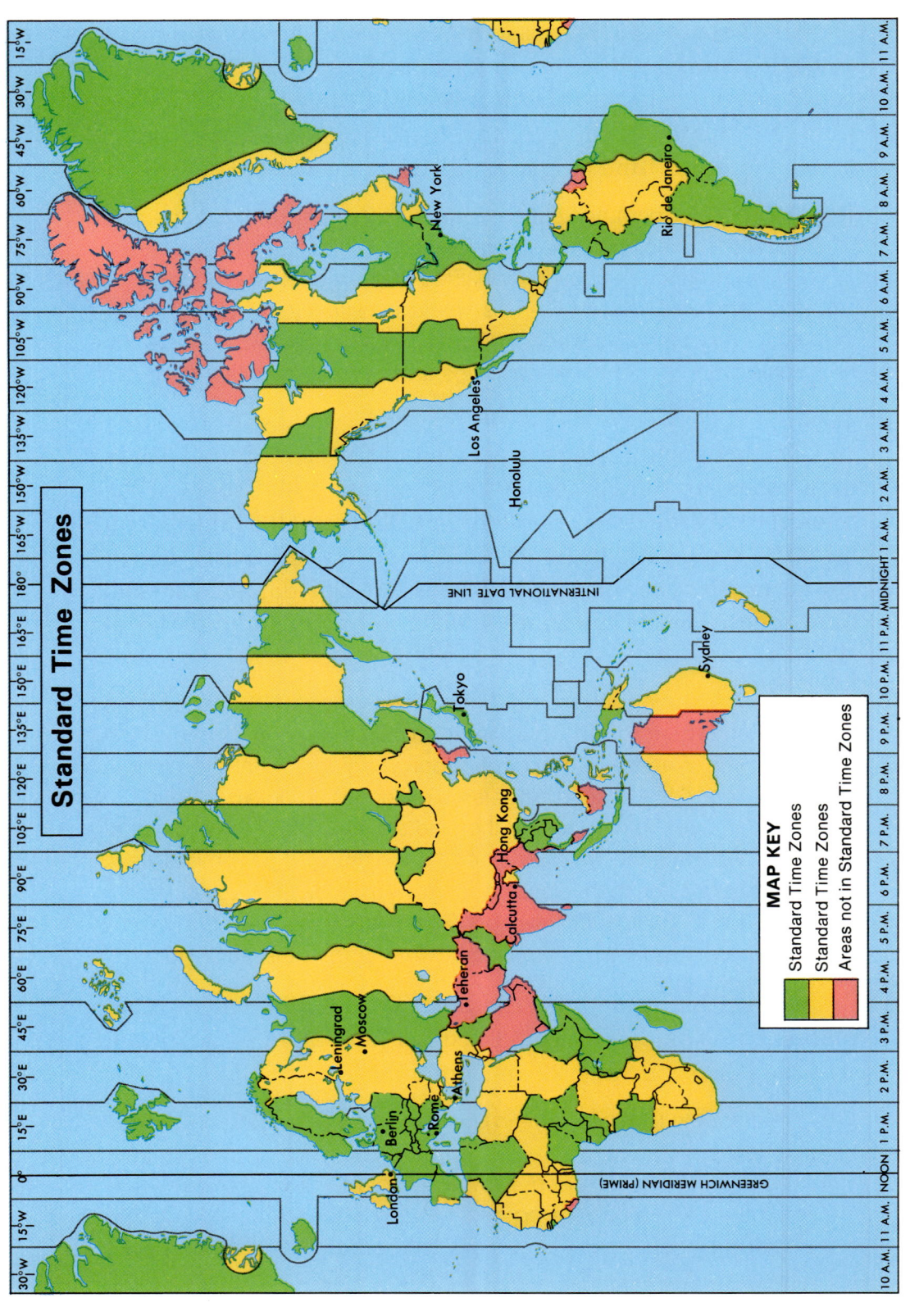

Measuring Time in History

How can we tell when something happened in history? We *could* just count backwards from this year. We could say such and such a thing happened 488 years ago. Then we would have to change the history books every year!

Instead we choose a certain date in history. Then we count all years forward or backward from that date.

Different peoples have had different calendars and different starting dates for counting the years. The starting date we use is the year when Jesus of Nazareth was born. That year is A.D. 1. **A.D.** is short for the Latin words *anno Domini*, "in the year of the Lord." For example, *A.D. 1* means "in the year of the Lord, number one."

There are two things we should know about A.D. First, historians say that the people who made our calendar were wrong about Jesus' birth. He was really born about four years earlier than A.D. 1. But we cannot change all the dates of history now. The other thing is that some people use the letters C.E. instead of A.D. **C.E.** stands for "Christian Era," or "Common Era." **Era** means a period of time.

A ▶ What year are we living in? How many years have passed since the year A.D. 100?

What about the years before A.D. 1? Many human beings lived during those years. We date those years by numbering them *backwards,* beginning from A.D. 1. Thus, the year before A.D. 1 is 1 B.C. (We write A.D. *before* a number and B.C. *after* a number.) **B.C.** means "before Christ." Look at the time line below to see how this works.

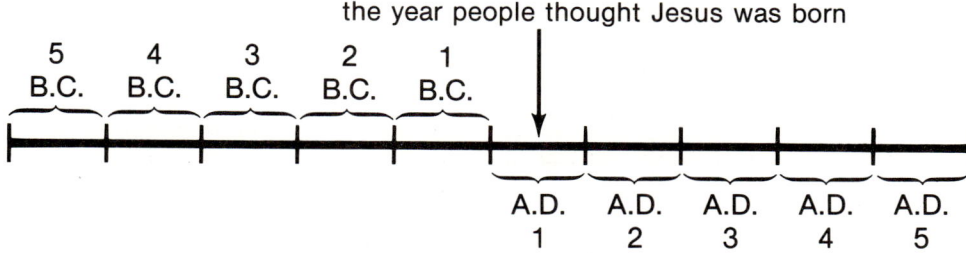

LOCATING OURSELVES IN TIME

B★ Compare this line with a number line for mathematics showing *positive* and *negative integers*. What difference can you see?

Numbering the Centuries

Let us look at a time line that shows longer periods of time. Here is one. It shows *centuries*.

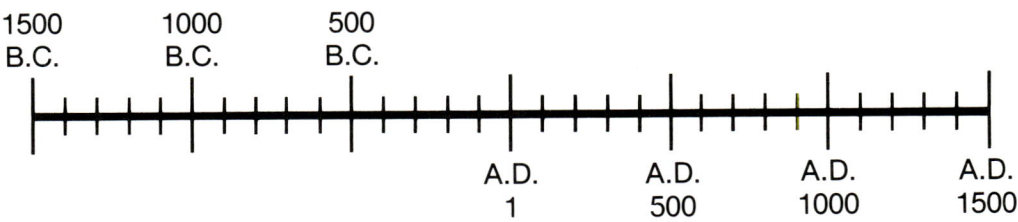

A▶ Point to 800 B.C. on the time line. Then point to these dates:
A.D. 400
1125 B.C.
A.D. 975
300 B.C.

How old are you? If you are eleven, you are in your *twelfth* year of life. If you are twelve, you are in your *thirteenth* year of life. Why? Think of newborn babies. They are in their *first* year of life. The day after their first birthday, they begin the *second* year of life. Still, we say that they are *one* year old. It is almost as if they were a year ahead of themselves. We number centuries in the same way. Look at the time lines below and on page 21 to see how this system works.

1st Century A.D.	2nd Century A.D.	3rd Century A.D.	4th Century A.D.
A.D. 1 — A.D. 100	A.D. 101 — A.D. 200	A.D. 201 — A.D. 300	A.D. 301 — A.D. 400

THE GROWTH OF CIVILIZATION

All the years from A.D. 1 *through* A.D. 100 are part of the first century A.D. All the years from A.D. 101 *through* A.D. 200 are part of the second century A.D. All the years from A.D. 1901 *through* the year A.D. 2000 are in the twentieth century A.D.

B▶ What years make up the third century A.D.? The fourth century A.D.?

C▶ What years make up the fourteenth century A.D.? The ninth century A.D.? The sixth century A.D.?

The same system is used for naming the centuries that came before Christ.

4th Century B.C.	3rd Century B.C.	2nd Century B.C.	1st Century B.C.
400 B.C. — 301 B.C.	300 B.C. — 201 B.C.	200 B.C. — 101 B.C.	100 B.C. — 1 B.C.

All the years from 100 B.C. *through* 1 B.C. are in the first century B.C. All the years from 200 B.C. *through* 101 B.C. are in the second century B.C.

D▶ What years make up the third century B.C.? The fourth century B.C.?

E▶ What years make up the eighth century B.C.? The thirteenth century B.C.?

F▶ In what century is each of the following years?
  331 B.C.   1350 B.C.
  A.D. 1776   A.D. 1861

LOCATING OURSELVES IN TIME   21

Summary

In order to study history, we need to know where we are in time and space.

Time is based on the earth's movements. The earth is like a clock that keeps perfect time. Its rotation gives us day and night. We divide the time of one whole rotation into 24 hours. Each hour is divided into 60 minutes and each minute into 60 seconds. The earth's revolution around the sun takes one year made up of 365 ¼ days. We add the four quarter-days every fourth year to make a leap year of 366 days.

The axis of the earth is the straight line that can be drawn through the earth from pole to pole. The axis is always tilted in the same direction. Because of the tilt, the length of day and night keeps changing through the year. On only two days each year are day and night equal. These are the equinoxes, on about March 21 and September 22.

Because of the earth's tilt, we use lines of longitude to measure time. These are called meridians of longitude. Each degree of longitude is equal to four minutes of time. Fifteen minutes of longitude equal one full hour of time. For people's convenience, the world is divided into 24 time zones.

In order to tell when something happened in history, we have to choose a certain date from which to count forward and backward. The date we use is the year in which people used to think Jesus was born. This year is A.D. (*anno Domini*) 1. All years after A.D. 1 are labeled A.D. Years before A.D. 1 are counted backwards. The year immediately before A.D. 1 is called 1 B.C. (before Christ). The year 301 B.C. was 301 years *before* Jesus' birth, just as A.D. 301 was 301 years *after* Jesus' birth.

Centuries are periods of 100 years. The first century A.D. goes from the first day of A.D. 1 through the last day of A.D. 100. The second century A.D. goes from the first day of A.D. 101 to the last day of A.D. 200, and so on. The first century B.C. is 100 B.C. through 1 B.C. The second century B.C. is 200 B.C. through 101 B.C., and so on.

Some Interesting Activities

1. Draw a diagram to show the rotation and revolution of the earth. Make sure the axis is tilted. Show the terminator.

2. Darken the classroom and have someone hold up a basketball or soccer ball. Ask another person to aim a flashlight at the ball. The student holding the ball should tilt it and slowly rotate it. This should help you understand what causes day and night. Explain what you have learned.

3. Examine a calendar for this year. How many days are in January? How many days are in April? How many days are in February? Why does February have fewer days than all the other months? An encyclopedia will help you to explain why.

4. Write a report on how the earth's rotation and revolution give us seasons of the year. Draw pictures to help explain your answer.

5. Explain the meanings of these words: *axis, calendar, decade, millennium, meridian, month, century,* and *terminator.*

6. Why do we have *time zones*? Use the time zone map in this chapter to answer these questions:
   a. What is the time in New York when it is 5 P.M. in Los Angeles?
   b. When it is 12:01 A.M. (one minute after midnight) on February 1 in London, what are the time and date in New York? In Moscow? In Tokyo?

LOCATING OURSELVES IN TIME

All regions have a location on the earth — a location that relates to another location. Maps and globes enable us to locate ourselves on the earth.

CHAPTER 2

Locating Ourselves on the Earth

Humans learned how to measure time. They also learned how to measure space. It is important to know how to pinpoint any place on earth. To do this we use *maps* and *globes*. A **globe** is a model of the earth. It shows the shape of the earth. A **map** is a flat drawing of the earth's surface.

Maps and Map Grids

A map can show all of the earth's surface or part of it. When we use a map, we must be able to match the area shown to the real area.

A▶ Here are some things you must look for when you use a map: compass directions, scale, and map symbols (shown in the map key). Explain what they mean.

B▶ Explain what these terms mean: *physical features, relief, cultural features.*

In order to tell where a place is on a map, we often use a *grid*. A **grid** is a checkerboard pattern of east-west and north-south lines. To make a *map grid*, we first draw a checkerboard on the map. Next we give numbers or letters to the spaces. Then we can tell where a place is by the number and the letter of its square.

C▶ Look at the map "Three Cities" below. Port is in B2.
1. What is the location of High?
2. What cultural feature is in D1?
3. In what square are the sources of the river?
4. Where are the mountains?

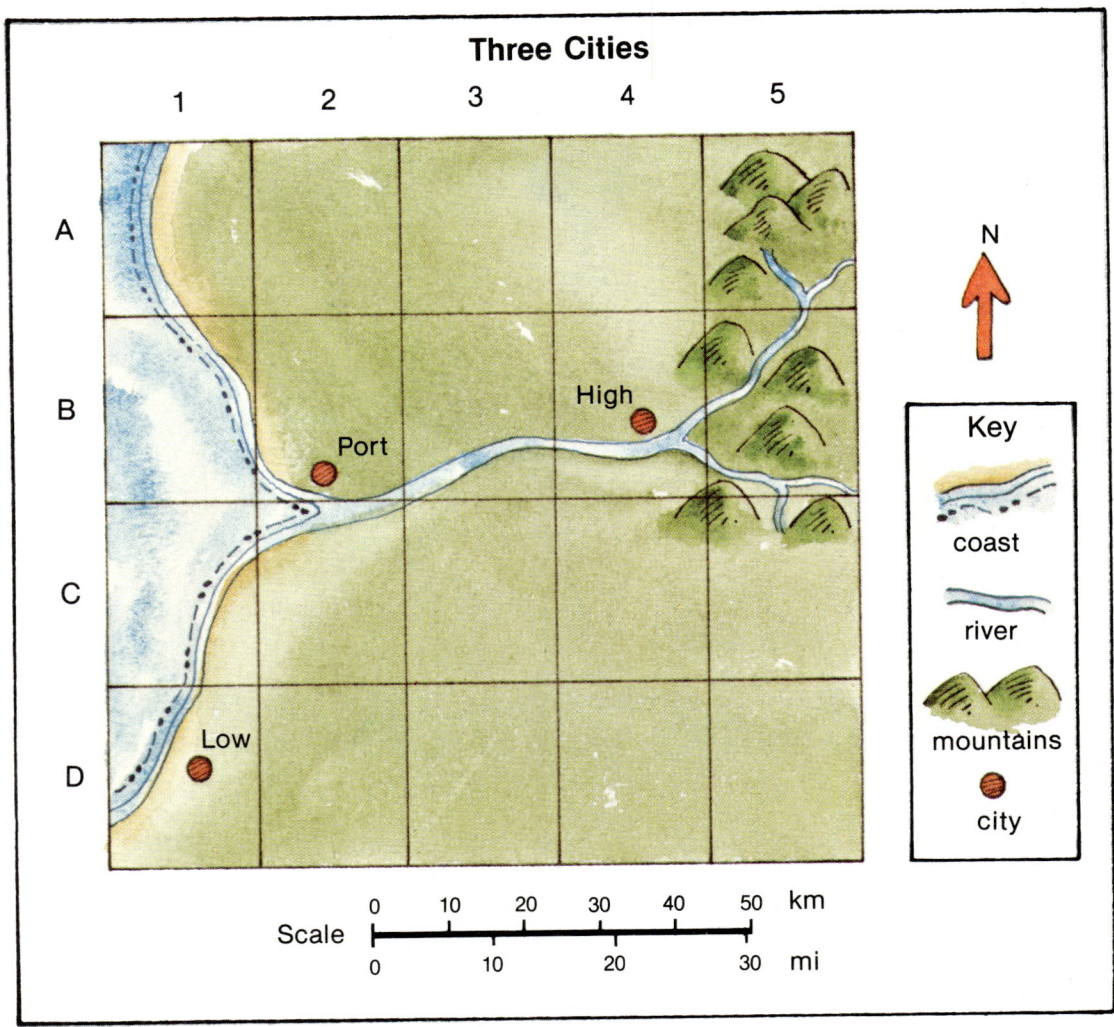

26   THE GROWTH OF CIVILIZATION

Global Grid

The grid system works very well for a flat surface. But the surface of the globe and the surface of our earth are not flat. They are curved. A grid system is difficult to make on a curved surface. But we need such a grid system so that we can tell locations. Geographers have therefore developed what is called a *global grid*.

A ● Put a dot on a ball. Now try to describe the location of the dot on the ball. Why is that so hard to do?

Our earth is not a ball that can roll in any direction. The earth rotates on its axis. The ends of the axis, the poles, are two fixed points. The North Pole and the South Pole are the only points on the earth's surface that remain fixed while the earth rotates.

B ▶ What are the lines that we draw through the poles around the earth? How do the lines help us in measuring time?

The meridians of longitude also help us to make a global grid. They divide the globe (or the earth's surface) into sections like those of an orange. You saw in chapter 1 that the meridians are numbered.

C ▶ How are the meridians numbered?

The other lines of the global grid are the *lines of latitude*. Lines of latitude run west to east around the globe. We need a fixed line from which to measure and number the lines of latitude. The fixed line we use is the *equator*. The **equator** is the latitude line that goes around the middle of the globe. It is halfway between the North Pole and the South Pole. All lines of latitude are *parallel* to the equator. We call them **parallels of latitude**.

D ▶ Look at the diagram "Parallels of Latitude" (page 28).
    1. Find the equator.
    2. What do we mean by *parallel lines*?
    3. How are the parallels of latitude numbered?

Parallels of Latitude

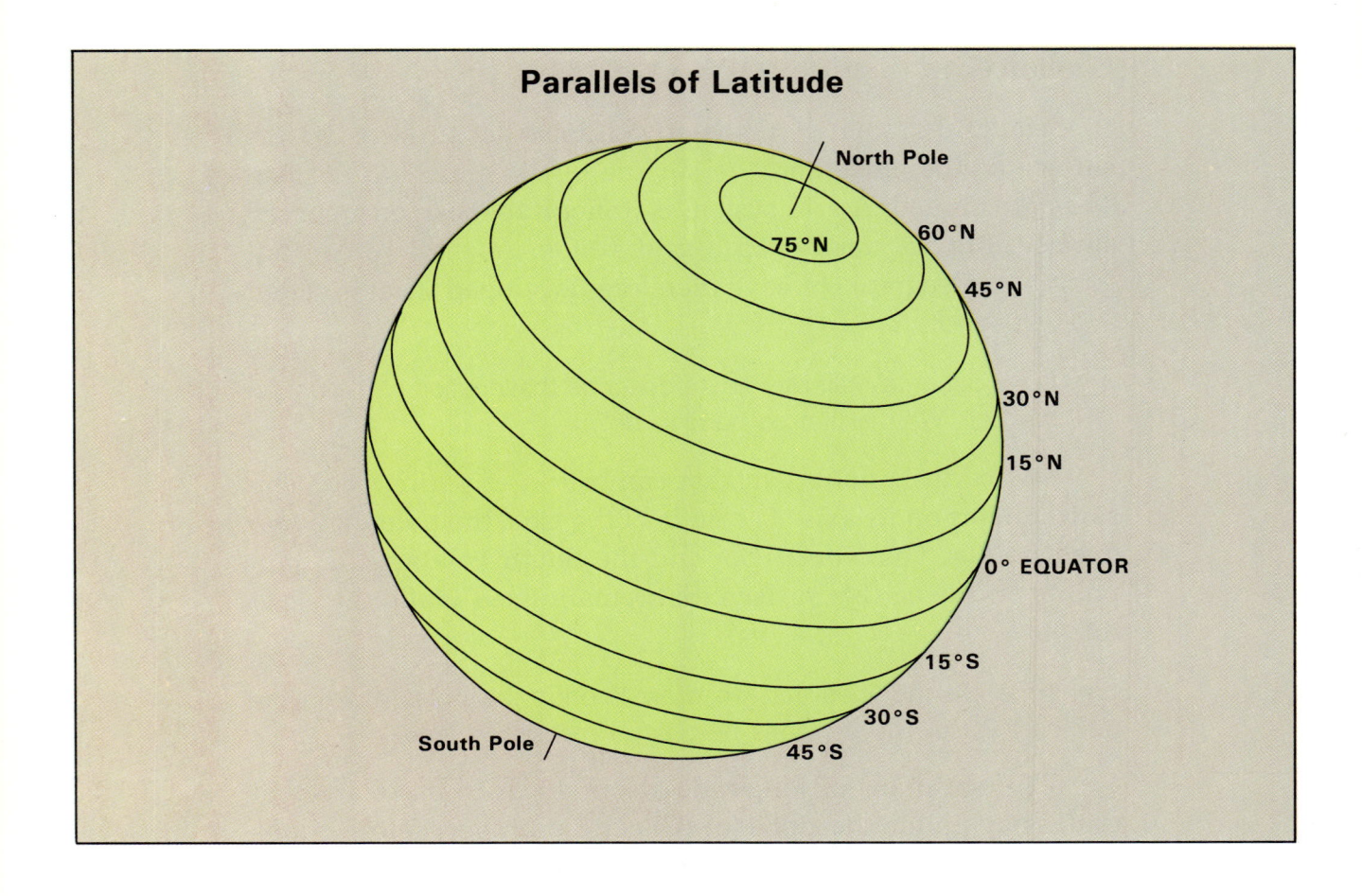

[Diagram of globe showing parallels: North Pole, 75°N, 60°N, 45°N, 30°N, 15°N, 0° EQUATOR, 15°S, 30°S, 45°S, South Pole]

If we put the lines of longitude and latitude together, we get a *global grid*.

E● Look at the diagram "Global Grid" (page 29).
  1. How can we use the parallels and meridians to give the location of a place?
  2. When we want to give a location on the global grid, we give the latitude and the longitude as exactly as we can. How is this different from giving the letter and the number of a square on a map grid?

F★ Look at a globe.
  1. Find the meridians and parallels.
  2. What big city is about 30° N, 30° E?
  3. Find Anchorage, Alaska. It is about 61° N, 150° W.

28 THE GROWTH OF CIVILIZATION

Measuring Longitude and Latitude

We have seen that longitude is measured in 360 degrees. Circles are always measured in this way.

A★ Look at the diagram "Measuring a Circle and Measuring Angles" (page 30).
1. Can a circle of any size be measured in degrees? Explain.
2. How do we measure *angles*?
3. There are 90 degrees in a *right angle*. What does a right angle look like? How many right angles make up a circle of 360°?

To measure and number latitudes, we need only 180 degrees. There are 90 degrees of latitude north of the equator and 90 degrees of latitude south of the equator. The North Pole is 90° north. The South Pole is 90° south.

B▶ Can there ever be a line of latitude 120° south? Explain.

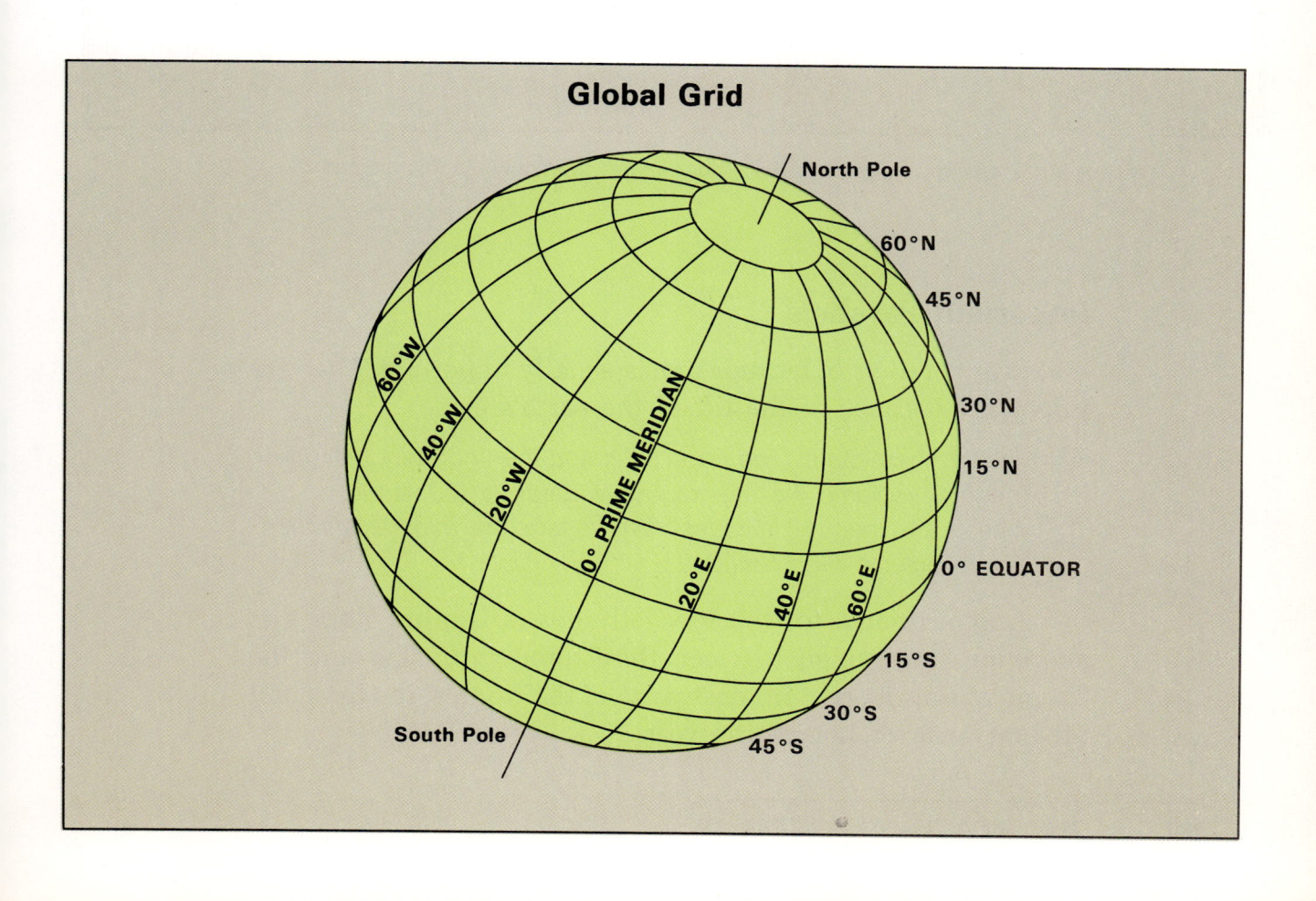

Global Grid

Measuring a Circle and Measuring Angles

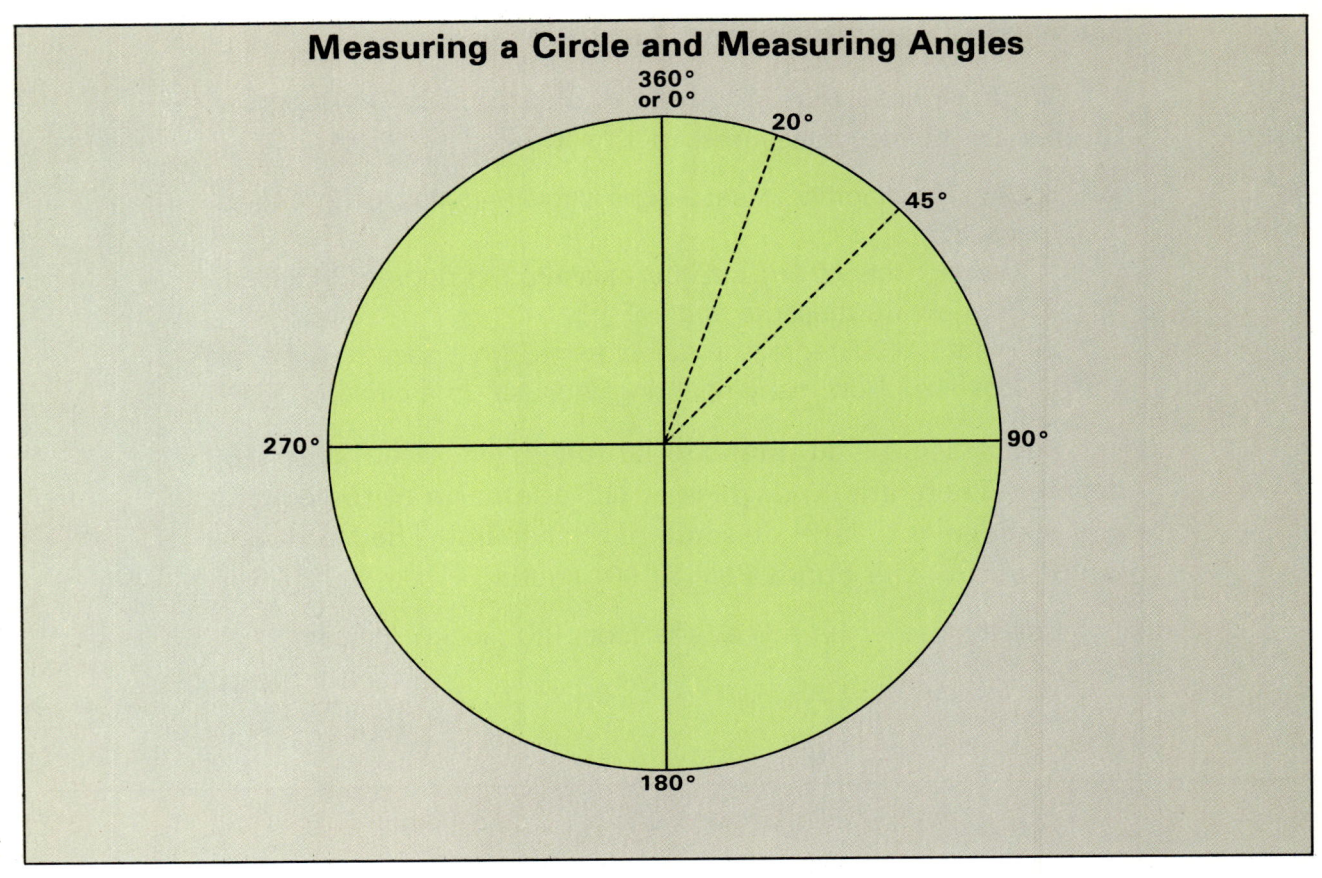

A 90° angle is a *right* angle. Four right angles are shown in this diagram.

Important Parallels

Five parallels of latitude are especially important. They are important because of the tilt of the earth's axis.

A ▶ Look at the picture "The Earth's Tilt and the Important Latitudes" (page 31). Name the five important parallels of latitude.
B ▶ Where are the *low latitudes*? Where are the *middle latitudes*? Where are the *high latitudes*?

Another name for the low latitudes is **tropics.** *Tropics* is short for "the region between the Tropic of Cancer and the Tropic of Capricorn." In most parts of the tropics, the land and air are warm or hot all the year.

30 THE GROWTH OF CIVILIZATION

Another name for the high latitudes is **polar regions.** These are the regions around the poles. In polar regions, it is very cold or cool all the year.

In the middle latitudes, it is cold or cool part of the year. It is warm or hot for the rest of the year. In the middle latitudes, most places have four seasons. Seasons happen because the earth's axis always tilts in one direction as it moves around the sun.

C ● Look at the picture "The Earth's Tilt and the Seasons in the Northern Hemisphere" (page 32). The picture shows the earth's orbit and four positions of the earth. Notice the earth's axis in the picture.
1. Does the tilt of the axis change at all?

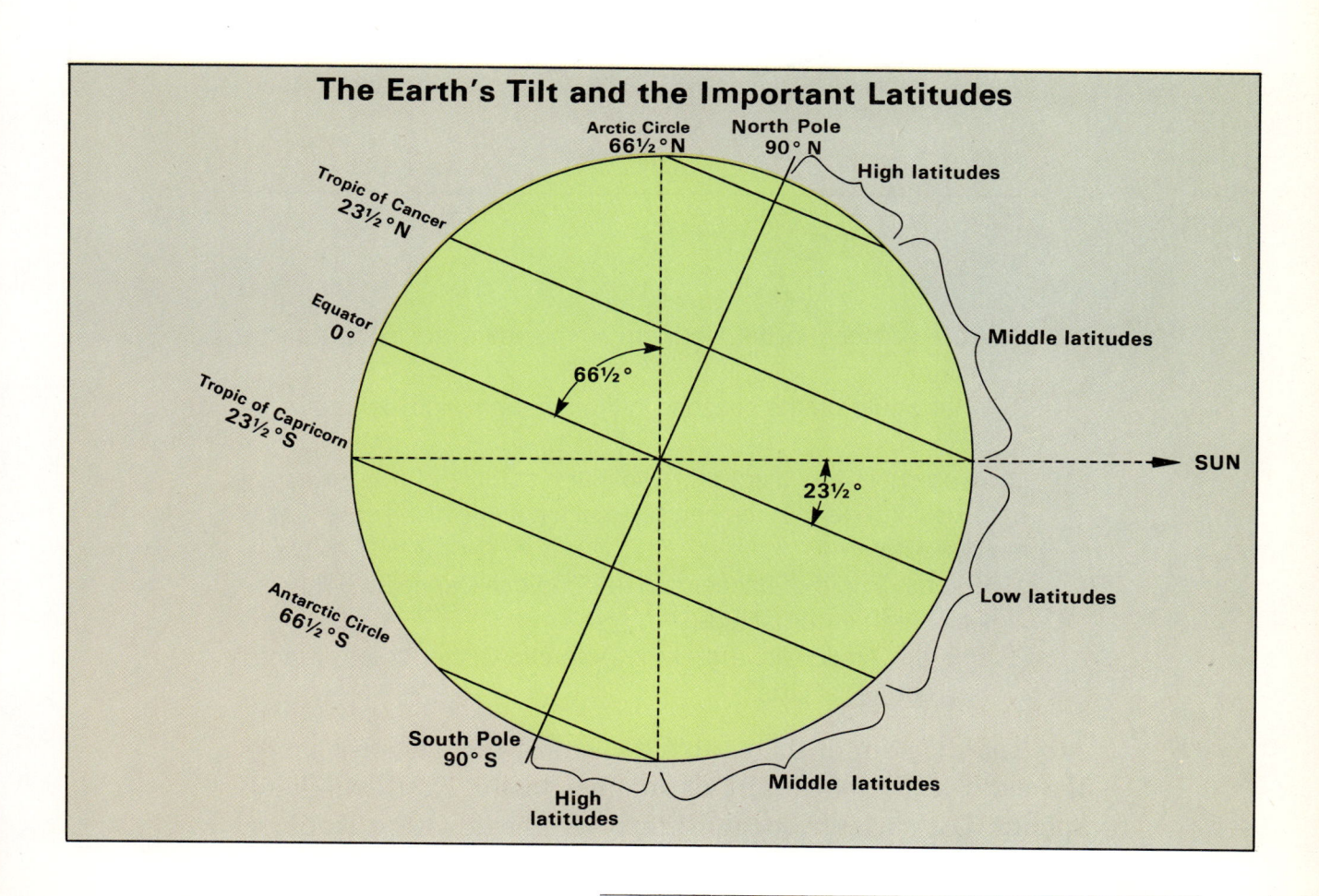

The Earth's Tilt and the Important Latitudes

LOCATING OURSELVES ON THE EARTH   31

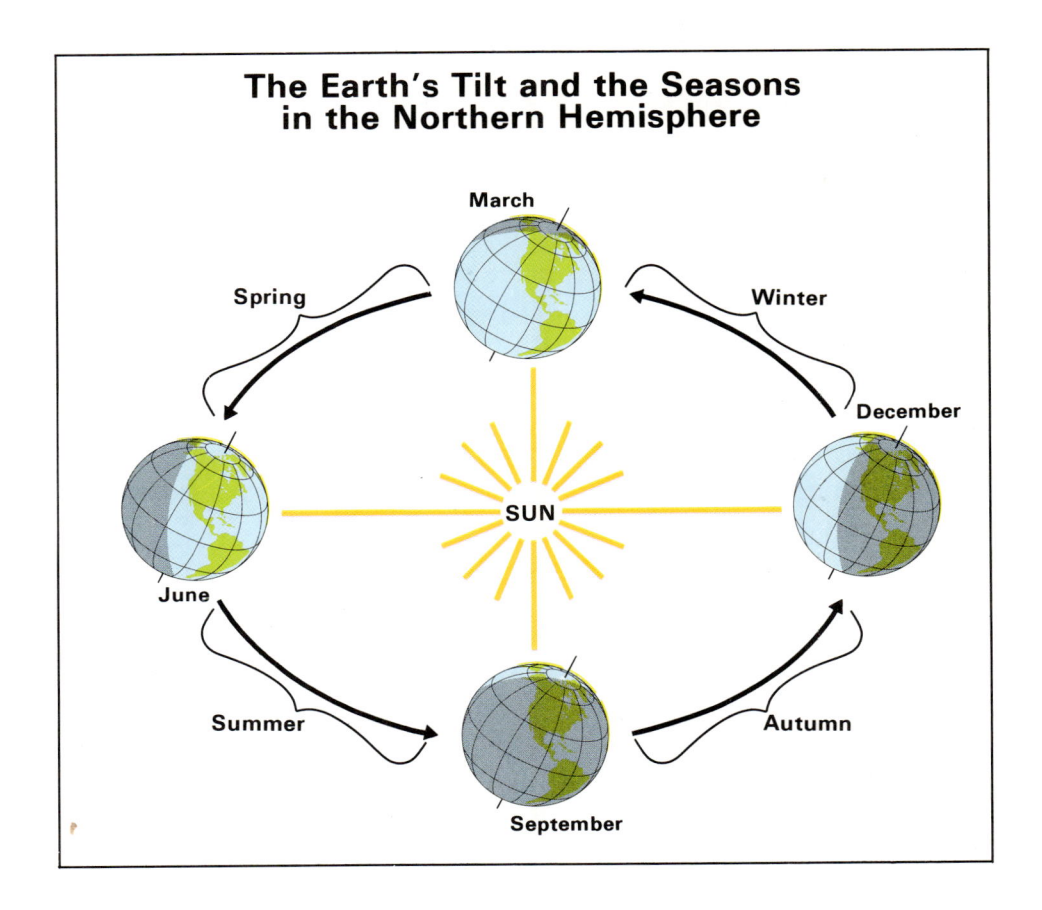

The Earth's Tilt and the Seasons in the Northern Hemisphere

2. What seasons in the Northern Hemisphere are shown in the picture?
3. What would be the seasons in the Southern Hemisphere in the picture?

D● Look again at the diagram "The Earth's Tilt and the Important Latitudes" (page 31). You can see that the *angle of the earth's tilt* is always 23½°.
  1. Find the Tropic of Cancer and the Tropic of Capricorn. What are their degrees of latitude?
  2. Find the Arctic Circle and the Antarctic Circle. What are their degrees of latitude?

The diagram of the earth's tilt and of the latitudes shows the earth at the beginning of summer in the Northern Hemisphere. The sun is vertical (directly overhead) at the Tropic of

THE GROWTH OF CIVILIZATION

Cancer. The Tropic of Cancer is the most northern parallel to receive the sun's direct rays. This happens about June 21. It is called the *summer solstice* [sol' stis]. **Solstice** comes from a Latin word meaning "a standing still of the sun." The summer solstice is the beginning of summer in the Northern Hemisphere. It is the beginning of winter in the Southern Hemisphere.

As the earth revolves in its orbit, different parallels come into line with the sun's vertical rays. Six months after the sun's vertical rays reach the Tropic of Cancer, they are above the Tropic of Capricorn. This is called the *winter solstice*. It takes place about December 22. It is the beginning of winter in the Northern Hemisphere and of summer in the Southern Hemisphere.

Halfway between the solstices are the equinoxes. The equator is in direct line with the sun's rays at the autumn equinox (about September 21) and at the spring equinox (about March 21).

E● Why is the earth's surface in the tropics generally hotter than other parts of the earth's surface?

F● Why are the Arctic Circle and the Antarctic Circle at 66½° N and 66½° S?

G● Why does the sun not "set" at the North Pole from the spring equinox to the autumn equinox?

Locating the Middle East

The Middle East is an important region in human history. We shall read much about it in the pages that follow.

A★ On a globe, find 35° N and 40° E. These lines cross the region called the Middle East.

B▶ Look at the map "Part of the Middle East, a Locator Map" (page 34).
  1. Find the Middle East. Compare the map with the globe.
  2. What three continents meet in the Middle East?

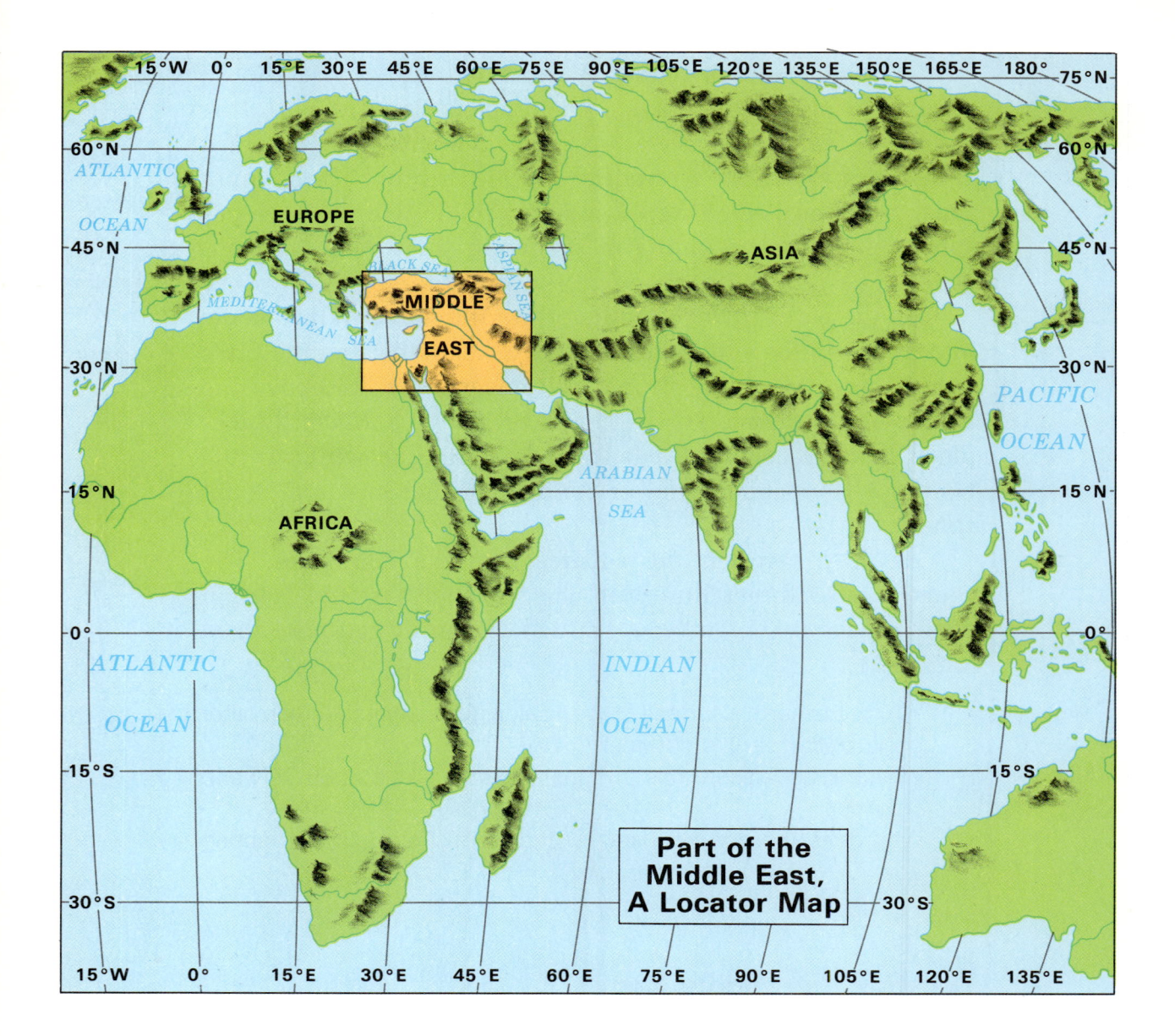

C ▶ Look at the "Grid Map of Part of the Middle East" (page 35).
  1. What is the latitude of X?
  2. What is the longitude of Y?
  3. Give the latitude and the longitude of Z.
  4. Is any part of the area shown on the map in the tropics?
  5. Give the latitude and the longitude of the city of Baghdad as nearly as you can.

34   THE GROWTH OF CIVILIZATION

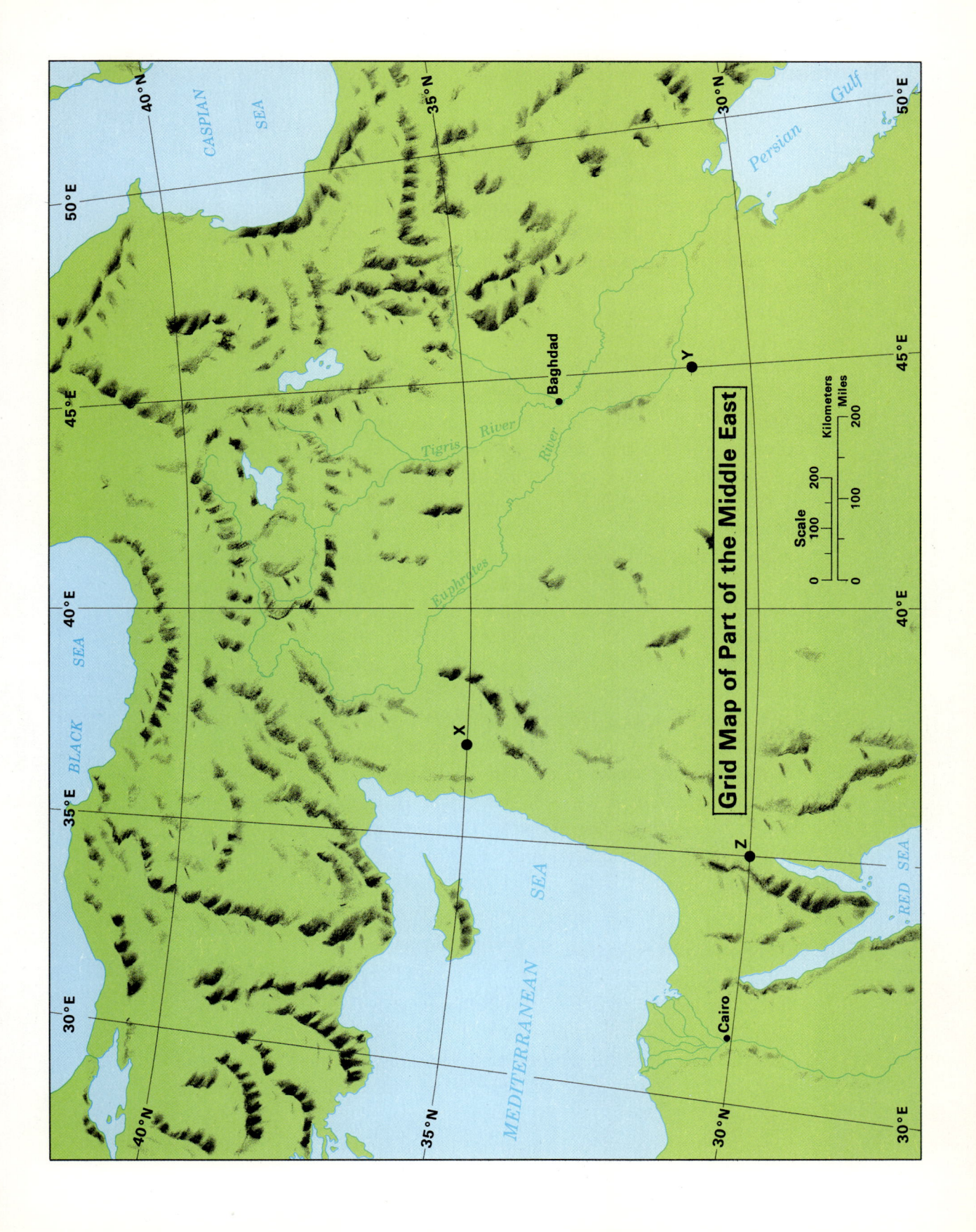

Grid Map of Part of the Middle East

Summary

To locate places on the earth, we use grids. On maps, which are flat pictures of the earth's surface, we use a grid like a checkerboard. Usually we label the grid lines with letters and numbers.

On globes and small-scale maps, we use a grid made of parallels of latitude and meridians of longitude. Latitude is measured in degrees north and south of the equator (0° latitude). Longitude is measured in degrees east and west of the prime meridian (0° longitude).

Five parallels of latitude are especially important: the Arctic Circle, the Tropic of Cancer, the equator, the Tropic of Capricorn, and the Antarctic Circle. The low latitudes lie between the Tropics of Cancer and Capricorn. Another name for low latitudes is tropics. The tropics region is warm or hot all year.

The high latitudes are regions between the poles and the Arctic and the Antarctic circles. In the polar regions, the weather is cold most of the year.

The middle latitudes are between the high and the low latitudes. Most of the middle latitudes have four seasons. The seasons are caused by the earth's revolution around the sun and the tilted axis.

As the earth revolves, the vertical rays of the sun are directly above different latitudes between the Tropic of Cancer (23½° north latitude) and the Tropic of Capricorn (23½° south latitude). When the vertical rays are at the Tropic of Cancer, the summer solstice occurs (about June 21). This marks the beginning of summer in the Northern Hemisphere and the beginning of winter in the Southern Hemisphere. When the sun is directly over the Tropic of Capricorn, the winter solstice occurs (about December 22). This is the beginning of winter in the Northern Hemisphere and of summer in the Southern Hemisphere.

Some Interesting Activities

1. Using a large map of the United States with a grid system, locate your city. What are its lines of latitude and longitude? Is your city in the high, middle, or low latitudes? How do you know? Write down your answers and keep them in your social science notebook.

THE GROWTH OF CIVILIZATION

2. Using a map of the world with a grid system, answer the following questions:
   a. Find Greenwich, England. (If Greenwich is not labeled, you can use London instead, since Greenwich is about 10 kilometers, or 6 or 7 miles, from the center of London.) What are the latitude and the longitude of Greenwich?
   b. Find Washington, D.C.
   c. What island is located at 35° N, 25° E?
   d. What two important cities are located about 42° N? (Hint: One is in North America; the other is in southern Europe.)

3. Collect as many kinds of maps as you can find in magazines, newspapers, books, almanacs. Display them in the classroom, and note similarities and differences among them.

4. Find out what a mercator projection and a polar projection are. Write a short report to explain both projections.

5. Use a pair of compasses and a ruler. Draw a globe showing the equator, the tropics, and the Arctic and Antarctic circles. Label the number of degrees of latitude of each parallel shown. Now draw the prime meridian and 45° E and 45° W. Label these.

6. Make a list of all the geographic terms in chapters 1 and 2 of your textbook. Put the words on file cards in alphabetical order. Write a definition for the term on each card. Include drawings when possible to help you remember the definitions. You may wish to add cards and definitions for other important words you have read in your textbook so far. Use the cards for review from time to time.

LOCATING OURSELVES ON THE EARTH

For many thousands of years humans had to live on whatever food they could get from their natural environment.

CHAPTER 3

The Great Leap Forward

In order to stay alive, humans had to learn to use their *environment.* For many thousands of years, they had to find what food they could in their *natural environment.* They did not know how to grow food. They were not strong enough to kill big animals with their hands.

Yet humans learned. For thousands of years they kept learning. A time came when they learned ways *to control* their environment. This was the *great leap forward.* It happened in three big stages.

First we will find out why humans were able to control their environment. Then we will study about the three big stages of the great leap forward.

How Humans Are Different from Other Creatures

Why can humans learn new things? Why can they change their ways of living much faster than other creatures?

A▶ Look at the box "Why Humans Are Different from Other Creatures" below. Look at points 1 and 2. Name some animals that also live in groups to protect their young.

B● Look at the box again.
1. How does growing up slowly lead to speaking a language?
2. How does speaking a language lead to points 4, 5, and 6?
3. Give examples of how humans plan for the future.
4. How do the things listed in the box help humans to change their ways of living faster than other creatures?

C★ The list in the box gives only *some* of the things that make humans different. Many people say that humans are different because they are "made in God's image." What does that mean? How does it explain the difference between humans and other creatures?

A group of humans living together is a **society.** Each society learns more and more as time goes by. The older persons pass the learning on to the children. Each society **educates,** or teaches, the children. The things that children learn are called the *culture* of the society. **Culture** is the whole way of life of a society. It is a people's way of living and thinking. Each society has its own culture.

D▶ Cultures have many parts. Look at the box "Some Parts of a Culture" (page 41). Name the parts and tell what they mean.

Why Humans Are Different from Other Creatures

1. Humans grow up more slowly than any other creatures.
2. Older humans and children must stay together for a long time.
3. Humans learn to speak a language.
4. Humans solve problems, and they invent things.
5. Humans pass their learning on.
6. Humans learn the difference between right and wrong.
7. Humans plan for the future.

THE GROWTH OF CIVILIZATION

E● What are some ways in which you have learned about the culture of your society?

Humans have always had to learn their society's culture. Today, however, we need to learn about other cultures as well. This is because faster and easier communication and transportation have brought the world's cultures closer together.

One way of learning about other cultures is to learn about people and cultures in the past. That is what we are doing in this book.

Some Parts of a Culture

1. Ways of getting food and other goods
2. Language
3. Families and other groups in society
4. Art, architecture, music, stories, poetry, dance
5. Religion and ideas of right and wrong
6. Laws and government

Prehistoric Times and Prehistoric Cultures

We call the age in which the earliest humans lived *prehistoric times*. Let us see what that means.

One meaning of *history* is "the whole story of the human race." However, a more special meaning of history is "the study of *written* records." The first writing was invented c. 3500 B.C. (You should know that *c.* stands for the Latin word *circa*, meaning "about.") **Prehistoric times** means "the times before written history."

We divide prehistoric cultures into two periods. The first period was the **Old Stone Age,** when people used stone tools and weapons for hunting. They made some tools sharp by chipping the edges with other stones. The second period was the **New Stone Age.** People in the New Stone Age used polished stone tools. But more important, they invented new ways of

THE GREAT LEAP FORWARD

getting food. Old Stone Age people had *to find food* in the natural environment. New Stone Age people learned how *to change and control* their environment. They learned how to tame wild plants and wild animals.

Old Stone Age People: Hunters and Gatherers

Old Stone Age humans were hunters and gatherers of food. How can we know how Old Stone Age humans lived? We have a number of clues. One clue is from the bones and tools of early people. Such things have been dug up by scientists. That is how we know that early people had knives and axes made of stone.

A second clue is the pictures painted by early people on the walls of their caves. These pictures show us how people hunted animals.

A third clue comes from discoveries made by explorers. Within the past 300 years explorers have found certain groups of people still living in about the same way *all* people lived 10,000 years ago. When these groups were discovered, they had only stone tools. They found all their food in their natural

This prehistoric painting of bison is from the Altamira caves in Spain.

A young Khoisan is digging up a root with a digging stick — a traditional tool used in foraging for food.

environment. They did not know how to grow food. The above picture shows a group of people living today the way Old Stone Age people used to live.

A★ Many members of the following societies live today the way people lived in the Old Stone Age:
1. the *Aborigines* of Australia
2. the *Batwa* ("Pygmies") of the central rain forest of Africa
3. the *Khoisan* [koi′ sän] ("Bushmen") of the Kalahari Desert in southern Africa

Try to find out about these societies in books or magazines in your school or public library.

Finding food in the natural environment was not easy. People had to learn what berries, seeds, and roots were fit to eat. Then they had to look for them. They had to learn what insects, animals, and fish were good to eat. Then they had to catch them. They had to invent tools and weapons to help them get food.

THE GREAT LEAP FORWARD 43

Natural environments are different in different parts of the world. Each society had to find a way of living that fitted its environment. This was one reason for the different cultures in prehistoric times.

B ▶ We call finding food in the natural environment *hunting and gathering.* Why?

C ▶ Look at the box "Hunting and Gathering in Some Different Natural Environments" below.
1. What were four environments where people lived in the Old Stone Age?
2. What were some foods people in the Old Stone Age ate?
3. What were some weapons nearly all Old Stone Age people used?

Hunting and Gathering in Some Different Natural Environments

Environment	Food Found	Special Tools Used
Grassland	Seeds, roots, insects, grass-eating animals	Digging sticks, traps, hunting spears
Lakes and rivers	Seeds, berries, fish, small animals	Fishing spears, nets, boats or canoes
Woodlands	Berries, roots, woodland animals and insects	Hunting spears, digging sticks, traps, and, later, bows and arrows
Seashores	Fish, shellfish, seals, seashore plants	Fishing spears, nets, boats, hunting spears

Note: Nearly all Old Stone Age people had knives of stone or bone, stone hand axes and hammers, wooden clubs, spears, and sacks made of skins.

THE GROWTH OF CIVILIZATION

D ● Why did people in each natural environment need some special tools? How might prehistoric people in different environments make some tools that were the same?

E ● What was a digging stick used for in a hunting-and-gathering society? (Think about roots that are good to eat.)

F ★ Prehistoric people had different sorts of traps to catch animals and birds. What is a *pit* trap? A *snare* trap? Can you name some other kinds of traps?

G ★ What ways of getting a living did the Eskimos have on the shores of the Arctic Ocean? What tools did they use?

Another name for the Old Stone Age is the **Paleolithic** [pā′ lē ō lith′ ik] **period.** *Paleolithic* is from Greek words meaning "Old Stone." All human groups had Paleolithic cultures until c. 8000 B.C.

The Paleolithic period came during the *Ice Age.* The **Ice Age** was a long period when the earth's climate was different from what it is today. The Northern Hemisphere was much colder than it is now. A huge *icecap* grew around the North Pole. The **icecap** was a thick mass of ice like the ice at the North and South poles today. It stretched as far south as the Great Lakes in North America. It also covered northern Eurasia.

The Ice Age lasted from c. 1,500,000 B.C. to c. 8000 B.C. During that time the icecap sometimes melted. Then it froze again. When the last of the icecap melted, heavy forests grew up in northern Eurasia, where ice had been. The grasslands that were south of the Mediterranean Sea turned into deserts. That is how the Sahara and the Arabian Desert were formed.

The Old Stone Age people lived south of the icecap. Their tools and cave paintings have been found in southern Europe and in Africa, Asia, Australia, and the Americas.

The Races of Humankind

Humans are all the same species. But the human species can be divided into a few big groups called *races.* A **race** is a group of people with similar *physical traits* [fiz′ə kl trāts]. **Physical traits** are things like skin color, kind of hair, shape of

A double-sided scraper, about 40,000–60,000 years old

Paleolithic (Old Stone Age) Tools

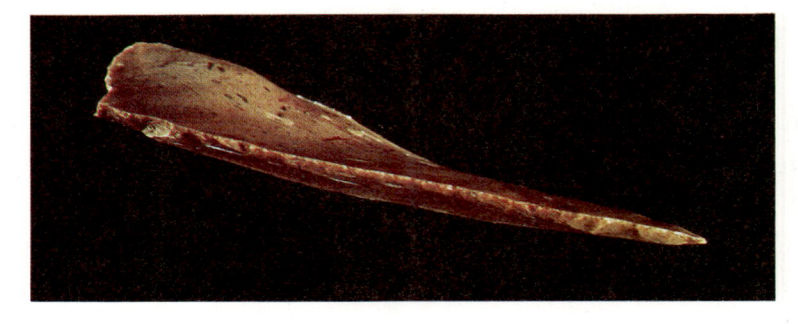

A point, about 40,000–70,000 years old

A point, about 40,000–70,000 years old

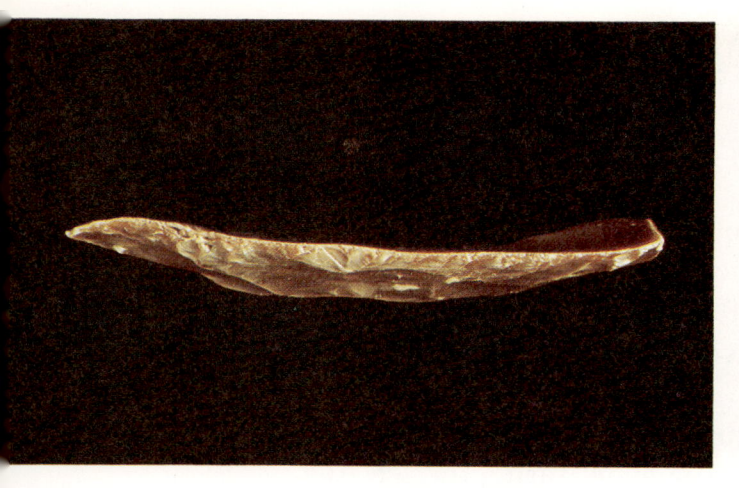

A side scraper, 40,000–60,000 years old   A hand axe, about 200,000 years old

Paleolithic (Old Stone Age) tools were made by hand of wood, bone, and stone. They were used in hunting and other food gathering activities as well as for domestic purposes.

eyes, color of eyes, shape of head, and body build. These things make people of one race *look different* in some ways from people in other races. How did these racial differences come about?

Scientists think that during the Ice Age human groups wandered and settled in different parts of the world. Then for long periods of time, these groups were cut off from one another. How were these early humans able to travel from one continent to another? Why were human groups cut off from one another?

During the Ice Age, the oceans had less water than they have now. That was because much of the earth's water was "locked up" in the great icecap. The sea level fell so low that there was dry land in many places that are covered with water today. The Bering Strait, which lies between Asia and Alaska, was a "land bridge." So was the North Sea, which lies between the British Isles and the mainland of Europe. Some of the shallow seas between Europe and Africa and Asia were dry land. Probably there were land bridges between the Malay Peninsula and Indonesia in Southeast Asia, and between New Guinea and Australia. There was never a solid land bridge all the way from Southeast Asia to Australia.

THE GREAT LEAP FORWARD

A ▶ Find these "land bridges" on a world map or globe: the Bering Strait, the North Sea, the Straits of Gibraltar, the Dardanelles and the Hellespont, and the islands and shallow seas of Indonesia. What areas did each "land bridge" connect?

Using the land bridges of the Ice Age, people were able to settle in most lands south of the icecap. The places they settled were far apart. Some people settled in southern Africa. Other groups settled in eastern Asia, western Asia, Europe, and the Americas.

Some groups settled in Australia during the Ice Age. However, in order to get to Australia even during the Ice Age, people must have used rafts to cross a few deep channels.

For thousands of years, people in one part of the world never met different people in other parts of the world. When the icecap melted, the oceans grew deep again. The land bridges were covered with water. Groups were more cut off than ever. Women of a group married men of the same group. Thus people in a group came to look alike in some ways. Many scientists think that racial differences probably came about in this way.

Scientists have found many racial differences among humans. There are, four main racial groups:

1. Australoid [ôs′ trə loid′]
2. Mongoloid [mong′ gə loid′]
3. Negroid [nē′ groid]
4. Caucasoid [kôk′ ə soid′]

B ▶ Look at the map "How Racial Differences Probably Came About" (page 49).
   1. Find the four main racial groups.
   2. In what parts of the world did each group stay for many thousands of years?

C ★ See if you can name the racial group to which each of the following belongs:

| Arabs | Eskimos | Japanese | Australian Aborigines |
| French | Germans | Black Africans | Native Americans |

Differences of race are not important, but sometimes people think they are. That is why we need to understand just what *race* means and how races came about.

48   THE GROWTH OF CIVILIZATION

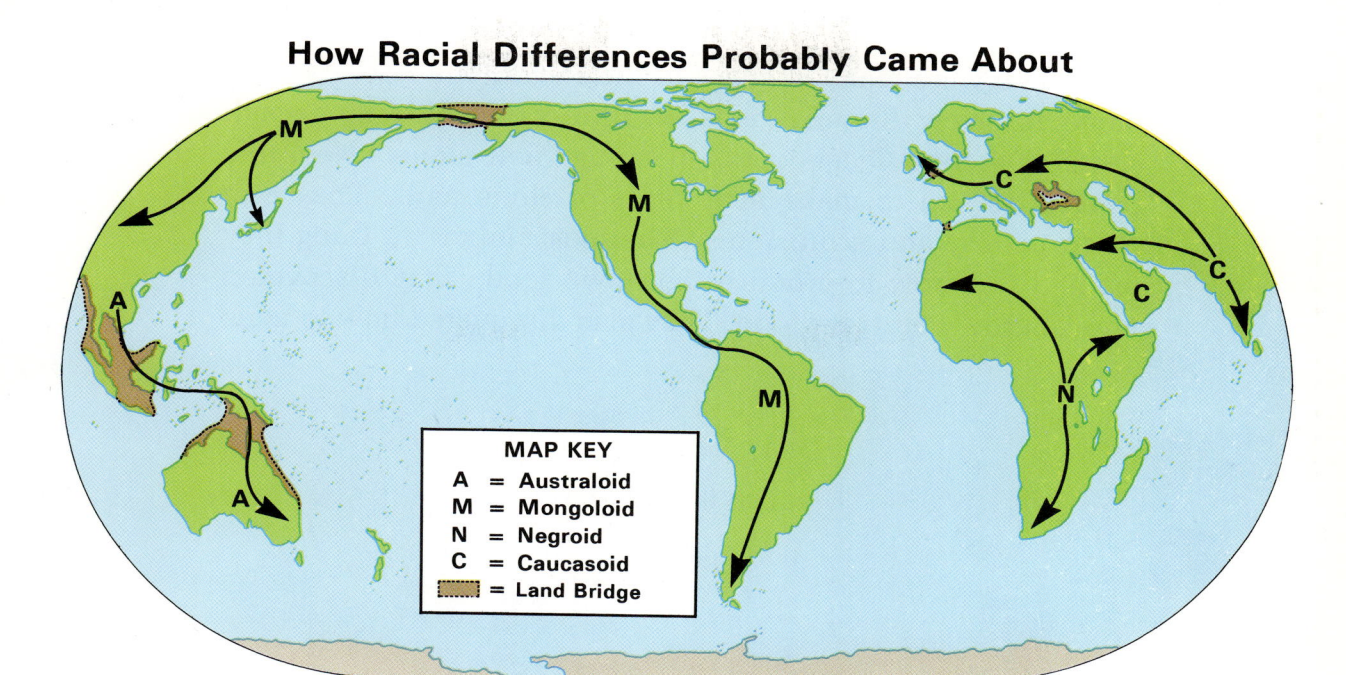

How Racial Differences Probably Came About

MAP KEY
A = Australoid
M = Mongoloid
N = Negroid
C = Caucasoid
▨ = Land Bridge

During the Ice Ages human groups wandered and settled as shown on the map. They used land bridges.

Until about 500 years ago, the four main races did not travel or mix much. Today, however, they mix more and more. Now people from different races can be found in many areas of the world. The United States, for example, has many people from every race.

D● Which will help you to understand other persons—knowing their race or knowing their culture? Explain.

Stage One of the Great Leap Forward

The great leap forward from the culture of the Old Stone Age to civilization was made in three stages. The first stage began about 8000 B.C.—the beginning of the New Stone Age. By this time, the Ice Age had ended. The climate had changed. Some parts of the world changed from forests and grasslands into deserts. People who lived in those areas began to look for better places to live. As their environment changed, humans were learning new things faster than they had learned before. Maybe the change in climate helped changes in cultures.

THE GREAT LEAP FORWARD 49

There were many changes in the New Stone Age. Another name for New Stone Age is **Neolithic** [nē′ə lith′ik] **period.** *Neolithic* is from Greek words meaning "new stone." Neolithic people learned to make new kinds of stone tools. They also made pottery and grindstones. The most important thing they learned was how to produce their own food. They discovered how to grow plants for food. They also discovered how to tame

Discovering Agriculture

This shows how a woman may have discovered how to grow crops.
1. She is cutting wild wheat and barley, using a wooden sickle with sharp stones for a blade.
2. She carries the seeds to the family.
3. She notices that a few seeds fall on the ground.
4. A month or two later she sees that wheat and barley plants have grown where she dropped the seeds.
5. She drops a lot of seeds on purpose.
6. A few months later she has a field of wheat and barley.

animals for food. These two discoveries are called **agriculture,** or farming. The discovery of agriculture was the beginning of the great leap forward.

How did people change from *finders* of food to *producers* of food? This great change did not take place all at once. People were not hunters and gatherers one day and farmers and herders the next. The change took place very slowly. Probably the first people who found out how to grow plants were women. Hunting-and-gathering cultures had a simple *division of labor.* **Division of labor** means that some persons do one job, while other persons do other jobs. This dividing the work is also called **cooperating,** or working together.

In hunting-and-gathering societies, men did the hunting and fishing. Women did the gathering of seeds, berries, and roots. Some women noticed something interesting about seeds that had dropped to the ground. The seeds grew into new plants! Some of the women had an idea. Why not plant seeds on purpose? Why not plant them where the new plants would be easy to find? The women had found a way of saving time. They had also found a safer food supply.

A ▶ How can planting seeds give people a "safer" food supply?

In the New Stone Age, someone had the idea of taming food animals. Old Stone Age hunters tamed dogs to help with hunting. But not until about 8000 B.C. did someone think of catching and taming wild goats and sheep. After 8000 B.C., people raised *herds* of goats and sheep. From their herds, people got meat, milk, wool, and leather. Soon people learned how to make butter and cheese. Later they tamed pigs and cows. Later still they tamed horses and camels. Another word for "taming" is **domesticating.** Humans learned how to *domesticate* plants and animals.

B● Suppose you wanted to domesticate an animal. How would you do it? Would you choose a young animal or an old one? Explain.

C● The animals that are easiest to domesticate are those that live in groups (herds, packs). Why is this so? Give examples of herd animals that have been domesticated.

THE GREAT LEAP FORWARD

The changes from hunting and gathering to agriculture came slowly. But they made a huge difference to humans and human societies. That is why the changes are called the **agricultural revolution,** or the **Neolithic revolution.** A *revolution* in this sense means a big change. The Neolithic revolution was the first stage of the great leap forward.

Some Changes Brought by the Neolithic Revolution

The Neolithic revolution was a revolution in **technology,** that is, it was a big change in ways of doing things and producing goods. Why did people take to the new technology of farming? They did so because farming was *more efficient* than the old technology of hunting and gathering. Farming was more efficient because it produced more goods by using less land and labor than hunting and gathering.

A hunting-and-gathering family needed a great deal of land for its food supply. Its members had to spend much time wandering—looking for seeds or trying to kill animals. A farming family could supply its needs with a field or garden for crops and a place where the tamed herds could graze. With the new technology of farming many more humans could live in the environment.

Societies did not switch suddenly from hunting and gathering to farming. For a long time many societies had a *mixed technology.* Part of their food came from hunting and part from farming. In the course of time, however, most societies in the Old World used farming only.

The revolution in technology led to other changes in societies. One change was that people now lived in *settled villages.* They could stay in one place for a long time. They learned how to build strong houses and fences. They could have storehouses, furniture, pots, and better clothes.

In a settled village there was more division of labor than in a hunting-gathering group. People were able to **specialize**—that is, learn special jobs. Some people became toolmakers. Some made pots. Some made cloth. Others looked after the herds. Still others grew crops. When people specialize, they are able to do a better job. They often have time to invent better tools. Neolithic people, for example, invented *spades* and *hoes*. These tools were more efficient than digging sticks.

A ▶ Look at the picture "A Neolithic Village after the Neolithic Revolution" below.
1. Point to the houses and storehouses.
2. Point to the oven for making pots.
3. Point to the women grinding wheat and barley into flour.
4. Point to the goats and dogs.
5. Point to the field of grain and the people bringing in bundles of wheat and barley.

A Neolithic Village after the Neolithic Revolution

The picture of the Neolithic village shows how people cleared an area for crops. They found that crops often grew best where trees had grown. Trees need plenty of water; so do most crops. In addition, the soil around trees is easier to dig up than grassland. But crops need sunshine. The farmers discovered how to kill a tree by slashing (cutting off) a ring of bark. When the trees were dead, the farmers set fire to the bushes and dead branches. The ashes made the soil better. Then the farmers dug the soil and planted seeds.

B ▶ Why is this way of farming called *slash-and-burn agriculture*?
C ▶ Why was land where trees grew good for agriculture?
D ▶ Why didn't Neolithic farmers chop the trees down? (Think about the tools they had.)

The Neolithic revolution brought another big change in societies. Now that people had settled in villages, they began to have more and more *property*. **Property** is the goods that people own. Rules about property were needed. People also needed to defend their property—their homes, fields, herds—against other groups. These needs led to stronger *government* and *laws*. Older persons with experience were leaders. They settled quarrels. They led the people when the group had to defend itself.

E ▶ What property did Paleolithic people have? What property did Neolithic people have?

The Neolithic revolution was the start of the great leap forward for the human species. Many more people could live on agricultural land than could live by hunting and gathering. Life was much safer. The supply of food was more certain.

In different parts of the Old World, people learned to grow many kinds of crops. Some societies grew rice or millet as their grain crop. Some grew bananas. Some grew peas and beans.

F ▶ What were the two great discoveries of the Neolithic revolution?
G ▶ How did Neolithic people learn to control the environment?
H ● Look again at the picture of the Neolithic village (page 53). What were some changes in human life brought by the Neolithic revolution? (Think of such things as food, work, use of spare time.)

THE GROWTH OF CIVILIZATION

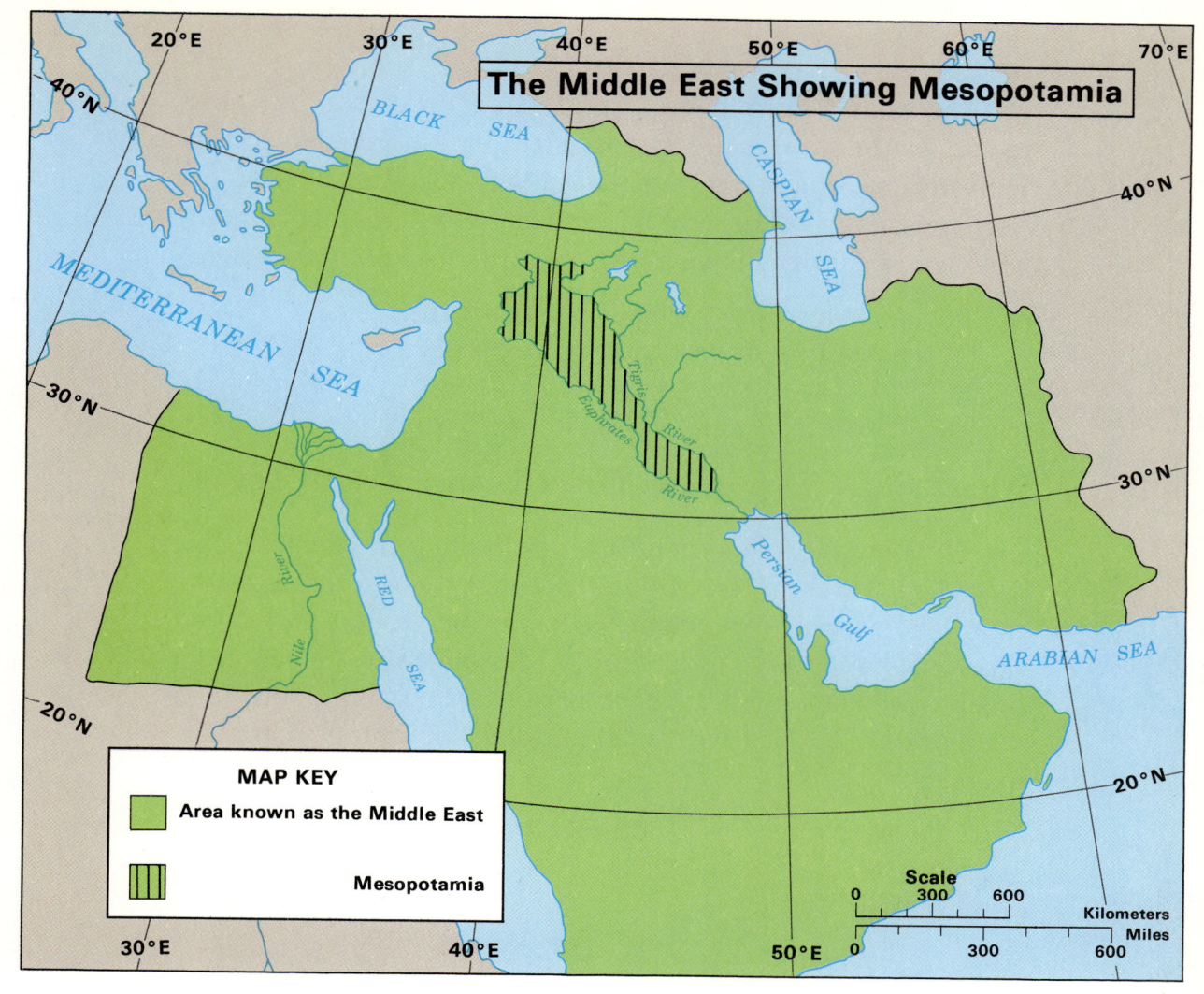

The Middle East Showing Mesopotamia

MAP KEY
- Area known as the Middle East
- Mesopotamia

This map shows the region now called the Middle East. Mesopotamia is the country now called Iraq.

People in the New World Discover How To Grow Food Plants

The Neolithic revolution happened in the Old World after 8000 B.C. By that time, the New World was cut off from the Old World because the icecap had melted. The land bridges had been covered by water, and the oceans had become deeper. But people in the New World also discovered how to grow food plants. They did not have wheat and barley. They had *maize* (corn), beans, and squash. Some people grew cotton for cloth.

THE GREAT LEAP FORWARD

The New World peoples had tame dogs, but not tame horses, cattle, or sheep. They had not yet discovered how to domesticate birds or pigs for food. Many societies in the New World still had a mixture of hunting and food-growing technologies when Europeans came to the Americas 500 years ago.

A▶ Why would a society that had no chickens, pigs, sheep, or cattle be likely to hunt as well as to grow crops?

Where Stage Two of the Great Leap Forward Began

Probably the first agriculture was in the hills of the Middle East. And it was in the Middle East that the next stage of the great leap forward was made. It happened in the land called *Mesopotamia* [mes′ ə pə tā′ mē ə]. Mesopotamia comes from Greek words meaning "the land between the rivers." This land was between the Tigris [tī′gris] and the Euphrates [yü frāt′ ēz] rivers.

A▶ Look at the map "The Middle East Showing Mesopotamia" (page 55).
   1. Find Mesopotamia.
   2. Find the two rivers that border Mesopotamia.
   3. What does *Mesopotamia* mean?
B★ Find the Middle East in an atlas. Find the following countries of the Middle East today: Iraq (what was its old name?); Iran (once called Persia); Saudi Arabia; Egypt.

A region's natural environment includes its physical features; soil, underground rocks and underground water; climate; and living things. Let us look at Mesopotamia's natural environment.

C▶ Look at the chart "Parts of the Natural Environment" (page 57). Why is each part important to humans?
D▶ Look at the map "Physical Features of Mesopotamia" (page 58).
   1. Find the highlands and the sources of the Tigris and Euphrates rivers.
   2. Find the lowland plain between the rivers.

56   THE GROWTH OF CIVILIZATION

PARTS OF THE NATURAL ENVIRONMENT

Physical features (landforms and bodies of water)

Soil, underground rocks, and underground water

Climate

Living things

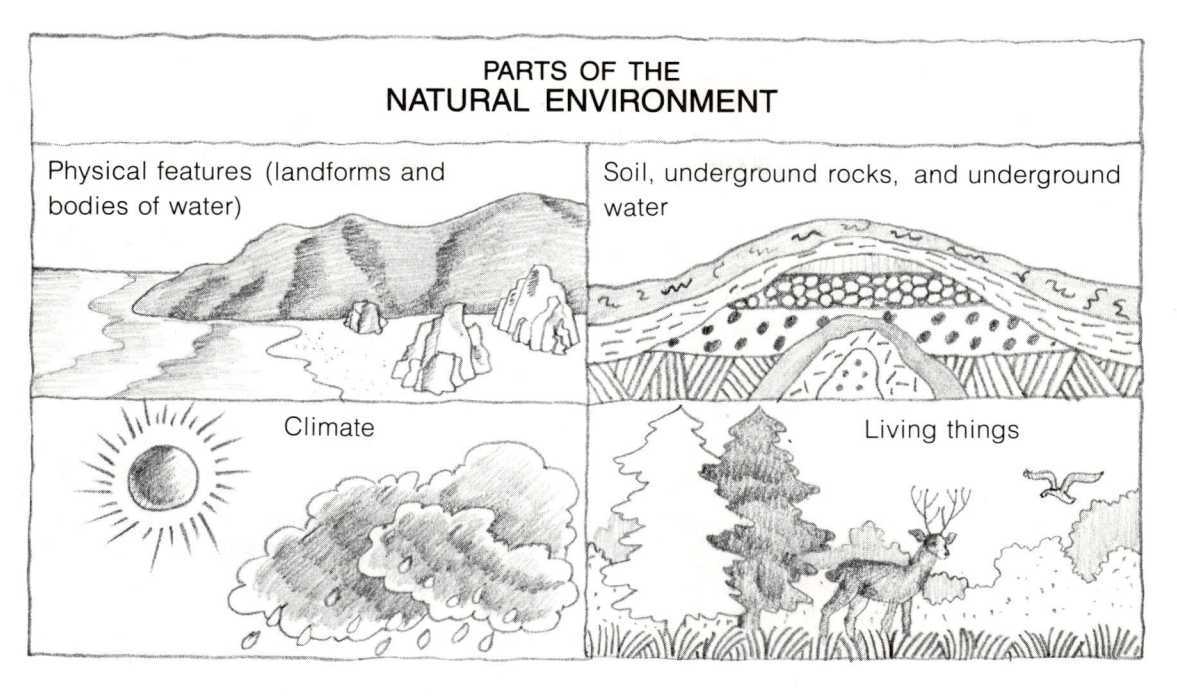

E★ In which part of Mesopotamia would you expect early slash-and-burn agriculture to begin? Why?

F● Look at the bar graphs "The Climate of Southern Mesopotamia" (page 59).
1. Look at the temperature graph. Does the temperature seem good for agriculture? Why or why not?
2. Now look at the precipitation graph. Do you think trees will grow in Mesopotamia? Do you think crops will grow there? Why or why not?

G● Look at the map "Rainfall of Mesopotamia" (page 60). What does the map tell you about southern Mesopotamia? The land southwest of the Euphrates River is desert. Would you expect southern Mesopotamia to be a desert too? Explain.

If we knew *only* the climate of southern Mesopotamia, we would expect it to be a desert. Yet the soil and natural living things tell a different story. The soil was rich. Grasses and trees grew there. For part of the year there were many miles of swamps and flooded land. Let us see why.

Every spring the snow melted on the northern mountains. Then the Tigris and Euphrates rivers became deep and strong. In southern Mesopotamia the rivers brought floods. In summer

THE GREAT LEAP FORWARD

the flooded lands dried slowly, and plants grew well for a time. Then the land dried out, and the plants died.

H▶ Why did the Tigris and the Euphrates overflow every year?
I★ Could people have agriculture in southern Mesopotamia? How?

For thousands of years people did not try to grow crops in southern Mesopotamia. Some herders lived there, but no farmers. Then the lands in the north became crowded. The soil began to wear out too. For those reasons, people in northern Mesopotamia had to find more land for agriculture.

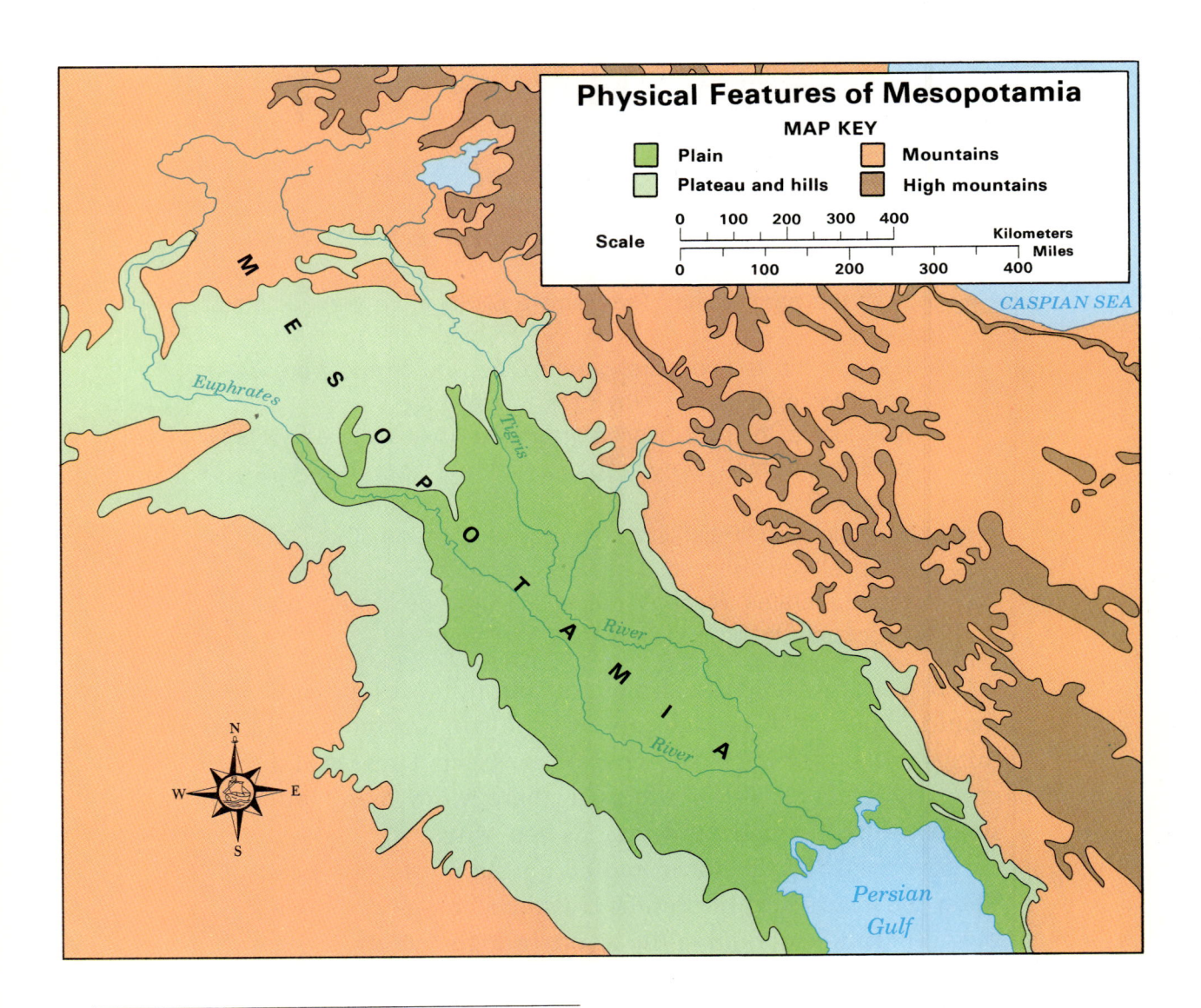

Physical Features of Mesopotamia

MAP KEY
- Plain
- Plateau and hills
- Mountains
- High mountains

THE GROWTH OF CIVILIZATION

The Climate of Southern Mesopotamia

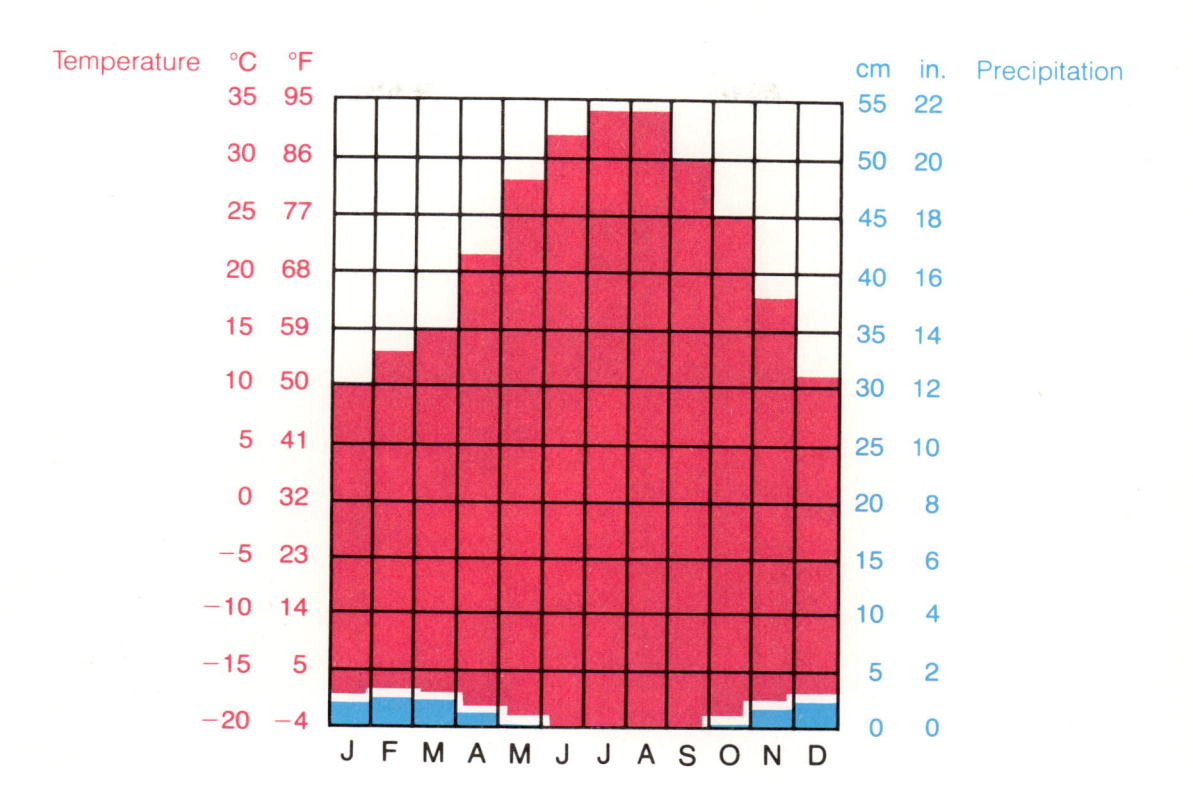

Temperature °C °F
35 95
30 86
25 77
20 68
15 59
10 50
5 41
0 32
−5 23
−10 14
−15 5
−20 −4

cm in. Precipitation
55 22
50 20
45 18
40 16
35 14
30 12
25 10
20 8
15 6
10 4
5 2
0 0

J F M A M J J A S O N D

Stage Two of the Great Leap Forward

The land of southern Mesopotamia was called Sumer [sü′mər]. It was in Sumer that stage two of the great leap forward took place. The people who lived in Sumer were **Sumerians** [sü mir′ ē ənz]. The Sumerians had a problem. They could *start* crops in the wet rich soil left by the river floods. But there was no rain. The hot sunshine dried the soil. Then the wheat and barley died before the food was ripe.

A▶ Why do most plants die if they get little or no water?

How could the Sumerians get water for their crops? They found an answer to the problem.

Every spring the flood waters left *silt* along the riverbanks. **Silt** is sand and soil carried along by the river waters. Year after year, this silt built up until it formed natural **levees** [lev′ ēz], or

THE GREAT LEAP FORWARD

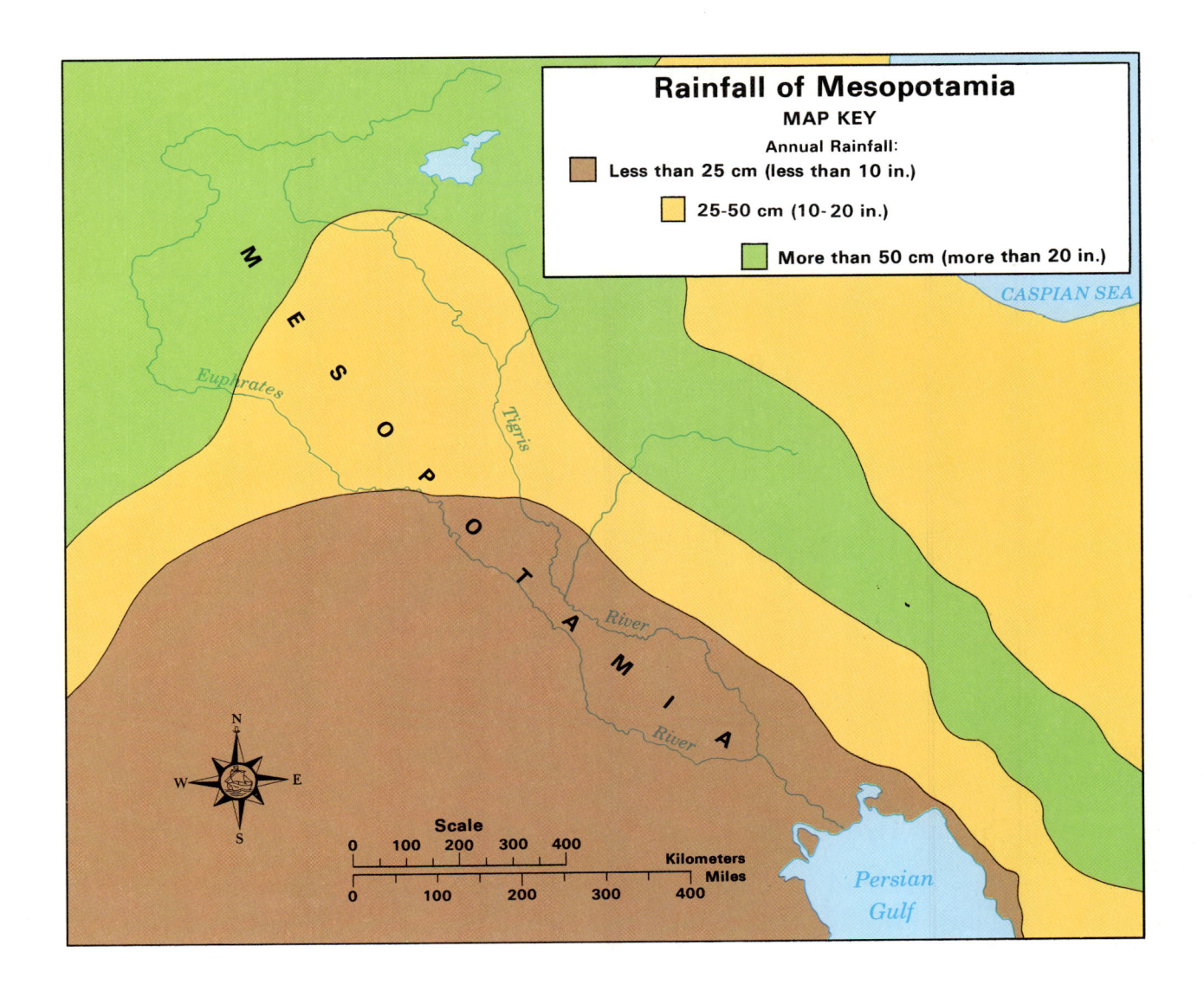

Rainfall of Mesopotamia
MAP KEY
Annual Rainfall:
- Less than 25 cm (less than 10 in.)
- 25-50 cm (10-20 in.)
- More than 50 cm (more than 20 in.)

banks of soil, on each side of the river. These levees gave the people the clue they needed to solve their water problem.

The Sumerians brought more soil to make the levees higher and stronger. Then the levees gave them some protection from the floods. The Sumerians used the levees in another way. When the fields became dry in the summer, the Sumerians made holes in the levees. The water would come pouring out. It flowed through ditches that the people had dug to carry water to their crops.

60   THE GROWTH OF CIVILIZATION

In time, the Sumerians made these ditches bigger. The ditches became *canals*. Many of the canals ran for many kilometers, bringing water to the crops. This way of watering the land is called **irrigation** [ir′ ə gā′ shən]. With irrigation, the Sumerians did not have to depend on rain to grow their crops. People were gaining more and more control over their environment.

In many ways irrigated agriculture was better than slash-and-burn agriculture. The soil was richer and deeper in the flood plains than on hillsides. The soil did not wear out so fast. It gave better crops.

Rain-watered crops *depend* on rain. In some years the rain fails to come. Then people starve. Yet the spring floods seldom failed. The mountain snow melted each year.

B★ There is one big danger when people rely on river floods. What is it?

Sumerians built up the levees and let water run out into the fields.

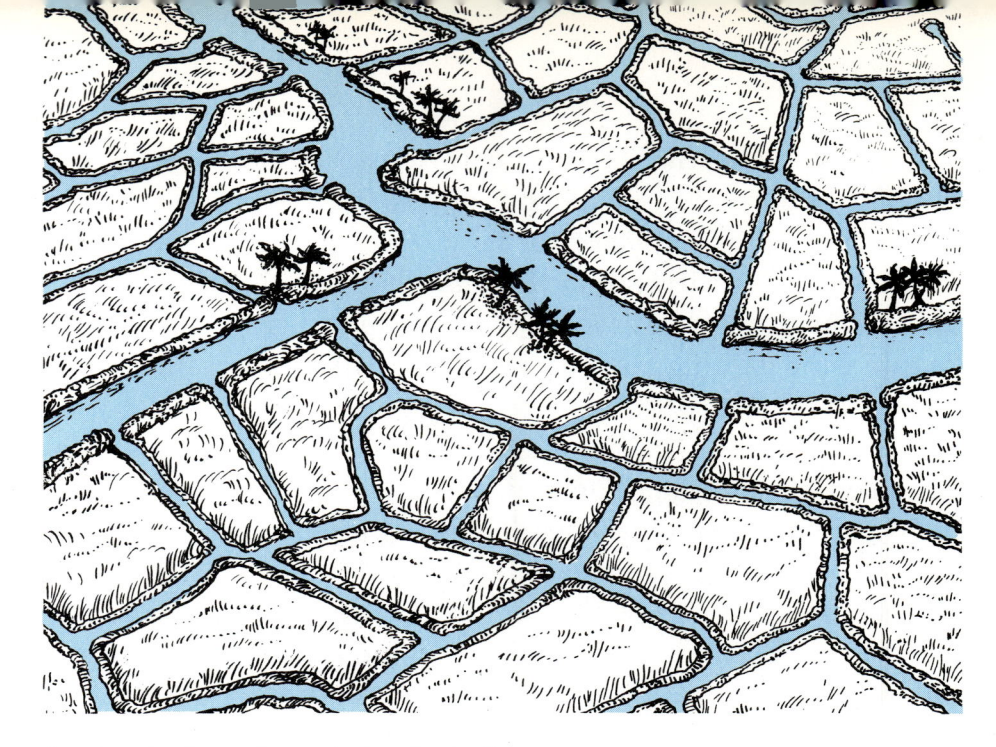

A network of canals carried water to the crops.

The irrigated agriculture of Sumer was the second stage of the great leap forward. The people of Sumer had more food for each person than humans had ever had before. They had more food than they and their families needed to eat. More people could specialize in jobs other than producing food.

C ▶ Why was irrigated agriculture a good invention?
D ● Why was it a good thing to have some people who did not have to work to produce food?

As Neolithic people learned more about irrigated agriculture, they invented better farm tools. The *plow*, for example, was invented in Neolithic times. Neolithic people had learned how to train animals to help them with their work. Some animals, such as oxen and donkeys, were trained to pull things. Animals that can pull things are called **draft animals.** Some Neolithic person had a good idea. Why not hitch oxen to a tool that would cut into the soil? This tool was the plow.

Another important invention of Neolithic times was the *wheel*. The invention of the wheel led to the invention of the cart. The use of draft animals to pull plows and carts saved a great deal of human labor.

THE GROWTH OF CIVILIZATION

E ▶ Look at the picture "An Early Plow" below. Why did the invention of the plow save humans a lot of hard work?

F ★ Find some pictures of plows used by farmers today. How are these plows pulled? Do they cut just one strip of soil (one *furrow*) at a time?

G ★ Name some draft animals. What animals did the Eskimos use as draft animals? Did those animals pull carts? Explain.

Stage Three of the Great Leap Forward

Big changes in technology caused more and more changes in society. Human life had changed very, very slowly in Paleolithic times. In Neolithic times, however, changes happened much faster. Changes grew like a snowball rolling down a hill. They were partly **economic changes**, that is, changes in the *production* and *consumption* (using) of goods.

Better technology meant that more people were free to do jobs other than producing food. These people became *specialists*. Some repaired the levees. Some repaired the canals. Some made pots or cloth or tools. Others took charge of groups of workers and showed them how to work together better. Those who took charge were managers.

In other words, there was more division of labor. Usually when there is a great division of labor, more goods are produced for each worker. Production is *more efficient*.

An early Sumerian plow

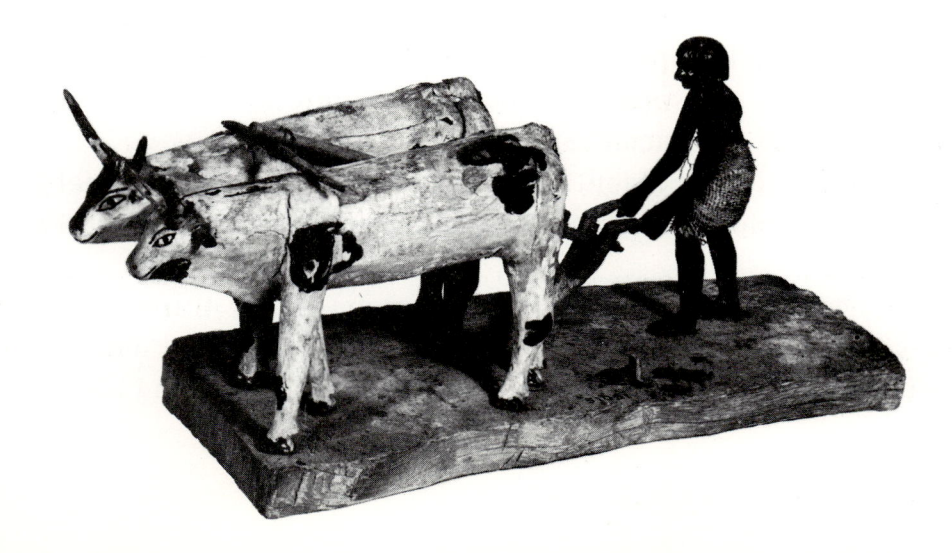

Another result of the division of labor was that villages grew larger. The villages grew into towns. Some early Sumerian towns had more than a thousand people. This meant that there was a bigger *market* for goods. **Market** means two things. It means the *place* where buyers and sellers meet to trade, or exchange, goods. It also means *all the trade that goes on between buyers and sellers*.

There are two kinds of goods: consumer goods and capital goods. When we use goods to satisfy our wants, we *consume* them. These are **consumer goods**, such as food, clothes, and houses. Some goods, however, are used *to produce* other goods. These are **capital goods**, such as tools, machines, and workshops.

Perhaps the most important economic change was that people had more capital goods than ever before. Paleolithic societies had capital goods, such as stone tools, nets, or traps. The people of Sumer had many kinds of capital goods: levees, canals, workshops, ships, plows, and tools of many kinds.

A ▶ Give some examples of capital goods that we use to produce goods today.

These economic changes came because humans kept inventing and learning new things. These new ideas were passed on.

Along with economic changes there were other changes in culture. People built the first cities. The first cities in Sumer were built about 3500 B.C. Society in cities was organized in groups called *classes*. There were farm workers. There were workers in workshops. There were traders, or merchants. There were learned persons, most of them priests. There were soldiers, who also acted as police.

Laws and government became more complicated. A society of 1,000 people is more complicated than a society of 20 or 30 people.

Ideas changed, too. Learned persons could think about religion. They discovered mathematics. They invented writing. (The photo on page 65 is an example of Sumerian writing.) With

A Sumerian accounting tablet (c. 1980 B.C.). The writing is cuneiform, a system invented by the Sumerians. Not only did the Sumerians have some knowledge of mathematics; they also had an understanding of medicine and astronomy.

the invention of writing the prehistoric period ended—at least for the societies that knew how to write.

When the snowball of change reached this point, a new kind of society existed in Sumer. We call it a *civilized society*, or **civilization**. Civilization was the third and last stage of the great leap forward that began with the Neolithic revolution. The first civilization, as far as we know, was made by the Sumerians. In the rest of this book we shall be studying different civilized societies in history.

Civilized societies are different from one another. They have different cultures. Yet there are certain things that all civilized societies have. Perhaps the easiest way to sum up the signs of civilization is by listing them as follows:

Civilization: A Stage of Human Societies

1. Efficient production of food and other goods
2. Great division of labor *(specialization)*
3. Savings: capital (better tools, roads irrigation canals, workshops)
4. Large market: wealth
5. Large communities: towns and cities
6. Big government: officials, soldiers, taxes
7. More learning: invention of writing and reading
8. Classes (learned persons, merchants, and so on)

THE GREAT LEAP FORWARD

B ▶ Look at the box "The Snowball of Change, 8000–3500 B.C." below. What things were found in all civilized societies? (Look at the end of Stage Two and at Stage Three.)
C ● Why could the Neolithic village in the picture on page 53 *not* have the things in Stages Two and Three?
D ● How do *savings* provide *capital goods*?
E ● How does a *larger market* lead to *greater wealth* or more goods per person? (Think of division of labor.)
F ● Why can a civilized society have *more learning* than a noncivilized one?

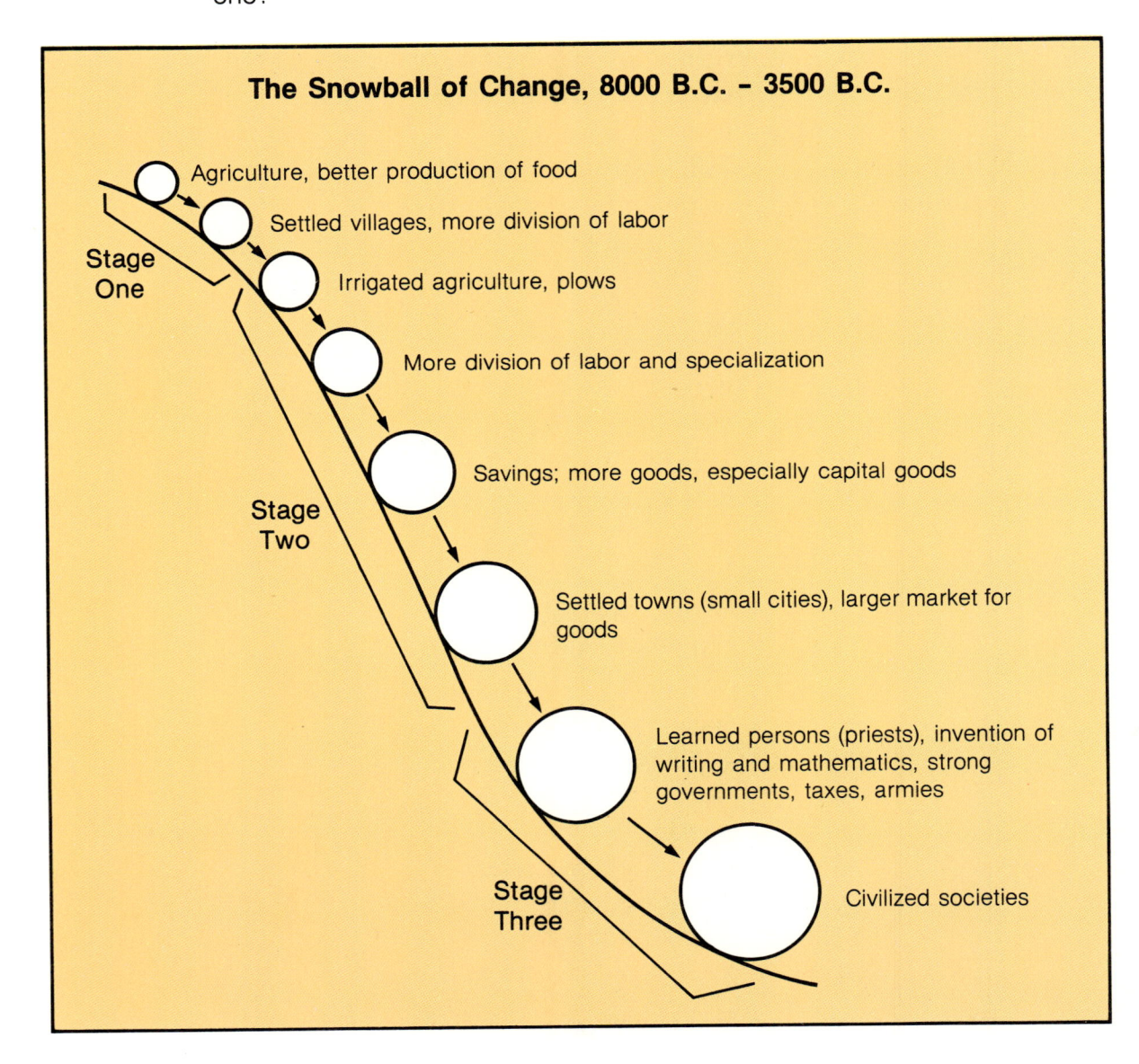

The Snowball of Change, 8000 B.C. – 3500 B.C.

Stage One
- Agriculture, better production of food
- Settled villages, more division of labor
- Irrigated agriculture, plows

Stage Two
- More division of labor and specialization
- Savings; more goods, especially capital goods
- Settled towns (small cities), larger market for goods

Stage Three
- Learned persons (priests), invention of writing and mathematics, strong governments, taxes, armies
- Civilized societies

66   THE GROWTH OF CIVILIZATION

G Look at the time line "Prehistoric Humans and Civilization" below.
1. Which part of the time line is shown in the box "The Snowball of Change" (page 66)?
2. About what date was agriculture invented?
3. About when did the earliest cities appear?
4. Where on the time line is the year you are living in?

H The scale of the time line from 50,000 B.C. is 2 centimeters = 10,000 years. How long would the time line be if we used the same scale from 1,500,000 B.C. to 50,000 B.C.? (1,500,000 ÷ 10,000 = 150. 150 × 2 cm = ?)

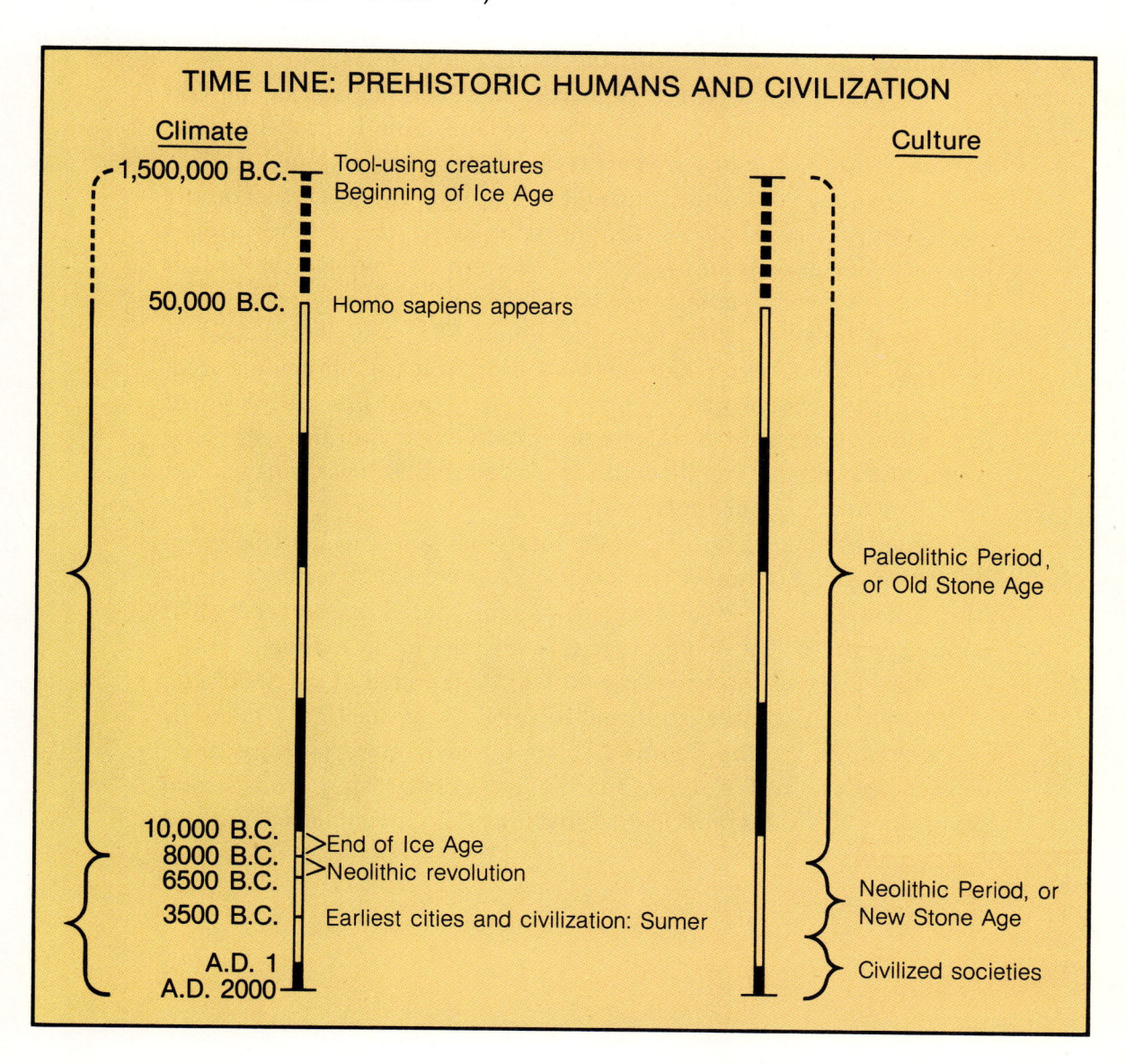

TIME LINE: PREHISTORIC HUMANS AND CIVILIZATION

Climate | | **Culture**

- 1,500,000 B.C. — Tool-using creatures / Beginning of Ice Age
- 50,000 B.C. — Homo sapiens appears
- Paleolithic Period, or Old Stone Age
- 10,000 B.C. — End of Ice Age
- 8000 B.C. — Neolithic revolution
- 6500 B.C.
- 3500 B.C. — Earliest cities and civilization: Sumer
- A.D. 1
- A.D. 2000
- Neolithic Period, or New Stone Age
- Civilized societies

THE GREAT LEAP FORWARD 67

Summary

This chapter covers a very long period. Prehistoric times were the times before there were any written records. Writing was invented only about 3500 B.C. Writing spread slowly. Many societies were still prehistoric while others had begun to use writing.

Human beings can change their ways of living because they can communicate and cooperate. However, for many thousands of years human societies and cultures changed very, very slowly. We call this period the Old Stone Age, or Paleolithic period. People had rough tools of stone and wood. They got food by hunting and gathering. The Paleolithic period lasted until the end of the Ice Age.

During the Ice Age, humans lived in different parts of the Old World. They did not mix with other groups. This is probably how humans came to belong to different races. However, people did move to other parts of the world during the Ice Age. The icecap made the oceans less deep in places. People were able to cross land bridges between Asia and America, between Western Europe and the British Isles, and between some other land areas.

About 8000 B.C., the Ice Age ended. The New Stone Age, or Neolithic period, began. During this period humankind made a great leap forward. Stage one of this great leap was the discovery of agriculture, called the Neolithic revolution. Food supplies were now much more certain. People could live in settled villages. They could save and make better tools.

Changes then came faster. In Mesopotamia—the land between the Tigris and Euphrates rivers—people invented irrigated agriculture. This was stage two of the great leap forward. Sumerians now had enough food so that some persons were free to specialize.

Stage three of the great leap forward happened about 3500 B.C., when Sumer became a civilized society, or civilization. Towns or cities were built. The people had more food, more savings, more capital goods, and a large market for goods. They had strong governments, armies, and learned persons who invented writing and mathematics.

Some Interesting Activities

1. Write a story about one of these topics:
   a. Living in a Paleolithic society
   b. The beginning of agriculture
   c. How people learned about irrigated agriculture

2. Use an encyclopedia to find out about some of these things:
   a. The Ice Age (sometimes called the *Pleistocene [plī′ stə sēn′] epoch)*
   b. Paleolithic (Old Stone Age) cultures and tools
   c. Neolithic (New Stone Age) cultures

3. Make a model or a drawing of a Neolithic village.

4. Write or tell about the following ideas: technology; division of labor, or cooperation and specialization; capital goods; and efficient production. Explain how they fit together.

5. Divide your class into groups of six or seven. Try to imagine that you are in the wilderness. Discuss how you should organize yourselves. How would you get food and shelter?

6. Make a model of river-valley irrigation. You can fill a large shallow pan with dirt or sand. To make canals, scrape the sand away and line the banks of the canals with aluminum foil. Carefully add water so it flows in the canals.

7. Find out what kinds of goods are produced in the area of the Tigris and Euphrates today. Do the people still grow crops there? What kinds?

THE GREAT LEAP FORWARD

Shown above are the ruins of an ancient Sumerian city on the banks of the Euphrates River. The site is located at what is now Mari, Syria.

CHAPTER 4

Discovering the Earliest Civilization: Sumer

In this chapter and the next, we shall see what the civilized culture of Sumer was like. We shall see why people liked civilized society and why other peoples copied Sumer. Once humans had invented civilization, they never lost it. However, no civilized society so far has lasted for more than about 2,500 years. Most have lasted for a shorter time.

A▶ What is a civilized society?

The story of the discovery of early civilizations has come to us through the work of historians and archaeologists [är kē ol′ ə jists]. **Archaeologists** are scholars who learn about the past by studying human-made objects that people have left behind. Such objects are called **artifacts**. Archaeologists usually dig in the ground to find artifacts.

B▶ What prehistoric artifacts have you learned about?
C▶ How do historians learn about the past?

An artist's reconstruction of the Hanging Gardens of Babylon, considered by the ancient Greeks to be one of the Seven Wonders of the World

Sumer Forgotten and Rediscovered

Many scholars believe that Sumer was the earliest civilization. No one knows for sure who the Sumerians were or where they came from. Working together, the Sumerians built a new kind of society. They organized workers and irrigated the land. They built cities. Sumerian civilization became rich and strong. It lasted for about 1,500 years. Toward the end of that time, it began to grow weak, or **decline**. Other civilizations took its place.

For more than 4,000 years, Sumer was forgotten. Historians did not learn about Sumer until early in the twentieth century. The people who found it were looking for traces of other civilizations. They learned later that these other civilizations came after Sumer.

Sumer was forgotten because other societies conquered the cities of Sumer. These societies copied Sumer's civilization. Sometimes they built new cities on the ruins of Sumer's cities. Sometimes they built cities in other places. Sumer's ruins either sank into the ground or were covered with silt from the river floods. What was left of the first civilization was deep underground.

How did people find out about Sumer? The steps leading to the discovery of Sumer read like a detective story. It is the story of how historians and archaeologists put together many clues to solve a great mystery. The clues led first to other ancient civilizations. Finally the clues led to Sumer. Before you read on, see if you can think of what these clues might have been. Use these questions to help you:

A ▶ Suppose you wanted to find out about a group of people who left no written records. How would you be able to find out about these people?

B ● Who would leave more clues—hunters or people who lived in cities?

First Clue: Historical Writings

Historical writings gave the first clues about Sumer. Three millennia after Sumerian civilization began, there was still a great civilization in Mesopotamia. It was called Babylon. Historians wrote about it.

A ▶ Babylon was where the town of Al Hillah, Iraq, now stands. Find Al Hillah on a map of the Middle East.

Let us read two old stories about Babylon. The first one comes to us from a Greek named Herodotus [hə rod′ ə təs]. Herodotus was a great historian of the ancient world.

A Story of Babylon

Very little rain falls in Babylon. There is just enough rain to make the grain begin to grow. After that, the plants must be irrigated with water from the Euphrates River. The waters of the Euphrates do not flood the grain fields naturally. Water must be spread across the land by hard work, canals, and buckets. The hard work produces wonderful results. Of all the countries that I have seen, no other produces so much grain.

Let me tell you how the Babylonians used to set up their marriages. Once a year, all the girls who were old enough to marry were brought together in one place. The men stood around them in a circle. Each girl in turn was offered up for sale as a wife. The pretty girls were sold first. Rich men who wanted wives bid against one another for the pretty girls. When all the pretty girls were gone, the plain girls were sold. The plainest girl would be asked to stand up. The poor men were asked who would take the least money to marry her. (The Babylonians thought that poor men had no use for pretty wives. They were paid to take the plain girls.) The poor men were paid with the money collected from the sale of the pretty girls. Marriages could be set up only in this way. It was against the law for a father to pick a husband for his daughter.

Other stories about the Babylonians are found in the Old Testament. (Most of what Christians call the Old Testament is the Hebrew Bible.) Our second story comes from the Old Testament. This Bible story tells about armies that marched out of Babylon to conquer the city of Jerusalem.

The Story of an Attack on Jerusalem

The servants of the king of Babylon (Assyria) came up to Jerusalem and attacked the city. And the king of Babylon came to the city while his servants were attacking it. And the king of Jerusalem gave himself up to the king of Babylon. He gave up himself and his mother, and his servants, and his princes, and his palace officials. The king of Babylon took him prisoner in the eighth year of his reign. And he also carried off all the treasures of the king's house and cut in pieces all the vessels of gold in the house of the Lord. He carried away captive all of Jerusalem. He carried away all the princes and all the brave warriors, 10,000 captives, and all the craftsmen. And none were left, except the poorest people of the land. Thus he carried away the king to Babylon and the king's mother, the king's wives, his officials, and the chief men of the land. And he took them all into captivity from Jerusalem to Babylon.

The Bible also tells how Abraham left a city called Ur [ėr]. We now know that Ur was one of the first Sumerian cities. It must have been about 2,000 years old when Abraham left it.

B★ In the Old Testament you can find that Abraham, the ancestor of the Jews, was born in "Ur of the Chaldees [kal′ dēz]." Look at the

Book of Genesis, chapter 11, verse 28. Other things in the Old Testament seem to hint at ancient Sumer. Look at the same chapter 11 of Genesis, verses 1 through 9. Historians think that the "land of Shinar" was Sumer. The brick Tower of Babel seems very like the high temples of Sumer and Babylon.

Second Clue: Tels and Tablets

The second clue to Sumer was discovered about 350 years ago by an Italian scholar, Pietro della Valle [pyā′ trō dāl′ lä väl′ lā]. Della Valle went to southern Mesopotamia. He looked for traces of ancient cities he had read about in the Bible and in old stories. He saw that the land of southern Mesopotamia was flat. Yet, here and there, he saw high *mounds*, or hills, that stuck up from the plain. The people of Mesopotamia called the mounds **tels**.

Excavation at this site in Babylon revealed a highly advanced civilization in an ancient Sumerian city. Note the tall brick buildings.

Della Valle wondered what the tels could be. They seemed to have been made by people. However, the people who lived in Mesopotamia could not explain what the tels were.

A ▶ To see what a tel looks like, look at the picture on page 75. The building on top of the tel is not very old.

Near one of the tels, Della Valle found some flat clay bricks, or tablets. The clay tablets were covered with little marks. The marks looked like the footprints of birds walking over wet sand. Della Valle thought that the marks might be writing. He took some of the clay tablets home with him. In Europe, other scholars studied the marks. They decided that the marks were a form of writing. However, scholars could not read the writing. The writing was called *cuneiform* [kyü nē′ ə fôrm]. **Cuneiform** is Latin for "shaped like wedges."

B ▶ Look at the picture of cuneiform writing. Is the name a good one?

The cuneiform writing on this clay tablet relates the end of the flood story from the epic poem of Gilgamesh (see pages 108–109).

Third Clue: Artifacts

Later, more and more cuneiform tablets were found near the tels. Then archaeologists began to dig into the tels. They discovered that the tels were made up of the ruins of ancient cities. Archaeologists usually found one set of ruins near the top of the tel. Underneath those ruins was another set of ruins. Still another set of ruins lay underneath those.

Many artifacts were buried in the ruins. Archaeologists dug up tools, dishes, toys, jewelry, and statues. They also found many clay tablets with cuneiform writing.

A ▶ What artifacts would help scholars know about the work of early people?

B ▶ Do the artifacts found in the tels show that the society had much division of labor?

C ● If you dig down deep and find three or more layers of ruins, what would you think about the age of the ruins? What layer is the oldest? (Think how long it takes for rubbish and soil to pile up over ruins.)

D ● Why would people keep building new houses where older ones had been? (Think about why the earliest cities were built in certain places.) Do we build new buildings where older buildings have been in our cities?

E ● Why might there be so many clay tablets with cuneiform writing in the ruins?

Fourth Clue: The Key to Cuneiform Writing

The fourth clue to Sumer's civilization was found in Persia, now the country of Iran. A huge rock, far from Mesopotamia, was the key to understanding cuneiform writing. Carved on the rock were some pictures and three messages. The messages were in cuneiform. Who had made the carvings on the rock? What did they mean?

One of the kings of ancient Persia was Darius [də rī′ əs] the Great. He wanted everyone in his kingdom to know that he was a great ruler. So Darius ordered that a record of his deeds be carved on a rock for all to see. Below the pictures, messages were carved to tell about those deeds. The messages were in three languages. All three languages were written in cuneiform. The picture below shows the carving.

Darius the Great seated on his throne at Persepolis (Iran)

A Do you know of any languages today that share the same alphabet? Give some examples.

The carvings on the rock were about 90 meters (about 300 feet) above the ground. Archaeologists had not been able to get near them. Finally, those who were interested in cuneiform figured out a way. They used long ladders, cables, and hooks. Then, dangling from the end of a rope, one man copied the writing.

The hardest work still lay ahead. The scholars had to find out what the writing said. One scholar had an idea. This person knew that many writings of the kings of Persia began like this: "So-and-So, the great king, the king of kings, son of So-and-So . . . ." The scholar thought that maybe the cuneiform writing on the rock also began with these words. He studied the cuneiform to test this idea. The order of the marks told the scholar that he was right.

With this key, scholars were able to figure out one of the messages. It described the king's victories in battle and the way in which he had gained his throne. Then the scholars used that message as a key to translate the other two messages. One of these two messages was written in the language of ancient Babylonia.

Scholars matched the Babylonian message with the writing on the tablets from southern Mesopotamia. The cuneiform writing on the tablets did not match the writing of the Babylonians! That puzzled the scholars. It made them suspect that the Babylonians had "borrowed" their writing from an even earlier people.

B Can you guess whose writing the Babylonians had "borrowed"?

Step by step, the scholars found the earliest writing of all. Then they learned how to read this writing. A whole new world opened up for them. The clay tablets gave up their secrets. The tablets led the archaeologists back past the Babylonians to the people who had invented cuneiform writing. These people were the Sumerians. The mystery of Sumer was almost solved.

DISCOVERING THE EARLIEST CIVILIZATION: SUMER

Fifth Clue: More Digging

Archaeologists dug deeper into some of the tels in southern Mesopotamia. Some tels had as many as 18 layers of city ruins! At the lowest layer were the oldest cities of all. Artifacts in the lowest layer were made about 3500 B.C. At last scholars had found what they believed was the oldest civilization.

Archaeologists must dig very carefully. Often the ruins are only shown by different colors of earth. The only traces of wood artifacts may be holes and stains in the earth. Even some metals can turn into fine powder. The diggers may have to use teaspoons or paint brushes. Sometimes archaeologists do not even use tools. They just blow the dirt off an artifact. Often the artifacts have been smashed into hundreds of pieces. All the bits must be collected carefully. At every stage of digging, the archaeologists must make lists and drawings and photographs of everything they find.

- A● Why must archaeologists take care not to mix up artifacts found at different layers of the "dig"?
- B▶ Look at the picture of the harp with a bull's head on page 81. Notice how the harp was crushed and flattened by the earth. Then see how skilled workers restored the artifact.
- C● At some layers archaeologists found artifacts of metal, especially copper and gold. But there is no copper or gold in Sumer's natural environment. What does this tell about the trade of Sumerian cities?

The City of Ur

Ur was one of Sumer's oldest cities. It lasted about 2,700 years. At times Ur was destroyed by conquerors. But it was rebuilt again and again.

- A● Look at the map "Sumerian Cities" (page 82). It shows some of the earliest cities of Sumer.
    1. About how many kilometers long from northwest to southeast was the land of Sumer?
    2. Find the city of Ur.

THE GROWTH OF CIVILIZATION

3. What has happened to the coast at the northwest end of the Persian Gulf since the time of Ur? What may have caused the change?

Between 1922 and 1934 Ur was dug up by a team of American and British archaeologists. Sir Leonard Woolley, a British archaeologist, was in charge of the team. Woolley and his wife, Lady Katherine Woolley, made discoveries that excited the whole world. Deep under the city of Ur, they found a huge grave. At the bottom of the grave were the skeletons of many

(above, left) A Sumerian harp with a bull's head as found in the ground. *(above, right)* The harp after it was restored.
(right) The plaster cast of the decayed wooden parts, used in making the restoration.

Sumerian Cities

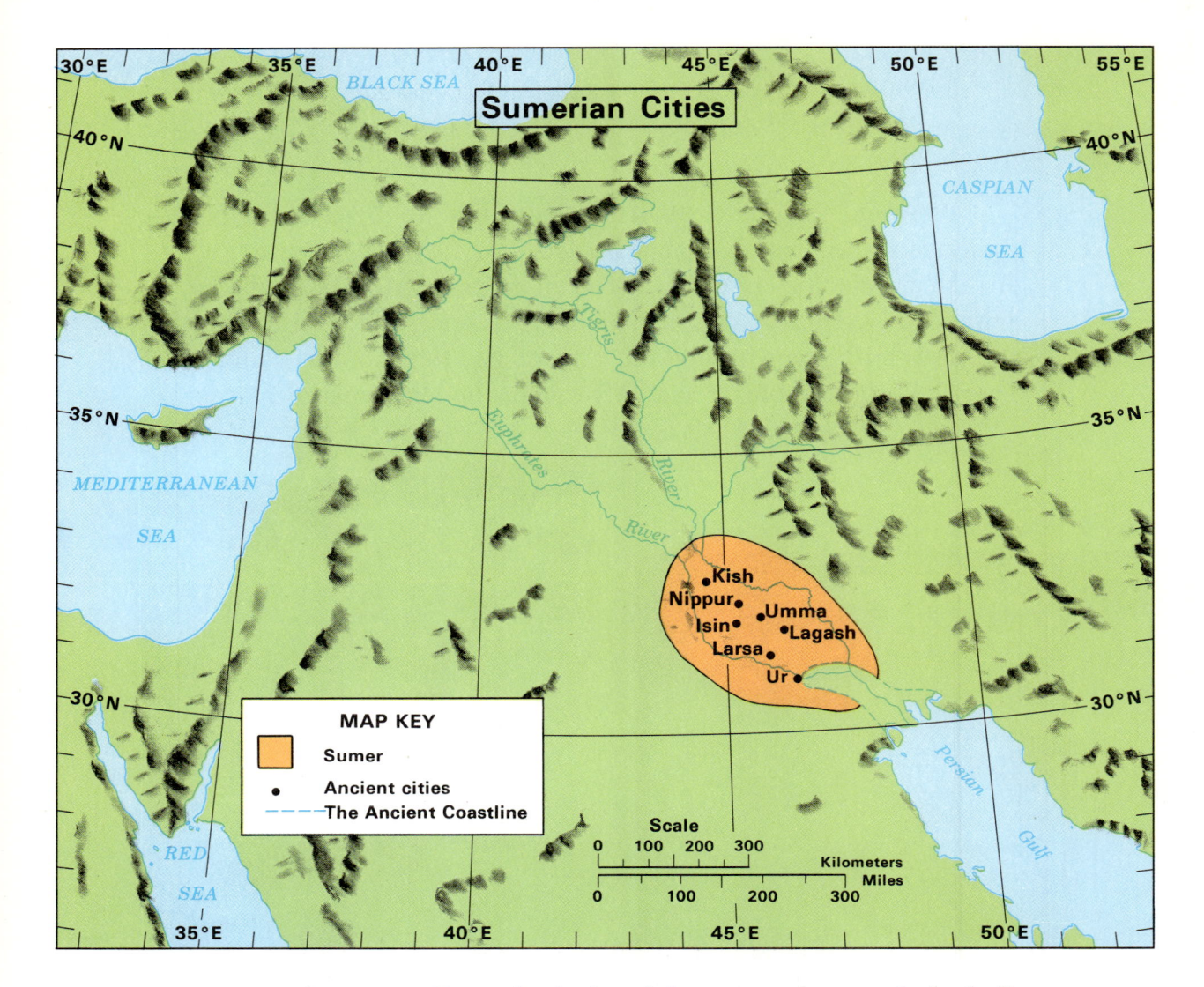

men and women. From the looks of the grave, the people had all been buried on the same day. The body of one woman was set apart from the other bodies. She had been dressed more beautifully than the other women. She wore a fancy headdress. Woolley believed that she was Queen Shubad. He thought that the people buried with her were the members of her court.

B ★ Read Genesis, chapter 11, in the Old Testament to find out what is said about the city of Ur.

The Woolleys found many things in the grave. They found the skeletons of some Sumerian men. On their heads were copper helmets. At their sides were spears. They probably were

THE GROWTH OF CIVILIZATION

the queen's soldiers. The Woolleys found the skeleton of one woman next to a harp. Her finger bones still lay across the strings of the harp. She must have been the court musician. Two wagons were found. The bones of oxen lay in front of them. In the wagons lay the bones of the drivers. There were skeletons of 64 women in the grave. They probably were ladies of the court. They were buried in wool dresses that had been bright red.

All the skeletons were found in neat, orderly rows. There were no signs of struggle or violence. All the men and women in the grave must have died peacefully. What did it mean? Woolley studied the clues to find out. One clue seemed especially important. Next to each body was a little metal cup.

C ▶ Before you read on, think about the clues and see how much of the mystery you can solve for yourself. Why were all the people buried with the queen? Why were there no signs of a struggle?

After studying all the clues, Woolley gave his explanation of what happened when Queen Shubad died. He believed that first a large, deep grave was dug in the ground. Queen Shubad's body was placed in the grave. Then all the queen's servants climbed into the pit. They knew they were going to die. When they were all in the pit, each one drank from a cup. The cups probably held some drug that put them to sleep and caused death. The pit was then filled with dirt. The funeral was over.

We will never know if Woolley's explanation was right. We do know that the grave was dug a very long time ago. Archaeologists have not found any other such graves in the remains from later periods of Sumer.

D ● Do you think archaeologists of the future will find out much about our civilization by digging up the graves of our important people? Why or why not?

E ● Can you guess why the queen was buried with many treasures? Why were her servants buried with her? Do you suppose the Sumerians believed in some kind of life after death?

F ● Look at the Sumerian artifacts of gold on pages 84–85. What ideas do they give you about Sumerian civilization?

G ★ Is gold a good metal for daggers and helmets? Explain.

DISCOVERING THE EARLIEST CIVILIZATION: SUMER

Two bowls of gold and a fluted gold tumbler

Sumerian Artifacts. The four photos show objects of gold excavated at Ur. The objects reveal the highly developed skill and artistry of the Sumerians in the use of metals.

A helmet of gold. It is believed to be that of a prince.

THE GROWTH OF CIVILIZATION

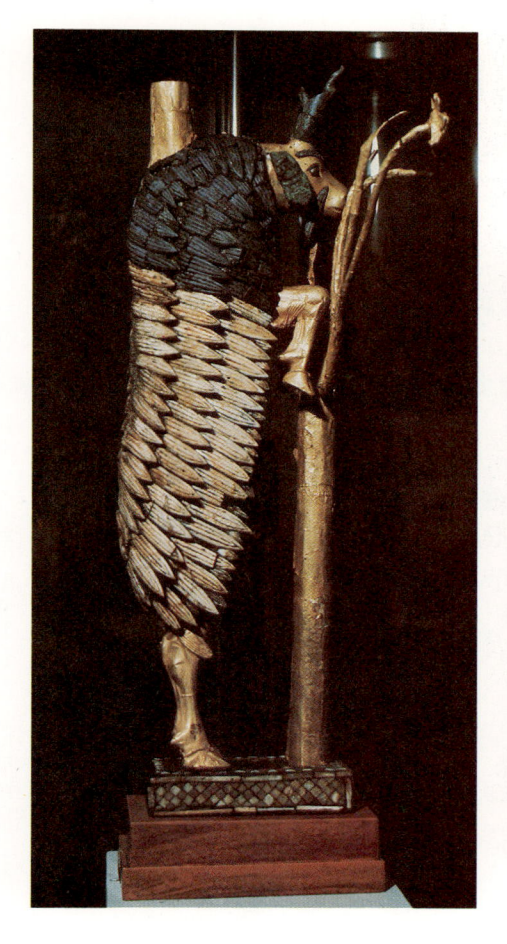

The goat in the thicket features gold and jewels; it also contains wood and shells.

A golden dagger and sheath

Metals Used in Sumer:

As early as 5000 B.C. some peoples had learned about copper, gold, and silver. Gold and silver were used in Sumer for ornaments. Copper was mainly used for tools, weapons, and armor. By 3000 B.C. people had learned how to make copper harder by mixing it with tin. This mixture is called *bronze*.

The Sumerians traded to get the metals they wanted. Sometimes tin was very hard to get. Copper could also be made harder by heating it, cooling it slowly, and hammering it. Bronze was better than copper, however.

A★ Sumerians used bronze and copper tools. People did not learn to use iron until about 1200 B.C. Why would iron or steel be better for tools and weapons than copper or bronze?

DISCOVERING THE EARLIEST CIVILIZATION: SUMER **85**

Summary

Historians and archaeologists help us to know about the past. Historians study written records. Archaeologists study artifacts—the human-made objects people have left behind. It is through the work of historians, archaeologists, and other scholars that we know about early civilizations.

The first civilization as far as we know was in Sumer, in southern Mesopotamia. For more than 4,000 years it was forgotten. Other societies conquered Sumer. They built new cities over the ruins of Sumerian cities.

Yet there were clues that hinted at Sumer. There were hints in the Old Testament (the Hebrew Bible) and in the history written by Herodotus. An Italian scholar in the seventeenth century A.D. found mysterious high mounds in Mesopotamia. He also found bricks with marks on them that scholars call cuneiform writing.

Later, archaeologists began to dig down into the mounds, or tels. They found that in each tel there were ruins of ancient cities. In fact, the layers in the mounds showed that the cities had become ruins and then had been rebuilt many times. The lowest layers were the oldest cities: the cities of Sumer.

Archaeologists also came upon tombs of Sumerians. One tomb was that of Queen Shubad. The tombs contained artifacts from Ur and other cities. The artifacts gave the archaeologists an idea of what Sumerian civilization must have been like.

From these artifacts, we learned about the Sumerians' style of building, their tools and weapons, their clothes, and their social organization. The artifacts tell us that the Sumerians used metal. Gold and silver were used for ornaments. Copper and bronze were used for tools and weapons. The Sumerians had to trade to get the metals they wanted.

Some Interesting Activities

1. Divide your class into groups of "archaeologists." Each group can write a letter and tear it into bits. Ask another group to see how quickly it can put the bits of a letter together. You can do the same experiment with a damaged clay pot or cup broken into pieces.

THE GROWTH OF CIVILIZATION

2. Collect artifacts of our twentieth-century culture. Choose things that would not rot if buried in the earth. Discuss what these artifacts may mean to an archaeologist a millennium later (in A.D. 3000).

3. Visit a museum that has artifacts of earlier cultures. Choose a culture and report on its artifacts.

4. Get a book about archaeology from the library. Choose one topic. Report the most important things you learn about your topic.

5. Imagine you are an archaeologist in A.D. 5000. You are digging down to an American city of the twentieth century. What sorts of things will still be in the ground after three millennia? Will our writings last as long as the clay brick tablets of Sumer lasted? Tell how you would try to solve the problem of learning how people lived in twentieth-century America.

6. Find out about one of the topics below. Report to the class about it. You may draw pictures (or use a map) to make your report more interesting.

    Where Copper Is Found in the World

    How Copper Was Used in Early Civilizations

    Some Present-day Things Made of Copper

    Some Things Made of Bronze (past or present)

    The Bronze Age

7. Make a sketch map of ancient Mesopotamia showing these things:

Tigris and Euphrates rivers	Sumer
Persian Gulf	plains
cities of Ur, Lagash, Nippur, and Kish	mountains and hills

    Make a map key and a map compass. Print all names on the map. Label the map. Color it neatly. You may use maps of Mesopotamia in Chapter 3 and in this chapter to help you.

DISCOVERING THE EARLIEST CIVILIZATION: SUMER

Known as the "Standard of Ur," these two panels were found in a grave in the city of Ur. In the top panel, the gods are holding a banquet, and people are bringing gifts of animals, grain, and other goods. The lower panel shows Sumerian soldiers in battle and leading prisoners to their king. These panels were made after kings had replaced the priests as rulers of Sumerian cities. However, they tell us much about the religion and work of the Sumerians from the time of the earliest cities.

CHAPTER 5

The Civilized Culture of Sumer

In this chapter we shall see what the civilization of Sumer was like. We have a long story to tell in a few pages.

Sumerian civilization began about 3500 B.C. It went through many changes before it disappeared. But Sumerian culture went on in southern Mesopotamia until about the eighteenth century B.C. Then the old Sumerian civilization died. Different civilizations rose up in new centers in northern Mesopotamia and other places.

Studying a Culture: The Social Sciences

The **social sciences** are the sciences that study societies. We will use the social sciences to help us learn about Sumerian society and culture. The social sciences will help us make a check list of the things we want to know about Sumer.

A ● Look at the box "Using the Social Sciences To Study a Culture" (page 91).
1. Make sure you know what each social science is about. Use a dictionary.
2. Look at the right-hand column. It tells the main things that each social science deals with. Make sure you understand each one.
3. Notice that the social sciences overlap. To understand any one social science, we need to know something about the other social sciences. For example: *changes that people make in the environment* are part of *geography*. But these changes cannot be separated from technology. Technology is part of *economics*. But technology cannot be separated from the *groups that make up society*. (The groups in society are found under sociology.)

B ▶ You have already learned about the geography of Sumer. Tell about its natural environment. How did the people use and change the environment?

C ● You have learned something about the early history of Sumer. What can you tell about its history?

Economic Life in Early Sumer

Now we shall look at Sumerian economic life in the early centuries of Sumer, from about 3500 B.C. to 3000 B.C.

Sumer's most important technology, or way of producing goods, was irrigated agriculture. It was so efficient that many workers were able to produce other goods besides food. This led to many other technologies, such as building places in which to live, work, and worship; clothmaking; and shipbuilding.

A ● Look at the pictures (on page 92) showing division of labor in Sumer. What different jobs can you see? What other jobs might there be in an early city and in the fields around it?

Using the Social Sciences To Study a Culture

1. GEOGRAPHY
Where is the culture?

What is the culture's natural environment?

What changes have people made in the environment?

2. ECONOMICS
What is the technology (how are goods produced)?

How are goods exchanged (or traded)?

How are goods distributed (shared)?

Is money used?

What capital does the society have?

3. ANTHROPOLOGY
What do the people look like?

How do they communicate?

How are children educated?

What recreation do they have?

4. SOCIOLOGY
What groups — families, tribes, classes, and so on — make up society?

5. RELIGION AND PHILOSOPHY
What do the people believe about God or gods or spirits?

What do they believe about the meaning of life?

What are their ideas about right and wrong?

6. POLITICAL SCIENCE
How are the people governed?

Do they have laws?

Are there struggles for power in the society?

What are their relations with other societies?

7. HIGHER CULTURE
What learning and science does the society have?

What are its art and architecture?

Does it have literature and music?

8. HISTORY
What has happened to the society as time passed?

Have changes been fast or slow?

Efficient production of food and other goods led to *saving*. We usually think of saving as "saving money." But saving really means much more than that. **Saving** means "to keep for future use." When we keep things that have been produced, we can use them to produce other goods. This is how savings provide capital goods.

These pictures show division of labor and some of the products of trade in Sumer. One man is carrying strings of fish, while another is carrying a load of wool or barley. In the picture of the dairy *(below)*, one person is milking a cow; others are straining milk and making butter.

92   THE GROWTH OF CIVILIZATION

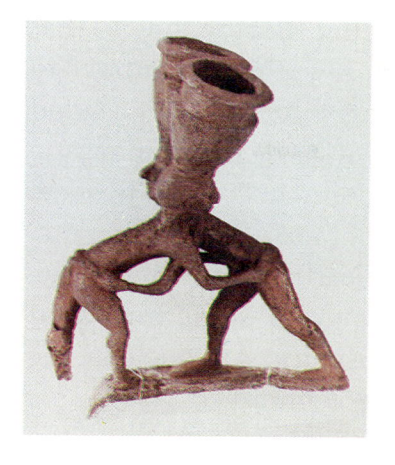

Sumerian crafts in bronze and clay (pottery). Two wrestlers form the base of the bronze statue. The votive vase, in the form of a doe, is made of red clay.

B▶ What was Sumer's most important technology?
C● Even prehistoric people had some capital goods. What tools did they have for hunting and gathering? What capital goods did a Neolithic village have? (Think of tools, cleared fields, storehouses, and anything else.)
D● What were the main capital goods of early Sumer?
E★ How does the division of labor help to produce capital goods? How do capital goods help to bring more division of labor?

Division of labor in a Stone Age group did not lead to trade. The group was small. People shared the goods. If one man made spears, he made them for all the others. The others shared the food they got with the spear-maker, and so on. If one person was lazy, the others punished that person.

But there had to be more complicated economic arrangements when people began to live together in large groups. In a city with thousands of people producing different goods, trade was necessary. There had to be a market for the exchange of goods.

F▶ Tell why a market is needed when thousands of people are producing different goods. How do people who sell goods in a market learn how much to produce?
G★ If people are lazy and do not produce enough goods, how do they get punished in a market?

THE CIVILIZED CULTURE OF SUMER

Barter was the earliest form of trading. **Barter** means that people exchange goods without using money. Producers have to find someone who wants their goods and who also has a good they want in exchange. For example, Tom gives his pen to Jane for three baseball cards. Mary trades John a French postage stamp for a candy bar.

In most societies today, trading is done by means of money. Money is a **medium of exchange.** Money is something that anyone can take in exchange for goods or work. Anyone can use the money to buy something she or he wants.

The Sumerians needed a medium of exchange. At first they used a good that everyone wanted. They used a grain from the fields: barley.

Then the Sumerians invented money. They began to use silver as a medium of exchange. Silver was better than barley. It was easier to use and easier to carry. Silver did not spoil, and it did not take up so much room as barley. At first the Sumerians weighed different amounts of silver dust. Then they used silver bars of different weights. These bars of silver were the first silver money in the world.

H▶ Why was barley a useful means of exchange?
I▶ Why was silver a better medium of exchange than barley? (Think of big, costly deals. Think of transporting and storing the barley.)
J● Is our money today mainly metal coins? What do we use as a medium of exchange?
K★ What gives value to the money we use today?

The Sumerians produced more food than they needed for themselves. They had grain and finished cloth to spare. But there were some things the Sumerians wanted that they did not have. Maybe they could trade their spare goods with foreign peoples. The Sumerians wanted copper, tin, silver, gold, and jewels. They also wanted certain building materials, such as wood and stone.

Sumerian merchants therefore began to trade with people in lands outside of Sumer. They began to *export* and to *import* goods. To **export** is to send goods to other countries for sale or exchange. To **import** is to buy goods from other countries. Sumerian merchants exported grain, cloth, and other goods. They imported gold, stone, wood, and other things that Sumerians wanted. Goods sent out of a country for sale or exchange are **exports.** Goods brought from other countries for sale or exchange are **imports.**

L ▶ Name some Sumerian *exports.* Name some Sumerian *imports.*

It took many centuries for regular trade to develop between the Sumerians and distant peoples. During these centuries, the Sumerians learned how to transport goods over long distances. It was the Sumerians who invented the wheel. By making carts and wagons they were able to transport goods overland. Groups of merchants traveled together for safety. These caravans could go overland to northern Mesopotamia.

The Sumerians invented the sailboat to transport goods on the rivers and on the seas. The Sumerians sailed down the river and across the Persian Gulf and even across the sea to what is now India. The boats took exports made by Sumer's skillful workers. They brought back imports the Sumerians wanted.

M ▶ Why do people trade with one another?
N ● Why does trade help to make people's lives better? Does trade between two societies help both societies to be better off? Explain.

A Sumerian cart and a Sumerian sailboat (models). The Sumerians' invention of the wheel and sailboat enabled them to engage in long-distance trade.

The Four Parts of Production

In a *civilized economy* four things are necessary. These things are the four parts of production. They are land and raw materials, capital, a work force, and managers. The *land* in Sumer was just right for irrigated agriculture. Irrigated agriculture gave plenty of food. There was no need for everyone to work at getting food. Some workers could work at producing *capital goods*. In Sumer the irrigation canals were capital goods. So were the cities, with their workshops, marketplaces, and other buildings. The farmers, canal diggers, and other workers made up the *work force* of the Sumerian economy. Who were the *managers*?

The managers directed the work. They also decided how to use capital. A civilized economy is not simple. Fields had to be plowed and planted and watered. Canals had to be dug and mended. Workers had to be assigned jobs.

Someone had to make plans. Someone had to decide how the water should be divided among the fields. Someone had to know when the spring floods would come. Certain people came to know these important things. They developed authority over the others. Their power grew.

The managers were the priests of Sumer. They had many skills. They knew how to figure out the seasons. They knew the right time for planting. They knew how to lay out the canals. The priests became very powerful. Their power became even stronger because of Sumerian ideas about the gods. The chart on page 97 shows how the four parts of production in early Sumer fit together. It also shows some goods that were produced.

A▶ What goods were imported?

Sumerian Religion: Fear of the Gods

The Sumerians feared and worshipped many gods. The people of Sumer had learned to control part of their natural environment. Still there were many things they could not

96 THE GROWTH OF CIVILIZATION

FOUR PARTS OF PRODUCTION

Work Force	Land and Raw Materials	Capital	Managers
farm workers canal diggers other workers	stone metal seed flood plains herds of animals imported wood	canals levees ships carts tools storehouses workshops	priests their helpers

GOODS

Capital Goods	Consumer Goods	Services
Savings used to build and repair capital goods	food clothing shelter	transport personal service education

THE CIVILIZED CULTURE OF SUMER

control. There were many things the Sumerians could not understand.

Sometimes huge floods washed away walls and canals and even whole towns. The Sumerians could not stop the floods. And they could not understand what caused them.

The Sumerians had many fears and questions about the *forces of nature.* Why did the rain fall? Why did the wind blow? Why did the sun rise and set? They knew only that they could not control these forces of nature.

The Sumerians came to believe that the forces of nature were alive. Thunder was alive. So was the sun. So were rain and wind. The Sumerians began to *worship* many of the forces of nature. Every natural force seemed a god to them. Their whole world became filled with gods—both male and female.

Let us read a Sumerian story. From this story we will learn what the Sumerians thought about the power of the gods.

The Sumerian Story of the Great Flood

In those days there were many, many people. The people made so much noise that the gods could not sleep. So the gods decided to kill all humans. They decided to send a flood to cover the earth.

One god felt sorry for the humans. He decided to warn one man that the flood was coming. He told the man to tear down his house and build a boat. The man listened to the words of the god. He built a boat. He loaded the boat with all his family and all his relatives. He loaded all kinds of animals, both wild and tame.

Then a black cloud arose in the sky. All that was bright turned into darkness. The rains came and the winds blew. Even the gods were frightened by what they had done. For six days and six nights, the flood went over the earth and killed all living things. On the seventh day, the rain and wind stopped.

The man looked out at the world from his boat. All was silent. He could find no land. He could see only water. The human species had turned to mud! This made him sad. He sat down and cried.

The boat sailed on. At last, the man saw a mountain. The boat moved toward the mountain. Suddenly, the boat stuck on the mountain. The man set loose a dove. The dove flew away but found no resting place because the waters had not gone down. The dove came back.

The Sumerian goddess Ningal, wife of Nanna, the god of the moon and city god of Ur

Later the man set loose a swallow. The swallow flew away but found no resting place. It, too, came back. Finally the man set loose a crow. The crow saw that the waters had gone down. It ate and flew around and cawed. It did not come back.

Then the sun god came out and warmed the earth. The man gave thanks that he was alive. He bowed before the sun god and sacrificed oxen and sheep.

A● What Old Testament story tells of a great flood sent to destroy human beings?
B▶ Who is the hero of the Bible flood story? How did he survive?
C● In the story you have just read, what clues tell you that the Sumerians were afraid of the power of the gods?
D● Name some other things that made the Sumerians afraid of the gods. (Think about the following: Did the Sumerians depend on the yearly floods? What would happen if the floods were too high? What would happen if they were too low?)
E★ Read the story of a flood in the Bible (Genesis: chapters 6-8). How does this Old Testament story explain the reason for this flood? What differences can you find between the idea of God in the Bible and the idea of the gods in the Sumerian story?

The Sumerians believed that the gods ruled everything. If the gods were happy, people would be happy, too. If the gods

THE CIVILIZED CULTURE OF SUMER

were angry, the whole world might fall apart. The gods could easily change their minds. One moment they might be happy. The next moment they might be very angry. The gods could do anything they liked.

The Sumerians made statues of the gods. From the statues we can see what they thought the gods looked like. Many gods looked like short people with round bellies. They had thin lips and big noses. They wore skirts made of sheep's wool. In fact, many statues of the gods looked like the statues the Sumerians made of themselves.

The gods of Sumer looked and acted like humans. They liked good food and nice clothing. They got married and had children. Sometimes they were kind. Sometimes they were cruel. Sumerians believed they had no control over what the gods did. The Sumerians believed that they were slaves of the gods. Their religion taught that the gods made human beings to work for them. The Sumerians believed that the gods would be angry if they did not work to provide food and clothing and temples for the gods.

F● What did the Sumerians believe was the main purpose of their lives?

G★ The Bible tells another story of how God created human beings. Read chapter 1 of Genesis, especially verses 26 through 31. Do Jews, Muslims, and Christians believe that humans are slaves of God? Explain.

The Power of the Priests

The priests of Sumer had great power. Being slaves of the gods was not easy. The Sumerians had to work hard to keep the gods happy. How could they know what would please the gods? Only the priests could tell them. The priests wrote down what happened year by year. They tried to learn what had pleased the gods in the past. The Sumerians obeyed the priests. By obeying them, they believed they were obeying the gods. So the priests were able to make the Sumerians work hard and long. The priests told the workers when to plant and when to harvest.

(above) This is what a ziggurat looked like long ago. Notice the stairways and the different levels. At the top is the temple, or holy place of the god, where processions of priests came. *(below)* Excavations at Ur uncovered this ziggurat dedicated to Nanna. The stairways shown are partly restored.

They told them when to dig canals and when to build earth walls. They told them when to make war and when to make peace. Priests played an important part in building the first civilization.

Each Sumerian city had its own special god. The priests of the city ruled in the name of this god. The priests had the people build a temple to honor the god. The temple was the largest and most important building in a Sumerian city. It rose above the city like a hill. Such a temple was called a **ziggurat** (zig′ ù rat′). The ziggurat was the "mountain of god."

A ▶ Look at the pictures of a ziggurat on page 101. Can you match the artist's drawing and the photograph? What happened to the top levels of the ziggurat as time went by?

Within a city, life centered on the ziggurat. The Sumerians believed that the god lived on top of the ziggurat. Three times a day the priests brought food to the god. Only the priests could enter the room where the god lived.

The farm workers brought grain to the temple. In return, the people believed the god would protect them and the city from harm.

B ● Look at the chart "The Sumerian Idea of Life" (page 103).
  1. Was religion an important part of Sumerian life?
  2. What effect did religious ideas have upon these five things?
     a. how the Sumerians were governed
     b. how the land was farmed
     c. who owned the land
     d. how grain was divided
     e. what the Sumerians thought about themselves

New Learning: Numbers and Arithmetic

The priests were rulers and managers. They were also learned persons. The priests of Sumer had to keep track of many important things. How much land was being farmed? How much grain was in the temple? How much grain should be given to the workers?

THE GROWTH OF CIVILIZATION

The Sumerian Idea of Life

GODS

FORCES OF NATURE

PRIESTS (understood the gods)

PEOPLE (were slaves of the gods)

THE CIVILIZED CULTURE OF SUMER

Later the merchants of Sumer had to keep track of their business matters. How much grain had they sold? What price did they get for the grain? How much stone or copper could they buy? How much profit had they made? **Profit** is the money left over from the sale of goods after production costs have been paid.

To keep track of these things, the Sumerians invented signs to represent numbers. They used these signs to develop a science of arithmetic.

A▶ Why did arithmetic develop?
B● Look at the chart "Sumerian Numerals" below. The Sumerians used two *bases* in arithmetic. They used *base 10,* as we do. They also used *base 60.*
  1. Why is 10 a "natural" base for humans to use?
  2. Find the numerals for 1 and for 60. What do you notice about them?

Sumerian Numerals

Value	Early	Late
1	D	𐏑
2	D D	𐏒
3	D D D	𐏓
4	D D / D D	𐏔
5	D D D / D D	𐏕
10	O	◁
60	D	𐏑
600	⌾ or D◯	𐏑◁

104 THE GROWTH OF CIVILIZATION

The Sumerians did not have a zero. Zero was invented in a later civilized society in India. However, by using base 60 as well as base 10, the Sumerians were able to do many calculations. We still use Sumerian measurements for time, circles, and angles.

C ▶ How many hours are there in a day and night? How many minutes in an hour? How many seconds in a minute? We are still using the base 60 system that the Sumerians invented more than 5,000 years ago!

More New Learning: Sumerian Writing

No Sumerian ever sat down and said, "Now I am going to write." Writing was developed over hundreds of years. Picture writing was the first step. The Sumerian priests began to write by drawing pictures of objects. They drew pictures of cows and sheep. They drew pictures of hands and feet. They drew pictures of stars and of many other things.

As time went on, some of the pictures began to stand for more than one thing. A picture of a foot might also mean "to stand," "to walk," or "to run." A picture of a star might also mean "the sky," "the heavens," or "the gods." This way of writing was confusing. The same picture could mean many different things. This way of writing was also difficult. What picture could the priests use to stand for ideas like "truth," "justice," and "courage"?

Slowly the Sumerian writing changed. Signs, not pictures, began to stand for words. Pictures changed into wedge-shaped marks. The Sumerians were able to put the wedge-shaped marks together in series. Then they could write sentences as well as words.

A ▶ What is this wedge-shaped writing called?

Some of the wedge-shaped marks began to stand for sounds instead of ideas or objects. A special mark would stand for each sound in the Sumerian language. Then each time someone

THE CIVILIZED CULTURE OF SUMER

needed to write a word with a certain sound in it, the wedge-shaped mark that stood for the sound was used.

The Sumerians wrote with hard reeds that were sharp and pointed. A writer pressed a reed into a tablet of soft clay. The reed left a wedge-shaped mark in the clay. When the writer finished, the tablet was baked in the hot sun or in an oven so that it would harden.

Writing was an important invention. It was too important for the Sumerians to keep to themselves. As their trade grew, the Sumerians sent more than products out of their country. They sent ideas, too. Sumerian writing spread to many parts of the Middle East.

- B▶ How did the Sumerians write their messages? Why did the writings last so long?
- C● Why is writing so important? Name some ways in which writing affects your life today.
- D● How would writing help the growth of business and trade in Sumer?

Writing on tablets was far from easy. Only a few Sumerians knew how to do it. Yet many Sumerians were engaged in business and trade. And every big business deal had to be put in writing. Then the writing had to be signed by the people who were making the deal. So the Sumerians invented the **cylinder seal.** They used the cylinder seal as a *signature*.

A cylinder seal and its signature

106 THE GROWTH OF CIVILIZATION

Cylinder seals were made of clay or stone. Every important Sumerian had a seal. It was usually carried on a chain worn around the neck. A different picture or design was carved on every seal. A person who wished to sign a tablet rolled the cylinder over the wet clay. The picture became the person's signature.

Thousands of Sumerian tablets have been found by archaeologists. Most of the tablets deal with business matters. Only a few contain stories or poetry.

E▶ Look at "From Picture Writing to Cuneiform" below. Notice how writing became simpler and faster as time went by.

From Picture Writing to Cuneiform

Objects	Early Picture Writing	Later Cuneiform Signs
Plow		
Boat (with Sails?)		
Chisel		
Axe		

Tablets showing early picture writing and later cuneiform signs

F How would writing and arithmetic help business and trade in Sumer?

G We have seen how archaeologists learned to read cuneiform. How did this help historians to know much more about ancient Sumer than artifacts such as ruins or helmets or pottery could tell them?

Archaeologists have learned many things about the knowledge and economic life of the Sumerians from reading tablets about business and trade. They have also learned a great deal about the Sumerians and their beliefs by reading the tablets containing stories and poetry.

Some of the tablets tell about the adventures of Gilgamesh (gil' gə mesh'), a Sumerian hero. Gilgamesh was strong and mighty. He was the first "superman." The story of Gilgamesh and his adventures was written as a very long poem. The following story (in prose) is based on part of the poem.

The Story of Gilgamesh

Gilgamesh knew all things. He knew all the countries of the world. He was wise. He understood mysteries. He knew secret things. The great god created Gilgamesh. They made him two-thirds god and one-third man. They made his body perfect. The sun god gave him beauty. The storm god gave him courage.

The gods decided that Gilgamesh should have a friend. So one goddess dipped her hands in the waters and pinched off some clay. Thus the noble Enkidu [en' ki dū] was created.

Enkidu ate grass in the hills. He played with wild beasts at the water holes. He loved the company of herds of wild game. He roamed over the hills with wild beasts, and he was happy. He was strong and brave. He was a match even for Gilgamesh.

Mighty Gilgamesh and Enkidu met and wrestled with each other. Each learned the strength of the other. Then they became friends.

• • •

In the forest of cedars lived a giant named Humbaba. No man ever went into the forest, for all men were afraid of Humbaba. Humbaba was the watchman of the forest. He never slept.

Enkidu warned Gilgamesh of all these things. But Gilgamesh said to Enkidu: "Only the gods live forever. Since we are men, our days are numbered. I must go to the forest. I must cut down the cedar. Then at

THE GROWTH OF CIVILIZATION

Gilgamesh, one of Sumer's early kings and hero of the poem "Epic of Gilgamesh"

least my name will be remembered." And so Gilgamesh and Enkidu went to the land of Humbaba.

When they got to the forest, Gilgamesh took an axe and began to chop down the trees. Humbaba heard the noise and grew very angry. He came out from his house of cedar. His face looked like a lion's. His teeth were like dragon's fangs. He charged at Gilgamesh and fixed on him the eye of death. Gilgamesh prayed to the gods for help.

The gods sent many winds to help Gilgamesh. They sent the great wind, the north wind, the whirlwind, the cold wind, and the dry wind. The winds beat against Humbaba until he could not move. Humbaba was frightened. He begged Gilgamesh to spare his life. He promised to serve Gilgamesh and make him lord of the forest.

Enkidu told Gilgamesh that Humbaba was trying to trick him. So Gilgamesh struck Humbaba with his sword. Then Enkidu struck a blow. At the third blow, Humbaba fell and lay deadly still. Confusion followed. The mountains and the hills were moved, for the watchman of the cedar lay dead.

H▶ Did even the mighty Gilgamesh need the help of the gods? Explain how the gods helped Gilgamesh.

I● Why did Gilgamesh want to go to the forest of cedars?

J★ Do you think Gilgamesh might have had another reason for going to cut down the cedars? (Clue: Look at an atlas. Find Lebanon. This land was famous for its cedars. Cedars did not grow on the flood plain of Sumer.)

THE CIVILIZED CULTURE OF SUMER   **109**

The Basic Group in Sumerian Society: The Family

Human societies have almost always had families to bring up the young. Sumerian families were similar to ours. The family was made up of a husband, a wife, and their children. Sumerian law said that a man could have only one wife.

The husband was the head of the household. If he was poor, he had one way to pay his debts. He could sell his wife and children as slaves for as long as three years. A Sumerian woman did have rights under the law. She could own property. She could carry on business. She could own slaves and sell slaves. She could be a witness in a court of law. When her husband went away, she could run his affairs, unless she had grown-up sons to take care of things.

Sumerian children had to obey *all* the older members of their family. They had to obey older brothers and sisters as well as parents. If children made their parents angry, they could be sent to another city. They could even be sold as slaves! Parents arranged marriages for their children. A marriage took place when a clay marriage tablet was made and signed before witnesses.

A Sumerian family (c. 3000 B.C.)

A▶ What were some of the rights of Sumerian women?
B● Compare family life in Sumer with family life in your town. What things are the same? What things are different?
C● Explain why you would, or would not, like to live in Sumer.

School in Sumer: An Important Social Institution

Often Sumerian schools were in the temples. These schools were called *edubbas* (ē dú bas), or "tablet houses." Pupils were taught religion and how to read and write. In another course, students learned arithmetic. They studied stories and poems of the past. There also was a course in which students learned the names of plants, animals, and minerals.

Because of Sumer's big markets for trade, it was important to teach young people how to read and write and to keep accounts.

Sumerian students did not have an easy life. They attended school from sunrise to sundown. They learned how to write by copying lines over and over on their tablets. Sumerian school children were afraid to break the rules. Every school had a very stern teacher. He was called "the man in charge of the whip."

Let us read a story about a school day in Sumer. This story is taken from one of Sumer's ancient clay tablets.

A Bad Day At School

Before going to bed, a schoolboy called Tolbi asked the family servants to wake him in time for class. But they failed to wake him. Tolbi slept late. When he did awake, he jumped out of bed and quickly dressed. He grabbed two rolls for lunch and ran all the way to school. He was filled with fear as he entered the classroom and bowed low before his teacher.

His low bow did not save him from a terrible day, however. Things continued to go wrong. First, he had been late. Then later on in the day, he forgot some lines in the lesson he wrote on his tablet. Next, he talked to a friend in class without permission. "The man in charge of the whip" beat him for all these things and also for breaking other school rules. But the boy had a rich father who invited the poorly paid teacher to dinner. The father gave the teacher new clothes, a ring for his finger,

A Sumerian boy training to become a scribe at a school in Ur. The school day was long, and the discipline was harsh.

and many other gifts. After this visit to the boy's home, the teacher began to treat his student more kindly.

Children in ancient Sumer sometimes fought. One clay tablet tells how two boys insulted each other. Each boy said that the other did not know how to write or multiply correctly. They called each other insulting names, like "windbag" and "chatterbox" and "bully." Finally the teacher came and put an end to the argument.

A ▶ What did Sumerian students learn in school? How did they learn?
B ● Compare the Sumerian school with your school. (Think about how teachers treated their students. Think about what the classrooms were like.)

The Classes in Sumerian Society

The big groups in Sumer were **social classes,** which were also **economic classes.** Each class had its own work to do.

A ● Look at the diagram "Sumerian Society" (page 113). This diagram shows society in early Sumer when the priests were also the rulers.

112 THE GROWTH OF CIVILIZATION

1. Why do we show "the gods" as part of Sumerian society?
2. What work did the priests do?
3. All city dwellers did not belong to the same economic class. What three groups are listed?
4. The two largest groups, or classes, were the farm workers and the slaves. What is a slave? Do you think that many of the farm workers were also slaves? Explain.

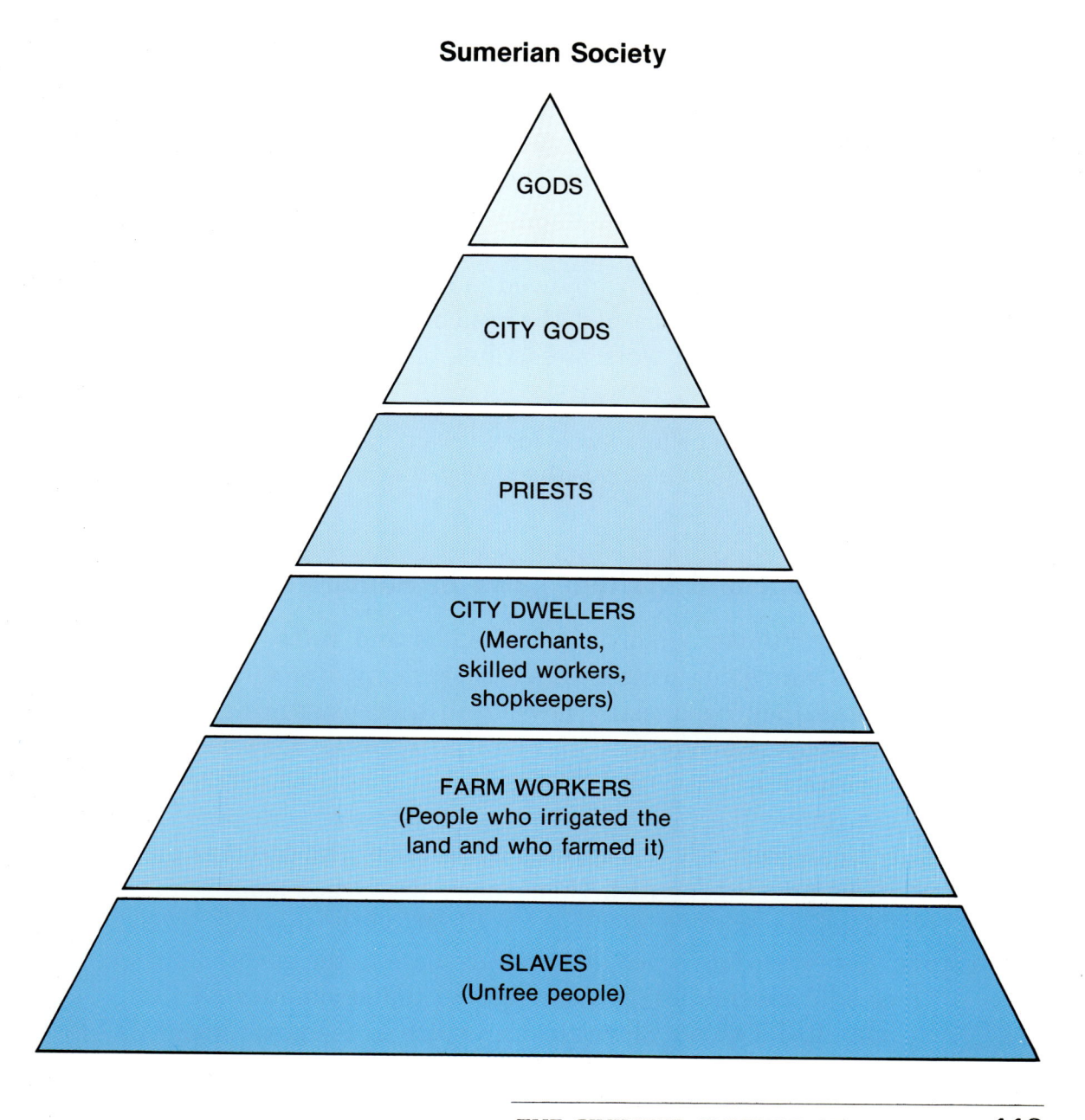

Sumerian Society

- GODS
- CITY GODS
- PRIESTS
- CITY DWELLERS (Merchants, skilled workers, shopkeepers)
- FARM WORKERS (People who irrigated the land and who farmed it)
- SLAVES (Unfree people)

THE CIVILIZED CULTURE OF SUMER

We have seen that Sumerians thought that all humans were "slaves of the gods." But Sumerians themselves had slaves to do the hardest work in society. Until about 400 years ago all civilized societies had this kind of **slave**—a person who had to work for an owner. Why did civilization lead to slavery?

One cause of slavery was war. One people would conquer another people. Then they made the conquered people into slaves.

Another cause may have been economic. Civilized societies had more goods and wealth than noncivilized societies. Yet they seldom had enough goods to give everyone a good wage. There are two ways of getting people to work hard. One way is to *pay them well* for hard work. The other way is to *force* them to work. Civilized societies for thousands of years used the second way. They took or bought slaves who could be forced to work. Sometimes poor people who owed money were sold as slaves. In Sumer, as we have learned, the head of a family might sell his wife and children to work as servants or slaves for as long as three years.

B ● Why is it much better to work for a reward than to work because you are afraid of being punished? Why does the first way give us freedom?

Government and Written Laws in Sumer

Every human society needs leaders and rules. Civilized societies are complicated. They have many different parts. Therefore they need many laws. And they usually have big governments. Governments in civilized societies may become very powerful.

In Sumer the form of government changed with time. In early times each city had its own government. For hundreds of years the priests governed. Then came a time when many of the city dwellers were economically well off. They were educated and were free. These people began to share in the government. They held **assemblies,** or meetings. In the assemblies all the freemen had a voice. Slaves had no voice in the government.

In Sumer people had obeyed certain laws for a long time. Then these laws were written down. For the first time, humans had *written laws.* Some laws were about marriage and families. Many were about crimes and punishments for crimes. Often crimes were punished by *fines.* For example, if a man hit

The limestone relief shows how the priest-kings received their power. It shows King Ur-Nammu of Ur being given the rod and line by the god Nanna.

THE CIVILIZED CULTURE OF SUMER

another man, the person who did the hitting would have to pay a fine to the person who was hit. A man who hurt another person badly would have to pay a much higher fine.

There were laws to protect weaker persons. Widows and orphans did not have to pay taxes. Even slaves had certain rights. They could earn money and buy their freedom.

A ● Were Sumerian laws like our laws? In what way? How were they different?
B ● Would you say that these Sumerian laws were good laws? Why or why not?
C ● Why are written laws needed in civilized societies? What can happen if people in the government change the laws whenever they like?

The Power and Danger of Government

In civilized societies, governments have great power. They tax the people. These taxes can be used in different ways. Often they are used for the good of the people. But also they can be used to make rich and powerful the persons who control the government.

Taxes can be used to pay an army. This army can be used to defend the society. But also the army may be used to terrify and crush many of the people in the society.

In any society there are people who are eager to get power for themselves. They want power because they enjoy having power over other people and because people who have power can make themselves rich. To get great power in civilized societies, it is usually necessary to control the government. Fighting to control a government is what we mean by "the struggle for power." Just such a struggle for power happened in Sumer.

A time came when the governments of Sumer were run by military leaders, called kings. Under these kings, the armies were strong, but Sumerian society was not healthy. In the next chapter we shall see how the civilization of Sumer disappeared and was forgotten after many years of military rule.

THE GROWTH OF CIVILIZATION

This detail from the Standard of Ur shows a procession of Sumerian soldiers. Sumerian soldiers were well trained in the science of warfare.

A★ What are some ways that civilized societies have used to stop governments from becoming too powerful? Look at the box "Ways of Controlling Governments" below. Do we use any of these ways in the United States? What ones?

> **Ways of Controlling Governments**
> 1. A written law, or *constitution,* that says how the government is set up and what things the government can and cannot do
> 2. A *bill of rights* protecting the freedom of the people
> 3. *Election* of government officials by the people
> 4. *Separation of powers* into *legislative* (lawmaking), *executive* (law-enforcing), and *judicial* (trying persons who may have broken the law)
> 5. *Jury trial* in courts of law
> 6. *Federalism:* dividing power between a central government and state governments

THE CIVILIZED CULTURE OF SUMER

Summary

The earliest big civilization about which we know a good deal is Sumer. Sumer grew up in Mesopotamia about 3500 B.C. The social sciences help us study the Sumerians. We have built a picture of the lives of the people by learning about Sumer's geography, economics, religion, education, and government and laws. And we have paid attention to events and changes in Sumer's history.

Sumer's main technology was irrigated agriculture. This was so efficient that many workers could do special work. Many workers produced capital goods, or goods used to produce other goods. The division of labor led to trade. Trade made it necessary to have money, or a medium of exchange. Trade began *inside* the society, but it later spread to foreign lands. In Sumer we find a clear example of the four parts of production: land and raw materials; labor (the workers); capital (savings and capital goods); and managers (who were priests in early Sumer).

The priests were important for many reasons. The Sumerians believed in many gods. They believed that humans must please the gods by being slaves of the gods. But only the priests knew how to please the gods. Thus the priests had great power over the people.

The priests were also the first learned persons. They invented arithmetic. They invented writing, first by pictures and then by wedge-shaped marks (*cuneiform* writing).

There were many different groups in Sumerian society. There was the family group, made up of husband and wife and their children. Other groups were social and economic classes: priests, merchants, skilled workers, shopkeepers, farm workers, and slaves. Later we also find kings, military leaders, soldiers, and government officials.

Like later civilized societies, Sumer had schools to train some children to read and write and do arithmetic. All societies educate the young, but civilized societies have schools that train special skills. Schools are part of the division of labor.

Finally, we looked at the laws and government in Sumer. The earliest written laws appeared in Sumer. As time went by, government became very powerful. Armies were raised and paid out of taxes. Kings, controlling the army, replaced the priests and the assemblies of freemen.

Some Interesting Activities

1. Make a chart similar to "Using the Social Sciences To Study a Culture" (page 91). Make an additional column, and write in it the information for early Sumerian civilized culture.

2. Examine the pictures in Chapters 3, 4, and 5. Then, make your own drawing of a ziggurat or of the irrigation network of Sumer.

3. Act a little play with your classmates. You could use the story of the Sumerian schoolboy, his classmates, his parents, and "the man in charge of the whip." Or you could have priests, merchants, and workers doing their jobs in Sumer. The priests could accept grain and money for the gods; they could plan work on the canals or decide when the river floods might be expected. The merchants could send ships with cargoes to India and decide what goods they would buy in India. Think of other ideas.

4. Write a short report telling why the struggle for power may cause trouble in a society. Tell why governments may have too much power. Tell some ways of controlling governments and of controlling the struggle for power.

5. Suppose you had to write down some rules ("laws") for your class. What rules would you suggest? Why would it be a good thing to have them in writing?

6. In the Old Testament, read the Jewish stories of Creation, the Flood, and the Tower of Babel. These stories are part of both the Jewish and the Christian religion. You will find them in Genesis, chapters 1 and 2, chapters 6-9, and chapter 11.

THE CIVILIZED CULTURE OF SUMER

The Ishtar Gate, Babylon (c. 575 B.C.), as reconstructed. The structure guarded the main entrance to the city.

CHAPTER 6

The Rise and Fall and Spread of Civilization

So far, the human species has never *lost* civilization. When one civilized society fell, there were others to carry on. Why do great civilized societies rise and then fall? Maybe one day social science will give us all the answers. Then perhaps *Homo sapiens* will get off the "ups-and-downs" of civilization.

There are several possible reasons for the fall of civilized societies. Among the reasons are (1) changes in the environment; (2) crowded cities and disease; (3) wars within the society and military rulers; and (4) wars with other societies. Let us see how these reasons were connected with the fall of Sumer.

Changes in the Environment

Changes in the natural environment played a part in the fall of Sumer. Over the years, the Sumerians kept irrigating their land. In the end, however, irrigation harmed the land. The water used for irrigation had a little salt in it. When the water dried up, the salt was left in the soil. Over the centuries, the amount of salt in the soil built up. Crops cannot grow in such soil. Little by little, less food was produced. The Sumerians did not understand why this was happening. The problem became serious between 2400 B.C. and 1700 B.C. In later centuries, the salting of the soil harmed farming throughout the irrigated lands of the Middle East.

A▶ Why was salting of the soil a serious problem?

B★ Try an experiment. Fill a glass about one-third full with tap water. Set it in the sun to let the water dry up. Do you see anything in the glass? Repeat the experiment several times without cleaning the glass. What has happened to the glass? Why?

Crowded Cities and Disease

Civilization brought crowded cities. Crowded cities led to many diseases that had not troubled villages and *nomads*. (**Nomads** are people who move from place to place and do not settle down.) When people are crowded together, diseases pass easily from one person to another. Rats, mice, dogs, and pigs carry diseases that can kill humans. The waste and sewage of cities carry diseases too.

Irrigated agriculture also brought disease. Farmers who work in water sometimes get a disease that makes them weak and tired.

Thus diseases often made civilized societies unable to fight back when another group of people made war on them.

A▶ Why do diseases spread more rapidly in a city than in a village?

B▶ How did having diseases make it hard for a society to fight and to win wars?

Wars within the Society and Military Rulers

When Sumer was young, the cities were quite small. There were stretches of swamp or desert land between the cities. Priest rulers from the temples in different cities often met to share ideas.

Over the years the population and the cities grew. The cities became city-states. A **city-state** was made up of the city itself plus an area around it.

Soon the grain fields of one city-state bordered on those of another. The rulers of the various city-states had nowhere to get new land for growing crops. The Sumerians began to fight one another. They fought over the boundaries of their land. And they fought over rights to water.

Early Sumerian city-states were not well organized for war. The Sumerians had always thought their main duty was to please the gods. If they now had to fight wars, they would have to do things in a different way. They would need weapons. And they would need someone to lead them into battle.

A▶ Why did Sumerians begin to fight among themselves?

In the early days, the assembly of each city-state put a military leader in charge whenever war broke out. The military leader was supposed to be in charge only as long as the war lasted. Every Sumerian man might have to serve as a soldier. Later on, these military leaders replaced the priests as rulers. They became kings and ruled even in times of peace. They passed on the kingship to their sons. The king's palace became stronger than the temple.

The Change from Priest Rulers to Military Kings

The figure at the far left in each drawing is a god.

THE RISE AND FALL AND SPREAD OF CIVILIZATION 123

Why did the ruling power pass from the priests to the military kings? The answer is that military kings *controlled the armies*. That control gave them real power. The military kings also claimed that they were close to the gods, just as the priests were. So they claimed the right to rule for both military and religious reasons.

> B▶ Look at the pictures "The Change from Priest Rulers to Military Kings" (page 123). What big change happened?

The wars between the city-states were long and hard. The armies had soldiers who fought on foot and other soldiers who fought from donkey-drawn carts. The soldiers wore copper helmets and leather kilts. They used spears and swords and shields. There were many bloody battles.

After a battle with another city-state, often the winning army would kill all its prisoners. The king of one city-state boasted that in just one battle he killed 3,000 of the enemy. Some prisoners might be made slaves. Some might be held for ransom.

Sometimes the captured city was robbed and destroyed. Then its temple would be knocked to the ground. That was the worst thing that could happen to a city-state. Destruction of the temple meant that its god had lost to the god of the winning city-state.

Over the years, kings of stronger city-states were able to bring several city-states together under their control. After 2375 B.C., the king of the city-state of Umma brought most Sumerian city-states under his control. When one ruler was able to gain power over many city-states, that was the beginning of the world's first *empire*. An **empire** is the rule of one government over a number of different societies. The ruler of an empire is called an **emperor**.

> C▶ What might happen to the people of a city-state that was conquered?
>
> D● Might it have been a good thing for the Sumerian city-states to have joined together in one united empire? Why or why not?

124   THE *GROWTH OF CIVILIZATION*

A Sumerian war cart drawn by a donkey

E● Do you think that people are very *loyal* to a king or emperor who rules them by force? Will they fight as hard for him as they would fight if they were free and sharing in the government of their society? Explain.

Wars with Other Societies

Around the edges of Sumer lived people who were not civilized. The name for noncivilized peoples on the edges of civilization is **barbarians**. Barbarians did not live in cities. Some were village farmers. Some were nomads who kept herds of animals. These people had their own way of life. However, many wanted a share in some of the good things of civilization. Unfortunately for the Sumerians, these people sometimes helped themselves. They attacked and robbed Sumerian cities.

Barbarians sometimes traded with civilized societies for the goods they wanted. Often, however, war broke out between them and the civilized societies. Sooner or later, the civilized

THE RISE AND FALL AND SPREAD OF CIVILIZATION 125

empire would become tired of fighting and grow weak. Then the barbarians took over the cities. The civilized people were killed or made into slaves.

In time the barbarians copied civilization. Later on, another set of barbarians appeared and the story was repeated.

- A▶ What things might make a civilized society weak and unable to fight off barbarians?
- B● What are some reasons for war between human groups or societies?
- C★ Think about the natural environment of Sumer. Was the area of Sumer easy to defend in the north and the northeast? Would there be many barbarians to the southwest? Explain.

Later Empires in Mesopotamia

Barbarians set up new civilized empires after Sumer fell. To the north of Sumer was the land of Akkad [äk′ äd]. Here the *Akkadian [ə kā′ dē ən] Empire* grew. Sargon I, king of Akkad, conquered Sumer about 2300 B.C. Before his death Sargon ruled all Mesopotamia. But wars kept breaking out, because new barbarians moved in.

In the eighteenth century B.C., the king of the city-state of Babylon conquered much of Mesopotamia. His name was Hammurabi [hä′ mu̇ rä′ bē]. He founded the *Babylonian Empire.* Much of the culture of Sumer and Akkad lived on in Babylon. But the cities of the first civilization were dying. The soil was worn out and salted. The floods and the sandstorms covered the ruins of the cities.

- A● Look at the map "Hammurabi's Empire" (page 127). Find the old area of Sumerian civilization. About how big was Hammurabi's empire from north to south?

There were empires based on Babylon for the next 1,200 years. Babylon ruled southern Mesopotamia until 539 B.C. Different barbarian peoples conquered Babylon during this long period, but they kept much of the culture and the civilization that had come down from Sumer.

Hammurabi's Empire

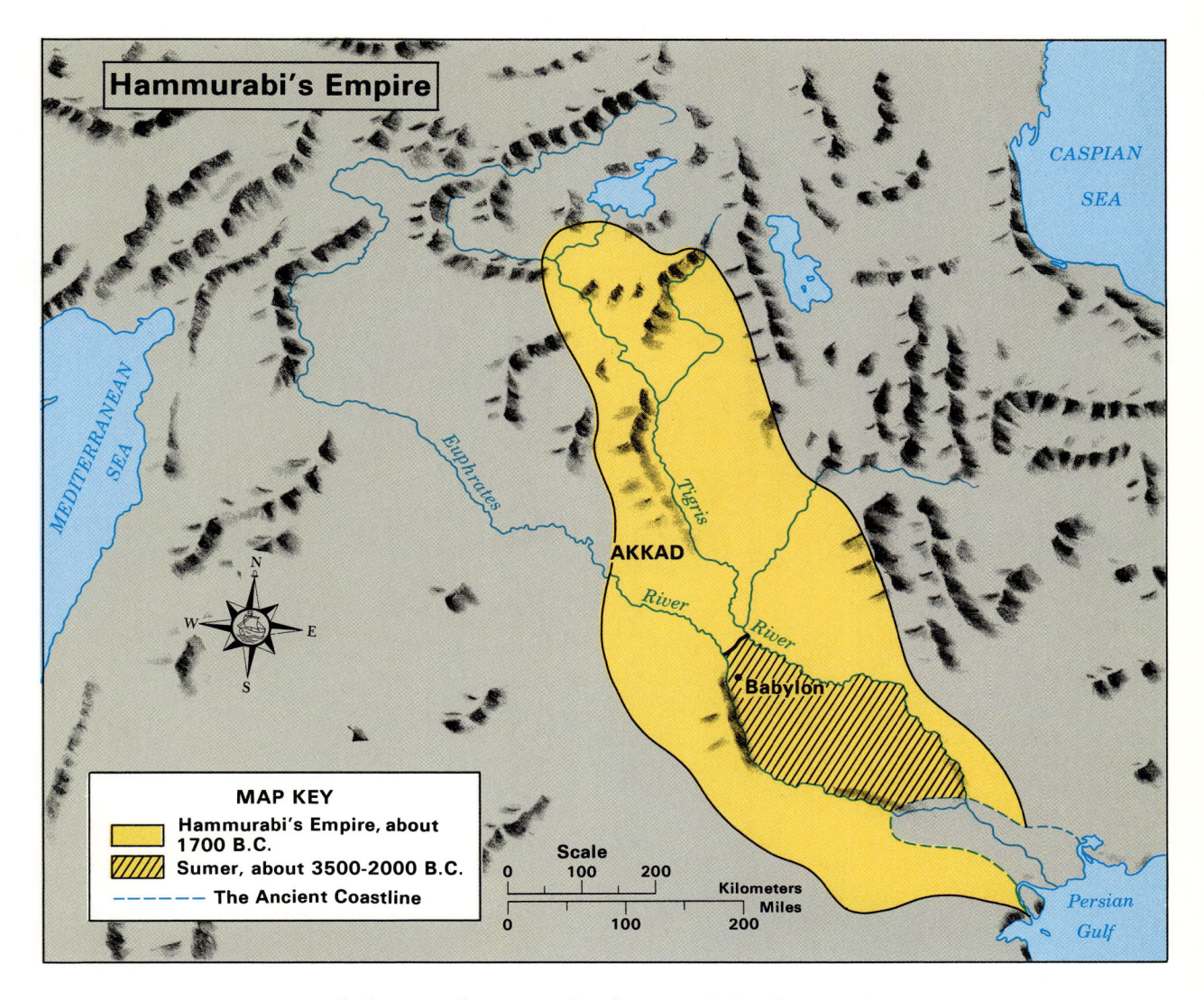

MAP KEY
- Hammurabi's Empire, about 1700 B.C.
- Sumer, about 3500-2000 B.C.
- ----- The Ancient Coastline

Meanwhile, civilization had spread far beyond Mesopotamia. Let us look at other branches of civilization.

Civilization Spreads to Other River Valleys

From Sumer, civilization spread to other river valleys. This happened because human beings can communicate ideas. They can copy good ideas. As early as 3100 B.C., traders from Sumer carried the idea of civilization to other places.

Until about 2100 B.C., civilization was possible only in great river valleys. Between 3100 B.C. and 2100 B.C., several

THE RISE AND FALL AND SPREAD OF CIVILIZATION

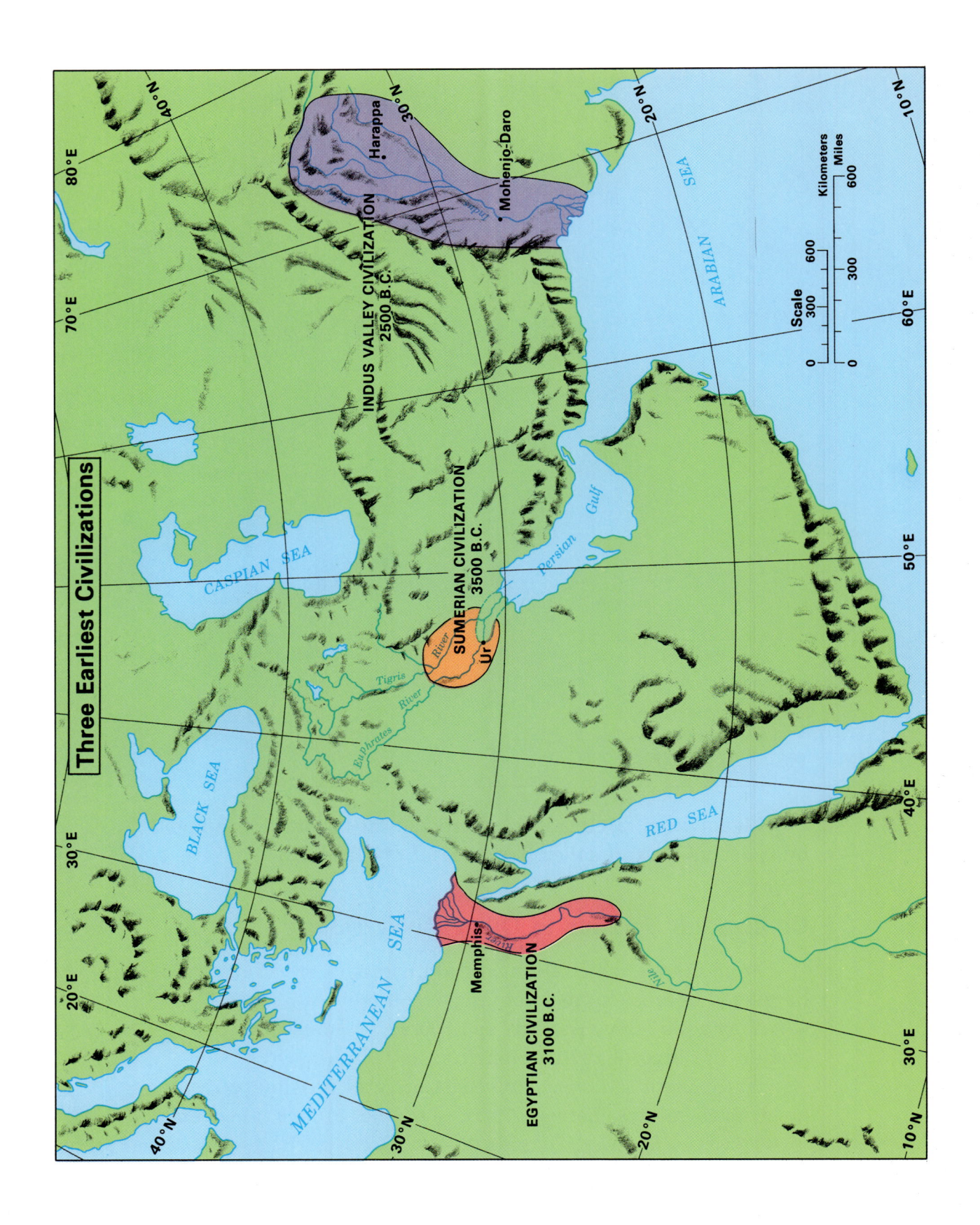

Three Earliest Civilizations

- INDUS VALLEY CIVILIZATION 2500 B.C.
  - Harappa
  - Mohenjo-Daro
- SUMERIAN CIVILIZATION 3500 B.C.
  - Ur
  - Tigris River
  - Euphrates River
- EGYPTIAN CIVILIZATION 3100 B.C.
  - Memphis
  - Nile

ARABIAN SEA, PERSIAN GULF, CASPIAN SEA, BLACK SEA, MEDITERRANEAN SEA, RED SEA

other civilizations developed. One was in the Nile Valley in Egypt. The other was in the Indus Valley in what is now Pakistan.

- A ▶ Look at the map "Three Earliest Civilizations" (page 128). Find the Nile and the Indus River Valley civilizations.

The Nile River Valley Civilization

Until a few years ago, people thought that civilization first appeared in Egypt. Then scholars learned about Sumer. Now they believe that Egypt was the *second* civilization, not the first.

Every summer the Nile overflowed its banks. The Egyptians dug ponds, or *catchment basins*, to hold the floodwaters. They planted seeds in the mud left by the floods. Then they used the water from the catchment basins for irrigation. They soon had large supplies of food. By working together they built a great civilization.

- A ▶ How was Egyptian irrigation different from Sumerian irrigation?
- B ● Why was irrigated agriculture the only *technology* for Sumer and Egypt?
- C ● Look at the pictures of Egyptian artifacts on pages 130–131. What do the pictures and the descriptions tell you about Egyptian culture?

The Egyptians developed many skills. They had a system of writing and figured out a way of making a kind of paper. We call the Egyptian writing *hieroglyphics* [hī′ ər ə glif′ iks]. **Hieroglyphics** means picture writing. (A sample of hieroglyphics appears on page 134.)

Egyptian civilization lasted much longer than Sumerian civilization. And it was never forgotten. Many Egyptian buildings were of stone. They have lasted longer than the brick buildings of Mesopotamia.

Egypt was much safer from barbarians than Mesopotamia. One reason Egypt was safer was that the land on each side of Egypt's flood valley is desert. Another reason for the long life of Egyptian civilization was its strong government. The Egyptians

A wooden stool, carved and painted to resemble leopard skin

Ancient Egyptian Art Forms

(below) Model figures who are carrying supplies to the tomb of the pharaoh

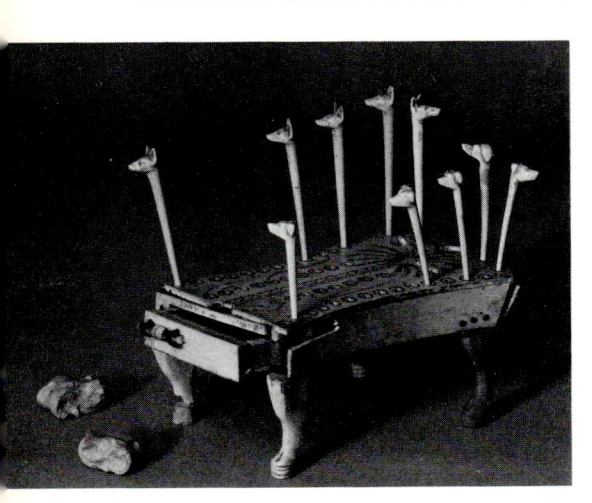

A game called "hounds and jackals"

A collar decoration in the form of a vulture (from the tomb of King Tut)

Huge pyramids were built as tombs for pharaohs. A tomb was filled with supplies for the pharaoh in his life after death (in which Eqyptians believed).

had strong rulers called **pharaohs** [fer′ ōz]. They did not, however, have strong armies. Therefore the Egyptians seldom tried to conquer lands outside the Nile Valley.

D▶ Look again at the map "Three Earliest Civilizations" (page 128.) How did the natural environment of the Nile Valley provide defense against barbarians?

E★ Read more about ancient Egyptian civilization. There are many books about it.

The Indus River Valley Civilization

The other early river valley civilization developed in the Indus River Valley. Cities grew up less than 1,800 kilometers (about 1,000 miles) east of Sumer. These cities were along the Indus River. When archaeologists began to dig in this area, they found two great cities. One was called *Harappa* [hə rap′ ə].

Harappa was in the north. The other city was *Mohenjo-Daro* [mō hen′ jō där′ ō]. Mohenjo-Daro was 680 kilometers (425 miles) southwest of Harappa. The sites of Harappa and Mohenjo-Daro are in an area that is now called Pakistan.

A▶ Find the Indus Valley on the map on page 128.

The Indus River people did many of the same things the Sumerians and the Egyptians did. They irrigated the land by using the water from a river. They produced a large supply of food. They had a division of labor. Some of the people did special jobs. And, in time, they built cities.

What were the Indus Valley cities like? They had wide streets, laid out in squares. Tall houses of baked brick looked out on the streets. The people who lived there had a knowledge of plumbing. They had bathrooms in their houses and drain pipes to carry away waste.

We know something about the religion of the Indus Valley people. They worshipped many gods. We also know that the priests learned to read and write. Their script appears on many seals. In the ruins of the cities, children's toys have been found. Many fine clay pots have also been found. The people were skillful in metal crafts. They worked with gold, silver, copper, and lead. The workers of Harappa and Mohenjo-Daro made beautiful small statues.

Like Sumer, but unlike Egypt, the Indus civilization was forgotten for thousands of years. The great cities died. They were not found again until after A.D. 1920.

Why did the cities die? Why was all trace of them lost? We cannot be sure. Perhaps the cities were ruined by invasions. Perhaps the people used up the soil around the cities. Perhaps the river changed its course. Perhaps, too, there were terrible floods. Or the climate may have changed. Another explanation might be that some illness killed off the people.

B● Look at the pictures of the Indus Valley artifacts on page 133. Find the example of plumbing (street drain). Does the culture of the Indus Valley remind you more of Sumer or of Egypt? Explain.

Copper hunting weapon from Mohenjo-Daro area (c. 1000 B.C.)

A child's toy

Artifacts That Illustrate the Life and Art of the People of the Indus Valley

A drainage ditch

Precision weights and measures

THE RISE AND FALL AND SPREAD OF CIVILIZATION   133

It is possible that the Indus Valley civilization fell without a barbarian invasion. We do know, however, that an invasion happened around 1500 B.C. About that time barbarians came across the northwest mountains. They called themselves *Aryans* [ar′ ē ənz]. They conquered all northern India. We do not know if they brought the Indus civilization to an end. The cities of Harappa and Mohenjo-Daro may have been ruined before the Aryans came. The Aryans did not use these cities. The Indus civilization gradually faded from human memory.

Archaeologists are still exploring in the Indus Valley. They have found written records. But they have not been able to understand these records. Archaeologists have not yet found a key to understanding this writing. This problem has made the study of the Indus Valley civilization difficult.

C ▶ Sumer's civilization was conquered and taken over by other people. What civilization then followed in Mesopotamia?

D ● Why is the study of the Indus Valley civilization difficult? How important are written records to historians in their study of ancient peoples? What difference will it make in the study of the Indus Valley people if archaeologists learn to read their writing?

E ★ Archaeologists were able to read hieroglyphics (Egyptian picture writing) because they found the *Rosetta Stone.* Find out about the Rosetta Stone. Was its discovery similar to the discovery that helped people to read Sumerian *cuneiform* writing?

This is how the written language of the ancient Egyptians looked. The Egyptians used pictures of an object to stand for a word, an idea, or a sound. Such pictures, or signs, are called *hieroglyphics.* Young Egyptian schoolboys who wished to become scribes had to learn about 700 signs and had to be able to draw the signs clearly.

The above are examples of picture writing from the Indus Valley.

Civilization Spreads to Rain-Watered Lands

About 4,000 years ago it seemed that civilization was possible only in river valleys. Such valleys were flooded once a year. People learned to use the floods for irrigation by digging canals or catchment basins. Irrigation made it possible to produce more food. With a good supply of food came division of labor and the growth of cities. As people settled down, they learned new knowledge. They set up new forms of government. Each early society that became a civilization went through these changes.

Could civilization grow in other environments? People were growing crops long before they found out about irrigation. The earliest agriculture was in **rain-watered lands.** These are lands that have enough rainfall to grow crops without irrigation. Rain-watered agriculture, like irrigated agriculture, could produce enough food for civilization to develop.

Civilization, however, began in irrigated river valleys. It came later to rain-watered lands.

THE RISE AND FALL AND SPREAD OF CIVILIZATION

A ● Why did civilization not develop in rain-watered lands for more than 4,000 years after the Neolithic revolution? Think about the following:
1. Where do people have more control of the environment—on rain-watered land or on irrigated land?
2. Which type of agriculture calls for the cooperation of many people—rain-watered or irrigated?
3. Which type of agriculture needs planners and managers?
4. Which type of agriculture frees many workers from farming?

By about 2000 B.C., people in the rain-watered lands began to copy civilization. This probably happened because of trade, wars, and conquests. Kings from civilized empires conquered the peoples in rain-watered lands. Then the kings organized the people along the lines of civilized societies. They got the farmers to produce more food. The extra food supported the armies and the government. Once again the division of labor grew. Cities were built.

Civilization developed in Asia Minor and in lands around the Mediterranean Sea. Civilization also developed around the Hwang Ho (Yellow River) in northern China. And civilization developed again in northern India after the Aryan conquest.

B ▶ How did civilization begin in the rain-watered lands?
C ▶ Look at the map "Civilization Spreads to Rain-Watered Lands" (page 137).
1. Find the Minoan civilization on the island of Crete in the Mediterranean Sea.
2. Find the Hittite civilization in Asia Minor.
3. Find the Aryan civilization in India.
4. Find the Hwang Ho (Yellow River) civilization in China.
D ● Which of these civilizations were partly river valley, using irrigation, and partly rain-watered?

Changes in Military Technology

It is a sad fact that wars have played a big part in history. After the rise of civilization, wars became bigger. They were also more *destructive*. As we have seen, wars sometimes brought the fall of a civilized society.

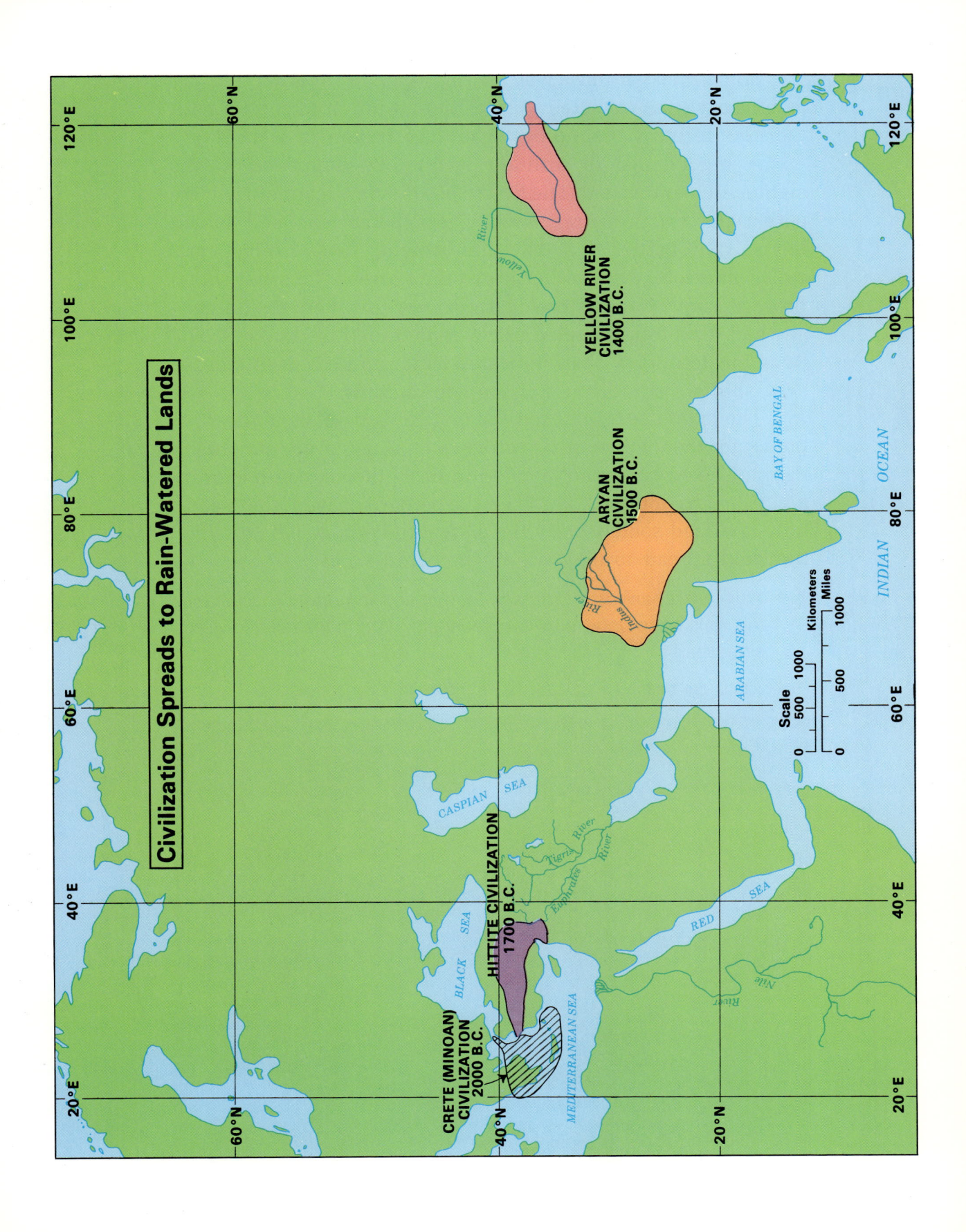

Civilization Spreads to Rain-Watered Lands

- CRETE (MINOAN) CIVILIZATION 2000 B.C.
- HITTITE CIVILIZATION 1700 B.C.
- ARYAN CIVILIZATION 1500 B.C.
- YELLOW RIVER CIVILIZATION 1400 B.C.

Sometimes a new way of fighting, or a new military technology, was invented. A society that did not keep up with the new military technology would be beaten in war.

A big change in military technology happened in the eighteenth century B.C. The first to use the new technology were barbarians from central Asia. These barbarians had tamed horses. For battle, they had lightweight, two-wheeled carts called **chariots.** One soldier drove the horses. The other shot a powerful bow. Long before chariots were invented, the Sumerians had used four-wheeled battle carts pulled by donkeys. The two-wheeled horse chariots were swifter and easier to handle. Foot soldiers could not stand up to chariots.

The *charioteers* attacked the civilized societies of Mesopotamia in the eighteenth century B.C. They even conquered Egypt. The Aryans who invaded India in the sixteenth century B.C. were charioteers, too. When the barbarians won, they set up new civilized societies. By the sixteenth century B.C., civilization had spread to all parts of the Middle East.

A ● Why are changes in *military technology* important? How does failure to keep up with military technology bring the fall of civilized societies?

Phoenicians are bearing a war chariot as tribute to King Darius.

During the fourteenth century B.C. there were more barbarian invasions of the Middle East. Once again the barbarians had a new technology. They had discovered how to use *iron* to make weapons and armor. With iron weapons, barbarians could defeat civilized charioteers. The *Bronze Age* was coming to an end. The *Age of Iron* was beginning.

Later Middle Eastern Empires: Assyria and Persia

The Assyrian Empire and the Persian Empire were the last two great empires in the Middle East. The Assyrian Empire rose in the ninth century B.C. Its center was northern Mesopotamia.

The Assyrians established a very powerful empire. They were, however, under constant attack from barbarians. Both the Assyrians and the barbarians used a new weapon—horse-soldiers. The horse-soldiers could shoot arrows.

The Assyrians were good soldiers. However, they were not able to govern their empire very well. The people who had to live under the Assyrian rule were not contented. Assyria had to spend much of its energy putting down revolts. These revolts weakened the Assyrian Empire. Finally, in 612 B.C., the Assyrian Empire fell.

The last great empire of the ancient Middle East was the *Persian Empire.* This empire was established in the middle of the sixth century B.C. by the emperor *Cyrus the Great.* It was the first empire to rule the whole of the Middle East. It even controlled land in northwestern India.

A ▶ What two things caused the Assyrian Empire to fall?
B ▶ Look at the map "The Persian Empire in 525 B.C." (page 140). This shows the empire after the emperor Darius the Great had conquered the Indus Valley and the European land called Thrace.
   1. Find Thrace. It is part of the *Balkan Peninsula.*
   2. Find *Sind* (the land of the Indus Valley).
   3. Find Persepolis [per sep′ ə lis]. This was the capital of the empire.
   4. Find Egypt, Assyria, Babylonia, and Persia.
   5. What sea is east of Thrace and north of Asia Minor?

THE RISE AND FALL AND SPREAD OF CIVILIZATION

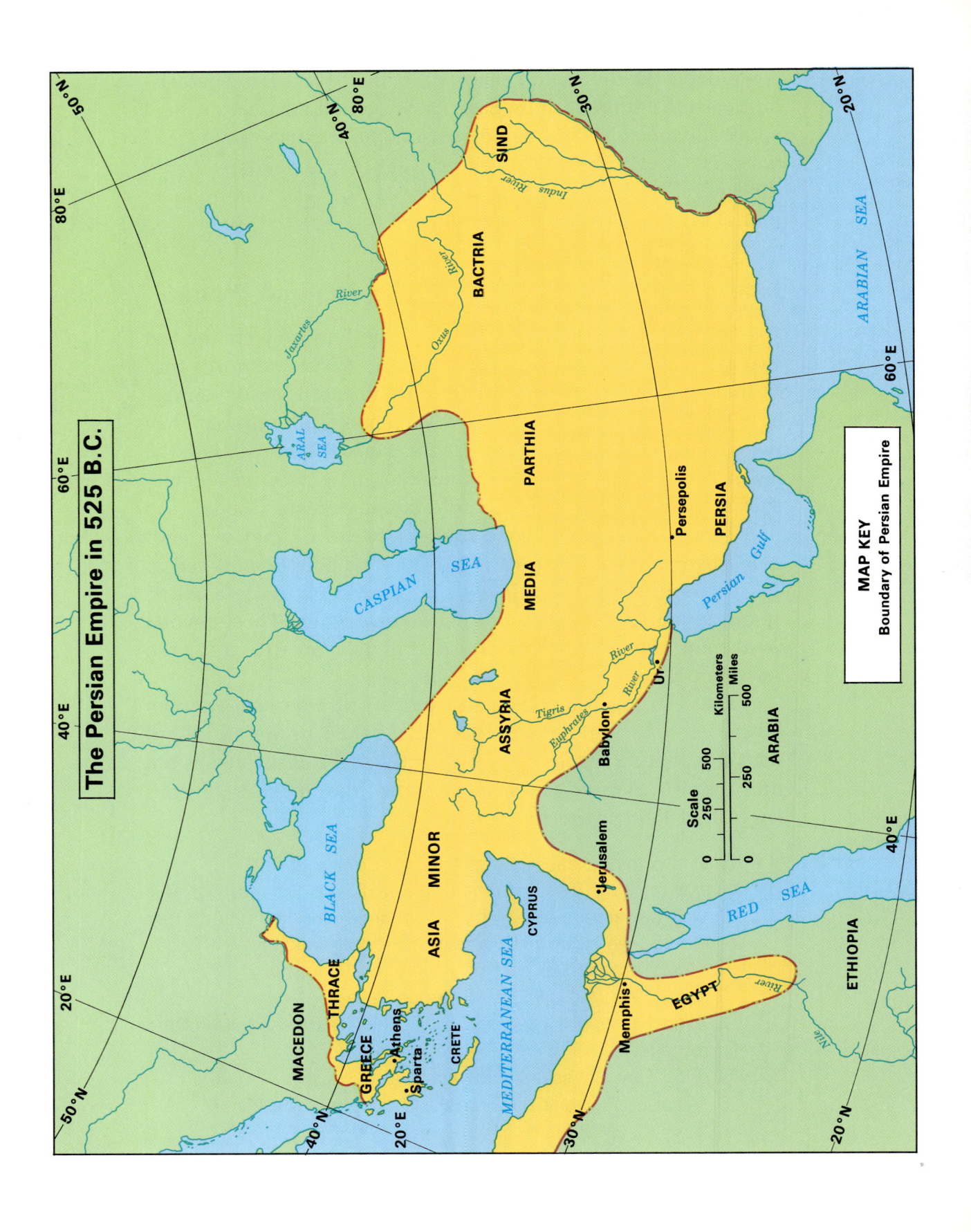

The Persian Empire in 525 B.C.

MAP KEY
Boundary of Persian Empire

The ruins of the Hall of the Hundred Columns at Persepolis, the ancient capital of Persia. Darius developed the city of Persepolis.

6. What is the gulf south of Persia? What two rivers flow into the gulf?
7. About how wide was the Persian Empire from west to east?
8. About how many degrees of longitude did this empire cover?
9. Between what degrees of latitude did the empire lie?
10. Was the empire in the tropics?

C ▶ The map also shows Macedon and Greece. Find them. Find the Greek city-states of Athens and Sparta. (The Persians tried to conquer Greece in the fifth century B.C. However, they failed.)

D ★ If the sun is setting in Sind, will it be daytime or nighttime in Persepolis? In Memphis, Egypt?

Periods of History

With the Persian Empire we come to the end of *ancient history*. Historians find it useful to divide history into *periods*. The period before writing was invented can be called *prehistory*,

THE RISE AND FALL AND SPREAD OF CIVILIZATION 141

or the prehistoric period. The period of the early civilizations is *ancient history,* or **ancient civilization.** This period lasted from about 3500 B.C. to the sixth century B.C.

In the fifth century B.C., we find that civilization had spread to the continent of Europe. In Greece the city-states were civilized. To the west, civilization was beginning in Italy also.

Of course, the end of ancient history is not a neat dividing line. People in the fifth century B.C. did not know that "ancient history" was ending. When we study history, however, it is useful to think of periods. Periods help us to keep events in order in our minds.

A ▶ Look at the "Time Line of Ancient Civilization" (page 143). It will help you to review what you have learned.
  1. Find the main civilized societies and their dates.
  2. How long was civilization found only in river valleys?
  3. When did civilization begin in China?

B ▶ What do we mean by "barbarians"?

C ● The growth of civilization brings changes to the government of a society. All the words listed below have to do with government. Can you explain why?

rulers	armies	taxes
officials	wars	empires
laws	power	monarchs

D ★ Can you think of any ways in which the growth of civilization would change the government of a society?

E ● Does civilization go with better control over the natural environment? Explain and give examples. Does civilization sometimes harm the environment? How?

F ● How may new ways of war bring changes in civilization and empires? Give some examples.

The Spread of Civilization and the Contact of Cultures

The culture of a society is the way of life of the people. Culture is learned by young people. It is passed on from one age-group to the next.

THE GROWTH OF CIVILIZATION

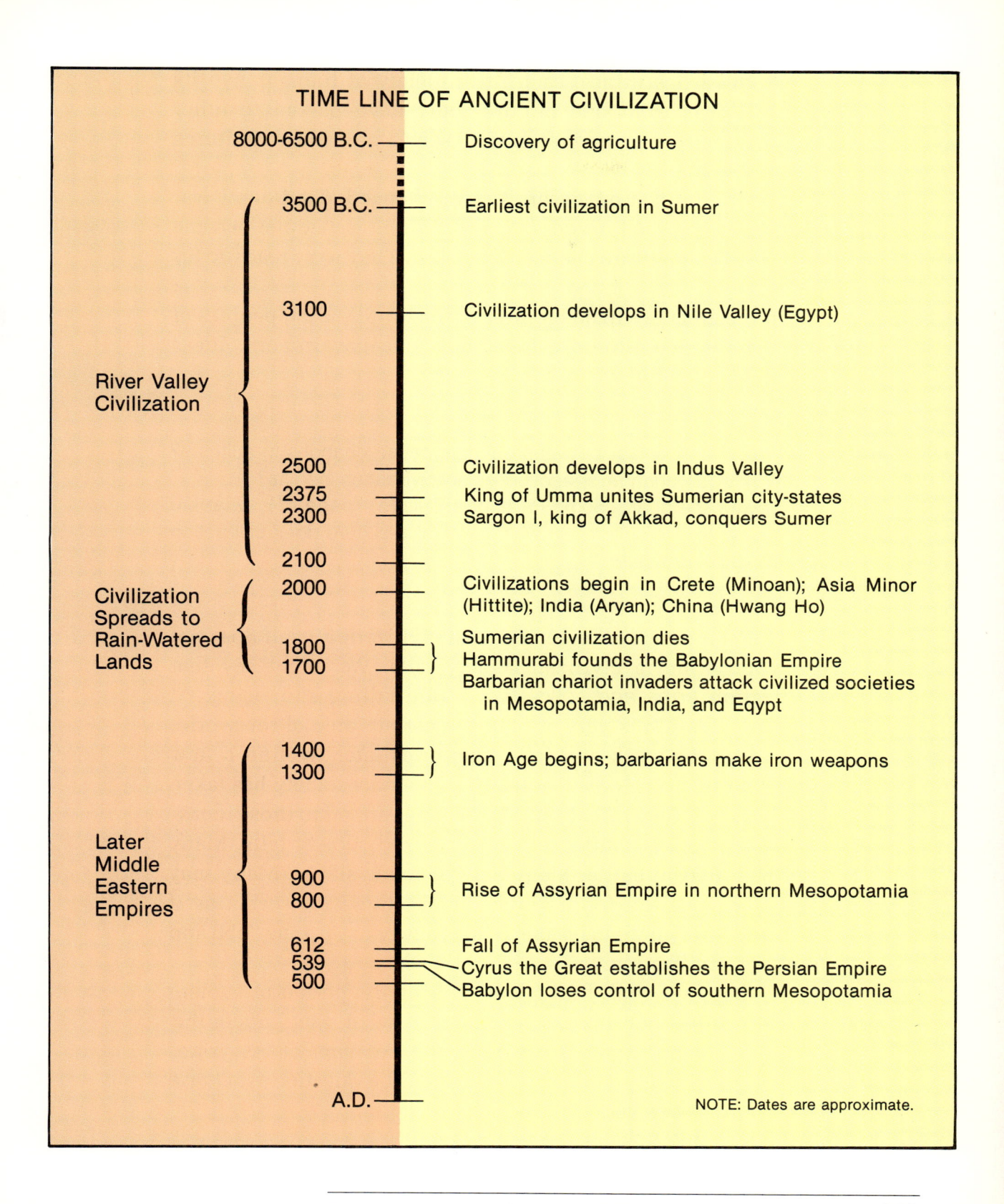

TIME LINE OF ANCIENT CIVILIZATION

	8000-6500 B.C.	Discovery of agriculture
River Valley Civilization	3500 B.C.	Earliest civilization in Sumer
	3100	Civilization develops in Nile Valley (Egypt)
	2500	Civilization develops in Indus Valley
	2375	King of Umma unites Sumerian city-states
	2300	Sargon I, king of Akkad, conquers Sumer
	2100	
Civilization Spreads to Rain-Watered Lands	2000	Civilizations begin in Crete (Minoan); Asia Minor (Hittite); India (Aryan); China (Hwang Ho)
	1800	Sumerian civilization dies
	1700	Hammurabi founds the Babylonian Empire; Barbarian chariot invaders attack civilized societies in Mesopotamia, India, and Eqypt
Later Middle Eastern Empires	1400, 1300	Iron Age begins; barbarians make iron weapons
	900, 800	Rise of Assyrian Empire in northern Mesopotamia
	612	Fall of Assyrian Empire
	539	Cyrus the Great establishes the Persian Empire
	500	Babylon loses control of southern Mesopotamia
	A.D.	

NOTE: Dates are approximate.

THE RISE AND FALL AND SPREAD OF CIVILIZATION 143

From earliest times, each little society of humans had its culture. Ideas from one culture must have passed to other societies. Yet there was not much exchange of ideas. Cultures changed very slowly.

When civilization began, things changed. Trade and war made ideas spread more quickly. When a people became civilized, their culture changed quite fast. They were ready to try new ideas.

In the great civilized empires of the Middle East, peoples of many different cultures came under one government. Ideas spread faster than ever.

A● Why does contact between cultures cause changes in cultures? Why does change speed up when civilization begins?

B● Review the chart "Some Parts of a Culture" (page 41). What are the parts of a culture? In what parts of a culture does civilization bring big changes?

It is important to remember that civilization itself does not die, even when a civilized society falls. We might say that civilization *ebbs and flows,* like a tide falling and rising. At times civilization is very strong in a certain area of the world. Then it grows weak and falls. Centuries later we find a new society in the same area—or nearby. The new society has taken over the ideas of civilization. Maybe it has added to those ideas.

Many persons suffer when a civilized society falls. Many may be killed in battle. Many may be made slaves. Many may starve because the food supply breaks down. It seems as if human beings ought to be able to find a way to stop the "ebb and flow" of civilization.

Perhaps we shall find a way. During the period of ancient civilization no one had a clear idea of what was happening. Today we know much more than the Persians or Assyrians knew about history and social science. The question is: *Do we know how to use our knowledge?*

THE GROWTH OF CIVILIZATION

> **Some Things That May Cause the Fall of Civilized Societies**
>
> 1. Damage to the physical environment
> 2. Disease
> 3. Population growth (leading to food scarcity)
> 4. Wars with other civilized societies
> 5. Changes in government (military empires)
> 6. Attacks by barbarians

C● What are some things that may cause the fall of civilized societies? (See the box above.)
1. Explain the things.
2. Give examples if you can.
3. Try to think of other causes, such as a change in climate or a terrible flood.

D● As you read on, think about the ebb and flow of civilization. Can *you* solve the problem? Is it still a problem today?

THE RISE AND FALL AND SPREAD OF CIVILIZATION

Summary

Despite the rise and fall of civilized societies, the human species has never lost civilization.

The civilization of Sumer declined partly because of the salting of its soil, disease, and wars. The wars between one city-state and another also brought a change in Sumer's form of government. The military leaders who led each city-state's army in battle used the army to take power from the priest rulers. Some of the new military kings were so powerful they were able to bring several city-states under their control. This led to the world's first empire.

Many of Sumer's city-states had groups of barbarians as neighbors. The barbarians frequently went to war with the civilized societies. This weakened the civilized societies. Finally the barbarians took over the cities. The barbarians copied civilization and set up their own civilized empires after Sumer fell. The Akkadian Empire reached a high point under King Sargon I about 2300 B.C. The Babylonian Empire followed the Akkadian Empire.

Another area where civilization appeared was the Nile Valley in Egypt. This civilization also used a form of irrigated agriculture. The Nile Valley civilization was safer from the barbarians because it was protected by large desert areas. As a result, Egyptian civilization lasted longer than the Sumerian civilization.

Civilization also grew in the Indus Valley of northern India. By about 2000 B.C., civilization came to rain-watered lands. This happened because of trade and because kings from civilized societies conquered peoples in rain-watered areas. The conquerors forced the people to follow civilized ways.

The role of wars has been very important in history. A society that did not keep up with military technology (ways of fighting) would be beaten in war. Barbarians from central Asia often introduced new military technology. These included the chariot, a powerful bow, and weapons made of iron. The Assyrian Empire successfully used these weapons, but was attacked by other barbarians. The Assyrians were followed by the Persians, who created the last of the great civilizations of the ancient Middle East. Under the leadership of kings Cyrus and Darius, Persia conquered lands from the Mediterranean Sea to the Indus River Valley.

The Persian Empire came at the end of ancient history. Historians find it useful to divide history into periods. The period before writing was invented is called *prehistory*. The period of the early civilizations is ancient history.

When people become civilized, their culture, or way of life, changes rapidly. Sometimes their civilization may fall, but civilization itself does not die. Other civilizations rise up. This is the "ebb and flow" of civilizations.

Some Interesting Activities

1. Draw a map of the Middle East, or use an outline map of the region.
    a. Color in Mesopotamia. Locate and label the capital cities for the Babylonian, Assyrian, and Persian empires.
    b. Label Egypt, the Nile River, Ur, Babylon, Persepolis.
    c. Label the Mediterranean Sea, the Red Sea, the Persian Gulf.
    d. Use arrows to indicate the directions in which civilization spread from Sumer.

2. Draw a donkey-drawn cart and a horse-drawn chariot. Use the pictures in the text to help you. Write the names of these battle wagons underneath and tell which civilization used them.

3. Make a time line of ancient civilization to put on the classroom wall. Make the line run from left to right, so that you can add more parts later on. Use a scale. Probably 30 cm (about 12 in.) for 500 years would be useful. You may add drawings to make it more interesting—a ziggurat for Sumer, a pyramid for Egypt, and so on.

4. Write a speech for a barbarian chief telling his followers why they should attack a civilized society. Choose one of the civilizations you have studied.

5. Use an encyclopedia to find out more about some things or people in this chapter—for example: Mohenjo-Daro, Sargon I, Hammurabi, Assyria, the Aryans, early Chinese civilization, the Persian emperor Darius the Great. Write notes and tell your class what you have learned.

Confucius at the Apricot Altar

CHAPTER 7

Some World Views at the End of Ancient History

Every culture has a *world view.* A **world view** is a whole way of looking at the world and our place in it. About the sixth century B.C., four world views became important. Each world view grew up in a different civilized culture area. The four areas were China, India, the Middle East, and Greece. Each culture had different ideas about religion and the meaning of life.

What Are Ideas? How Do We Get Ideas?

Sometimes we think we have a new idea, but most of our ideas are not new at all. Most of the ideas we have were thought of by men and women who lived centuries ago. Many of these ideas are shared by millions of people today.

Suppose you are asked: "What is your idea of an elephant?" This means: "Can you think what an elephant is like when you hear the word *elephant*?" It also means: "If you saw a certain kind of animal in a zoo or came upon it in a jungle, could you say, 'Aha! an elephant'?" You could—if you have a picture of an elephant in your mind. Many ideas are mind-pictures of things we can see, touch, hear, taste, or smell. We use these mind-pictures—and the words that describe them—all the time. They help us to think. They help us to tell others what we are thinking.

Not all ideas are mind-pictures of things we can see or touch. We also have ideas of things like "happiness." We cannot picture a thing called "happiness." Yet each of us has an idea of what "happiness" means. An idea like "happiness" is harder to describe than a mind-picture like "elephant." Jim might think that "happiness" means learning to play the guitar. Anne might think that "happiness" means having an exhibit at the science fair. It is the same with ideas like "beauty," "goodness," and "danger." They mean different things to different people.

A● Discuss what the idea *house* means. Can everyone agree on a meaning?

B● Discuss what the idea *beautiful house* means. Can everyone agree on the meaning? Would *beautiful house* mean the same thing to a Sumerian and an Eskimo? Explain.

Where do ideas come from? How do we get them?

We get some ideas through our *senses*. We touch something that is "too hot." On a snowy, windy day we feel "too cold." We see that the sun is shining and know that it is daytime. We hear our names called and know that someone wants us. We taste ice cream and decide that ice cream tastes good.

We also get many ideas from our *communities*. A **community** is a group of people living or working together. It is also the *place* in which a group lives.

There are different kinds of communities. Each of us belongs to many of them. A family is one kind of community. A group of friends, a church, and a school are all communities. A

QUESTIONS ABOUT CONTROLLING IDEAS

1. What *is* the world and the universe? (What is it made of? How was it made? What can our senses tell us about it?)

2. What should human beings try to do with their lives? (Why are we here? What is our aim? What are our rights and duties?)

3. How can men and women know what is good and what is bad, or what is right and what is wrong?

4. Are human beings mainly good, or mainly bad, or a mixture of good and bad?

5. What is happiness? How can men and women find happiness?

6. Is there life after death?

7. Does God (or do the gods) exist?

8. Does God (or do the gods) care about human beings?

9. Are any of the controlling ideas of this particular people shared with other people? Are some shared with all men and women?

town or city is a community. Even a whole nation can be called a community. From each kind of community, we get ideas. Sometimes we may get the same idea from more than one community.

C ▶ Many people think that it is a good idea to study hard. From what communities would you probably get that idea?

D • Where did you get your ideas about the following?

love	God	good manners	continents
time	words	freedom	happiness
loyalty	laws	obedience	cooperation
	sorrow	mathematical sets	

Many of the ideas we get from our communities are part of our culture. Such ideas have been handed down to us from long ago. They come from many generations of people and from many parts of the world.

The cultures we know today have been formed over thousands of years. They began when travel and trade were not easy. Thousands of years ago people knew little about the cultures of other societies. Yet ideas did travel. Sometimes societies copied ideas from other cultures. That is how civilization spread across the Old World.

Controlling Ideas and World Views

Civilization led people to think about the meaning of life. They tried to find out how human beings could be happy. They wondered about the best kind of government. Some people questioned whether there were many gods.

Important ideas about the meaning of life may be called **controlling ideas.** These are ideas that guide or *control* our ways of thinking and behaving. A *set of controlling ideas* makes a world view. Cultures have different world views because some people's ideas are different from others.

Some ideas and ways of thinking are called *values*. **Values** are beliefs that we think are important. Our values guide us in everything we do. Values *can be* controlling ideas. Some values are honesty, bravery, patience, love, and loyalty.

- **A ▶** How would having such values make a person act?
- **B ▶** What communities might teach a person those values?
- **C ●** There are many other values. What values can you think of?
- **D ●** Look at the box "Questions about Controlling Ideas" (page 151). These are the questions that humans try to answer. They are questions that we can use as we study a world view. Make sure that you understand the questions. Why are they important?
- **E ▶** What controlling ideas did the Sumerians have?

Most of us get our world view from our culture. However, as we learn more, we use our *reason* (the power of thinking) to form our own personal world view.

Four World Views

Each of the four world views that we will study took form in a civilized society. These world views became strong near the end of ancient history. Yet they have been very important in the history of the world since that time. They molded the cultures of many later civilized societies.

Four World Views That Became Strong by the Sixth Century B.C.

World View	Culture Area
Confucianism [kən fyü′ shən iz′ əm]: the teaching of Confucius about human duties and good behavior	China
Buddhism [bü′ diz əm]: the teaching of Buddha about life	India
Judaism [jü′ dē iz′ əm]: the religion of the Hebrews (later Jews) about one God and obedience to His laws	Middle East
Naturalism: the idea that humans can find out about nature and human life by reason	Greece

A▶ In what civilized society did each world view grow?

B▶ Look at the box "Four World Views That Became Strong by the Sixth Century B.C." (page 153). The list names the four world views we are going to study. What are the four views called?

Each of the four world views grew out of different cultures. However, all four views moved forward from the idea that priests knew all about the gods. The world views told people how to think and how to act in order to live good lives.

C● What would you say was the Sumerians' world view about 3000 B.C.? How did Sumerians get their world view?

The teachings of Confucius and Buddha were set down in books. The history and beliefs of the Hebrews were written in many books. These books are collected in the Hebrew Scriptures, also called the Old Testament. The writings of Greek thinkers are found in many books that have been passed down to us. All of these ideas are very much alive today.

In this chapter, we will study Confucianism, Buddhism, and Judaism. We will study the ideas of Greek thinkers in the next chapter.

THE CONFUCIAN WORLD VIEW

Early Chinese Civilization and Confucius, the Teacher

Chinese civilization began in the Hwang Ho Valley in the fifteenth century B.C. For centuries there was a strong empire in northern China around the Hwang Ho Valley. But by the sixth century B.C., the Chinese Empire had become weak. It was divided into provinces. The rulers of these provinces fought one another. It was a time of troubles. In this time of troubles, Confucius lived and taught. He was born in the province of *Lu* in 551 B.C.

A▶ Look at the map "China in the Sixth Century B.C." (page 155).
   1. Find China today on a globe or a world map.

THE GROWTH OF CIVILIZATION

2. Compare China of the sixth century B.C. with China today.
3. Find the province of Lu.
4. What big cities are in or near Lu today?

Confucius was a *philosopher*. A **philosopher** is a person who loves wisdom. Confucius felt that in times of trouble—and indeed in *all* times—the thing people need most is wisdom. Wisdom teaches us to lead a good life.

For four years Confucius was an important official in the government of Lu. He got rid of crime in that province. But in the long run the ruler of Lu would not do what Confucius advised. So Confucius left the government and spent the rest of his life in teaching wisdom. But he kept hoping that rulers would take his advice.

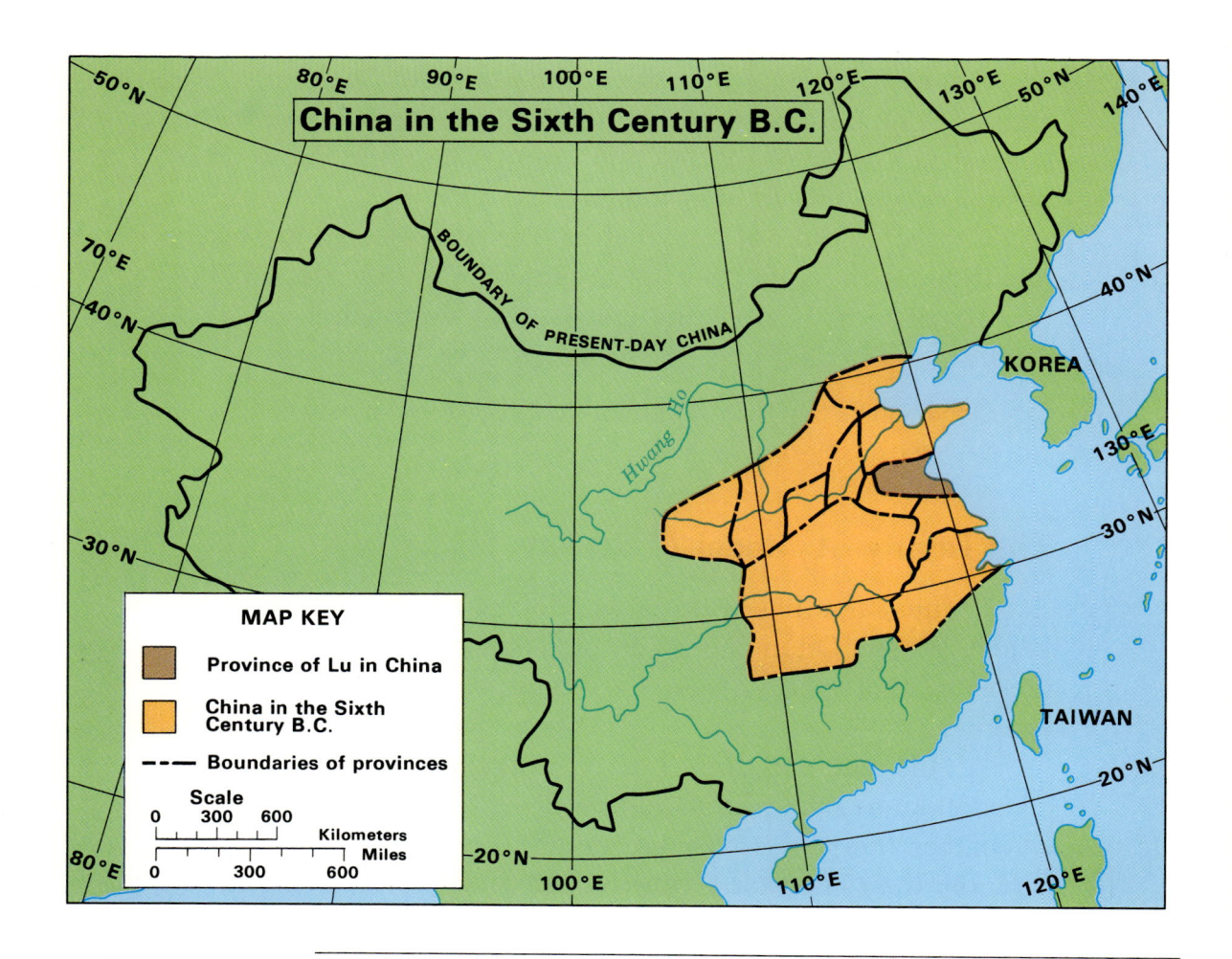

China in the Sixth Century B.C.

MAP KEY
- Province of Lu in China
- China in the Sixth Century B.C.
- --- Boundaries of provinces

SOME WORLD VIEWS AT THE END OF ANCIENT HISTORY

How does one learn wisdom? Confucius said that people must first *read* what wise persons have written in the past. So he and his pupils studied ancient Chinese books. Confucius also said that people must *listen* to wise persons. Above all, people must learn how to *choose* and to *think* rightly.

B▶ How did Confucius think that one learns wisdom?
C● Do you think that wise persons in most civilized cultures would agree with Confucius? Explain.

Confucius said that people should try to follow the *Way of Heaven*. This **Way of Heaven** is the path to wisdom and goodness in human lives.

Confucius taught, above all, that people should know how to behave toward others. They should be truthful and kind. They should be loyal. People should always be polite and should always keep their tempers.

Order in society was very important to Confucius. He explained how each person should fit his or her behavior to the behavior of other people. In any group, one must know what person or persons to obey.

Confucius did not say what heaven was. He did not teach much about the gods. But he accepted many things that the traditional religion of China taught. One such belief was that divine power ruled over the world.

D● Do you think that learning about Confucius's ideas may help us to be wise? Why or why not?

The Family: A Model of Society

Chinese families were large and the members of families kept together. Often hundreds of members of a family lived close together in a village. They were able to work the land together.

All the members of the family knew how they were related. They all knew that they shared the same *ancestors*. They could remember their ancestors for many years back. And they all honored their ancestors. They believed that the spirits of their

A present-day nuclear family in Taipei (Taiwan). The teachings of Confucius placed a great deal of importance on a strong, united family.

ancestors watched over them. Such a large family is called an *extended family*. An **extended family** is parents and children, grandparents, aunts, uncles, and cousins. A **nuclear family** is one set of parents and their children.

The extended family worked very well in China. Every member helped all the other members. The oldest man was the leader. And the younger people honored and obeyed the older men and women.

For Confucius the extended family gave a model for order in society. In a time of troubles the family stayed strong.

A ▶ Who is part of the extended family?
B ● Honoring ancestors is sometimes called *ancestor worship*. Can you see why?
C ● Why did honoring their ancestors hold large Chinese families together?

SOME WORLD VIEWS AT THE END OF ANCIENT HISTORY

Five Social Relationships

Confucius said that there are five *social relationships*. A **social relationship** is the way in which two or more persons get on together. For each person in each relationship, there is a proper way to behave.

The first and most important relationship is the one *between parent and child.* Someone asked Confucius: "How can a person become a good person?" Confucius answered: "First of all by being a good son." Confucius said that when we learn to obey our parents, we are learning to be good. He also taught that parents had duties to their children.

A● Why did Confucius say that the parent-child relationship is the most important relationship?

Another social relationship is that *between friends.* Confucius believed that friends are equals. Friends owe respect to each other. Each must be worthy of the other's respect.

The three other relationships are those of *older and younger child, husband and wife,* and *emperor and subject.* Confucius taught that these relationships are like the relationship between parent and child. In each of these, one person is the leader. The other person should obey. Confucius believed that people would get along together if they followed the duties in the five relationships.

B▶ What is the most important social relationship?
C● Look at the picture "The Five Social Relationships" (page 159).
   1. Which relationships are inside the family?
   2. Which relationships show one person who is leader?
   3. Which relationship shows persons who are equal?
   4. What do you think of Confucius's ideas about relationships between people? Are they the same as your ideas? Explain.

What Confucius Taught about Government

Confucius did not teach that people should be made to do anything the leaders like. The leaders have duties, too. They

The Five Social Relationships

must follow the Way of Heaven by treating others as they would want to be treated themselves. That is wisdom and the way to the good life.

Confucius said that government was like the head of a family. People should think of the emperor as a parent. Therefore they should show the emperor great respect. The emperor had certain duties. He should rule wisely and fairly. Then people would obey happily. However Confucius knew that governments are not always good. When they are bad, the people do not obey. Then there are times of trouble. When there is a time of trouble, it means that the government has not followed the *Will of Heaven.* The **Will of Heaven** is the great spirit of wisdom that helps a ruler to govern well. Sooner or later a bad government falls. And civilized society might fall with it.

Let us read a story that tells about Confucius's belief about government.

SOME WORLD VIEWS AT THE END OF ANCIENT HISTORY

One day Confucius saw a woman weeping by a tomb. He said to her, "You weep as though you are very sad."

"So I am," replied the woman. "In this place, my husband's father was killed by a tiger. My husband also was killed by a tiger, and now my son has been killed, too."

"If this is so, why do you not leave this terrible place?" asked Confucius.

The woman replied, "Here there are tigers, but at least the government is not bad."

"My pupils," Confucius said, "hear and remember. Bad government is worse than a fierce tiger!"

To this day China has kept this idea of government and the Will of Heaven. The people expect that governments will be good. Yet they know that bad governments happen. Then they expect a time of troubles until a new, good government arises and obeys the Will of Heaven.

Confucianism and Chinese Culture

Most of us probably agree with most of Confucius's ideas about the Way of Heaven. But some of his ideas are different from ours.

- A● Think about Confucius's idea about government. What could make a government good? What could people do if government was bad?
- B● Look at the box "Ways of Controlling Governments" (page 117). Why did Confucius not think of any of these ways?
- C★ Is it likely that a government that has *unlimited power* will always be good and fair? Explain.
- D● Do you think Confucius was right to compare a government and the people to a parent and family? What is the big difference between a parent's leadership and a government's leadership?
- E● How did the ideas of Confucius explain the ebb and flow of civilization?

Confucius had many pupils who became teachers and workers in government. Yet Confucius himself was not able to keep an important job in government. He was never able to persuade a ruler to follow his teachings. He died believing that he had failed.

But Confucius had not failed. His ideas became known to all Chinese people. For about 2,500 years after the death of Confucius, the people of China followed his teachings. *Confucianism*—all the teachings of Confucius together—became part of the Chinese way of life. For many centuries Confucianism was the most important controlling idea in China.

Today mainland China has a Communist government. The Communists do not like many of Confucius's ideas. They do not want the family to be strong. It will be interesting to see if the people of China give up the world view that has been so important to them for two and a half millennia.

A painting on silk of a prosperous fourteenth or fifteenth century Chinese family.

THE BUDDHIST WORLD VIEW

Another world view that was important in China was Buddhism. Buddhism and Confucianism were often found in the same areas of China. But Buddhism began in a very different culture area: in a kingdom in northern India. Today most of that land is in the country called Nepal. It is on the slopes of the Himalayas [him′ a lā′ əz], the highest mountains in the world.

Before we learn about Buddhism, we need to know about a still older religion—*Brahmanism* [brä′ mə niz′ əm].

Brahmanism and Reincarnation

From about 2400 B.C. there had been civilized societies in India. In the sixth century B.C. the culture of India had a religion called Brahmanism. **Brahmanism** taught that there were many gods. It taught that all living things were part of a great spirit.

Brahmanism also taught that whenever a living thing died, it was born again as another living thing. This was true of human beings as well as of other creatures. This idea is called *rebirth,* or **reincarnation.**

The idea of being born again may seem strange to us. Yet many people say they remember the lives they led before. One of those people was a little girl who lived in the country of Burma about 80 years ago. Let us read what she said about her other life.

Why I Love Puppets

When I was very small, I did not remember my last life. I was just like any other little girl—except for one thing. I loved puppets. They were my favorite toys. My mother and my father got me some to play with. I was only three then. Yet I could handle puppets better than a grown-up could. My parents wondered if I had handled puppets in my last life. Then, when I was four, a wonderful thing happened.

Mother and Father took me to a puppet show one day. What a surprise we all got! I recognized the puppet booth! It was mine, I told them. I remembered my last lifetime. I had been a man named Maung

Mon. That was my booth. I could prove it. I knew all the puppets' names. I even knew what lines they said in the plays. How pleased we all were! Now we know why I loved puppets so much.

No one can be sure if the little girl really remembered her past life. Perhaps she only thought she did.

The Caste System of Brahmanism

Another part of Brahmanism was the *caste* [kast] *system.* A **caste** is a special kind of group, or class, in society. In a caste system, people are born into a caste. They cannot change their caste. They must marry a person in the same caste. Their children are in the same caste, too.

A▶ Look at the box "The Four Main Castes and the Outcastes" below.
1. What is the highest caste?
2. What are the three other castes?
3. What work does each caste do?
4. Who are the outcastes?

The Four Main Castes and the Outcastes

Brahmans (brä′ mənz)	Priests and learned persons
Kshatriyas (kshat′ rē əz)	Soldiers and rulers
Vaisyas (vīs yəz)	Farmers and merchants
Sudras (sü′ drəz)	Workers in many trades
Outcastes	The lowest people, who belonged to no caste. They did the dirtiest jobs.

The caste system depended on reincarnation. Brahmanism taught that a person's caste depended on the way that person had acted in earlier lives. Those who obeyed the rules of

SOME WORLD VIEWS AT THE END OF ANCIENT HISTORY   163

religion would be reborn into a higher caste. Those who did not obey would be reborn into a lower caste, or they might have no caste at all. They might even be reborn as animals.

Life was not bad for the three upper castes. For the people below them, however, life could be very difficult. Most of the lowest caste, the Sudras, were very poor. Few were able to read or write. And they were not allowed to own land. Yet, compared with the outcastes, even the Sudras had good lives.

The lives of the outcastes were miserable. Outcastes were allowed to do only the dirtiest of jobs. No outcastes could go to school or even to religious services. They could not use the wells or streams used by the castes. They could not touch or be touched by someone of another group. Even their shadows were considered unclean.

Historians think that the caste system began after the *Aryans* conquered India. The top castes were Aryans. The Sudras and outcastes were probably descendants of the people who were conquered. As time went by, however, the system became part of the religion. It is part of the religion called *Hinduism*, which came from Brahmanism.

The religion of Brahmanism kept order in Indian society. Nearly everyone obeyed the laws. It is interesting to see how the belief in reincarnation stopped people from envying those in higher castes. People believed that their next life on earth would be better or worse depending on their behavior in their present life. Reincarnation taught people to accept their caste and to do their work.

B● Why would people in higher castes not care if the lower castes were unhappy? Whose fault was it if a person was a poor outcaste?

Gautama Becomes the Buddha

Toward the end of the sixth century B.C., a prince was born in a tiny kingdom in northern India. He was Prince Siddhartha Gautama [sid där′ ta gō′ tə mə]. We shall use the name Gautama. There are many stories about his early life. Here is one of them.

Under the caste system, outcastes were assigned the lowliest jobs. Here an outcaste in New Delhi sweeps the sidewalk.

The Story of Gautama's Birth

In a previous life, Gautama had been a saint. His name had been Kasappa [kä′ sä pə]. When Kasappa was dying, he made a promise that he would be reborn as a great teacher.

One of his servants decided to find the reborn Kasappa. He traveled all over, looking at newborn babies. Then he saw Gautama, who was only two days old. The baby raised a hand to bless the servant. The servant believed that this was Kasappa reborn. The servant told Gautama's mother what he believed. He said that her son would be a great teacher. He also said that Gautama would give up all his power and wealth and that he would travel to seek the truth about life. People would remember Gautama's name forever.

The king, Gautama's father, became very worried when he heard this. He wanted his son to rule the kingdom someday. How could his son give up everything? The king ordered that no one should ever tell Gautama what the servant had said. Gautama would learn to be a prince. He would not learn to be a teacher. He would have everything he wanted. No sick people or poor people would be allowed to come near the palace. Gautama would never see anything unpleasant or unhappy. He would never want to give up his life in the palace.

Prince Gautama had a happy life in his father's palace. He had many servants. He had everything he wanted. Of course, Gautama had to go through some hard training. He had to learn to ride. He had to learn to drive a chariot and to use a bow. A ruler had to be a mighty soldier. He also had to learn about how to rule a kingdom.

SOME WORLD VIEWS AT THE END OF ANCIENT HISTORY   **165**

Yet Gautama became unhappy. This was the beginning of his *awakening.* By the time he was 29 years old he found out that most people were less fortunate than he was. He worried about life. Why were people unhappy? Why were people sick? Why were people sometimes cruel? Must people go on being born again and again? Gautama wondered if people could ever escape from trouble and suffering.

Gautama decided to give up his own pleasant life. He left wealth and comfort. In a simple robe, with no money, he set out to find the truth about the world and life.

For years he wandered. He lived sometimes with holy men who tried to find peace by living very simply. But still Gautama worried.

One day Gautama sat down beneath a tree and thought and thought. After 49 days he found the answer. Gautama felt his mind clear up. At last he understood the truth about life. The cause of human suffering was that people did not understand the world and human life. Suddenly Gautama saw that everything around him was *not real.* Human life was a *dream*—an unhappy dream. If people understood this, they could escape from suffering. A person who really knew that the world was unreal could escape from being born again. There was no need to keep going through the troubles of life.

This discovery of Gautama's is called his **enlightening.** This means that he saw the light of truth after years and years of

Gautama sat under the sacred bodhi tree to think about the meaning of life. After 49 days of meditation, he achieved the enlightenment he was seeking.

darkness. That was why people called him *Buddha.* **Buddha** [bü′ də] means "enlightened one."

Nirvana

Guatama had found freedom from suffering. He called his freedom *nirvana* [nir vä′ nə]. **Nirvana** means "cooled." In *nirvana,* a person is "cooled" from the "fevers" of life. Buddha said that nirvana is the only important goal for people. When people reach nirvana, they have no greedy wants, no fears, no hatreds. Such people are free from the *dream* of life. Now they can join the great spirit of the universe.

Nirvana is hard for most of us to understand. It is a state of mind that few of us can reach. The idea that life is only a dream is very different from our ideas about science. It is quite different from our ideas about the importance of technology and the idea that people will be better off with more goods, better health services, and so on. It is far from Confucius's idea that people should be attached to parents, family, friends, and society. It is unlike religions such as Christianity, Judaism, and Islam, which teach the love of God and of our fellow humans. To Buddha and to his followers all these things are part of the foolish dream—the dream that life is real or important.

What about rebirth? Buddha believed in rebirth. Yet he believed that people can escape from being reborn. They will escape when they reach nirvana. A person can live many times without reaching nirvana. Reaching nirvana has nothing to do with caste. A Sudra worker might reach it in just one lifetime. A learned Brahman priest might never reach it. It would all depend on how a person acted.

Buddhism Spreads and Changes

During his life Buddha taught his ideas to many people. Many of these people taught the ideas to others. During the following centuries the ideas of Buddha spread through most of Asia. After a while different forms of *Buddhism* (Buddha's teachings) developed. However, all the forms agreed that the world and this life are dreams.

During the fourth century B.C., Buddhism split into two major schools of thinking. One school believes that Buddha was a human, a holy person, and a wise teacher. Many scholars believe that this was how Buddha saw himself. The second school of thought sees Buddha as a god and savior. Today one or another form of Buddhism is important in China, Korea, Japan, Sri Lanka, Vietnam, Laos [lä′ ōs], Kampuchea (Cambodia), Tibet, and Mongolia.

In India, Buddhism changed Brahmanism. Buddha's idea of life as a dream became part of the religion called *Hinduism.* Hinduism, now the main religion in India, developed from Brahmanism. However, Hindus kept the caste system. To Buddha the caste system had been part of the dream of life.

A ▶ Did Buddha believe that a member of the lowest caste could reach *nirvana*? Explain.

B ● At the end of his life, Buddha said: "Remember this. Everything in this world will decay." How does this help us to understand the Buddhist world view?

C ▶ If you were a Buddhist, would you try to get a better government or try to rise above worrying about bad government?

D ▶ Would a Buddhist try to have more goods and better technology or try not to care about such things?

E ● Look at "Questions about Controlling Ideas" (page 151). How would a Buddhist answer the questions? How would a Confucian answer them?

THE WORLD VIEW OF JUDAISM

Another world view began about the same time that Confucianism and Buddhism were becoming important in China and India. This new world view, Judaism, grew up in the Middle East. Judaism began as a set of controlling ideas for the Hebrew people. Before we study Judaism, we should review the earliest people's ideas about gods.

The Earliest Religions: Animism and Polytheism

Nature is often hard for people to understand. Sometimes nature helps us. Rain falls, the sun shines, crops grow. Sometimes nature seems unkind. Storms, floods, or earthquakes wipe out our work.

People have always tried to explain the forces of nature. In the earliest times, people said that there were *spirits* everywhere. People thought that even trees and rocks had their own spirits. These spirits, people believed, made nature behave as it did. This belief is called **animism** [an′ ə miz′ əm]. *Animus* is Latin for "spirit" or "breath."

In chapter 5, you learned how the Sumerians went from fearing spirits in nature to believing that these spirits were gods. These gods looked like people. They acted in the same ways that people act. The gods quarreled with one another. Sometimes they were kind. Sometimes they were unkind. The Sumerians did their best to please the gods by giving them grain and other gifts.

Belief in many gods is called **polytheism** [pol′ ē thē iz əm]. *Polytheism* comes from two Greek words: *polus* (many) and *theos* (god).

A★ Here are some words derived from *animus, polus,* and *theos:* animal, animated, theism, theology, polysyllable, polygon. What do the words mean?

The front part of the Temple of Hathor at Abu Simbel in southern Egypt. Hathor was the ancient Egyptian goddess of heaven and beauty.

169

Myths: The Stories of the Gods

Ancient peoples loved to tell stories about the wonderful adventures of their gods. These stories are called **myths** [miths]. As people told the myths over and over again, the stories grew and changed. After many, many years, the myths were written down. They became a part of early literature. We still enjoy hearing and reading these myths.

We can learn some things about ancient people from reading their myths. First of all, the stories tell us about early religion. We can learn what people thought about the gods and which gods were their favorites. We can learn how the gods acted: their loves, hates, quarrels, and mistakes. Second, many of the myths tell us about early science. The myths were people's first attempts to explain why things around them were the way they were. The myths tried to explain why things happened the way they did.

Here is an example of a Greek myth. It explained to the early Greeks the reasons for the changes of the seasons.

Hades and Persephone

Hades [hā′ dēz] was the god of the Underworld. He hated light and seldom left his gloomy home. One day, however, he visited the earth. There he saw the beautiful Persephone [pər sef′ ə nē] and fell in love with her. He grabbed Persephone and put her in his black chariot pulled by coal-black horses. He struck the earth with his spear, and the earth opened. The chariot plunged deep into the Underworld. Then the earth closed over them. Hades made Persephone the goddess of the Underworld.

Persephone was the daughter of Demeter [di mē′ tər], the goddess of the harvest. Demeter missed her daughter. She looked everywhere for her. All she could find was the sash that Persephone had dropped before being carried into the Underworld. Demeter was filled with grief. She blamed the earth for taking her daughter away, and she punished it. She refused to let anything grow until Persephone came back to her. Flowers wilted and died. Leaves fell from the trees. Fields became cold. Cattle died. Seeds did not spring up and grow. The whole earth became brown, icy, and lifeless.

Then Demeter found out that the earth was not to blame. Persephone had been carried away by Hades. Demeter needed help in getting Persephone back. She went to Zeus [züs], the king of all the gods. Zeus said that if Persephone had not eaten anything in the Underworld, she could return to earth. A messenger of the gods took the news to Hades. Hades told Persephone she could leave. He did not tell her that she must not eat. As she was getting ready to leave, Hades gave her some fruit to eat. Persephone had been very sad in the Underworld. She had refused all food. But this time Persephone accepted the fruit. The messenger tried to stop her from eating—but too late! She had eaten six seeds of the fruit. Hades demanded that Persephone spend six months of each year with him, one month for each seed she had eaten.

Persephone returned to Demeter. Every year, however, she returned to the Underworld and lived with Hades for six months. During those months, Demeter was heartbroken. Nothing grew. The earth became cold and brown. Winter came to the world. When Persephone returned, Demeter was happy. Then she made the earth warm and green. She made it rich with crops and bright with flowers. The return of Persephone brought joy to Demeter and springtime to the world.

A● Suppose you met an ancient Greek. How would you explain the change of seasons to him or her?

B● Do you think all the ancient Greeks believed myths like this one? Why or why not?

People began to wonder why the gods they worshipped did not set good examples for them. People can learn to live good lives only if they have good examples to follow. The gods had to be worthy of people's praise. Over the centuries people began to wonder more and more.

As different cultures came into contact with one another, people learned that there were many different gods for the same natural forces. People began to wonder how there could be only one sun but many sun gods. When people lost battles, they wondered if it meant that their gods had lost their power. Often people who lost wars adopted the gods of the people who had won. But changing gods made many people wonder even more about the gods. Some societies, including the Babylonian and the Egyptian, decided that there was one main god and that the other gods were lesser gods.

(below, left) A prayer written in Hebrew. *(below, right)* A young man proudly reads from the Torah during the ceremony in which he becomes Bar Mitzvah (a "son of the commandment"), assuming the responsibilities of an adult Jew. The ceremony takes place near the boy's thirteenth birthday.

Monotheism

Very slowly people changed from polytheism to *monotheism* [mon′ ə thē iz′ əm]. **Monotheism** means belief in one god. Like the word *polytheism,* it is made by putting together two smaller Greek words. *Monos* means "one." *Theos* means "god." A person who believes in one God is a **monotheist.** The change in controlling ideas from polytheism to monotheism marked a very important point in the human adventure.

Monotheism began when certain peoples started to believe that one God had created the earth and the heavens. Thousands of years ago a group of people, the Hebrews, began to believe in one God. This small group of people from the Middle East is very important in the story of monotheism and in our study of controlling ideas. Their religion is alive today. It is called *Judaism* [jü′ dē iz′ əm].

The Hebrews Learn about God

The Hebrews kept records of past events. These records told how their God had helped the Hebrews and how He had punished them. The records told how some of the Hebrew leaders had direct contact with their God. Direct contact with a god is called **revelation.** That means that God made his will known to humans.

The records of the Hebrews are called *Holy Scripture.* **Scripture** means "writing." The Scriptures were first collected and put together in the sixth century B.C. Additions to the Scriptures were made during the next four centuries.

The first five books of the Scriptures are the **Torah.** *Torah* is a Hebrew word that means "law," or "teaching." The Torah is also the first five books of the Christian Bible. Other books are part of the Scriptures, too. Some of these books were written by *prophets.* **Prophets,** in religion, are persons who speak with God and pass God's words to the people.

A▶ What do we call the religion of the Hebrews?
B★ What is another meaning of *prophet?*

SOME WORLD VIEWS AT THE END OF ANCIENT HISTORY

C★ Look at the *Holy Scriptures* of the Jews and at the Christian *Old Testament.* Look at the table of contents. Find the names of the first five books also known as the *Torah* (or the *five books of Moses*). How many other books are in the Hebrew Scriptures?

D● The Jews are often called "people of the law" and sometimes "people of the book." Why?

The History of the Hebrews to the Exodus

Hebrew history begins when the family of Abraham left Mesopotamia in the nineteenth or eighteenth century B.C. A nomadic herder, Abraham was a rich man. The Scriptures tell how God made a promise to Abraham. God said that Abraham was to be the ancestor of a great nation. God also said that Abraham's descendants must set an example for all people.

With his herds, Abraham and his family traveled from Mesopotamia to Egypt and then back to Palestine, or the land of Canaan [kā′ nən]. This was the land that God promised to Abraham and his family if they would worship Him.

The Old Testament tells why Abraham left Mesopotamia:

> Now the Lord said to Abraham, "Go from your country and your father's house to the land that I will show you. And I will make of you a great nation, and I will bless you and make your name great so that you will be a blessing. I will bless those who bless you and curse those who curse you. And through you will all the families of the earth be blessed."

A● Look at the map "Palestine in the Ancient Middle East c. 2000 B.C." (page 175).
  1. Trace Abraham's travels—from Ur through Babylon to Haran; then to Egypt and back to Palestine.
  2. Where is the *Fertile Crescent*? Why would a herder follow the Fertile Crescent?
  3. What is Palestine called today?

After Abraham died, his descendants stayed in Palestine as herders. The Torah tells how Abraham's great-grandson Joseph became an official of the Egyptian pharaoh. It also tells how the Hebrews moved into Egypt about 1700 B.C. For about three

174 THE GROWTH OF CIVILIZATION

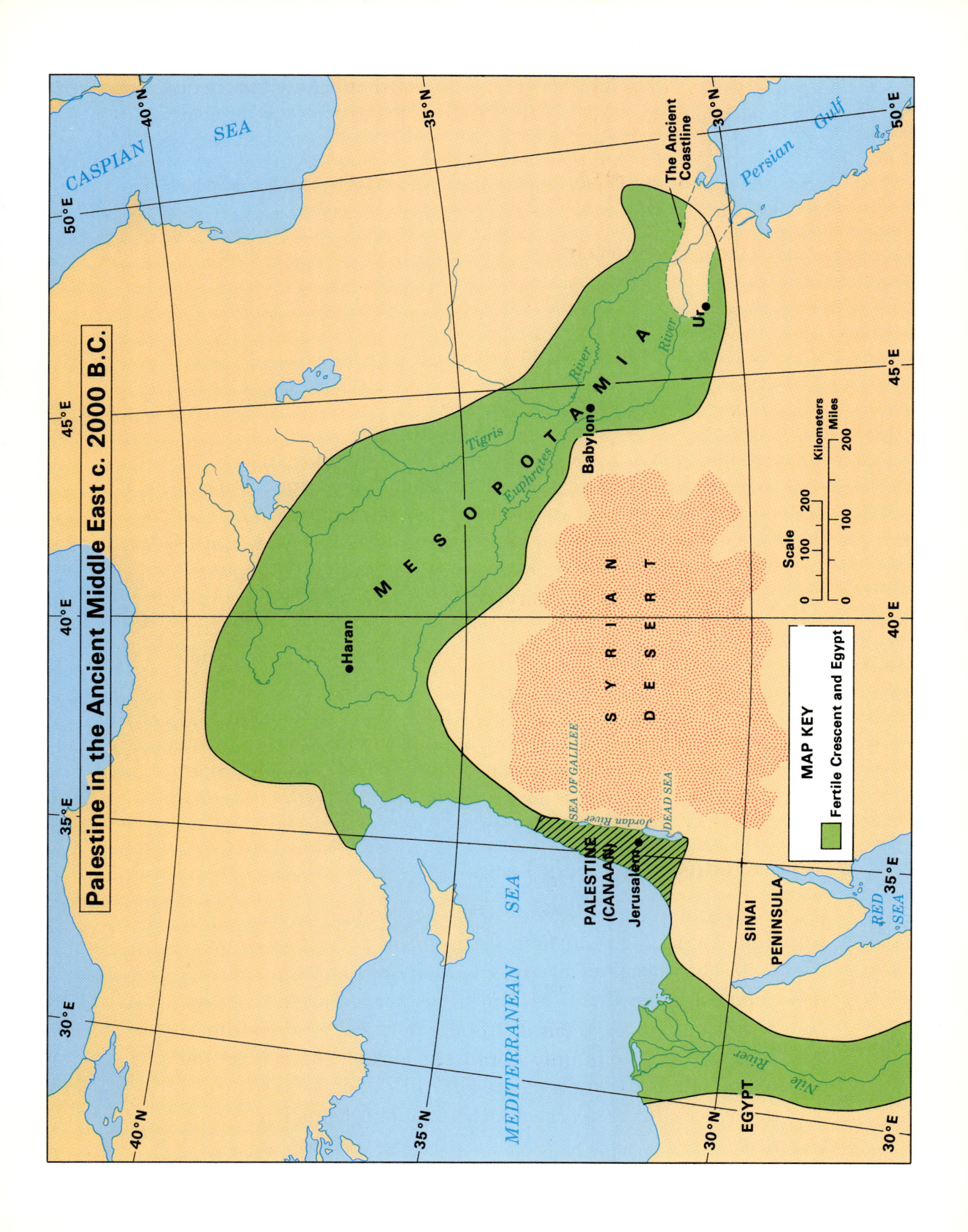

Palestine in the Ancient Middle East c. 2000 B.C.

MAP KEY
- Fertile Crescent and Egypt

Locations labeled:
- CASPIAN SEA
- MESOPOTAMIA
- Tigris River
- Euphrates River
- Babylon
- Ur
- The Ancient Coastline
- Persian Gulf
- Haran
- SYRIAN DESERT
- SEA OF GALILEE
- Jordan River
- DEAD SEA
- PALESTINE (CANAAN)
- Jerusalem
- MEDITERRANEAN SEA
- SINAI PENINSULA
- RED SEA
- EGYPT
- Nile River

centuries the Hebrews did well in Egypt. Then a new family of pharaohs came to power. From about 1500 B.C., the Hebrews in Egypt were made slaves.

B★ You can read the story of Joseph in Genesis, chapters 37 and 41–45.

In the thirteenth century B.C., the Hebrews in Egypt found a leader. His name was *Moses.*

C★ Read how Moses was saved from being killed along with other baby boys. This story is in Exodus, chapter 2, verses 1–10.

The Torah says that Moses was chosen by God. God told him to free the Hebrews from the Egyptians.

Moses went to the pharaoh and asked him to set the Hebrew people free. The pharaoh refused. Then *plagues* [plāgz] fell on Egypt. **Plagues** are troublesome happenings. The Hebrews believed they were punishments sent by God. Cattle owned by Egyptians died of disease. Insects ate the Egyptians' crops. Storms ruined the harvest. In all this the Hebrews saw the hand of God. They believed God was punishing the Egyptians. Finally the pharaoh agreed to free the Hebrews. They then began the **Exodus** [ek′ sə dəs], or *journey out of Egypt.*

To the Hebrews the Exodus is a great event in their history. It showed them more about God. It taught them that their God had the power to save a whole nation. Their God was more powerful than the pharaoh's army and all the gods of Egypt.

The Exodus and God's Laws

For about 40 years Moses led his people through the desert of Sinai [sī′ nī]. During their long journey the people were nomads. They became very weary. Many of them thought that God had forgotten them. At times they turned against Moses. But Moses convinced them that God would not let them die in the wilderness. At one time during the journey, Moses left the group and climbed a mountain to talk with God. Because he did not come back for many weeks, the people became frightened.

They decided to make an idol to help them. They made a golden calf and prayed to it.

When Moses returned and saw the golden calf, he was angry. He saw that the people had turned away from God. Moses smashed the idol. Then he told the Hebrews about the laws that their God had given them. These laws are the **Ten Commandments.**

A● Look at the box "The Ten Commandments" below.
  1. Which commandment is about *monotheism*?
  2. Which forbids *idols*?
  3. Which forbids *lying*?

B● Why did the Hebrews think they were "God's chosen people"?

C★ Do you think that Confucius and Buddha would have agreed with some of the commandments? What ones? Why do you think so?

The Ten Commandments

I am the Lord your God, who brought you out of the land of Egypt, out of a state of slavery. You must have no other gods besides me.

You must not carve an image for yourself in the shape of anything that is in the heavens above, or that is on the earth below, or that is in the waters under the earth. You shall not bow down to them or serve them.

You must not misuse the name of the Lord your God.

Remember to keep the sabbath day holy.

Honor your father and your mother.

You must not commit murder.

You must not be unfaithful to your husband or your wife.

You must not steal.

You must not bring a false charge against your neighbor.

You must not desire your neighbor's home. You must not desire your neighbor's wife, nor his servant, nor his ox, nor his donkey, nor anything that is your neighbor's.

(Based on Exodus 20:2–17)

SOME WORLD VIEWS AT THE END OF ANCIENT HISTORY

The Ten Commandments became the *basic laws* of the Hebrews. Moses gave them many other laws, too. Under these laws all the people were equal. Some laws told them how to worship. Some were about health. Most of the laws told the Hebrews how to behave toward one another.

D ▶ Why was Moses angry with his people when he returned from the mountain?
E ▶ What do we call the basic laws of the Hebrews?
F ● How are the controlling ideas of these laws different from the controlling ideas of polytheistic religions?

The Hebrews in Palestine

At the end of their travels, the Hebrews settled again in the land of Palestine. Moses had died just before the Hebrews entered the land. A new leader was chosen. The leader's name was *Joshua*.

These tablets show the Ten Commandments written in Hebrew. They remind people of the stone tablets that Moses brought down from the mountain.

For many years the Hebrews fought with the farmers who were already living in Palestine. After a time the Hebrews became farmers themselves. They lived in *tribes.*

At first the Hebrews did not have a central government. But in the eleventh century B.C., they faced a new danger. A people called the *Philistines* tried to conquer them. The Philistines came across the Mediterranean Sea in ships. In order to fight back successfully, the Hebrews chose a king to lead them. The tribes united under *King Saul.*

A▶ Why did the Hebrews need a king to lead them at this time?

After the death of King Saul, the Hebrews were ruled by *David.* David was a great leader. He made Jerusalem the capital of his kingdom. Jerusalem is often called "the city of David."

B★ Read the story of how young David killed the Philistine giant Goliath, in I Samuel, chapter 17.

The third king of the Hebrews was David's son, *Solomon.* King Solomon was very wise. Under his rule the Hebrew people were strong and rich. After Solomon's death in 930 B.C., the kingdom was divided.

C▶ Look at the map "The Divided Kingdom, 931 B.C." (page 180). What were the two kingdoms? What two countries were neighbors of the Hebrews?

Dividing the kingdom weakened the Hebrews. The northern kingdom, Israel, was conquered by the Assyrians under King Sargon I. The Assyrians captured Samara, the capital of Israel. They forced many Hebrews to leave the kingdom. Those Hebrews went to live in other lands of the Middle East.

Judah, the southern kingdom, was stronger than the kingdom of Israel. Judah survived until 586 B.C., when the Babylonians under King Nebuchadnezzar conquered it. You read this story in Chapter 4. The Hebrews in Judah were either killed or carried off to Babylon as slaves. The Hebrews remained in Babylon for 59 years. During this time the Hebrews began to be called *Jews.* The name came from the kingdom of Judah. They will be called Jews from this point in the story.

SOME WORLD VIEWS AT THE END OF ANCIENT HISTORY

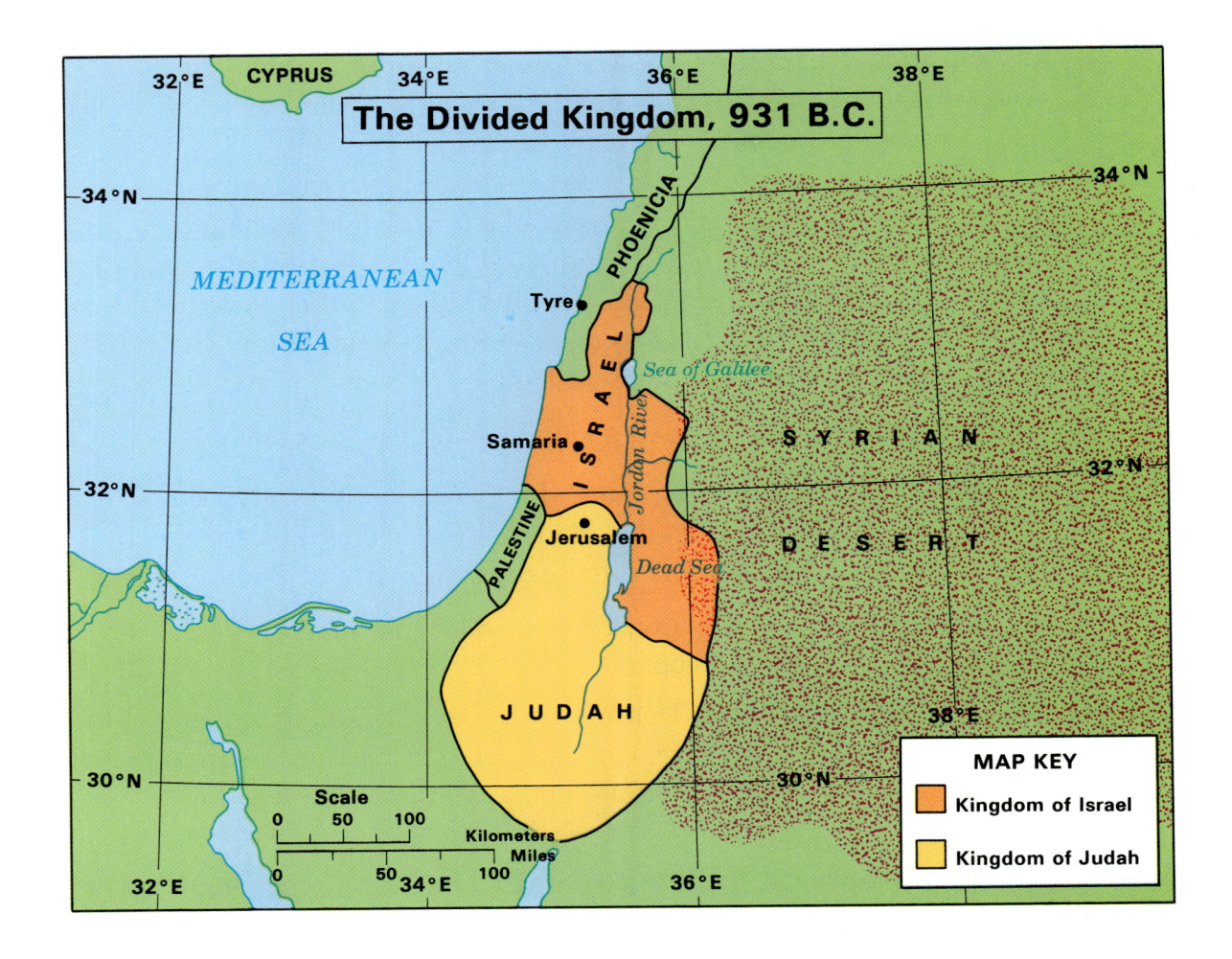

The Prophets

During the captivity in Babylon, the Jews tried to find out what they had done wrong. The prophets became even more important in Jewish life.

A ▶ What did prophets do?

The prophets told the people that their sufferings were a punishment for breaking God's laws. But God would give them great blessings if they were faithful.

The Jewish people became stronger in their faith. At this time the Scriptures were put together. The Holy Scriptures set forth the world view of Judaism. The Jews had new ways of worshipping God. They learned that each person could pray to God. And they believed that God was everywhere.

Things got better for the Jews. In 539 B.C. the Persian Empire conquered the Babylonians. The Persians freed the Jews, who went back to Palestine. After their return, the Jews again built Jerusalem and the temple.

Some Jews, however, remained in parts of the Persian Empire as soldiers or merchants. Here is a story about the Jews who remained in Persia.

The Story of Queen Esther

In the third year of the reign of King Ahasuerus (Xerxes [zirk' sēz]) in the early fifth century B.C., the king was angered by the disobedience of his queen. As punishment, he took the title of queen away from her.

Xerxes searched long and hard for a new queen. Finally, he was attracted by the beauty of Esther. Esther was the foster child of Mordecai [môr' də kī], a Jewish adviser to the king. Xerxes chose her as his new queen.

After the celebrations in honor of Queen Esther were over, Mordecai heard of a plan to kill the king. He told Esther, and she told the king.

Xerxes was very grateful and wanted to reward Mordecai for warning him of the plan. This came as bad news to Haman, the king's chief general. Haman was jealous. He did not want anyone else in the kingdom to receive more honors and rewards than he did.

Haman knew Mordecai was a Jew. He tricked the king into approving the death of all Jews in the empire.

Mordecai heard of Haman's plan. He asked Queen Esther to plead with the king for the safety of the Jews. Esther told the king the whole story. Xerxes had not realized Esther was a Jew.

King Xerxes was so angry at being tricked by Haman that he ordered Haman to be hanged on the very gallows Haman had built for Mordecai. The king also gave permission for the Jews to kill all their enemies in Persia before their enemies tried to kill them.

In this way the Jews of Persia were saved from death. The deed of Esther and Mordecai is remembered every year at the Jewish holiday of Purim.

The Problem of Evil

The controlling ideas of the Jews made up a world view. In later years Judaism continued to grow, but the major ideas were clear by the sixth century B.C. Part of the world view of Judaism was about the problem of evil.

Humans have always faced the problem of evil in the world. People suffer. They can be cruel to one another. Nature can bring suffering, too. Polytheistic religions say that evil comes from differences among the gods. Buddhists say evil comes from human desires. Indeed, for Buddhists evil is part of the *dream* of life. It does not come from gods. Confucians think that human evil comes from wrong behavior. It does not come from heaven. It comes when people do not follow the Way of Heaven.

How did Judaism explain evil in the world? The Jews believed in one perfect and loving God who created everything. Did God then create evil? The story of Adam and Eve at the beginning of the Torah, or Old Testament, gives an answer.

The story tells how God created everything and made everything good. He created the first man and woman, Adam and Eve. He gave them a beautiful land to live in, the Garden of Eden. He made them completely free to do what they wanted, except for just one thing. They were forbidden to eat the fruit of *one* tree in the garden. But Adam and Eve did eat the fruit of the tree.

Angry because Adam and Eve had disobeyed, God drove them out of the beautiful garden. From that time, there was evil in the world, and humans had to fight against evil. Adam and Eve's act of disobedience is known as the **Fall of Man,** because humans fell from the goodness that God had given them.

A★ You can read the story of the Fall in Genesis, chapters 2 and 3.
B▶ How did polytheistic religions explain good and evil?

The world view of Judaism (or Judaic world view) got its idea of human nature from this story. Human beings are mixed. They are partly good, because God made them. They are partly

Adam and Eve are driven out of Eden in this wood engraving by the famous French artist Gustave Doré (1833–1883).

bad, because they did not, and do not, always obey God. And they are *free.* God made people free. They know the difference between good and evil and are free to choose.

Judaism Spreads and Grows

The Holy Scriptures of the Jews set forth the world view of Judaism in the sixth century B.C. At the same time, far away in Asia, Confucius and Buddha were teaching.

As we have seen, the Judaic world view gave the Jews their controlling ideas. Look at the box "The Judaic World View" (page 184). This list does not cover all the controlling ideas of

> **The Judaic World View**
>
> 1. The world and the heavens were created by God.
> 2. The duty of human beings is to worship and to obey God.
> 3. Humans can know right and wrong from the laws that God gave them.
> 4. Humans are often sinful, yet they can learn to be good.
> 5. Humans must love one another, just as they love God and as God loves them.
> 6. There may be life after death, but this is not the reason for obeying and worshipping God.
> 7. God cares greatly about human beings. Human beings can communicate with God.

Judaism. Notice the idea about life after death. Some Jews believe in life after death, but this belief is not central in Judaism.

A▶ What ideas on the list show the view that God loves people?
B● Look at the box "Questions about Controlling Ideas" (page 151). See if you can answer these questions for Judaism.
C● What controlling ideas are shared by the three world views you have studied?

The Judaic world view became part of two important religions—Christianity and Islam. The Judaic world view spread all over Europe and to many cultures in other parts of the world.

The story of the Jewish people continues today. After the Jews returned to Palestine, they established another kingdom in that land. Later, Palestine became part of the Roman Empire. Still later, some Jews became Christians.

Both Christians and Jews were badly treated by the Romans. In A.D. 70, Roman soldiers destroyed Jerusalem. Most of the Jews

THE GROWTH OF CIVILIZATION

were driven out of Palestine. They settled in many parts of Europe, Asia, and North Africa.

At this time the *rabbis,* who were learned men, went on building Judaism on the Torah and other Scriptures. The rabbis' writings are called the **Talmud.** The Jewish religion kept on growing. The Jewish people have kept their faith. And they have kept the feeling of being one people.

Today many Jews live in Europe and in the Soviet Union. There are many, too, in the Jewish state of Israel, which was founded in 1948. The largest Jewish community in the world is in the United States.

D★ Find out about these Jewish holy days: Shabbat, Pesach, Shavuot, Sukkot, Rosh Hashanah, Yom Kippur, Chanukah, and Purim.

The rich traditions of Judaism continue to be observed. Here a rabbi prepares young boys for their Bar Mitzvah at the Great Wall, Israel.

SOME WORLD VIEWS AT THE END OF ANCIENT HISTORY

Summary

Every culture has controlling ideas. These are the ideas that guide people's behavior. When a set of controlling ideas explains the meaning of life and the nature of the world, we can call it a world view. About the sixth century B.C. four important world views grew in four different civilizations. The civilizations were in China, India, the Middle East, and Greece.

The Confucian world view grew up in China. Chinese civilization ebbed and flowed for many centuries. Its main controlling ideas came from a man who was born during a time of troubles. This man was Confucius. He taught that humans should follow the "Way of Heaven," or the way of wisdom. He said that order in a society was important. For him the extended family was a model for order in society.

The Buddhist world view began in northern India at a time when Brahmanism was the chief religion. Brahmanism divided all humans into four castes and the outcastes. A person born into one caste could not rise into a higher one. However, Brahmanism also taught belief in reincarnation. By obeying the rules of religion, a person could be born again in a higher caste.

A man named Gautama, later called Buddha, questioned many teachings of Brahmanism. He said that human life, with its fears, wants, attachments, and hatreds, is an unhappy dream. Castes, too, were dreams. A person can be free of the dream of life in nirvana. He or she can stop the cycle of being reborn. Anyone who tries hard can find nirvana. Buddha's teachings are called Buddhism.

Buddhism has a very different world view from Confucianism. Buddhism had a great influence on Brahmanism, which later became the religion called Hinduism. Both Buddhism and Hinduism are among the chief religions of Asia today.

Many people in the ancient world were animists, believers in the forces of nature. Most became polytheists, believers in many gods. A few ancient people became monotheists, believers in one god. The most famous ancient monotheists were the Hebrews.

The religion of the Hebrews is Judaism. This was the third world view in the ancient world. Judaism rose in the Middle East about 2000 B.C. At that time God made a promise to Abraham that his descendants would be blessed. After Abraham came many leaders. It was through Moses that the Hebrews received the Ten Commandments, their basic laws. The Hebrews' God tested their loyalty many times. They were forced to wander from country to country. They were enslaved by the Egyptians and the Assyrians.

The Scriptures were written to tell the history of God and the Hebrews, now called Jews. The Scriptures tell the world view of Judaism. Judaism is strong today. It also influenced the religions of Christianity and Islam.

Some Interesting Activities

1. Use an encyclopedia to find out more about Confucius and Buddha.

2. Read the questions under "Questions about Controlling Ideas" on page 151. Form three committees in your class. One committee will be Confucianists; one, Buddhists; and one, Jews. Have each committee answer the questions, using its own world view. Then have a discussion of the answers.

3. In a book of Greek myths, read the story of Pandora and Epimetheus. This story tells how the Greeks—who were polytheists—explained evil. Can you see any similarity to the story of Adam and Eve? Discuss.

4. The Scriptures tell about many battles fought by the Hebrews in Palestine and of the way in which God helped them. One story tells about two women who brought victory to the Hebrews over the Canaanites. Read the story of Deborah and Jael in the Old Testament, Judges, chapter 4.

5. The Jews had many poems praising and thanking God. They are called the Psalms. Some psalms were written by King David. Read David's Psalm 23. What does it tell you about Jewish beliefs?

6. Make two large maps of the Middle East. On the first, show the cities and boundaries of important civilizations as they were about 500 B.C. On the second map, show the location of cities and boundaries as they are today. Are many of the cities the same? Point out the differences in boundaries between the old and the new civilizations. What are the nations that make up the Middle East today?

Poseidon, the powerful god of the sea. The ancient Greeks believed that their fate depended on him when they were at sea.

CHAPTER 8

The Classical Civilization of Greece

About the sixth century B.C. the period of ancient civilization, or ancient history, ended. In the area around the Mediterranean Sea a new period of history began. Historians of Europe call this period **classical civilization.**

For centuries students have studied the *classics*. The **classics** are the writings and art of the civilized cultures of Greece and Rome.

In the sixth century B.C. there were many civilized cultures in the world. There was the great civilized empire in Persia. There were civilized empires in China, Southeast Asia, and India. In the Sudan region of Africa and in North Africa there were civilized societies. Civilized societies also developed in the area now called Mexico.

Historians often talk about the "classical period" of these and other civilized societies. For Europeans, however, classical civilization means the civilized cultures of Greece and Rome. The classical period of European history lasted from about 600 B.C. to about A.D. 500.

Grouping Cultures

With the growing numbers of civilized cultures, the task of studying them becomes harder. The job is made easier when we divide the cultures of the world into groups.

The cultures of the Old World are divided into two main groups: *Eastern cultures* and *Western cultures.* Cultures that grew up in the eastern part of the Old World are called **Eastern cultures.** These include the cultures of China, Japan, and India. Cultures that grew up in the western part of the Old World are called **Western cultures.** Western cultures spread to many parts of the world. Today we find Western culture in North America, South America, South Africa, and Australia.

There are many other large culture groups in the world. There are African cultures, Pacific cultures, Central Asian cultures, and Middle Eastern cultures.

The region of the Middle East is an area where Eastern and Western cultures meet and mingle. For example, Judaism began in a Middle Eastern culture. But Judaism helped to make Western cultures.

A▶ What countries are part of the Eastern cultures?

B● Did Confucian and Buddhist controlling ideas have much effect on Western cultures in the past? Why or why not?

C● Look at the map "Some Civilized Cultures c. 500 B.C.–A.D. 100" (page 191).
1. What mountains separate Europe from Asia?
2. Why was the Middle East so important in the spread of civilization and ideas?
3. Do you think that civilization spread in North Africa and the Sudan from the Middle East? How would it happen?
4. Find the Mesoamerican civilized culture. **(Mesoamerican** means "Middle American.")
5. There were many other cultures at this time. There were many societies in the Americas, Africa, Central Asia, Australia, and the islands of the world. Why are these not shown on the map?
6. In which latitudes were civilized societies at this time (500 B.C.–A.D. 100)?

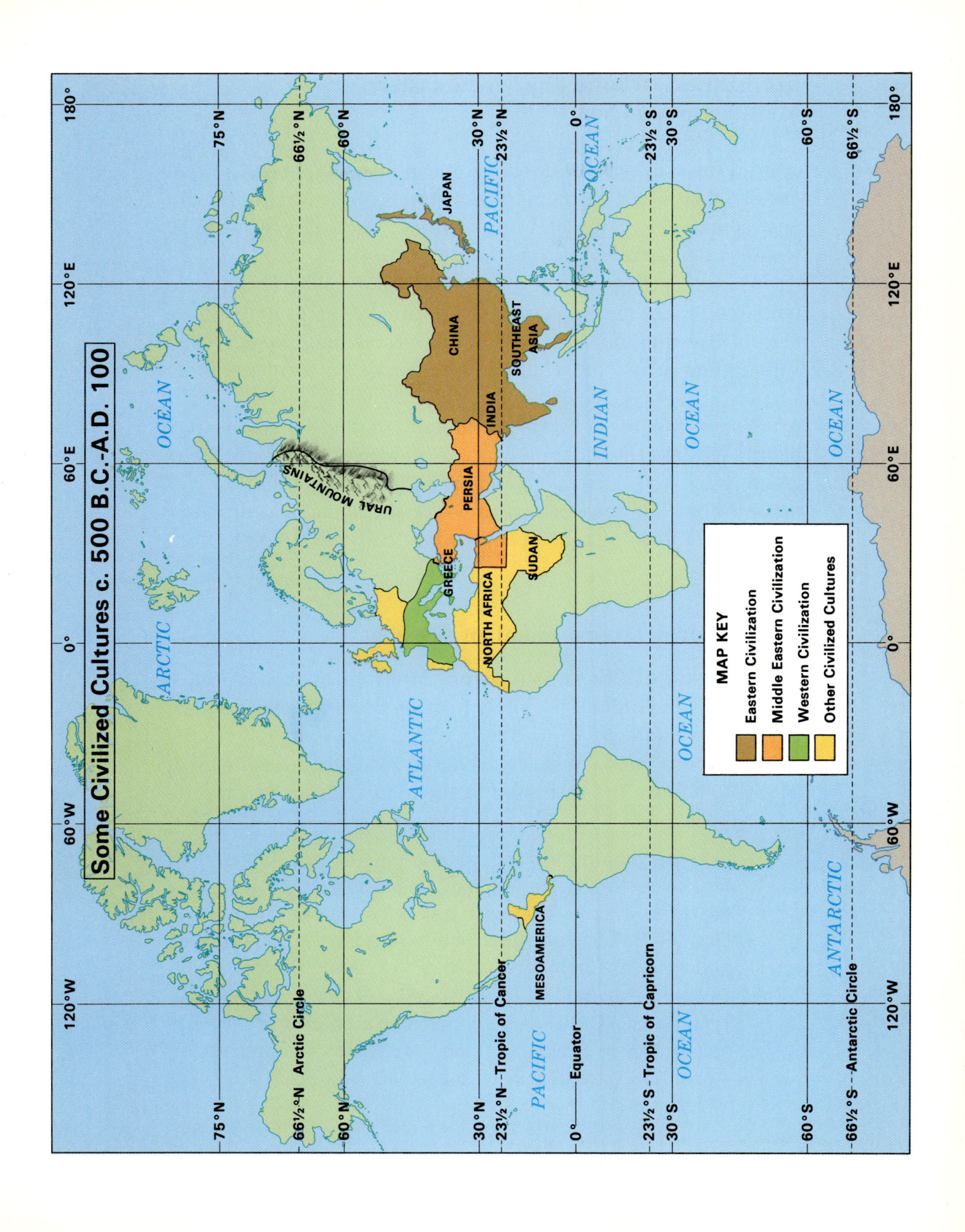

Some Civilized Cultures c. 500 B.C.–A.D. 100

MAP KEY
- Eastern Civilization
- Middle Eastern Civilization
- Western Civilization
- Other Civilized Cultures

Labels on map: JAPAN, CHINA, SOUTHEAST ASIA, INDIA, PERSIA, GREECE, NORTH AFRICA, SUDAN, URAL MOUNTAINS, MESOAMERICA

Oceans: ARCTIC OCEAN, ATLANTIC OCEAN, PACIFIC OCEAN, INDIAN OCEAN, ANTARCTIC OCEAN

Latitude lines: 75°N, 66½°N Arctic Circle, 60°N, 30°N, 23½°N Tropic of Cancer, 0° Equator, 23½°S Tropic of Capricorn, 30°S, 60°S, 66½°S Antarctic Circle

Civilization around the Northeastern Mediterranean Sea

By 1600 B.C. civilization had spread to the other areas around the northeastern Mediterranean Sea. People had settled on the islands and on the northern shores of the Mediterranean Sea. Small city-states grew up. Around each city were rain-watered fields for crops and herds.

Each city-state was separate and ruled itself. The people who lived in these city-states did not think of themselves as one nation. But they *did* think of themselves as *one people.* They called themselves the **Hellenes** [hel′ ēnz]. We call them the Greeks.

The Hellenes, or Greeks, thought of themselves as one people because they shared the same language and beliefs. They worshipped the same gods. They had the same stories and heroes. They had the same culture—a culture that was different from the culture of other peoples. We call the Greek culture **Hellenism.**

The Natural Environment of Greece

The land of Greece is different from other lands we have studied. The mainland is mostly hilly and rocky. It has no great flood plains and no wide river valleys. And it has few large rivers. Greece does, however, have the sea. The sea is its great gateway. It links the mainland to the many islands of Greece.

A ▶ Look at the map "Physical Features of Greece" (page 193).
1. Find this area on a globe or on a map of the Old World.
2. Find Asia Minor, the Aegean Sea, Crete. The first island civilization was on Crete. We call it the *Minoan* civilization.
3. Find the Balkan Peninsula. Find the Peloponnesus. The Peloponnesus is a peninsula south of the Balkan Peninsula.
4. Notice all the islands in the Aegean Sea. A large group of islands such as this group is called an **archipelago.**
5. Notice Greece's neighbor to the west. What is this land called?
6. About how wide from west to east is the Peloponnesus at its widest part?

Physical Features of Greece

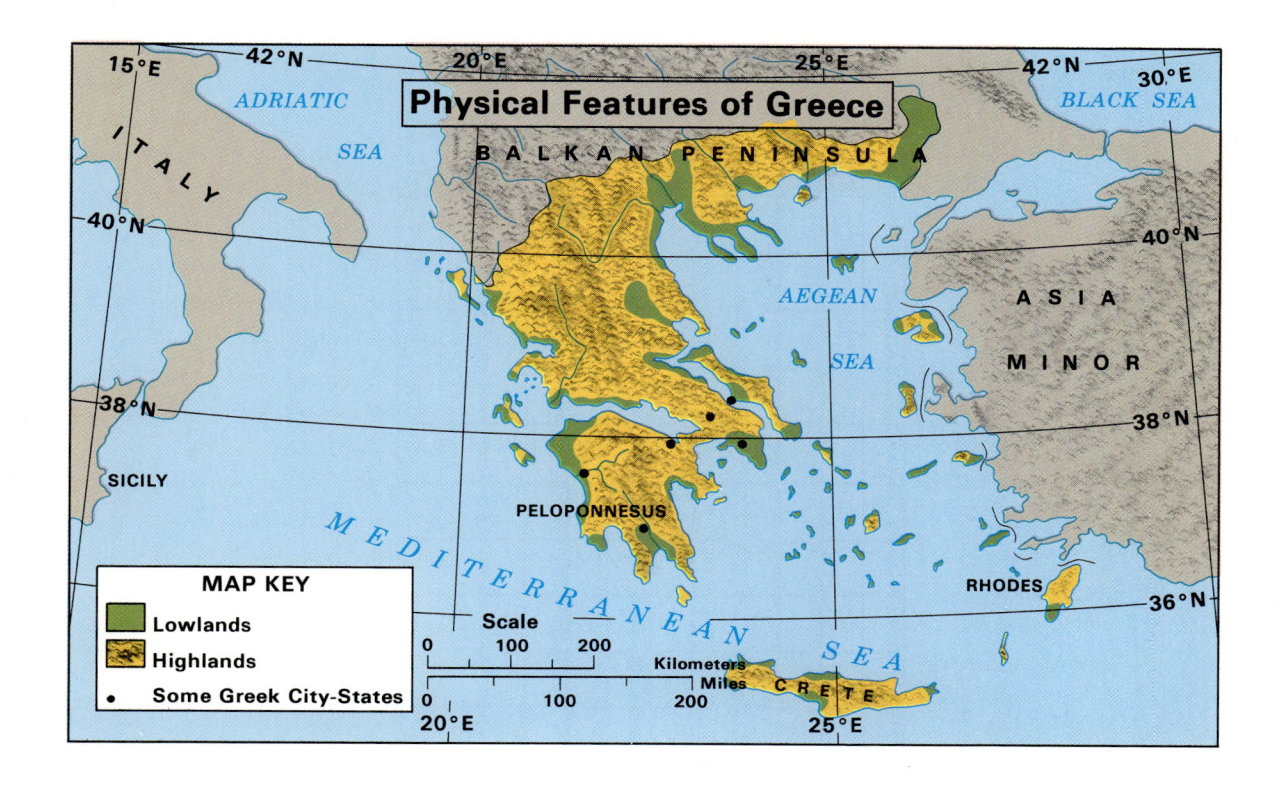

MAP KEY
- Lowlands
- Highlands
- • Some Greek City-States

7. Find the city-state of Athens. It is 38° N and nearly 24° E.
8. Is Greece in the tropics or in the middle latitudes?

B ▶ What do you think was the main form of transportation between city-states?

The climate of Greece is pleasant. It is called a **Mediterranean climate.** It is mild in winter and not too hot in summer. Summers are dry, and winters are wet. We find the same type of climate in California. It is suited for growing oranges, lemons, olives, grapes, cork-oaks, and some grain.

C ● Look at "Climate Graph: Athens" (page 194).
1. Which five months have the most precipitation?
2. What is the lowest average temperature? In what months does Athens have its lowest temperature?
3. What is the highest average temperature? In what months?
4. Does Athens have frosts that kill plants every year? How can you tell?
5. Is the climate good for growing crops? Explain.

THE CLASSICAL CIVILIZATION OF GREECE

Climate Graph: Athens

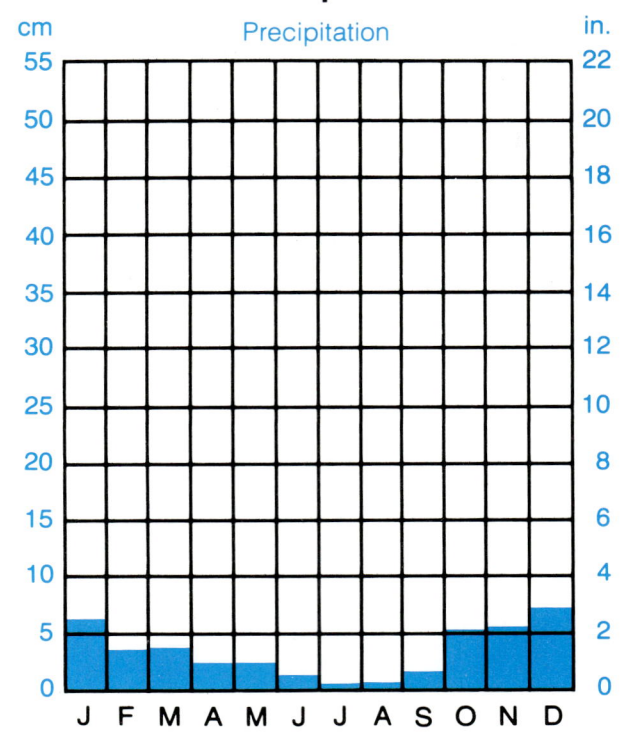

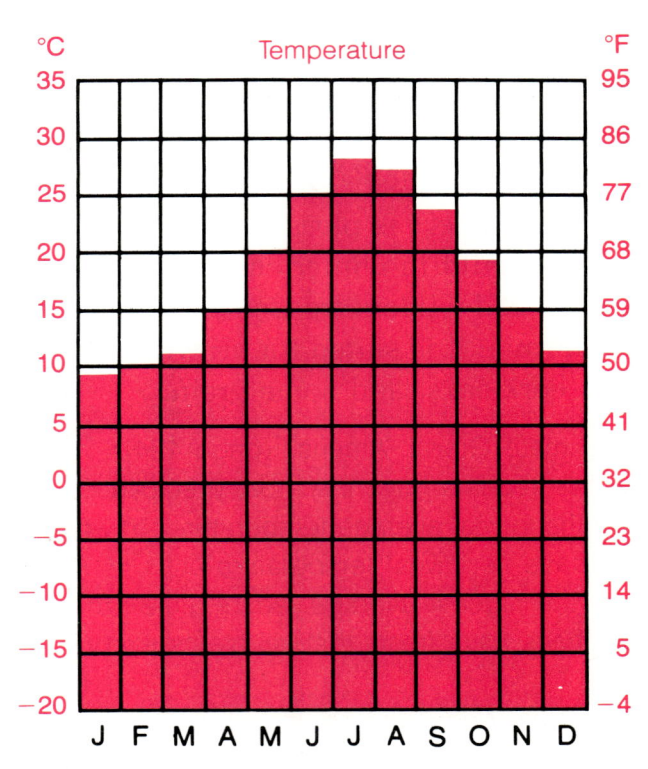

How the Greeks Used Their Environment

Since much of Greece is mountainous, good soil is scarce. The natural plant life is grass and *scrub*. **Scrub** is low evergreen plants with a few trees. Except high in the mountains, the precipitation is too low for dense forest.

The climate and the soil of Greece are good for growing only certain crops. Wheat and barley will grow in the valleys and lowlands. Grapevines and olive trees grow well on the hillsides. The roots of the vines and trees help hold the soil in place during the hard rains of winter. Sheep and goats can feed on the hills. The Greeks thus had three main crops: grain, olives, and grapes. These gave them bread, oil, and wine. The sheep and goats gave milk, cheese, meat, wool, and leather. From the sea, the Greeks had fish.

The sea was important in another way. The Greeks were sailors. The sea became their highway for trade and travel. Merchants, sailors, even pirates went to sea for a living. In the summer months they sailed far and wide. In the winter they stayed ashore because of high winds and heavy rains.

An olive grove on a Greek hillside. The ancient Greeks used olive oil for cooking, making soap, and lighting their lamps.

The Greeks were fascinated by the sea. One of their earliest and greatest poems tells of it. This poem is thought to have been written by Homer. It tells the story of a journey homeward by sea. The hero is Odysseus [ō dis′ ē əs], and the poem is called the *Odyssey* [od′ ə sē]. The adventures of Odysseus in storms and shipwrecks were favorite Greek stories. It took Odysseus ten years to get home. He might have gotten home more quickly by land. But no Greek would go by land when he could sail!

Let us read two descriptions of the sea taken from the *Odyssey*.

The Sea—As Friend

The ship sprang through the dark purple waves of the crashing sea. The ship cut steady and straight through the fish-filled water. The falcon was the fastest of all birds. But not even the falcon could keep up with her.

The brightest of stars arose to announce the dawn. The seaworthy boat approached a harbor. This harbor is dear to the Old Man of the Sea. It is sheltered on two sides by cliffs. The walls of the cliffs give shelter from winds and waves. Ships can be left in the harbor without moorings. They are completely safe. They stay where the sailors leave them. Near the water of the harbor is an olive tree. Near the olive tree is a cool, shadowy cave. Inside the cave the honeybee hives its honey. There, too, young girls weave cloth. And the cloth is deep purple—the same color as the sea. It is wonderful to see. And into this beautiful harbor, they sailed easily. For the sailors knew the waters very well.

As in ancient times, fishing is an important part of the economy of Greece.

The Sea—As Enemy

Suddenly the god of the sea appeared. He gathered the clouds and stirred up the sea. The winds began to blow and blast. In a cover of clouds the land and sea were hidden. Night rushed over the earth.

Out of the whirling waters came a great wave. Odysseus was frightened. The towering wave came crashing down over him. He and his boat were spun around with terrible force. The oar was wrenched out of his hands. The mast of the boat snapped in the middle. Odysseus was thrown far from the boat.

Then the god of the sea raised another great wave. The planks of the boat were scattered—like dry heaps of straw. Odysseus climbed onto one of the planks. He rode it as though he were riding a wild horse.

Two days and two nights passed. Odysseus was tossed by the waves. But on the third day the rosy streaks of dawn broke through the clouds. The winds grew calm. Odysseus was raised high on the top of a wave. He looked straight ahead. There—close by—was land.

We have learned something about the land and sea of Greece. Now we are going to read a Greek myth. From the myth we will begin to learn about Greek ideas.

The Greek Myth of Prometheus

Far away a giant is chained to a mountain. Eagles come every day to attack him. They tear at him with their sharp beaks and claws. Every night his wounds heal, but every morning the eagles return.

The giant's name is Prometheus [prə mē′ thē əs]. He has been chained to the mountain since the early days of time. He is being punished by the gods. Yet people love him. What has he done to be punished?

Long, long ago the gods created everything on the earth. They gave a special gift to each creature. They gave courage to the lion. They gave strength to the ox. They gave speed to the deer. When humankind's turn came, the gods had nothing left to give. They had given all the gifts away. There was nothing left for humans.

Humans became slaves to the other animals. They lived in dark caves, afraid to come out. They were weak and slow and timid. They lived in fear and ignorance. Life seemed hopeless.

Prometheus felt sorry for humans. He did not think such treatment was fair, so he plotted to help them. The gods lived in a great mountain

THE CLASSICAL CIVILIZATION OF GREECE

palace. There they kept the sacred fire. One night Prometheus crept into the mountain palace. Taking a burning log from the fireplace, he rushed out before the gods could see him. He went to the dark caves where humans lived, and he gave them fire.

Fire was the gift from Prometheus to humankind. With this gift humans scared away the wild beasts. They warmed themselves and cooked food. They melted metal for tools and weapons. They made the dark caves shine with light. They became rulers of the world.

Soon the gods saw what had happened. Prometheus had stolen fire from them! That is why they punished him. But that is why people love Prometheus. His gift had set them free.

THE WORLD VIEW OF GREEK NATURALISM

Some Greek Controlling Ideas

The Greeks looked at the people in the great empires of the Middle East. They saw people who were under powerful governments. They saw people who were ruled by soldiers and emperors. To the Greeks, these people seemed little better off than slaves. The Greek citizens shared in the government of their small city-states. Because of this the Greeks felt that they were special. They felt like free people.

The importance of humankind was one of the strongest controlling ideas for the Greeks. This idea guided the way the Greeks acted and the way they thought. The Greeks believed that people could use their minds to help explain the world of nature around them.

The Greeks were always trying to find out things. They were interested in nature. They began the studies that we call *natural sciences.* They were also very interested in *human nature.* The Greeks felt that the human mind was a wonderful thing. They saw that humans could create things like statues, buildings, and poetry. They believed, too, that humans could think of better ways of living and of governing. Thus the Greeks also began the social sciences that we have today.

A★ Today most of our scientific words come from the Greek language. Use a dictionary to find the meanings of the following words: *physics, geography, politics, hydrology, philosophy, biology, economics, thermometer, anthropology, photography.* (Some dictionaries also tell the Greek words used to form these words.)

The Religion of the Greeks

Long before they became scientific, the Greeks had a religion of many gods and goddesses. Their polytheism taught that the gods were selfish and quarrelsome and very much like humans. There were *Zeus,* the chief god, and *Hera,* the wife of Zeus. There was the god of the sun and of health, *Apollo.* The goddess of love was *Aphrodite.* The god of war was *Ares.* There were many more gods and goddesses. We can learn about these and other gods and goddesses by reading Greek myths. You have already read some Greek myths in this book.

A▶ What is a myth?

B★ You might enjoy reading the stories about *Perseus* (and how he cut off the Gorgon's head) and *Pandora and Epimetheus* (and how evils came into the world).

The two greatest poems of the Greeks are the *Iliad* and the *Odyssey.* They are very long poems, known as *epics,* which tell of the mighty deeds of great heroes. The *Iliad* describes the events of the Trojan War and the part played in it by a Greek hero, Achilles. The *Odyssey* describes the adventures of Odysseus.

Apollo, the Greek god of the sun, poetry, music, prophecy, and healing. Shrines to Apollo were built on Mt. Delphi and on the sacred island of Delos.

Athena, the Greek goddess of wisdom and of the arts and the daughter of Zeus. She was also the protector of the home and the guardian of Athens.

Many Greeks loved the myths about the gods. The early Greeks believed that there were many gods in nature. These gods caused the things that humans could not understand. The myths often explained human problems in a special way. The early Greeks were full of questions about their world. Their first answers to these questions were simple ones. They looked at the forces of nature and explained them with myths. What was lightning? It was the spear of the god Zeus. What made an earthquake? The sea god stamping his foot.

Many earlier peoples had asked these same questions and had found answers that were much alike. Some of these peoples had gained much useful knowledge while looking for answers. The Babylonians, for example, had learned about astronomy. The Egyptians had learned how to practice medicine. The Sumerians had worked out a system of mathematics. The Greeks learned much from these peoples. However, they did not stop with what other people had learned. The Greeks went further.

The Greeks never grew tired of asking why things happened and how things happened. The more they asked, the less they liked the old answers. Could they learn more about lightning than the myth about Zeus told them? Could they explain an earthquake without thinking of the sea god? The Greeks thought that men and women could get answers to such questions by using their minds and by observing the universe. People could figure out the "why" and "how." What if there were laws in nature? Perhaps people could understand these laws.

Naturalism and Humanism

In most ancient civilized societies, the learned persons were priests or religious leaders. But in Greece, as in China, learning was not tied to religion. Some of the cleverest Greeks put their minds to work studying nature and studying human beings.

These Greek thinkers were not against religion. But they thought that the first problem for humans is to learn to understand themselves. They saw that polytheism stopped people from thinking about the *natural* causes of things. Indeed, some Greek thinkers were close to monotheism. (Monotheism, you will remember, is the belief in one creator, or one ruler of the universe.)

This Greek world view is called *naturalism.* The word **naturalism** means seeking truth in nature and natural causes. We may also call this world view *humanism.* The word **humanism** means studying human beings to find the meaning and purpose of human life.

How could the Greek thinkers study both nature and human life? First of all, they used observation. They *observed,* or watched, nature. They looked at humans and human societies.

Next, the Greeks *thought.* They tried to think of *explanations.*

Then they tried to find *general rules* that fitted the facts. They called these rules the *laws of nature.* They found rules for physical nature, or the environment. They also found rules for human nature, or the behavior of men and women.

The Greeks had a name for the persons who sought truth through observation and thought. They called such persons *philosophers.* **Philosophy** comes from two Greek words meaning "love of wisdom."

THE CLASSICAL CIVILIZATION OF GREECE

A▶ What do *naturalism* and *humanism* mean?

B▶ What does *philosopher* mean?

C★ Was the philosophers' way of trying to find truth the same as our *natural science*? If not, what differences can you see between philosophy and modern science? How might Greek naturalism and humanism and philosophy lead to modern science?

D● About 300 years ago our early modern scientists called their study "natural philosophy." Can you see why?

E● Read the story "Thales [thā′ lez] of Miletus [mī lē′ təs]" in the box below.

1. How did his study of nature help Thales?
2. What *law of economics* had he also noted?
3. How did he use a law of economics to make a fortune?
4. What things might philosophers think more important than riches?

Thales of Miletus

In the Greek city-state of Miletus, on the coast of southwestern Asia Minor, lived one of the finest Greek philosophers. His name was Thales. Thales lived there from 624–546 B.C. He was one of the first philosophers. He studied mathematics and astronomy and earth science. Thales was poor. People teased him about his poverty. "What is the good of philosophy," they asked, "if it can't make you rich?"

Thales knew by his observations that the weather would bring a huge olive crop the next year. He borrowed money and bought all the olive presses for many miles around. When the big olive crop came, nobody could turn their olives into oil unless Thales would let them use his presses. Thales made them pay high prices to rent his presses. As a result, he made a fortune.

"You see," he said "philosophers *can* be rich, if they want to be rich. However, philosophers think there are *more important things than riches.*"

202 THE GROWTH OF CIVILIZATION

The Discus Thrower — a Roman copy of a Greek sculpture. The discus throw was one of the five events in the pentathlon, a major contest in the Greek Olympics. A flat disk either of stone or metal came to be the standard discus used. A stone disk could weigh as much as 15 pounds. Observe how well the sculptor has captured the qualities of strength and grace of the performing athlete.

Greek Art and Athletics

The Greek world view can also be seen in the statues and painted pottery that have come down to us. Never before had any culture made such *natural* copies of human beings. Greek artists tried to see exactly how human bodies were made.

They were interested in more than just copying nature. They wanted to show the beauty and strength that humans could have. So their statues and painted pottery nearly always show especially fine human bodies and faces. The artists seem to be saying, "Look how great human beings can be!"

For the same reason, the Greeks loved *athletics*. They trained young people to build their muscles. They trained them to be healthy and strong. Men and boys competed in running, jumping, wrestling, and boxing. They threw the *discus* (a metal or stone disc) and the *javelin* (a long spear). Sometimes the Greeks admired an athlete more than they did a politician.

Every four years the best athletes from all the city-states (such as Athens and Sparta) met in the city of *Olympia* in the Peloponnesus. There they competed for prizes. These competitions were known as the *Olympic Games*.

A● Do we have Olympic Games today? Where did the idea come from? How did the Greek Olympics show one Greek controlling idea about human beings?

THE CLASSICAL CIVILIZATION OF GREECE

The Beginning of Political Science

The Greeks tried to have fine minds as well as fine bodies. They tried to think of answers to questions about society and government. They asked many questions that other civilized societies had not asked.

A● Look at the box "Some Questions the Greeks Tried To Answer" below.
1. Which of these questions are "new" in the sense that earlier civilized societies had not tried to answer them?
2. How would Confucius have answered the questions "Which kinds of governments are good? Which kinds are bad?"

The Greeks saw that a society and its government were things that *humans could control.* These things were made by humans. Therefore humans can change these things. Humans can make society and government better *if they know enough.* The Greeks started **political science,** or the study of government.

The word *politics* comes from the Greek word for city-state: *polis.* This tells us something. In the city-states the citizens took part in governing. The great empires did not have political science. The rulers of empires would not let people talk about changing their government.

B● Look again at the questions in the box below. Why would the rulers of empires not allow people to discuss such questions?

Some Questions the Greeks Tried To Answer

1. What is justice, or fairness?
2. Can there be different kinds of governments? Can people choose the kind of government they want?
3. Which kinds of governments are good? Which kinds are bad?
4. What is freedom?
5. Should people love their city-state and be loyal to it?
6. How should young people be educated? What should they learn in order to be free people?

The Greeks thought that people ruled by emperors were slaves. Living in a Greek city-state, or *polis,* was different. The *polis* was made by the people, and some of the people shared in the government. Equally important, the people loved their *polis.* They would defend their *polis.* Although the great empires had large armies, many of the soldiers were forced to join. The army of the *polis* was made up of free men. Every Greek farmer or craftsman was ready to be a soldier or sailor when the *polis* needed him.

Freedom and loyalty to the city-state went together. People could not have freedom without loyalty. That was one of the controlling ideas of Greece.

However, not all people who lived in a *polis* were free. Most city-states had slaves as well as citizens. As we have seen in chapter 5, slavery and civilization went together for thousands of years. Yet the Greeks did not want slaves to be soldiers. And some of the Greek philosophers said that only foreigners (people who were not Greeks) should be slaves.

C ▶ What made the Greeks proud of their *polis*?

D ● What do you think of the idea that in a society where people are free, the people must also be loyal to the society? Do Americans today have the same idea? Explain.

E ● Why would free persons usually be better soldiers than slaves would be?

Different Forms of Government

The philosophers studied governments. They saw that there were different forms of government. Sometimes one person ruled. This is a **monarchy** (from *monos,* meaning "one"). Sometimes a small number of people ruled. That can be either an **aristocracy** or an **oligarchy** (from *aristos,* meaning "best," and *oligos,* meaning "few"). Sometimes the *majority* of the men ruled by voting. That is **democracy** (from *demos,* meaning "ordinary people"). **Majority** means *more* than half or the greater number. The opposite is *minority.* **Minority** means *less* than half or the smaller number.

THE CLASSICAL CIVILIZATION OF GREECE

The philosophers knew that each form of government might be bad or good. The bad governments were selfish. They cared nothing for the people. They did not obey the laws. Good governments worked for the good of the whole *polis*. They ruled according to the laws.

A▶ What is the meaning of majority and of minority?
B● Look at the box "Good and Bad Governments" (page 207).
   1. Why should governments obey the laws?
   2. Why should governments rule for the good of the whole society?
   3. How can the majority be unfair to minorities in democracies?
C● The philosophers wanted people to understand the differences between governments. How might understanding these things help people to have better governments?
D★ Are any of the Greek ideas about governments helpful to us today? Explain.

The Different Parts of Government

The governments of Greek city-states were different in many ways from governments today. Yet, in this chapter, we will see how American governments owe much to the political science of the Greeks.

Greek political science taught that governments have different jobs to manage. One official of the government could not do all the things that a government had to do.

Greek philosophers taught that good government needs *specialization*. Government should be set up in such a way that different people would do special jobs. The way in which a government is organized is set forth in its *constitution*. A **constitution** is the basic set of laws of the whole government.

How could good governments be kept? Most philosophers thought that education was important. The people of the *polis* should learn about their government and its constitution. In this way they would learn to obey the laws. They would know how to keep their constitution.

A● Do you think that free people need to learn about their government and constitution? Explain.

Good and Bad Governments

Ruling Persons	Good Government	Bad Government
One person: *monarchy*	A monarch rules according to law and for the good of all.	A *tyrant* rules selfishly and by force.
A few persons: *aristocracy* or *oligarchy*	*Aristocracy:* The best persons rule for the good of all.	*Oligarchy:* A few persons oppress the rest of the people.
All men can vote: *democracy*	Rule under law: respect for all groups.	The majority oppresses minorities and may be led by bad politicians.

The Greek Wars with the Persian Empire

In the fifth century B.C. the Greeks had to fight for their freedom. The Persian emperors, *Darius* and *Xerxes,* tried to conquer the Greek city-states. Just before the wars between Greece and Persia, the Persian Empire had conquered all of Asia Minor, including the Greek cities there. They had also conquered the area of Europe called Thrace.

A● Look at the map of the Persian Empire on page 140. Compare the size of the empire with the area of the Greek city-states. Remember, the city-states were not united. Were the Greeks likely to win a war against the Persian army and navy? Why or why not?

THE CLASSICAL CIVILIZATION OF GREECE

B● Look at the map "Some Greek City-States, Fifth Century B.C." (page 209). Use the inset map as well as the large map.
1. The most important city-states were Athens, Sparta, Corinth, and Thebes. Find each of them.
2. Macedon was a kingdom north of the Greek city-states. It later became very powerful. Find Macedon.
3. If the Persians marched west through Thrace and south through Macedon to Greece, which important city-states would be in danger first?
4. The four big battles between the Greeks and the Persians were at Marathon (490 B.C.), Thermopylae [thər mop′ ə lē] (480 B.C.), Salamis (480 B.C.), and Plataea (479 B.C.). Find these places.

About 500 B.C., the two strongest city-states were Athens and Sparta. Athens had a strong navy. It was a sea power. Sparta, in the Peloponnesus, was a land power.

In 499 B.C., the Greek city-states in Asia Minor revolted. The people did not want to be ruled by Persia. Athens sent ships and soldiers to help the Greek city-states against the Persians. Darius the Great, king of Persia, defeated the Athenians.

In 490 B.C., Darius set out to punish Athens. A big Persian army sailed across the Aegean Sea and landed in Greece at Marathon, 43 kilometers (26 miles) northeast of Athens. Athens was in great danger. The Persian army had twice as many soldiers as the Athenian army. Yet the Athenians were able to defeat the Persians at the Battle of Marathon. The Persian troops were driven back to their ships.

C★ Find out why a long foot-race today is called a "marathon."

The Athenians guessed that the Persian emperor would try again to conquer them. Athens started to build a stronger navy.

D● Look at the picture of an Athenian warship, or *trireme* (page 210). The main power of a trireme was from its rowers. There were probably three rowers to each oar. Notice the sharp *ram* at the prow, or front, of the ship. How do you think the ram was used in a sea battle?

'08   THE GROWTH OF CIVILIZATION

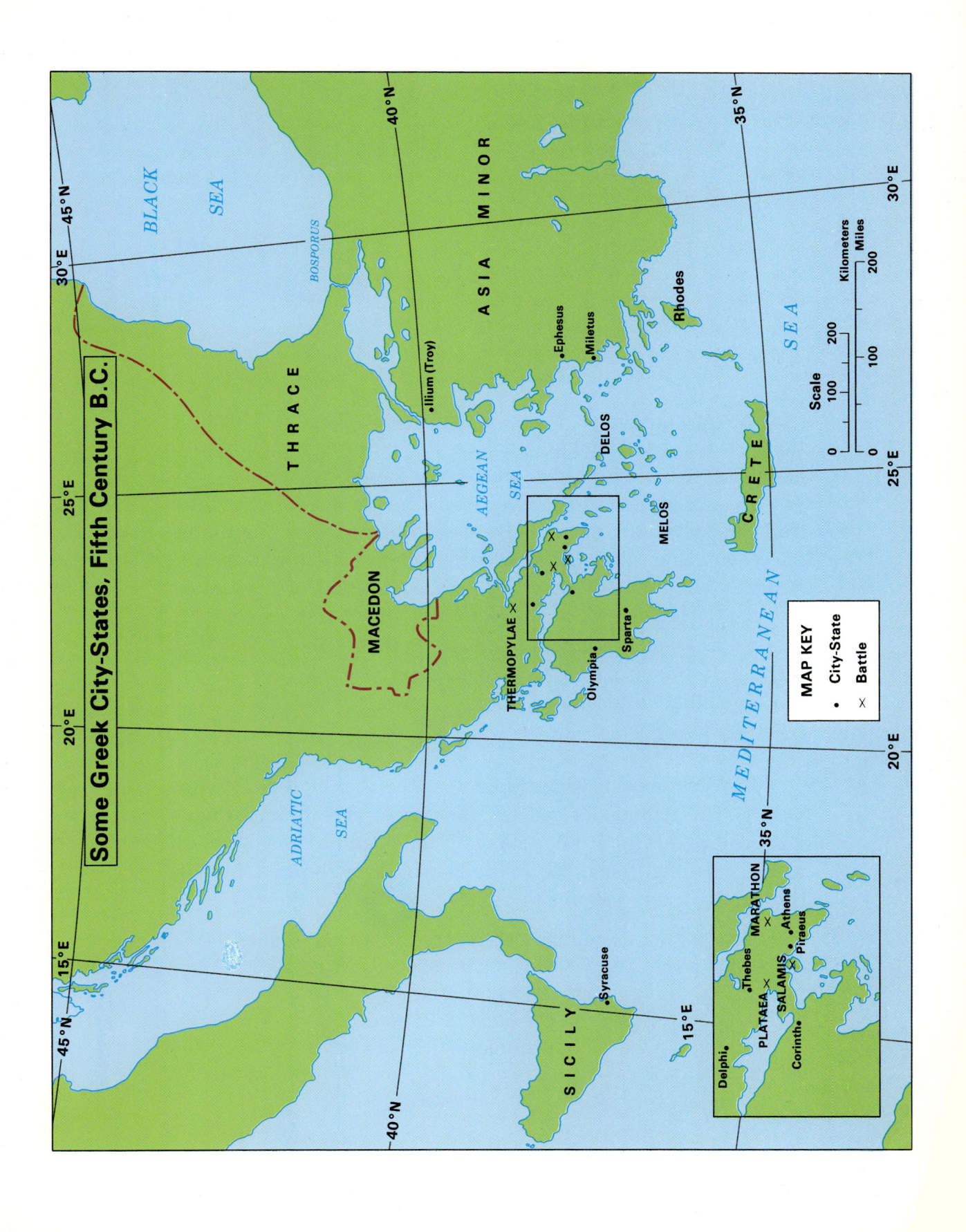

Some Greek City-States, Fifth Century B.C.

- BLACK SEA
- BOSPORUS
- THRACE
- MACEDON
- ASIA MINOR
- Ilium (Troy)
- Ephesus
- Miletus
- Rhodes
- AEGEAN SEA
- DELOS
- MELOS
- CRETE
- MEDITERRANEAN SEA
- THERMOPYLAE ×
- Olympia
- Sparta
- ADRIATIC SEA
- SICILY
- Syracuse
- Delphi
- Thebes
- PLATAEA ×
- MARATHON ×
- Athens
- SALAMIS ×
- Piraeus
- Corinth

MAP KEY
- • City-State
- × Battle

Scale: 0–200 Miles / 0–200 Kilometers

An Athenian warship, or *trireme*

In 480 B.C., Xerxes, Darius's son, attacked Greece. This time the Persians struck by land and sea. A huge army marched west and south from Thrace. A great navy sailed to Athens.

Twenty of the largest city-states joined to fight the Persians. The Greeks tried to stop the Persians at the pass of Thermopylae. Fewer than 4,000 Greeks were sent to hold the pass. The Persians were able to take the pass, and 3,000 of the Greeks retreated. However, part of the army, the Spartans and the Thespians, said they would die rather than retreat. And they did die. In the end, only two Spartans came back alive. One of the two killed himself for shame.

E▶ Find Thermopylae on the map on page 209.

The Persians next marched to Athens. But the city was empty. The Athenians had left their city. The Athenian navy was waiting for the Persian navy off the island of *Salamis* close to the port of Athens. While the Persian army burned Athens, the Persian navy set out to attack the Athenian fleet.

F● Look at the picture map "The Battle of Salamis" (page 211).
1. Find the port of Athens, named Piraeus [pī rē′ əs].
2. Find the town and island of Salamis.
3. Notice how narrow the *strait* of Salamis is.
4. How did the Athenians trap the Persian navy?
5. What sailors knew the strait of Salamis? How would this knowledge help them in the battle?

THE GROWTH OF CIVILIZATION

Many Persian ships were destroyed in the battle of Salamis. Most of the Persian army went back to Thrace. The rest of the Persian army was defeated the next year at *Plataea,* west of Athens. The Greeks in this battle were from Sparta and other city-states of the Peloponnesus. The Persian wars were over.

Athenian Democracy

By the fifth century Athens had a democratic government. Athens was the first civilized democracy that we know much about.

Democracy means "rule of the ordinary people." However, Athenian democracy differed from America's democratic republic in a number of ways. In the first place the city-state was small. It had only about 1,800 square kilometers (700 square miles.) The population of Athens was about 350,000. Of these people many were foreigners and about 150,000 were slaves.

A★ How big is the United States? How many people live in the United States?

THE BATTLE OF SALAMIS

An outdoor marketplace in Athens today. It is small by comparison with the agora in ancient Greece.

Secondly, only adult male citizens could share in the government. They numbered about 40,000.

Thirdly, Athenian voters did *not* elect *representatives.* Instead, the male citizens would go to a big meeting, or Assembly. In the Assembly each citizen voted for or against any law that was proposed. This is direct democracy.

- B★ Explain the difference between *direct democracy* and *representative democracy.* Is there any direct democracy in the United States?
- C● The Greeks thought that only small societies (city-states) could have freedom. They thought that in large societies ordinary people could have no share in government. Why did they think so?

Even in Athens all the citizens could not meet every day. So 500 citizens were chosen each year to carry on the government. This *Council of 500* was chosen *by lot.* **Lot** means picking names at random, as in a *lottery.* Nearly all the officials of Athens were chosen by lot every year.

- D● What are the good things about choosing government officials by lot, or chance? What might be some bad things about this method?

There were ten jobs that were not left to chance. These ten jobs were those of military leaders. Every year ten experienced *generals* were elected by the Assembly. One of them was chosen *commander in chief.*

- E● Why were the generals *not* chosen by lot?

12   THE GROWTH OF CIVILIZATION

The Athenian law courts were different from ours. Whenever someone had to be tried, a jury was chosen by lot from the Assembly. Athenian juries were large. They were made up of 301 or 501 men. Sometimes a jury had 1,001 men. The jury heard the evidence. Then it voted *guilty* or *not guilty*. If the majority of the jury found a person guilty, the jury then voted the punishment. There were no judges.

F★ How big are juries in the United States? Do American juries use a *majority* vote to decide if a person is guilty? What role do *judges* play in the United States?

G★ Why were there differences in the size of juries in Athens?

Athenian democracy was different from American democracy. Yet our representative democracy owes much to Athens. Athens showed that a civilized society could also be a free society.

H● Look at the charts "The Government of Athens" and "The Government of the United States" (page 214).
1. Explain how the laws are made in the two governments.
2. Which judicial system might be fairer? Why?
3. Who is the commander in chief of the United States? How is that person chosen? How was the commander in chief of Athens chosen?

I★ What does *executive* mean? Compare the executive in Athens with the executive in the national government of the United States.

Athens in the Age of Pericles

After the Persian wars, the navy of Athens ruled the eastern Mediterranean. Although the city of Athens had been burned by the Persians, the spirit of the people of Athens was high. They began to rebuild their city.

About twenty years after the victory over the Persian Empire, the people of Athens elected Pericles as commander in chief. He was the leader of Athens from 461 B.C. until his death in 429 B.C. Under Pericles, Athens reached its highest power. The years that Pericles was Athens' leader is known as the *Age of Pericles*.

THE CLASSICAL CIVILIZATION OF GREECE

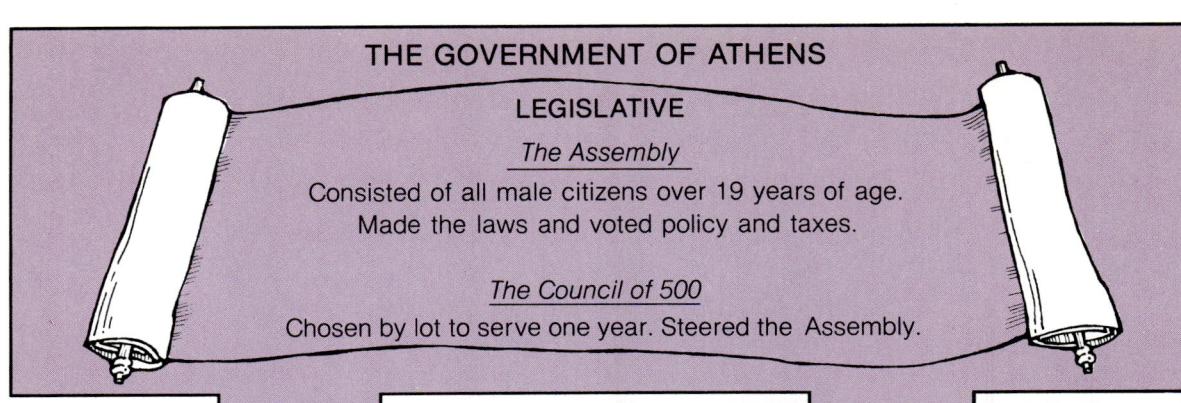

THE GOVERNMENT OF ATHENS

LEGISLATIVE

The Assembly
Consisted of all male citizens over 19 years of age. Made the laws and voted policy and taxes.

The Council of 500
Chosen by lot to serve one year. Steered the Assembly.

EXECUTIVE

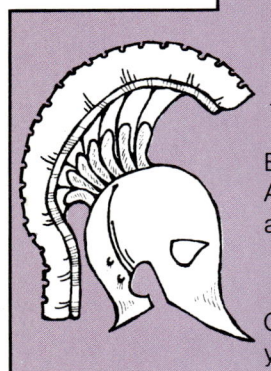

The Commander in Chief and Nine Generals
Elected annually by the Assembly. Directed policy and the armed forces.

Other Officials
Chosen by lot to serve one year.

JUDICIAL

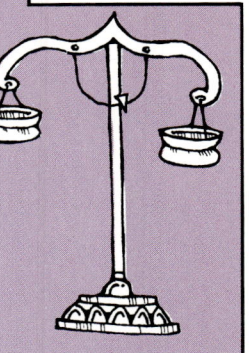

Juries
Consisted of members of the Assembly, who were chosen by lot. Tried all law cases.

THE GOVERNMENT OF THE UNITED STATES

THE CONSTITUTION

EXECUTIVE
Carries out laws and commands the armed forces.

The President
Elected by the people every four years. Appoints other officials.

LEGISLATIVE
Makes laws, votes taxes, declares war.

The Congress
Elected by the people.

Senate
Two senators from each state, elected for six years.

House of Representatives
Each member is from a district, elected for two years.

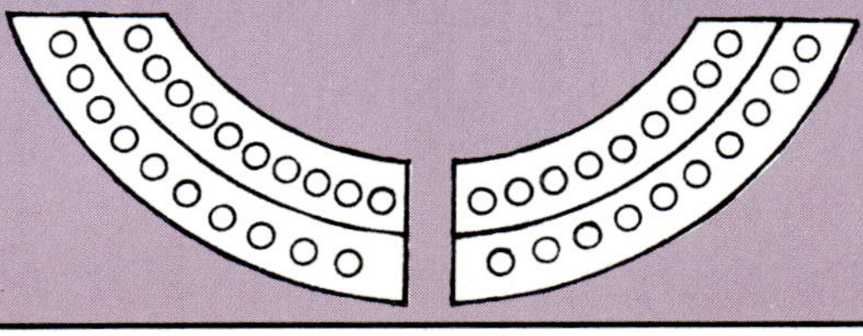

JUDICIAL
Says what laws mean and whether a law has been broken.

The Supreme Court and Other Federal Courts
Appointed by the president with agreement of the Senate.

Pericles — statesman, orator, and military commander — governed Athens from 461 to 429 B.C. Under his leadership, Athens reached the height of its culture, wealth, and power, and the period is known as "the Age of Pericles." Literature and the arts flourished. Pericles' building program included the construction of magnificent temples on top of the Acropolis. He also introduced many domestic reforms and civic improvements.

During the Age of Pericles the Athenians became even more proud of their *polis*. Here is part of a speech that Pericles once made. It was a funeral speech for Athenian soldiers. Notice that Pericles did not talk about the dead soldiers. Instead, he talked about what they had died for. He talked about Athens.

I will not talk about the battles we have won. I will not talk about how our ancestors became great. Instead I will talk about our spirit and our way of life. I will talk about those things that have made us great.

Our government does not copy those of our neighbors. Instead, ours is a model for them. Ours is a democracy. The power is in the hands of the people. It is not in the hands of a small group. Everyone is equal before the law. We do not care what class a man belongs to. We care only about his ability. No one is kept from taking part in government because he is poor.

Our political life is free and open. So is our day-to-day life. We do not care if our neighbors enjoy themselves in their own way. We are free and tolerant. But in public affairs we obey the laws. We especially obey the ones that protect the lowly.

THE CLASSICAL CIVILIZATION OF GREECE

Here is another point. When our work is done, we enjoy our free time. There are ceremonies and contests all year. In our homes there is beauty and taste. Our city brings us good things from all over the world.

And our city is open to the whole world. We never keep people out for fear they will spy on us. We have no secrets. We do not rely on trickery. We rely on our own hearts and hands. We are brave in facing danger. Our love of beauty does not lead to weakness. Our love of mind does not make us soft.

Everyone here is interested in the *polis*. We do not say those who are not interested in politics are minding their own business. We say they have no business here at all!

Looking at everything, I say Athens is a school for the whole of Greece. Future ages will wonder at us. The present age wonders at us now. Everywhere we have left memorials of our greatness. For this great city of ours, these men fought and died. Each of us who still lives should gladly work for our great city.

I could tell you what we gain by defeating our enemies. Instead, I would rather have you gaze on Athens' greatness every day. Then you would fall in love with our city. You would realize Athens' greatness.

Make up your minds to this. Our happiness depends on our freedom. And our freedom depends on our courage. Because of that, I will not mourn the dead. In their lives, happiness and death went hand in hand.

A● Why did Pericles want Athenians to "fall in love" with their city?
B● What does this speech tell us about how Athenians felt about their *polis* and other cities?
C● Do you think Athens was "a school for the whole of Greece"? Do you think it has been a school for the whole world? Explain.

For more than 30 years Pericles was the political leader of Athens. At great cost, Pericles made the city beautiful. Marble temples were raised on the Acropolis, the hill in the middle of the city. Sculptors made beautiful statues. Men wrote histories that are still read today and plays that are still read and performed. To this day we use Greek words to describe the two main kinds of plays. **Tragedies** are serious plays that help us to understand human problems. **Comedies** are plays that poke fun at human foolishness.

216 THE GROWTH OF CIVILIZATION

From their plays, the Athenians learned a lot about themselves. They could see what brave people and foolish people were like. They could see how people, great and weak, handled problems. The plays helped the Athenians to understand their own problems better. The plays also gave the people a chance to enjoy themselves.

D▶ How could the people of Athens learn from plays?

E● Why would a democracy encourage plays in theaters? (Who would watch the plays? Does a democracy usually encourage *free speech*?)

F● Athenian comedies poked fun at political leaders and at philosophers. Would a society ruled by monarchs or by priests allow such things? Why or why not?

G★ Look at the pictures of Athenian buildings and sculpture below and on page 218. These will help you to understand what the art of classical civilization was like.

The Porch of the Maidens on the Erechtheum [i rek′thē əm], a temple built on the Acropolis. The temple was named after Erechtheus, a legendary king.

217

(above) Ruins of the Parthenon. Begun in 447 B.C. and completed in 432 B.C., this magnificent temple was dedicated to the goddess Athena. *(below)* The Acropolis, a hilltop overlooking Athens, was adorned in Pericles' time by such architectural masterpieces as the Parthenon and the Erechtheum.

1. The Parthenon was the temple to Athena, the goddess who protected the city. People think that the temple's beauty lies in its *simplicity* and its *proportions*. What do people mean when they say this?
2. Why would this style of architecture suit the Mediterranean climate?
3. Have you seen American or later European buildings that copy the style of the Parthenon? Where?
4. Do the sculptures help you to understand Greek *humanism*? Explain.

The Rise and Fall of the Athenian Empire

An *empire* is the rule of one government over a number of different societies. In the period of ancient civilization there were many empires. They were ruled by monarchs and nobles. In the fifth century B.C., under Pericles, Athens was able to gain an empire. But the Athenian empire was not ruled by a monarch.

The Greeks were able to defeat the Persians because the Greek city-states were united. Before the Persian wars, some of the city-states had joined leagues. The Greek successes in the war with Persia showed all the city-states how much more strength they had when they were united. After the war they did not forget this.

Many of the city-states formed a league. These city-states made the island of Delos [dē′ los] their headquarters. They called themselves the *Delian* [dē′ lē ən] *League*. Each *polis* agreed to give ships or money to the league. These gifts added up to a large fleet. Who was going to command the fleet? Athens had given more ships than any other *polis*. Athens had the most powerful navy. So Athens was chosen to command the fleet.

By 465 B.C. Athens controlled the Delian League completely. Other city-states had to ask Athens' permission to sail or trade. The city-states paid money to keep the league running. The Athenians used much of this money to rebuild their city. The Athenians were convinced that no other *polis* was as good as theirs. They stopped treating the other city-states as equals.

Athens allowed most of the city-states to keep their own assemblies, juries, and laws. However, the city-states also had to obey laws made by the Athenians. The league had turned into an empire.

The members of the league became angry. They loved their freedom as much as the Athenians did. They resented the Athenians' wealth and power. Before long, they rebelled against the Athenians.

An important *polis* that had never joined the Delian League was Sparta. Sparta was an aristocratic military *polis*. Many of the league members turned to Sparta for help. The Spartans had seen Athens' wealth and power growing. They had not wanted to interfere, however. Sparta had a treaty with Athens. A war with Athens would be long and costly. Besides, the Spartans were land fighters. They had no interest in ruling the sea.

Athens attacked one of Sparta's allies. Sparta took action. The Spartans demanded that Athens break up the league. Athens refused. Sparta declared war. The war lasted almost 30 years. It is called the Peloponnesian [pel′ ə pə nē′ zhən] War because the leading states that fought Athens were in the Peloponnesus.

A▶ Look at the map "The Athenian Empire, c. 450 B.C." (page 221).
1. Had Athens taken over parts of the Persian Empire? Which parts?
2. Was this a sea or land empire?
3. Find the Bosporus. How did Athenian control of the Bosporus enable Athens to trade with countries on the Black Sea?
4. Name two city-states that were *not* in the Athenian Empire.
5. Was the peninsula of the Peloponnesus in the Athenian Empire?

B● What might the Greeks in city-states ruled by Athens feel about that rule? What might Greeks in Sparta, Corinth, and other city-states *not* in the empire feel?

Pericles died soon after the Peloponnesian War started. The Athenian leaders who came after Pericles were often reckless men. The Assembly listened to them. Some foolish decisions were made.

After almost 30 years of war, Athens was worn out. Its best men had been killed in fighting. Its money had been used up. Many of Athens' allies had left her. Finally, in 404 B.C., Athens was forced to surrender. The Spartans broke up the empire. They set up a rule of 30 men in Athens. About a year later, the Athenian people overthrew these men, called the Thirty Tyrants. Democracy was in power in Athens again, but the great days of the city were over.

C▶ About how long did the great power and empire of Athens last?

Athenian Empire c. 450 B.C.

MAP KEY
Athenian Empire and boundaries

Socrates: A Great Philosopher

Athens had lost its empire. The Athenians did not like to be reminded of the mistakes they had made. New leaders tried to flatter them. More and more, the city was governed by poor and

THE CLASSICAL CIVILIZATION OF GREECE

uneducated people. These people did not like to be criticized or even to be questioned. They got rid of a great man who dared to criticize.

This man was the philosopher Socrates [sok′ rə tēz]. Socrates thought and talked about what makes human life worth living. He had given up all private business to search for truth. "What is justice?" he asked. "What is beauty? What is friendship?" He listened to the answers given by Athenians. When he thought them wrong, he tried to lead people toward the truth by argument. Socrates believed deeply that an unseen godlike power can help us become good men and women. He said that the truly wise human being is a good human being.

Socrates did not have a school or regular students. He simply went about Athens talking to people. They knew he was brave, but also the Athenians found Socrates amusing. Funny descriptions of Socrates were included in Greek comedies. Yet Socrates made Athenians think about their faults as people and about their mistakes in public affairs. Many Athenians did not enjoy being reminded of such things. They decided that Socrates was dangerous. They accused him of being unfaithful to the gods and of teaching young men false things. Socrates was put on trial.

Before the Athenian jury, Socrates did not beg for his life. Instead he spoke about truth. The jury found Socrates guilty and voted for the death penalty. Socrates was ordered to drink a poison called hemlock. Thanking the jury, Socrates said that they had given him a fine chance to learn what death was. Perhaps they were doing him a favor.

A month later, surrounded by his friends and family, Socrates calmly drank the hemlock. He died believing that he was right and that it was better to die than to live falsely.

A ▶ Do you think the Athenians were wrong in condemning Socrates for his beliefs?

B ● In a democracy, do we expect people to be killed for thinking differently from the majority? Was Athens a democracy?

C ★ Do any governments today punish people for their ideas? What kind of governments are they? Give some examples.

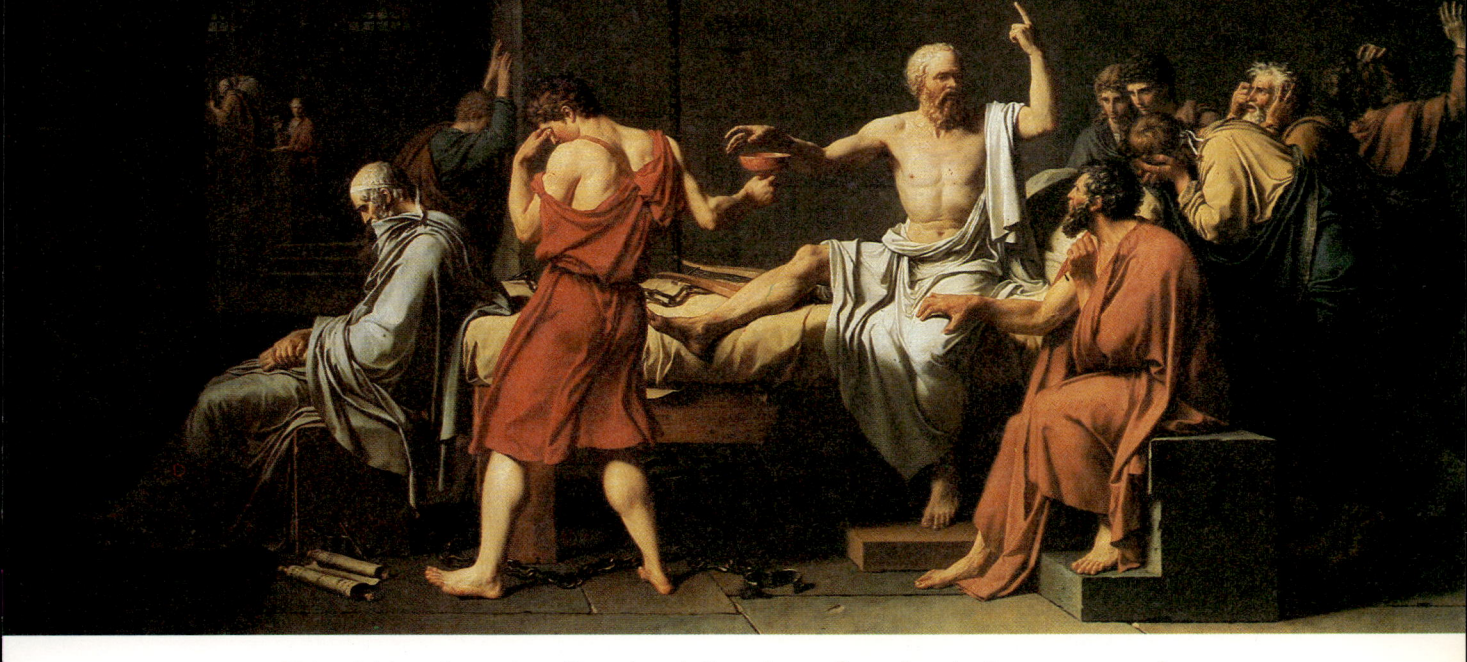

This eighteenth-century French painting shows Socrates, in the company of friends, about to take the cup of hemlock.

The End of the Classical Age in Athens

Although the Athenians put an end to Socrates, they could not kill his ideas. One of Socrates' students was Plato, who became a great poet as well as a great philosopher. Plato wrote down many of the conversations of Socrates. It is Plato who tells us what Socrates said at his trial and just before he died.

Plato taught about the human soul. Also he tried to describe what the best state would be like. He said that the real and lasting world is a world of ideas—not just the world we see around us. Among his many pupils was Aristotle, who later became Alexander's tutor.

Aristotle was the greatest of Greek scientists. His scientific studies included what we call physics, biology, zoology, and other branches of scientific knowledge. Also he wrote books about ethics and about politics that still are studied in many countries. So it is that, through Plato and Aristotle, the civilization of Athens influences the world even today.

Pericles had been right in saying, "Future ages will wonder at us." In Greece today one can still see buildings and statues that remind us of the great age of Athens. We still read the works of Athenian writers and thinkers. We still continue the great Athenian experiment: the idea of democracy. We try to avoid the mistakes that Athens made. We have learned from Athens' daring experiment.

A★ Find out more about Plato and Aristotle.
B★ The oracle at Delphi said that Socrates was the wisest man in Greece. How did Socrates explain his wisdom?

Alexander the Great and Hellenistic Culture

After the Peloponnesian War, the Greek city-states lost their power and their glory. Yet their culture and ideas spread far and wide. How did this come about?

It began in 338 B.C., when Philip II, king of Macedon [məs' ə don], conquered the mainland of Greece. From that time on, the Greek city-states were ruled by foreign powers.

In 336 B.C., a new king came to the throne of Macedon. He was a brilliant young man named Alexander. As a boy he had the philosopher Aristotle as his teacher. So Alexander learned to love Greek culture.

Alexander meant to conquer the world. In 334 B.C. he led an army against Persia. There were many Greeks in his army. In battle after battle Alexander's army quickly swept its enemies aside. Alexander was unbeatable.

There is a myth that explained to the Greeks why Alexander was able to make so many conquests. Here is the story.

The Gordian Knot

The gods had told the people of Phrygia [frij' ē ə] that the next man who entered the city in a wagon would be their new king. A little later, a poor wagon-driver named Gordius entered the city with his wagon. He was immediately accepted as king by all the people.

Gordius was so happy to become king that he wanted to offer his wagon to the gods. He did so by tying the wagon to the temple. He used a very strong and difficult knot. It was called the Gordian knot.

Many years later, people said that whoever could untie the Gordian knot would become lord of all Asia. Over the years, many hopeful men tried to untie the knot, but no one was able to do so.

Then Alexander stopped in Phrygia with his army. Since he wanted to conquer all of Asia, he thought he could untie the knot. He tried very hard. He tried many times. But even he could not untie the Gordian knot. Alexander became angry. He felt he had to succeed so he could show the world that he could really conquer Asia. Finally, after a few more unsuccessful attempts, he took out his sword and cut the knot with it.

A▶ Later, Alexander did conquer all of Asia. People thought it was because he had "untied" the Gordian knot. Do you think that was the reason? Why or why not?

Alexander the Great, king of Macedon, in battle. One of the world's greatest generals, he conquered Greece, the Persian Empire, and Egypt. His rule extended from the Danube River in the Balkans to the Indus River in India.

Alexander conquered the Persian Empire and Egypt. He marched over the Himalayas and conquered a kingdom in northern India. From India, Alexander and his men went back to Persia.

In 323 B.C., Alexander died suddenly at Babylon. He had lived only 33 years. He had been king for just 13 years. No wonder he is known to history as Alexander the Great.

One result of Alexander's conquests was the spread of Greek ideas throughout the Middle East. Another result was that Eastern ideas were brought into Europe. The mixture of Greek and Eastern cultures produced a culture that is called **Hellenistic.** Some of the ideas of that culture became a part of our Western culture.

B● In the third century B.C. the Hebrew scriptures were translated into Greek. What does this tell us about *culture* contact and exchange of ideas in this period?

C▶ Look at the map "Conquests of Alexander the Great" (page 227).
1. Trace the route of Alexander's army from Sardis to Alexandria. By 332 B.C. all the lands around the eastern Mediterranean were conquered.
2. Follow the route from Memphis to Ecbatana. By 330 B.C. Alexander had defeated the Persian army.
3. Follow the route from Ecbatana to Sogdiana. What difficult physical features had the army to cope with?
4. Never losing a battle, Alexander marched east and south down the Indus Valley. Find Taxila and Patala.
5. In 326 B.C., the army would go no farther. Alexander turned back to Persepolis. Follow his route. Part of his army went back to Persia in ships. What would their route be?
6. In 323 B.C. Alexander died at Babylon. Trace his route to Babylon.
7. Find the city founded by Alexander in Egypt. The city bears his name.

In the next chapter we will study the people who conquered the whole Mediterranean area. These were the Romans. The Romans took over the western parts of Alexander's empire, as well as southern and western Europe and northern Africa.

THE GROWTH OF CIVILIZATION

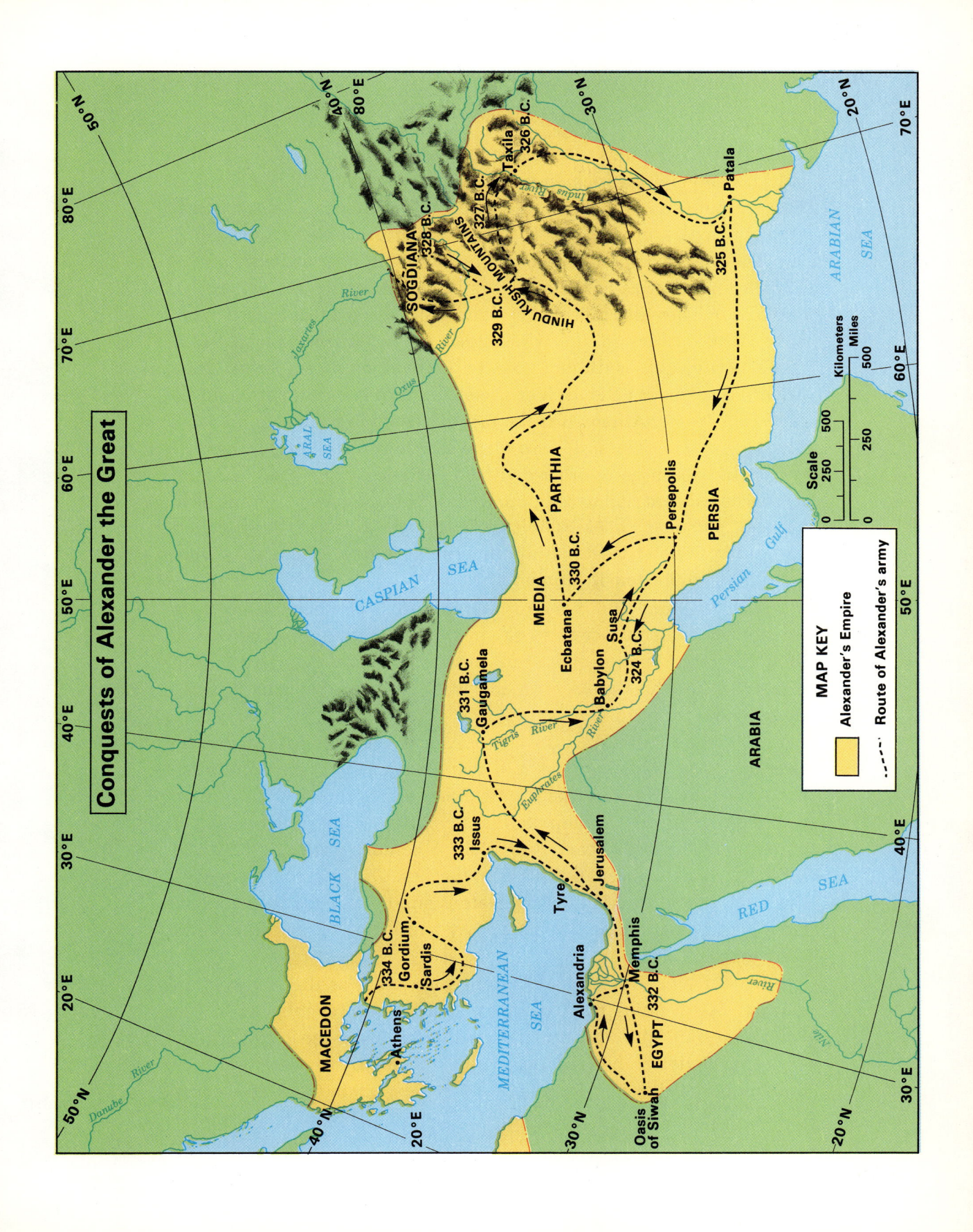

Conquests of Alexander the Great

MAP KEY
- Alexander's Empire
- ----- Route of Alexander's army

Summary

In earlier chapters we learned about Eastern and Middle Eastern cultures and civilizations. In this chapter we studied the beginning of Western culture in the classical civilization of Greece. Greek civilization reached its high point in the fifth century B.C.

The Greeks had long been organized into independent city-states. Their economy was based on agriculture, especially grains, grapes, and olives. They also raised sheep and goats and got fish from the sea. Many Greeks were sailors who traded in the Mediterranean Sea.

The Greek cities did not want to be governed by emperors. They preferred to govern themselves. Every form of government could be found in Greece. Athens was the first city-state to have a democracy. The Greeks felt free and were always trying to find out things.

Unlike learning in other civilized societies at the time, learning in Greece was not tied to religion. Religious leaders were not the only learned persons. Greek scholars developed a world view called naturalism. They tried to study the laws of nature. The Greeks were especially interested in human nature.

The freedom and way of life of the Greek city-states were threatened in the fifth century B.C. by the Persian Empire. There were four important battles between the Greeks and Persians during 490–479 B.C. The Greeks won the wars, and the Persians did not invade Greece again.

After the Persian Wars the city of Athens became the leader of the Greeks. Its government was a direct democracy. Athenians were proud of how all the citizens were equal before the law. They were proud of the fairness of their court system. Athens became the head of an empire. The city became very rich. Athenians used the wealth to build new and beautiful buildings in the city. This period is known as the *Age of Pericles.* Many of the statues and buildings of the ancient Greeks still exist today. The plays they wrote are still performed and read today.

By 431 B.C., Athens had become unpopular as the leader of an empire. Many cities tried to break away. These events led to the Peloponnesian War. The enemies of Athens were led by Sparta.

After Pericles, the leaders of Athens were not as effective. Since the Peloponnesian War lasted almost 30 years, Athens grew weaker and finally had to surrender in 404 B.C. Athens never again recovered its earlier importance.

The new Athenian leaders did not like to be criticized. One man who they thought was criticizing them was the philosopher Socrates. Socrates was tried and killed for his beliefs.

Although Sparta had won the Peloponnesian War, it was not strong enough to protect Greece from outside invaders. Philip II, king of Macedon, conquered Greece in 338 B.C. His son, Alexander the Great, made more conquests and created the largest empire the world had ever known.

Alexander was an amazing man. He appreciated Greek culture. He helped to unite Greek culture with the cultures of the Middle East. The new culture is called Hellenistic.

Some Interesting Activities

1. Use the list of "Questions about Controlling Ideas" on page 151.
   a. Review how Confucians, Buddhists, Jews, Greek humanist-naturalists would answer the questions.
   b. Which world view stressed finding out about nature? About the best society and best government?
   c. Which two world views were especially important in Western (European) cultures?
   d. Would the two world views that formed Western culture fit together easily? Why or why not?

2. Use an encyclopedia to find out about Solon (leader of Athens in 594 B.C.). What was Solon's great work? What do we mean when we call persons "Solons" today?

3. Find out more about Pericles. Read again his funeral speech on pages 215–216. Write a list of the main things he said about Athens and its glory. President Abraham Lincoln made a similar speech about American ideals in the soldiers' cemetery at Gettysburg during the American Civil War. You might read the Gettysburg address and compare it with Pericles's speech. Do you think that Lincoln was thinking of Pericles when he wrote the address?

4. Find out more about Greek triremes. Make a drawing of a trireme.

THE CLASSICAL CIVILIZATION OF GREECE

The Arch of Titus, located near the Roman Forum, commemorates the military victory of Titus at Jerusalem. Titus later became emperor of Rome.

CHAPTER 9

The Roman Republic and Empire

Greek and Hellenistic culture passed on to another strong civilized society. That society began in the city-state of Rome, in Italy. Rome became the center of an empire. The Roman Empire at its greatest extent covered western Europe, northern Africa, the Balkans, and the western lands of the Middle East. Rome fell after its civilization had lasted more than 1,000 years. The language spoken throughout that long period was Latin. The Greek language continued to be used in the eastern part of the Roman Empire.

To educated Europeans and Americans up to the early part of the twentieth century, the *languages* of the Greeks and the Romans were important. Even more important were the *ideas* of the Greeks and the Romans. European and American people have been interested in Greek and Roman ideas for a very good reason. They know that many of their own controlling ideas come from the Greeks and the Romans. To understand their own culture, they know they must understand its beginnings. They know that those beginnings lie in the classical world.

A ▶ Why is Roman civilization as important as Greek civilization to Western cultures?

B ● Many of our words come from Greek. Many other words come from *Latin,* the language of Rome. For example, the following words come from Latin: *constitution, senate, civic, president, legal, dictator, government, republic.* What do these words mean?

Italy's Natural Environment

The peninsula of Italy lies just west of Greece. Italy and Greece are at about the same latitudes. They both have a *Mediterranean climate.*

A ● Look at pages 193–194. Describe a Mediterranean climate.

B ▶ What crops were grown in classical Greece? What animals were raised there?

C ● Look at the map "Ancient Italy and Its Physical Features" (page 233), and compare it with the map of Greece on page 193.
1. In what ways are the physical features of Italy like those of Greece?
2. Does Italy have more plains and large rivers than Greece? Name the three rivers shown on the map of Italy.
3. Notice the high mountains to the north of Italy. What are these mountains called?
4. Along which river is the city of Rome?
5. Give the latitude and longitude of Rome to the nearest degree.

How Rome Began

Rome began as a tiny farming village in Latium [lā′ shē əm]. Latium is a plain in central Italy, south of the Tiber [tī′ bər] River. The early settlers of Latium were called *Latins*—that is, "people of Latium." In Latium, the Latins found lakes and springs. They found woods and good pastureland. And they found a number of hills rising from the plains. On these hills, they built their early settlements. The Latins also found a good climate—a Mediterranean climate. The summers are hot and sunny, with little rain. The winters are rainy but not cold.

232   THE GROWTH OF CIVILIZATION

Ancient Italy and Its Physical Features

The Latins discovered that wheat grew well in this Mediterranean climate. Winter rains made the grass grow thick and long. The Latins could keep oxen, goats, and sheep. They could keep pigs and chickens. They learned to plant fruit and olive trees. Olive oil became very important to Rome, just as it had been to Greece. It was valuable for trade.

The village of Rome began on one of the hills that was settled by the Latins. This hill was later called the Palatine [pal′ ə tīn]. The hill had several advantages. It was close to the Tiber River. That meant the settlers could easily use the river for transportation. The Palatine was surrounded by six other hills. That made it easy to defend. It was also close to a small island in the Tiber River. This island was a good place for crossing the river. The Palatine was a good place for controlling the island. Whoever controlled the Palatine commanded both the river and the plain.

The Legend of How Rome Began

We do not know the earliest history of Rome. The Romans believed that the city was founded in 753 B.C. They dated their years from the year they thought Rome was founded. Their year 1 is the year we count as 753 B.C.

There is a famous legend that tells how Rome was started. Let us read it.

The Legend of Romulus and Remus

Rome was founded by two brothers, Romulus [rom′ ū ləs] and Remus [rē′ məs]. They were twin sons of the war god, Mars. Their wicked uncle, who was a king, planned to kill them. He put the two babies in a basket and set it afloat on the river Tiber. But the gods were watching over them. The babies did not drown.

The basket floated gently down the Tiber. At last it drifted to shore. Just then a she-wolf was drinking at the river. Not long before, the she-wolf had lost her cubs. She looked at the babies and wondered. Could these be her lost cubs? Eagerly she pulled them from the basket and took them to her den. There she fed and cared for the two babies as if they were her cubs.

Soon after, a shepherd killed the she-wolf. When he searched for her cubs, what a surprise he got! Instead of cubs, he found two healthy, husky babies! The shepherd took them home. He and his wife brought them up as their own sons.

Romulus and Remus grew into brave young men. They became the leaders of a band of young shepherds and farmers. With this band, they decided to found a new city. Then trouble began. Who would rule the new city? Both Romulus and Remus wanted to rule. They agreed to let the gods decide which one it should be.

Remus stood on top of a hill later called the Aventine [av′ ən tīn]. Romulus stood on top of the Palatine. Both brothers waited for a sign from the gods. Soon six vultures flew over the Aventine. The followers of Remus cheered. Before they could name him king, however, there was another sign. Twelve vultures flew over the Palatine, where Romulus was standing. The two brothers and their followers began to quarrel. In the end, Romulus was named king.

The artist draws on the legend of Romulus and Remus, illustrating the delivery by the shepherd to his wife of the two husky babies that he had found.

On that very same day, Rome fought its first "war." Romulus had just begun to build a wall for his city. The wall barely came up to his knees. Remus was still angry and began to make fun of his brother. "Do you call that a wall?" he asked. "This is what your enemies will do to it!" He jumped over the wall.

"Then this is what the city's enemies will get!" cried Romulus. He attacked Remus and killed him. So Romulus became the founder of the city and its first king. He named the city after himself. He named it Rome.

That, according to legend, is how it all began. Romans began to *prophesy* (tell what would happen). "Twelve vultures flew over Romulus," they said. "Each vulture stands for 100 years in the life of the city. That means the power of Rome will last for 1,200 years."

A ▶ How close did the Romans come to being right? (Rome began in 753 B.C. In A.D. 476, the last emperor to live in Italy gave up his throne.)

B ▶ Do you think the early Romans were polytheists or monotheists? Why do you think so?

Marcus and Claudia: Children in Early Rome

What was life like in early Rome? Marcus and Claudia are twins. They were born in 560 B.C., that is, 193 years after the founding of the city. We will learn about their lives when they were 11 years old.

Marcus and Claudia have to work hard to help their family. Marcus and his brothers help their father with the work on the farm. Claudia and her sisters help their mother to run the house, to spin yarn, to weave cloth, and to store food.

The family house is made of mudbricks. It is inside the city wall for protection. The fields where Marcus and his brothers work are outside the walls. Grain and olives and grapes grow there. There are grassy fields, too, for sheep and goats.

Marcus and his friends are training to be soldiers. Enemy tribes may attack their city and its farmlands. Marcus and his

This sculpture of a family in early Rome suggests how important family life was to the early Romans.

friends learn to stand heat and cold. They learn to swim and to run long distances. They learn to fight with wooden swords and spears.

When they grow up, Claudia and Marcus will live in much the same way as their parents live. Claudia will be a wife and mother. She will manage a big family. Marcus will be a farmer and a Roman citizen. They both understand two controlling ideas of their culture: *discipline* and *authority.*

Discipline is from a Latin word meaning "teaching" and "training." To Marcus and Claudia, *discipline* means "good behavior." That means obeying older persons. It also means controlling oneself and not being sorry for oneself. Discipline goes with **authority,** which is the right to give orders, or commands. For Marcus and Claudia, authority belongs to their parents and grandparents. At the head of the family is grandfather. Grandfather is lord and master of all his sons, their wives, and the grandchildren. He *owns* the family. To disobey him would be a disgrace or even a crime.

THE ROMAN REPUBLIC AND EMPIRE

We can see how the early Romans came to be stern and tough. They learned discipline and loyalty in the family.

A ▶ Where do people first learn the controlling ideas of their culture?
B ● What values of Roman culture were like those of Confucianism? How were they different from Confucianism?

The early religion of Rome was bound up with the family. Each family had its special gods. There was a god of the *hearth,* or fireplace. There were gods of the plow, of seeds, and of trees.

C ▶ Look at page 169. What is animism? Were the Roman family gods like the spirits in animistic religions?
D ● How did the idea of family gods make the Roman family strong?

Later the Romans came in contact with the Greeks. They copied the polytheism of the Greeks. However, they changed the names of the gods.

E ● Look at the box "Some Gods of Greece and Rome" (page 239).
  1. How many names of planets can you find in the list?
  2. Where does our word *cereal* come from?
  3. The names of our months come from Rome. Find two gods for whom two months are named.

The Roman Republic

There were many small societies in Italy. Yet Rome conquered them all. What made Rome so powerful? No one can give an exact answer. One thing that helped was the toughness of Romans. A second thing that helped was their loyalty to their city.

Another helpful thing was that Rome became a *republic.* **Republic** is from two Latin words *res publica.* The Latin words mean "the public thing" or "the public good." In a republic all the citizens (the "public") share in the government and the good of society.

A republic need not be a democracy. In Athenian democracy, all the votes of the citizens were equal. The *majority* ruled. In the Roman republic, people were divided into *classes.* One

Some Gods of Greece and Rome

Special Function	Greek Name	Latin Name
King of the gods and ruler of the heavens	Zeus	Jupiter
Queen of the gods and protector of marriage and of women	Hera	Juno
Goddess of love and beauty	Aphrodite	Venus
Little god of love	Eros	Cupid
God of war	Ares	Mars
God of the sea	Poseidon	Neptune
God of the sun, prophecy, music, medicine, and poetry	Apollo	Apollo
Ruler of the underworld	Hades	Pluto
Goddess of harvests	Demeter	Ceres
Messenger of the gods	Hermes	Mercury
God of fire	Hephaestus	Vulcan

class was the **patricians,** or the people of noble families. The other class was the **plebs** [plebz], or the ordinary people. In the republic each class had *representatives*. The representatives of each class had to agree on laws.

At one time the Romans were ruled by kings. The last king of Rome was *Tarquin the Proud*. He was driven out of Rome by the patricians because he was cruel. This happened sometime between 510 B.C. and 474 B.C. Instead of a king, the Romans decided to elect two leaders called *consuls*. The **consuls** were the executive branch of the new Roman government.

Patricians and plebs agreed on a republic. However, they quarrelled about the government. In the new government the consuls were patricians. The patricians also made up one part of the legislative branch. This was called the *Senate*. The plebs made up another part, the Assembly of the People. The Assembly included all adult male citizens who were not patricians. The plebs also had two special representatives

THE ROMAN REPUBLIC AND EMPIRE

known as the **Tribunes of the People.** The Senate, the Assembly of the People, and the Tribunes made up the legislative branch of the Roman republic. In addition, there were elected judges called *praetors* [prē′ tərz].

A ● Look at the box "The Government of the Roman Republic" below.
  1. Why do you think there were *two* consuls?
  2. How would the *division of legislative power* help both patricians and plebs to feel that their interests would be taken care of?

B ● The government of Rome was a mixture of parts of monarchy, aristocracy, and democracy. The Romans liked this **mixed government.** Why do you think the Romans wanted a mixture of different forms of government?

THE GOVERNMENT OF THE ROMAN REPUBLIC

EXECUTIVE

Two Consuls
Elected yearly by voting men
Had almost kingly powers

Other Magistrates
Elected yearly by voting men
Helped the consuls with the day-to-day business of government

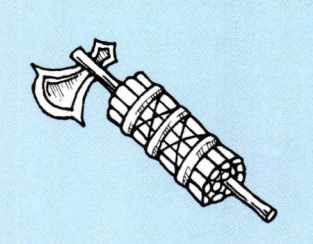

LEGISLATIVE

Senate
Included 300 members who served for life
Advised the consuls and proposed laws

Assemblies of the People
Included all citizens
Had power to declare war or to agree to peace terms.

Tribunes of the People
Elected yearly (after 494 B.C.) by the Assembly
Protected the rights of the plebs

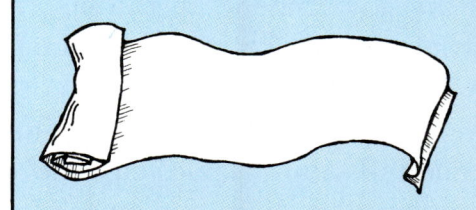

JUDICIAL

Praetors
Elected yearly by voting men
Acted as the judges of Rome

---

240   THE GROWTH OF CIVILIZATION

C● Look at the box "The Government of the United States" on page 214.
1. Do you think that the United States Constitution was partly copied from the Roman Republic? Explain.
2. Which officer in the United States is like the consuls in Rome?
3. How are the Senate and House of Representatives chosen in the United States?

D★ Another word for republic is "commonwealth." Is this a good translation of the Latin words? Why? Are any of the states in the United States called commonwealths?

War with the Etruscans

The Roman Republic was hardly set up before it was tested. To the north of Rome lived the Etruscans [i trus′kənz]. They were a powerful people. Tarquin and his followers asked the Etruscans for help. They agreed to help Tarquin win back Rome.

The war with the Etruscans began. Romans and Etruscans fought each other, off and on, for more than 200 years. To win the wars, the Romans needed loyalty and discipline. Could a republic expect loyalty and discipline from its citizens? If people were free, would they obey their commanders? Would citizens fight well without a king? These were important questions. To answer them, let us read two famous Roman legends. The first story is about a Roman soldier's courage and his loyalty to Rome.

Horatius at the Bridge

The Etruscans were at war with the Romans. Suddenly the Etruscans moved toward the city of Rome. The Romans, taken by surprise, fled behind the city walls. They forgot to destroy the narrow bridge over the Tiber. The Etruscans poured toward the bridge. If they captured it, the whole Etruscan army could get into Rome.

A young Roman soldier rushed onto the bridge. His name was Horatius [hə rā′ shəs]. He knew the Romans had to hold the bridge. "Stand and fight!" he called to the other Roman soldiers. The others would not help. They were terrified at the size of the Etruscan army.

THE ROMAN REPUBLIC AND EMPIRE

Horatius defending the bridge

"Then at least break down the bridge!" Horatius called. "I will try to hold them off alone!" The Romans were too ashamed to disobey. They began to chop down the bridge.

Horatius turned to face the Etruscans alone. He dared them to fight. "Who is brave enough to face a single Roman?" he shouted. The Etruscans answered with a shower of spears. Horatius did not retreat. He met the Etruscans at the end of the bridge, fighting like a hero. One Etruscan after another fell dead or wounded. Two more Romans rushed out to help their comrade. They were not enough. It looked as if the enemy could not be held much longer.

Behind them, the Romans were chopping at the wooden bridge. It was giving way. "Go back before the bridge falls!" Horatius ordered his two companions. They dashed back across the bridge. Horatius, left alone, fought desperately to hold back the enemy.

Suddenly a large section of the bridge gave way. The broken timbers plunged into the Tiber. Now Horatius turned and dived into the water. Spears whistled through the air. They splashed into the water all around him. His heavy armor pulled him down, yet he swam on.

Wounded and tired, Horatius reached the Roman shore. Grateful soldiers helped him up the bank. They welcomed him as a great hero. Rome had been saved.

The second story is about the loyalty of the Romans toward Roman law.

Brutus and His Sons

Brutus [brü′təs] was one of the patricians who had rebelled against Tarquin. Brutus was a wise man who loved his country. He became one of the leaders of the new republic.

The sons of Brutus did not feel the way their father did. They joined a group of younger patricians who wished to bring back Tarquin as king. They planned to betray their city. Secretly, at night, they would open up the gates of Rome. Then Etruscan soldiers could sneak into the city. By morning, Rome would once again belong to Tarquin.

The plot became known ahead of time. Angry Romans seized the young patricians and took them to be judged. Brutus was one of the judges. The people were shocked. The penalty for this crime was death. Would Brutus treat his sons the same as he treated the other young men? Would he find them guilty? Could a judge pass judgment on his own sons?

The evidence left no doubt. The young men were guilty. Brutus joined the other judges in passing sentence. Then the judges took their seats to see the sentence carried out. The young men were beheaded.

The people turned to look at Brutus. His face remained stern and grim. His heart was full of sorrow. Still, the Roman law came before his love for his sons. Brutus did his duty before the law. He proved himself a loyal Roman.

A ▶ What does the story of Horatius tell us about the Romans? What qualities did they admire in soldiers?

B ● Why are discipline and loyalty needed to win a war?

C ● What does the story of Brutus tell us about the Romans? What qualities did they admire in political leaders?

D ● How had free Athenians managed to keep discipline in their army and navy? Did this take great pride and patriotism? Why or why not?

Mixed Government and the Rule of Law

The mixed government of the Romans had advantages. There was strong leadership in time of trouble (the consuls). The rich people (the Senate) had a strong voice in the government. The ordinary people (the Assembly and the Tribunes) also had a strong voice in the government. The Roman Republic lasted much longer than Athenian democracy. Romans said that their mixed republic was *more stable* than any simple government. It was not easy for the government to act foolishly. It was not easy for the government to treat one class badly. All Romans had a share in the republic. They were loyal to it.

The Romans had another thing that was stable. They soon began to write down the laws. This made it possible to have a *rule of law.* When a praetor (judge) heard a case, he had to obey the law. Whenever one praetor ruled that the law meant a certain thing in a certain case, later praetors had to follow the same rule. Changes in the written laws had to be agreed to by the Senate, Assembly, and Tribunes. Almost every possible crime was written down side by side with a penalty. No one could be accused of a crime that was not written down.

A ● Rome had the *rule of law.* What does this mean? How does the rule of law help people to have rights and freedom?
B ● Do we have the rule of law in the United States? Explain.
C ● How would the Roman government help Rome to become powerful?

Rome Conquers Italy

Their culture and government gave Romans unity and power. Soon they were winning wars. By 265 B.C., they had conquered most of Italy south of the Po River. The language of Rome, Latin, and Roman laws spread through Italy. The Romans usually ruled over the conquered people fairly and justly. Many of the conquered peoples became Roman citizens.

The Romans built fine roads linking the towns of Italy. This made travel faster and easier. The new roads were used by

A part of the Appian Way still in use today. This Roman military road was one of a network of roads linking Rome with many cities and towns in Europe.

traders and travelers. This helped increase Roman trade. Troops could also use the roads to go quickly from one place to another. This made keeping the peace easier.

At first these changes did not change the life of the Romans. They did not change the "old ways" of discipline and hard work. Even senators were proud of being able to plow a field. Rome was strong because of the "old ways," people said. For many years, this was true. Rome was growing, however. Things began to change for everyone.

A ● Why do you think good roads between towns made it easier to keep the peace?

Wars with Carthage: The Punic Wars

Rome fought three great wars in the third and second centuries B.C. They are called the *Punic* [pyü′ nik] *Wars*, because the powerful enemies of Rome were the people of Carthage, who spoke the Punic language.

The city of Carthage in North Africa was a great center of trade and wealth. Its empire covered western North Africa, part of Sicily, part of southern Spain, and the islands in the western Mediterranean. Its navy ruled the western Mediterranean Sea.

THE ROMAN REPUBLIC AND EMPIRE

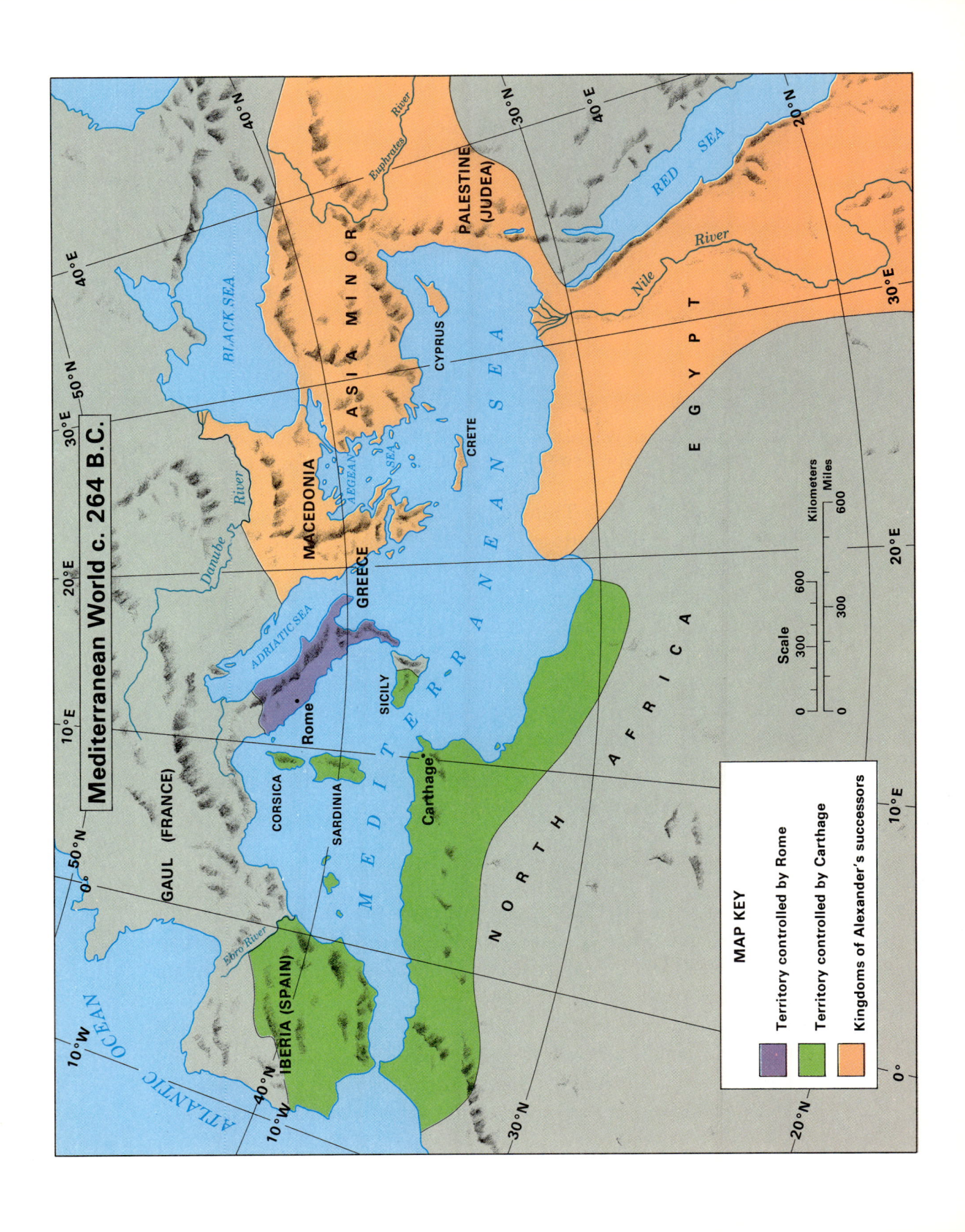

Mediterranean World c. 264 B.C.

MAP KEY
- Territory controlled by Rome
- Territory controlled by Carthage
- Kingdoms of Alexander's successors

Labels on map:
ATLANTIC OCEAN, GAUL (FRANCE), IBERIA (SPAIN), Ebro River, CORSICA, SARDINIA, Rome, SICILY, Carthage, NORTH AFRICA, MEDITERRANEAN SEA, ADRIATIC SEA, Danube River, MACEDONIA, GREECE, AEGEAN SEA, CRETE, BLACK SEA, ASIA MINOR, CYPRUS, Euphrates River, PALESTINE (JUDEA), RED SEA, Nile River, EGYPT

Carthage was a great sea power. But Rome was a land power. It controlled Italy. Rome's navy was small and weak.

The Carthaginians wanted to make their empire in the western Mediterranean greater. They already controlled the western half of the island of Sicily. They wanted to control all of Sicily. The leaders of Rome did not want the empire of Carthage to get any larger. As a result, Rome and Carthage came into conflict.

The First Punic War started in 264 B.C. The Romans had to find a way for their foot soldiers to fight on the water. And they did find a way. They put swinging gangplanks on their ships. Then a Roman ship could pull beside an enemy ship and lower the gangplank. The Roman foot soldiers could rush across the gangplank to fight the enemy. This helped Rome to win the First Punic War. The Carthaginians were forced to give up Sicily.

A ▶ Why did Rome and Carthage go to war with each other?
B ▶ Did Carthage or Rome have stronger sea power?
C ● On the map "Mediterranean World c. 264 B.C." (page 246), find the following:
  1. Carthage's empire
  2. lands controlled by Rome
  3. Sicily

Both Carthage and Rome were now sea powers. They both wanted to control the western Mediterranean. Another long war followed late in the third century B.C. This was the Second Punic War. Although a Carthaginian army invaded Italy, Carthage lost the war. Rome gained control of the Iberian Peninsula at the western end of the Mediterranean Sea. The war was followed by about 50 years of peace. By 150 B.C., however, Carthage showed signs of becoming too powerful again.

Many Romans believed that unless Carthage were destroyed, it would remain a terrible threat to Rome. One of these Romans was a senator named Cato. Every speech he made in the Senate ended the same way: "Carthage must be destroyed!"

A third war came in 146 B.C. Carthage was defeated for the final time. The Carthaginians were killed or made slaves. Salt

THE ROMAN REPUBLIC AND EMPIRE

was scattered over the ruins of the great city, so that nothing would grow on that site.

- D★ You may wish to find out more about the Punic Wars. Read about Carthage's general *Hannibal,* who came close to defeating Rome in the Second Punic War (218–201 B.C.).

Empire, Culture Change, and Social Problems

At the time of the Third Punic War, Roman armies also conquered Macedonia, in the Balkan Peninsula. The Romans went on to conquer all the Greek city-states. The Romans liked the Hellenic culture, so they began to copy Greek ways. Greek artists and teachers came to Rome—some of them as slaves. As time passed, Greek culture and Roman culture were mingled. The mixture is called **Greco-Roman culture.**

By the middle of the second century B.C., Rome had gained a vast empire. Taxes paid by conquered peoples and profits from trade made Rome rich. Greek art and philosophy spread among Rome's educated classes.

During the wars, many thousands of enemies had been taken prisoner by the Roman legions. Most of these prisoners were made slaves and were put to work on the estates of rich Roman landowners. Many free Roman farmers had lost their land while they were serving in the army. Now these small farmers tended to drift into Rome and the other cities. Their place on the land was taken by slave labor.

- A▶ Why were there many people without jobs in Rome after the Punic Wars?
- B● What Romans besides landowners might grow wealthier after a war?

Many of the older Romans did not like the changes brought by the Punic Wars. Most Roman citizens had not expected to gain an empire by conquest. They thought they had been fighting to defend Rome. Yet by winning the wars they had gained much territory. Most of the "old Romans" were alarmed at the changes that resulted from conquest. They believed in the

THE GROWTH OF CIVILIZATION

The Colosseum, built A.D. 72–80, was a huge amphitheater in Rome that held about 45,000 spectators.

old ways of Rome. They hated seeing new riches tempt people away from old customs and beliefs.

Many of the younger Romans enjoyed their new wealth and luxury. "Why be poor and simple when we can be rich and comfortable?" they asked. "Rome is strong and powerful. It is Rome's destiny to rule the world!"

Most of Rome's new wealth went to a few families. The gap between rich people and poor people grew bigger. More and more Roman citizens who had lost their land lived in Rome's slums. Romans of all classes did not work as hard as their fathers and grandfathers had worked. Slaves did the work. In the Roman armies, more and more of the soldiers came from far parts of the empire, not from Rome.

The old discipline and loyalty of Roman society were hurt by these changes. Respect for law broke down. Riots and street fighting happened often, and then civil wars. Rome suffered nearly a century of unrest and bloodshed.

- C ● How would Roman life be changed by the new wealth from conquest and trade? Would it take as much discipline and hard work to make a living in the city as it had when most Romans were farmers? How might this change affect Roman ideas?
- D ● Do you think it is possible for people like the "old Romans" to keep society from changing? How could they try to do that?

THE ROMAN REPUBLIC AND EMPIRE

To try to keep mobs from causing more trouble in Rome, the Roman government gave the people free food. The government also gave "circuses," or big public shows, to keep city people contented. The Roman crowds enjoyed watching several chariot drivers race on a special track called a *hippodrome*. Chariot racing was more popular in Rome than it had been in Greece. It was a dangerous sport. Chariot drivers often were injured, and some were killed. Romans cheered their favorite charioteers in the way that Americans today cheer their favorite football or baseball players.

Many Romans liked to watch the savage fights of *gladiators*. **Gladiators** were armed men who fought one another, sometimes to the death. In other shows, hungry lions or tigers were let loose on prisoners. Sometimes groups of prisoners taken in war were forced to fight one another for public amusement, until all were dead. Thousand and thousands of people in the city of Rome watched these terrible shows, screaming with excitement.

E▶ What do you think about the Roman shows? Is it good for people to enjoy the sufferings of others?

The Baths of Caracalla, located near Rome, were built during the reign of Emperor Caracalla (A.D. 211–217). These elaborate public baths — offering cold, warm, and steam baths — covered 33 acres and held 16,000 people at one time.

F● Some Romans argued that gladiators' fights helped to keep Romans warlike. What do you think? (Is being a soldier ready to fight in war the same as being a person who enjoys watching a bloody fight?)

The End of the Republic

Free bread and circuses did not get rid of the social problems. Some of the poor Romans who had been farmers tried to get back the land that they or their ancestors had lost. Politicians fought for power. Political parties began to use weapons against one another. To stop such fighting, military leaders seized power. In the first century B.C., there came several *military dictators*. By **military dictators** we mean rulers whose power is based on the army. Some dictators favored the rich. Some favored the poor. The fighting continued. The old laws had broken down!

A▶ Why did military dictators seize power?
B● What was happening to the mixed, balanced government of the Roman Republic? Why was this happening?
C● Why do many people welcome a *dictator* when law and order break down?

In 49 B.C., after nearly 100 years of trouble, a great general marched his army into Rome and seized power. That general was Julius Caesar. Caesar was a politician who later turned to soldiering. He became a military dictator who governed for five years.

Julius Caesar had more power than the kings of early Rome. Some senators plotted to kill him and bring back the republic. They stabbed Caesar to death in the Senate in 44 B.C. However, the senators could not bring back the mixed government of the republic. The people had lost the values and habits that made the republic work. There were 14 more years of civil war before peace and order came again.

D● How had the Romans lost the values, or controlling ideas, that made the Roman Republic work in the past?

THE ROMAN REPUBLIC AND EMPIRE **251**

Caesar Augustus, the first emperor of Rome (27 B.C.), brought peace to the Roman people. He also encouraged literature and the arts and did much to beautify Rome. The period of his reign is known as the Augustan Age, which is also considered the golden age of Latin literature.

The Roman Empire

The Romans were tired of war. They were ready to make a hero of anyone who could stop the fighting. The hero was Octavian [ok tā′ vē ən], a nephew of Caesar. Octavian's armies won the civil war that followed Caesar's death. Octavian became ruler of Rome in 27 B.C.

Octavian was a clever politician. He knew that the Romans wanted peace more than anything. His victory had brought them peace. Octavian also knew that many Romans still dreamed of the old ways. He gave his soldiers money and land. He did away with many debts that were facing poor Romans. And he began a huge program to improve the city. This program gave many jobs to the Romans who had no work.

Octavian knew that the Romans feared a dictatorship. He could have forced everyone to obey him. Yet he did not do this. Octavian pretended to rule in the old, honored ways. That kept people happy. Many felt that Octavian had brought back the republic. But Octavian had much more power than the people realized. He was really a military dictator.

Rome was under one-person rule. Even so, the people were grateful to Octavian. They gave him the title of *Augustus.* This title means "grand" and "holy." (From this point on we will refer to Octavian as Augustus.) Soon he held four offices. He was consul, tribune, high priest, and senator—all at once. Augustus had become an emperor. The word *emperor* comes from the Latin *imperator. Imperator* was a title given to victorious Roman generals.

Under Augustus, Rome only *seemed* to be a republic. It was really a monarchy. From this point in history, we speak of the **Roman Empire.** The name *Roman Empire* means the new form of government under an *imperator* (military dictator).

A● "Empire" has another meaning. What? Was the Roman Republic an "empire" in the usual meaning of the word? Explain.

Roman civilization did not end with the republic. It continued for 500 more years in the area around the western Mediterranean Sea. In the area at the eastern Mediterranean, Greco-Roman civilized society lasted for 1,500 more years.

B● What can we learn from the history of Rome? Look at the box "Why the Roman Republic Became a Military Dictatorship" (page 254).
  1. Was any one of these causes the "most important"? Which?
  2. Why should we study these things? What lessons might they have for us today?

The Roman Peace

The Romans had lost their political freedom. But they had gained peace and order. For many years the empire was strong. There was much wealth. The government went on giving free bread and entertainment to keep poorer people "happy."

Augustus began to rebuild Rome. He said that he found Rome built of brick but left it built of marble. The ruins of the Roman Forum (marketplace) today give us an idea of the grand buildings of Augustus's Rome.

The people were pleased with Augustus. They felt that he respected the old ways and the old gods. Augustus urged people to remember the Roman past. Under Augustus the citizens again took pride in Rome.

> **Why the Roman Republic Became a Military Dictatorship**
>
> 1. Roman conquests brought great wealth. The wealth caused corruption in politics. It made bitter divisions between rich and poor. Free bread and entertainment made people lose their self-respect.
> 2. Many millions of people became "Roman citizens." The old constitution was not designed to serve such large numbers of citizens.
> 3. The Roman armies were made up of *paid soldiers*, not citizen-soldiers. The new armies were loyal to their generals, not to the Republic.
> 4. The old Roman cultural values broke down.
> 5. Civil wars and street fighting made most people agree to give up their political freedom if they could have peace and order.

Augustus improved the life of citizens who lived in the provinces, or places far away from Rome. Taxes were made fairer. Land and other property were protected by special laws. People in the provinces were especially grateful for these things. New cities were built in the provinces. Old cities prospered.

During the rule of Augustus the empire stretched from the North Sea to the Caspian Sea to the Red Sea. The Roman peace lasted for almost 200 years.

A ▶ Look at the map "Empire of Augustus, A.D. 14" (page 257).
    1. Trace the boundaries of the empire.
    2. Find the North Sea and the Danube River.
    3. Find the Caspian Sea.
    4. Find Britain and Germania. Britain (now England) later became part of the empire, but Germania was never conquered.

B ● How would the power of the Roman Empire help trade and wealth all over the empire?

THE GROWTH OF CIVILIZATION

The Rise of Christianity

During the Roman peace a new controlling idea began. The idea grew and spread until it became the religion of the Roman Empire. It was *Christianity*.

Already the ideas of Judaism were known to many non-Jewish people in the area around the eastern Mediterranean. Hellenistic culture came from the mixing of Greek culture and Middle Eastern cultures.

In the first century B.C., Rome conquered Palestine. Many Jews hated the foreign rule. They fought against it. But Roman rule went on. It was during this time that Jesus was born in Galilee, in the northern part of Palestine.

A ▶ Look at the map "Palestine at the Time of Jesus" (page 258).
 1. Notice the three divisions of Palestine. What are they called?
 2. Find Nazareth, where Jesus was born.
 3. How far is Nazareth from Jerusalem?
 4. Notice the river from the Sea of Galilee to the Dead Sea. This is the Jordan River.

The followers of Jesus believe that he is the *Christ* or the *Messiah* [mə si′ ə]. The words **Christ** and **Messiah** mean the same thing, *anointed*. *Christ* is a Greek word; *Messiah* is a Hebrew word.

When we study about Jesus, we must remember two things. First, Christians believe that Jesus is the person who the Hebrews' God promised would save the people. Second, for some non-Christians, Jesus is a great and wise teacher. They learn about him in their religion.

The teachings of Jesus and his followers are recorded in the New Testament of the Bible. These teachings became the controlling ideas of *Christianity*. Also in the New Testament is some information about the life of Jesus. Yet there is much about Jesus' life that we do not know.

Like other Jewish children, Jesus studied the Torah. He learned about Judaism and Jewish worship. For much of his life he worked as a carpenter.

When he was about 30 years old, Jesus began to teach. He taught about God's love. He taught that people should love one another. He taught the ordinary people. Many people loved him and followed him. However, two groups in Palestine disliked Jesus' teaching. One group was made up of some Jews who thought that Jesus was trying to change the Jewish religion. The other was made up of Roman officials who feared that Jesus would lead another revolt against Rome.

Three years after he began to teach, Jesus went to Jerusalem for the Passover holiday. There he was accused of being a troublemaker. He was tried before the Roman governor, Pontius Pilate. He was sentenced to be crucified (put to death on a cross). This was the usual Roman death penalty at that time.

The New Testament tells that after Jesus' death, his followers believed that Jesus was still with them. They began to spread his teachings far and wide. They taught that Jesus would save everyone who believed in him.

A large number of early converts to Christianity were Jews. In addition, more and more people in the rest of the Mediterranean world became Christians. Christianity spread, and many **churches** (groups of Christians) were formed.

Jesus' Teaching

Jesus was not an Alexander who carved out a great empire. He was not a Pericles who led a great city. He was not an Aristotle who wrote great books of philosophy. His public career lasted no more than three years. During those years, he spent most of his time just talking to ordinary people. How could Jesus have left such a deep and lasting mark on the human adventure? What was his teaching that helped so many people?

Much of Jesus' teaching was already found in Judaism. He used simple, everyday speech. Everyone could understand it. His message was about the love of God. Jesus told people to follow the law of Moses:

You shall love the Lord your God with all your heart, and with all

Empire of Augustus, A.D. 14
ATLANTIC
OCEAN
NORTH
SEA
BRITAIN
GAUL
(FRANCE)
IBERIA
(SPAIN)
Ebro River
Po River
GERMANIA
Danube
River
ADRIATIC
SEA
CORSICA
Rome
SARDINIA
SICILY
MEDITERRANEAN
SEA
MACEDON
AEGEAN
SEA
CRETE
BLACK
SEA
CASPIAN
SEA
ASIA MINOR
CYPRUS
SYRIA
PALESTINE
Tigris
River
Euphrates
River
Alexandria
EGYPT
Nile
River
RED SEA
NORTH AFRICA
MAP KEY
Roman lands
Site of Old Carthage
Provincial boundaries
Scale
0
300
600
Kilometers
Miles
0
300
600
20°W
10°W
0°
10°E
20°E
30°E
40°E
50°E
60°E
60°N
50°N
40°N
30°N
20°N

your soul and with all your might. . . . And you shall love your neighbor as yourself.

Jesus taught that everyone could have God's love. He showed how God could comfort those who were sad or poor or ill. He showed how those who had done wrong could have forgiveness.

Jesus told people that they must not be proud or angry. They must love even their enemies. He told them that God could see into a person's mind. Someone who was full of pride

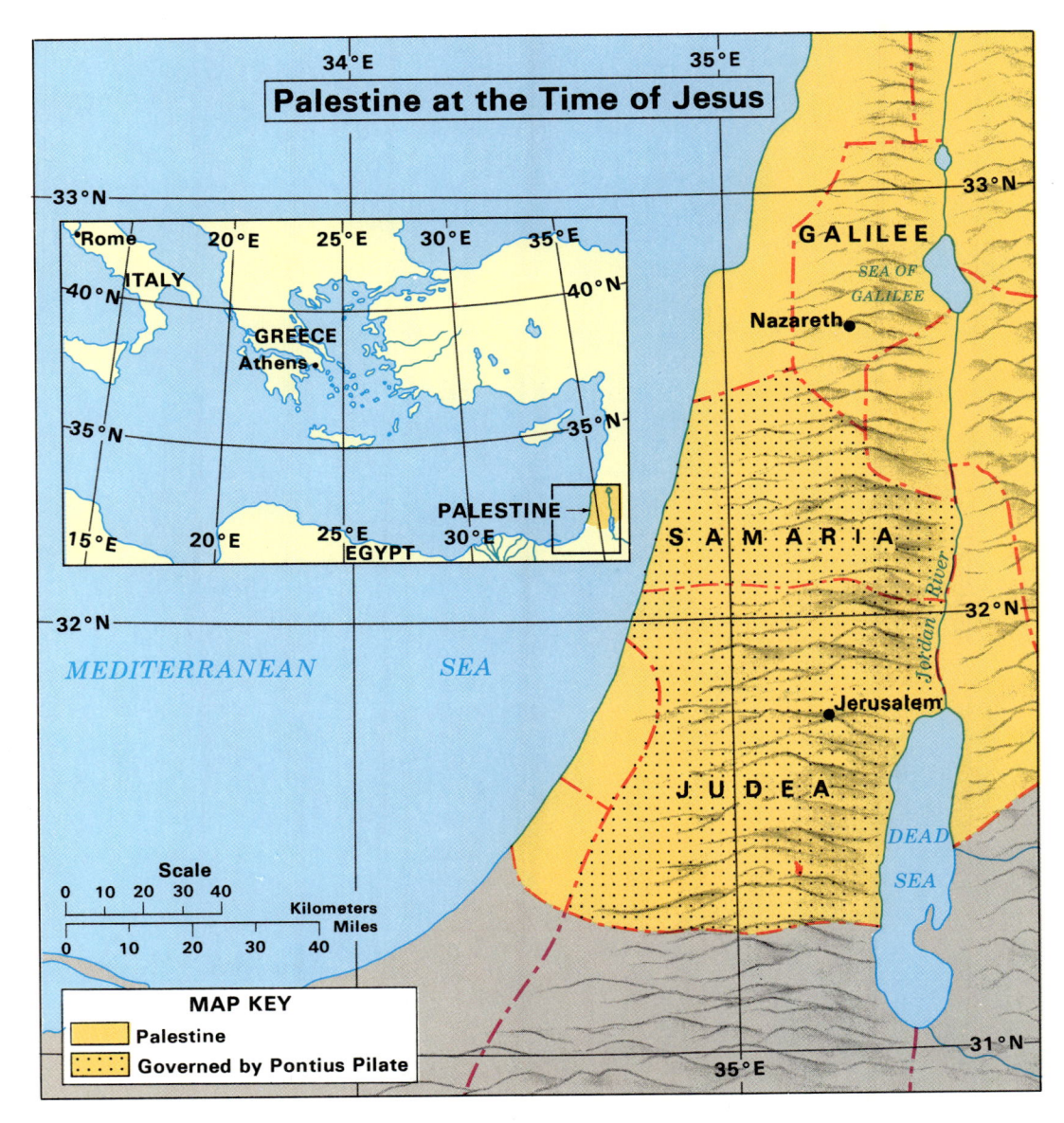

Jesus delivers the Sermon on the Mount (of Olives).

or anger was evil (bad), even if that person did not do *wrong* or let others know what he or she was feeling. How could anyone be so good? Jesus answered that people could be good if they loved God and also their neighbors.

Above all Jesus told people that if they had faith in God, they would find the kingdom of God. God loved them all. All people are precious to God. That was why God had sent Jesus to them. Jesus showed kindness even to the lowest people (even to criminals).

A★ You can read more about Jesus' teaching in the *Gospels* (the first four books of the New Testament).

The Early Church and Persecution

Jesus' followers, who were called disciples [dĭ sī' plz], traveled to many places. They taught as Jesus taught. They said that Jesus had given his life to save all people. They believed he would come back to bring the kingdom of God.

Soon there were churches in many cities of Asia Minor, Egypt, and Greece. There were churches in Rome, Sicily, and Spain.

The Roman government began to attack the new religion. Christianity taught that in God's love, poor people and slaves were equal to the greatest persons. By this time the emperors claimed to be gods. Christians and Jews would not agree to this idea. The government said they were *disloyal*.

A ▶ Why did the Roman government not like Christianity?
B ● Why might a Roman who was a polytheist not mind saying that the emperor was a god? Why could Christians and Jews not say this?

In A.D. 66 the Jews in Palestine revolted. It took Rome four years to end the revolt. The Roman army destroyed Jerusalem. Most of the Jews were forced to leave Palestine.

The government in Rome tried to stop the growth of Christianity. It was against the law to be a Christian. For centuries Christians had to meet in secret. In Rome, for example, they met in underground rooms. Christians were often *persecuted* (treated cruelly) to make them give up their faith. Some Christians were tortured and killed. Some were killed in cruel shows to entertain the people. Even with these persecutions, the number of Christians continued to grow.

The Empire Grows Weak and Troubled

One reason that people turned to Christianity was that the Roman Empire had begun to weaken. Some emperors, such as Augustus, governed well. Other emperors, however, were bad rulers. The army then became the real power. However, by the third century A.D., the army was not able to defend the empire against barbarians.

Barbarians from Germany and eastern Europe and Asia had always been a problem. In the third century A.D., attacks by barbarians happened more often. The attacks also became more successful. Roman armies were busy defending Rome's borders. Trade was difficult. Many people died from plagues. More and more citizens doubted the ability of the government to defend and to help them.

So many people looked for a new set of controlling ideas to give meaning and hope to their lives. Among the religions and philosophies to which people turned was Christianity.

Near the end of the third century A.D., the Roman Empire was divided into two parts, mostly for better military defense. One emperor governed in the west, another emperor in the east. But early in the fourth century, these two halves were joined again for a time under the rule of Constantine the Great.

Constantine and Christianity

Constantine had been commander of the Roman army in Britain when his soldiers proclaimed him emperor. He marched to Italy, where he defeated the emperor of the west. Later Constantine said that during the battle he had seen a cross in the sky. And beside the cross he had seen the words: "In this sign you conquer." The cross was the sign of Christ. After that, Constantine became the great friend of Christians in the empire. He used Christian symbols on his banners and on his soldiers' shields. He won battles—and all the empire. A year after his victory in Italy, Constantine sent out an *edict,* or order. This edict said that all religions were free to exist in Rome. It mentioned Christianity in particular. Christians were not to be persecuted. Any property that had been taken from Christians had to be given back.

A marble sculpture of Constantine

This was a great turning point in the history of Christianity. For the first time, it was lawful to be a Christian. Christians could enjoy the full rights of Roman citizens. They could hold offices in the government. Soon it even became popular to be a Christian.

THE ROMAN REPUBLIC AND EMPIRE

After Constantine's victory in the west, he conquered the eastern half of the empire. He made his capital in the eastern city of Byzantium, renaming it Constantinople, "the city of Constantine." This location was good for trade and for defense. It made a safe and strong capital.

The Roman Empire Dies in the West

The strong rule of the empire came to an end with the death of Constantine. After that, the empire grew weak again. Once more it was divided.

In A.D. 410, the barbarian Goths captured Rome and looted the city. Other barbarians overran Gaul (France) and Spain. They crossed over into North Africa. All these provinces were lost to the western empire. In A.D. 476, the empire in the west came to an end.

In place of the empire in the west, a number of barbarian kingdoms were set up. Civilization in the west broke down for a time. Yet the Christian Church remained. The bishop of Rome became the head of the church in the west. A bishop is a clergyman of high rank who has charge of all the churches in a certain area. The bishop of Rome was called the *pope*. Many barbarians became Christians. As a result, the Church was able to carry on Roman civilization.

The Christian Church began to do many things that government was no longer able to do. It began to feed the poor and care for the needy. It provided leadership for the people. Roman law had once guided the people. Now the Church guided them by its teachings. More and more people turned to the Church and depended on it. The Church became the source of order and peace in Western Europe.

A ▶ What caused the western empire to break down?
B ● Why was the Church able to go on through these centuries of trouble? Why did the barbarians not get rid of the Church? What might have happened in Western Europe if the Church had been wiped out?
C ● In what period of Roman history would you have preferred to live?

The Roman Empire Lives in the East

The western empire was gone. In the east, however, Greco-Roman civilization went on. It was also a Christian civilization. The emperors ruled from Constantinople. Roman laws were carefully written down in the Byzantine Empire. To this day Roman law is used in many western countries.

The Church in the Byzantine Empire later became separated from the Roman Church in the West. The Byzantine Church became the *Greek Orthodox church.* The western Church became the *Roman Catholic church.*

For ten centuries after the fall of the empire in the west the Byzantine Empire lived on. It fought back many invaders. But its lands grew smaller and smaller. At last, in A.D. 1453, Constantinople was captured by barbarians called the Ottoman Turks.

A Byzantine mosaic showing Theodora, a Byzantine empress, and her court attendants. Byzantine art combined influences from Greece and Rome.

Santa Sophia (the Church of Holy Wisdom) at Constantinople. Originally a Christian church, it later became a mosque. It is now a museum of Byzantine art. It is considered one of the world's finest examples of Byzantine architecture.

SOME IMPORTANT EVENTS IN THE CLASSICAL PERIOD

Europe and the Mediterranean

Sixth Century B.C.
- Greek city-states emerge as civilized societies
- 636–546 Life of Thales
- 509 Roman Republic is founded

Fifth Century B.C.
- 494–479 Persian wars
- 460–429 Age of Pericles in Athens
- 431–404 Peloponnesian War

Fourth Century B.C.
- 469–399 Life of Socrates
- 427–347 Life of Plato
- 356–323 Alexander the Great
- 338 Macedon conquers Greece
- 384–322 Life of Aristotle

Third Century B.C.
- Rome conquers Italy
- 264–241 First Punic War
- 218–202 Second Punic War

Second Century B.C.
- 149–146 Third Punic War
- 146 Rome conquers the Balkans and Greece
- 146–27 Social troubles and military dictators in Rome

Middle East and Asia

Confucius and Buddha are teaching
The Hebrew prophet Jeremiah
The Jews in Babylon
539 Persian Empire is founded

494–479 Persians invade Greece
446 Persia signs a peace treaty with Athens

334–326 Alexander the Great conquers Persian Empire, Babylonia, Parthia, etc.
322–275 Alexander's empire is divided

274–236 Buddhism, India's religion under Emperor Asoka
230–221 Golden age of philosophy in China

Jewish Kingdom under the Maccabees
184 Brahmans regain power in much of India
136 Confucianism, China's religion

A ▶ King Tarquin was driven out of Rome in 509 B.C. The Byzantine Empire ended in A.D. 1453 How long had the Roman Republic and Empire lasted (in one form or another)?

B ● Byzantine civilized culture was quite different from earlier Greco-Roman culture. Look at the pictures of Byzantine art on page 263. Compare them with earlier Greco-Roman art. Did the Roman Republic and Empire *really* last so long? Discuss your answers.

C ● Look at "Some Important Events in the Classical Period" above. Many other things happened in the world in this period, but the

THE GROWTH OF CIVILIZATION

	Europe and the Mediterranean	Middle East and Asia
First Century B.C.	49–44 Julius Caesar dictator of Rome 27–A.D. 180 Roman peace 27–A.D. 14 Octavian (Augustus) emperor of Rome	63 Rome takes Palestine 47–30 Reign of Cleopatra as queen of Egypt 4 Birth of Jesus of Nazareth
First Century A.D.	Spread of Christianity Roman Empire outlaws Christianity	Ministry of Jesus; spread of Christianity 70 Jerusalem is destroyed
Second Century A.D.	113–117 Roman Empire under Trajan reaches greatest extent 166–175 German barbarians invade Roman Empire	132–135 Jews revolt against Romans in Palestine but are crushed
Third Century A.D.	Barbarians weaken Roman Empire 284 First division of Roman Empire	c. 200: Beginning of the Talmud Another Persian Empire, which fights with Rome
Fourth Century A.D.	306–337 Constantine the Great reunites Roman Empire 364 The Empire divides again	Barbarian invasion (Huns) from Asia Hindu philosophy and art at their height in India
Fifth Century A.D.	410 The Goths sack Rome More barbarian invasions 476 Fall of Empire in the West	
Sixth Century A.D.	The Empire in the East continues 527–565 Emperor Justinian 590–604 Pope Gregory the Great	Buddhism spreads to China, Korea, Japan A series of wars between the Persian Empire and the Eastern Roman (Byzantine) Empire

dates shown will help you to have a "pattern" in your mind.
1. When did Socrates, Plato, and Aristotle live?
2. What conquests brought Hellenistic culture?
3. In which century did four important world views become established? Name these world views.
4. In which century did a fifth world view begin? What is it called?
5. In what year did the barbarians first sack Rome?
6. Name the Roman (or Byzantine) emperor who had Roman law written as a *code*. In what century was this done?

THE ROMAN REPUBLIC AND EMPIRE

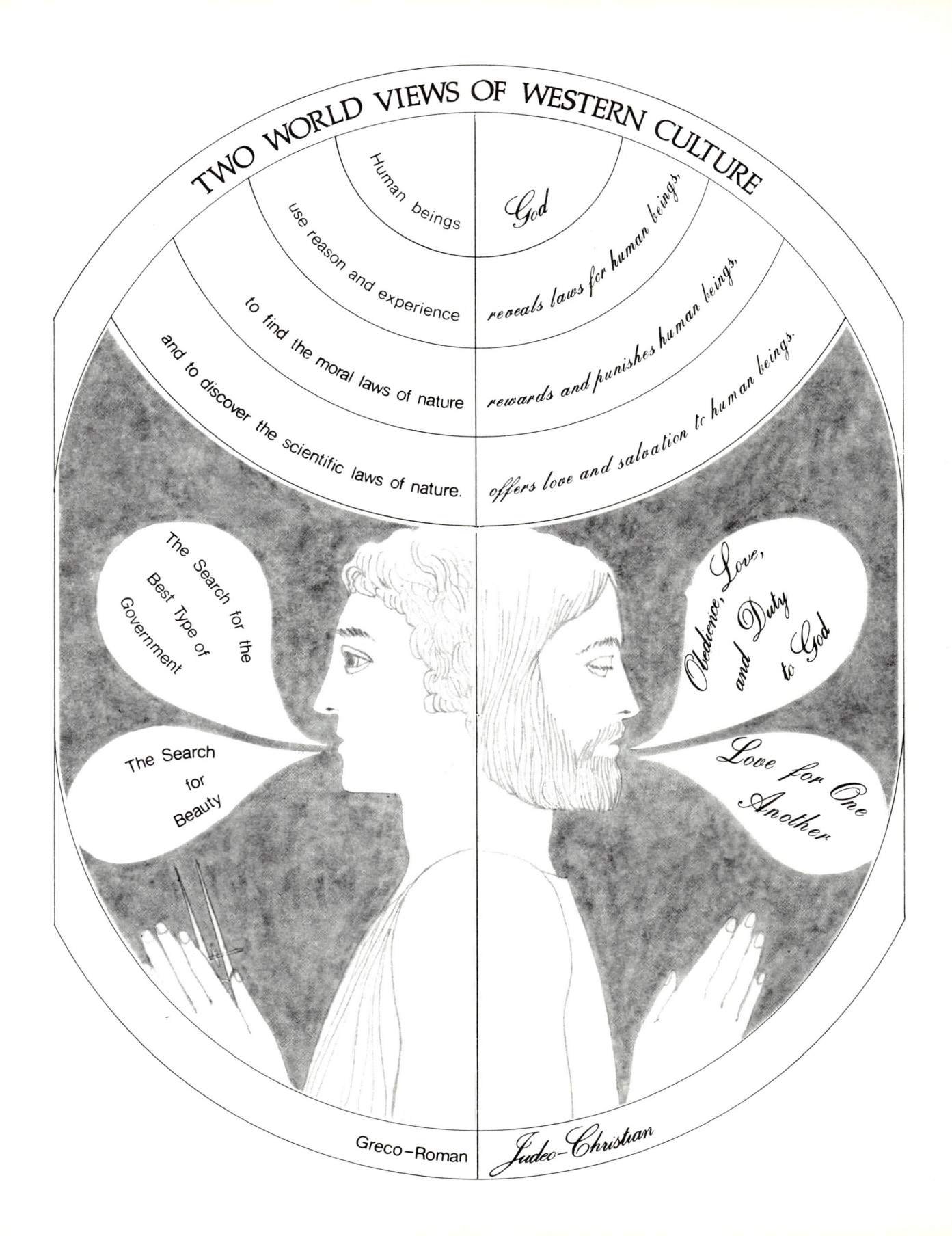

TWO WORLD VIEWS OF WESTERN CULTURE

Human beings / God

use reason and experience / reveals laws for human beings,

to find the moral laws of nature / rewards and punishes human beings,

and to discover the scientific laws of nature. / offers love and salvation to human beings.

The Search for the Best Type of Government

The Search for Beauty

Obedience, Love, and Duty to God

Love for One Another

Greco-Roman / Judeo-Christian

A Look Forward to Western Civilization: Two World Views

In a later chapter we shall see how civilization grew once more in Western Europe. At that point we shall notice something that made Western cultures unlike most (perhaps all) earlier cultures.

People in Western cultures had to live with *two quite different world views*. One world view was *Greco-Roman*. It was *naturalistic* and *humanistic*. It led people to look at nature and human life to understand the world. The Greeks and Romans were scientific. They searched for the *laws of nature*. The Greco-Roman world view also stressed the power of the human mind. It believed that humans—with knowledge—could control their societies and their lives. It was interested in politics, government, and human laws.

The other Western world view was *Judeo-Christian*. This world view led people to look to God for guidance and understanding. It saw human beings as weak and often unhappy. It did not think that humans could make their own laws. It did not believe that humans could make good and lasting societies or governments. To the Judeo-Christian view, faith in God was far more important than using our minds to solve our problems.

A ● Look at the picture "Two World Views of Western Culture" (page 266).
1. Tell about the difference between the two world views.
2. Why would it be hard to live with *both* world views?

After the fall of the Roman Empire in the west, the Judeo-Christian world view was very strong in Western Europe. Slowly, however, people turned again to the great writings and art of Greco-Roman culture. Since that time, Western cultures have had the "double world view."

B ● Some people think that the "double world view" makes Western civilized societies restless and changing. What do you think?

THE ROMAN REPUBLIC AND EMPIRE

Summary

Greek and Hellenistic culture passed on to Rome. Rome had begun as a small city-state in central Italy. Through discipline, hard work, and good technology, Rome soon conquered most of the Italian peninsula.

Roman government was at first a monarchy. Later the people of Rome revolted, and Rome became a republic—the first republic with a mixed government. Romans believed in the rule of law.

Roman government worked well until the end of the third century B.C. Then new conquests in north Italy, Carthage, and the Balkans created new wealth. The old values and habits of loyalty, strong family, hard work, discipline, and courage began to weaken. Rich people preferred to buy slaves or to hire other people to do things they used to do.

Cooperation between classes broke down. Many Romans became poorer. There were many riots and disorders. The rich tried to buy votes in the Senate and Assembly. After almost 100 years of trouble, Julius Caesar became military dictator. A group of senators killed him in 44 B.C. After a period of confusion, Caesar's nephew, Octavian, became ruler of Rome in 27 B.C. Octavian, or Augustus, was also a military dictator, but he made people believe he was restoring the old ways of the republic. He encouraged the arts and literature. He had many beautiful new buildings built in Rome and in the provinces.

During the first century A.D., Christianity began. It was based on the teachings of Jesus. He offered a way to heaven to all who would believe in him. Jesus' followers grew in number. For almost three centuries, Christians had to meet in secret. Finally, in 313 A.D., the emperor Constantine made Christianity legal.

Some emperors who came after Augustus were bad rulers. The army began to control the emperors. There were many barbarian attacks across Roman borders. There were shortages of goods and several plagues. All these things led to civil wars. People lost hope in the ability of the government to defend them.

These bad conditions encouraged more people to become Christians. Christianity offered more hope than the empire did. After the empire in the west collapsed, Christianity continued to grow. In the east, the Byzantine Empire went on until A.D. 1453. It kept alive both Greco-Roman and Judeo-Christian ideas.

Some Interesting Activities

1. On a map of southern Europe, the Mediterranean, and the Middle East, show the boundaries of the Roman Empire when it was at its greatest extent (about A.D. 117). You can get information from the map showing the empire of Augustus, A.D. 14 (page 257), but you must add the following:
    a. England (then called Britain), as far north as the border of Scotland
    b. Romania (then called Dacia)—north of the Danube River
    c. Iraq (then called Mesopotamia), the area between the Tigris and the Euphrates rivers
    d. Bulgaria (then called Thrace), the area northeast of Macedon
    e. part of Turkey (then called Cappadocia)

    When the empire was divided, the boundary between the western and eastern empires was roughly along 18° east longitude. Show this boundary and label it "Division of the Empire, Fourth Century A.D."

2. Dramatizations:
    a. Divide the class into two parts. One half will play the role of senators arguing in favor of accepting Julius Caesar as military dictator for life. The other half will oppose Caesar. Base your arguments on what you know of the later period of the Roman Republic.
    b. One student may play the role of a Roman campaigning for office (consul or tribune of the people) in the middle of the third century B.C. The audience should offer support or objections.
    c. The class may pretend they are Romans during the later empire (say the fourth century A.D.). They live in Gaul and work at specific trades. Romans will discuss barbarians, high taxes, a faraway government that doesn't protect them, obeying the emperor, and worshipping him as a god.

3. Rudyard Kipling's *Puck of Pook's Hill* has stories about English history. Three stories are about a Roman officer on the Roman Wall that was built to keep out the barbarians who lived in what is now Scotland. The stories are "A Centurion of the Thirtieth [Legion]," "On the Great Wall," and "The Winged Hats." Read and report on the stories.

THE ROMAN REPUBLIC AND EMPIRE

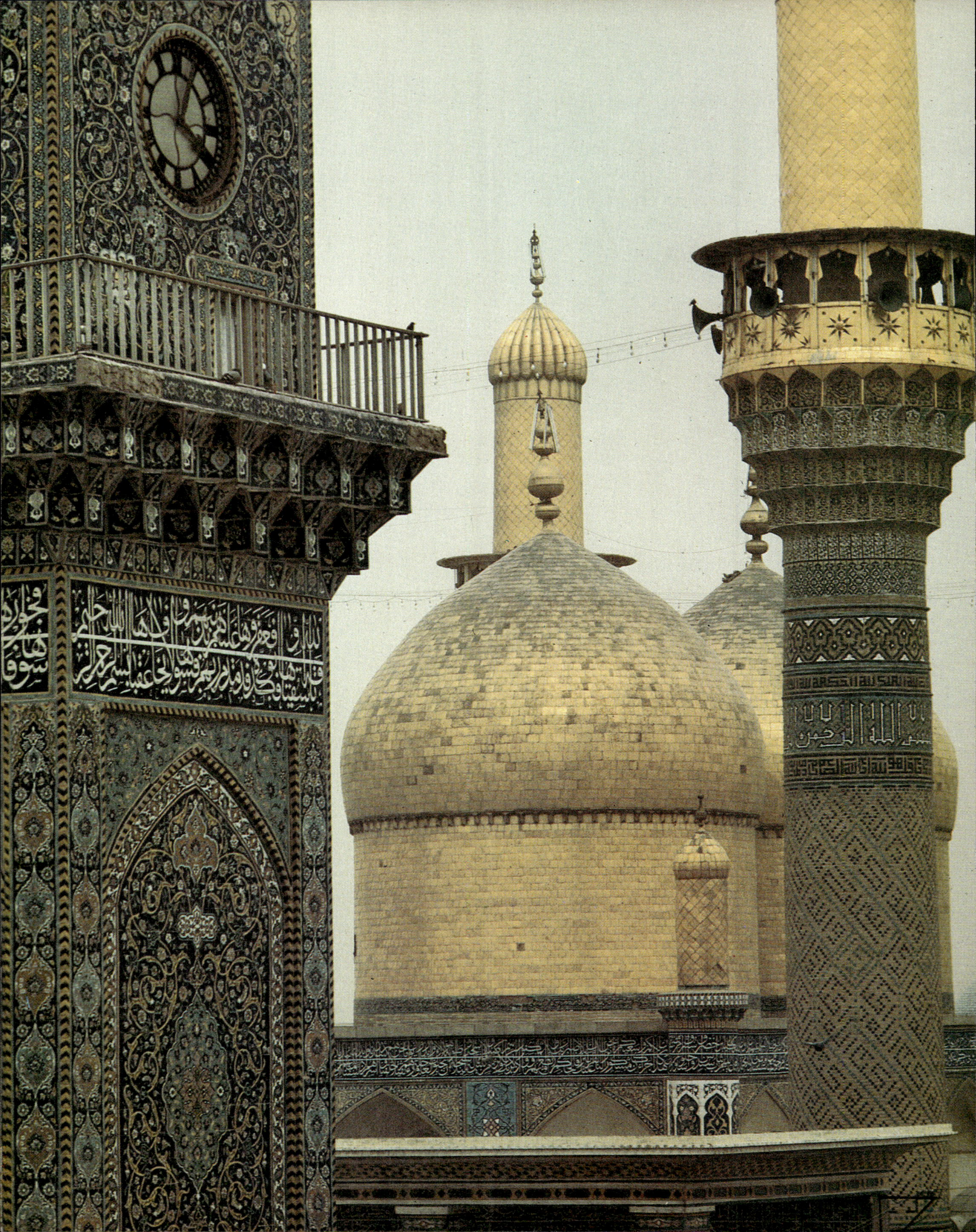

CHAPTER 10

Islam and the Arab Empire

About 100 years after the end of the Roman Empire in the west a prophet was born in Arabia. His name was *Muhammad* [mů ham′ əd]. He taught a religious faith that is called **Islam.** Islam became the religion and world view of many people in the Middle East. From this area, Islam spread to other peoples in Asia, Africa, and Europe. Today Islam is one of the world's great religions. People who follow Islam are called **Muslims**.

A ▶ What is the name of the religion started by Muhammad?
B ● Look at the map "The Muslim World Today" (page 273).
   1. In which areas of the world is Islam the main religion?
   2. Find Mecca. This is where Muhammad was born. It is the holy city of Islam.
   3. Notice how Islam spread west, south, and east over land. How might Islam have come to Indonesia and Malaysia?

The Arab Bedouin and the Land of Arabia

The Arabs were a group of peoples who had learned to live in a hard environment. They lived on the Arabian peninsula. This peninsula is south of Mesopotamia. Arabia is a hot land. Most of it is desert. During the summer months some areas of Arabia have temperatures as high as 49° C (120° F).

Arabia has some of the world's driest land. Sometimes years pass without a drop of rain. This land is cut by many *wadis* [wä′ dēz], or dry river beds. Water flows in them only after rain. Most of the time, the Arabs can use the wadis as roads for crossing the desert.

In the northern half of the Arabian peninsula, hot winds sweep across rocky ground. The desert surface is mostly stones and pebbles. There are a few thin patches of grass. Farther south, the desert is sandy. The winds blow the sand into hills that look like huge waves. These hills of sand are called sand dunes. Some sand dunes may be as high as 210 meters (almost 700 feet). During storms, the sand is blown into the air. People caught in sandstorms can hardly see or breathe. Whole armies have been lost and buried in the sand.

A ● Look at the map "Annual Rainfall of the Arabian Peninsula" (page 274).
1. How can you tell that most of the peninsula is desert?
2. Which parts might have some rain-watered agriculture?
3. Where are the hilly regions?
4. How much of Arabia is in the tropics? Would you expect Arabia to be very hot as well as very dry? Explain.

B ★ Look at a map of the Arabian peninsula today. Find the following nations: Saudi Arabia, Iraq, Jordan, Oman. What other Arab states are in the region? There are also Arab nations along the coast of North Africa. Name some of them.

For many centuries most Arabs lived the life of *nomads*. They were called **Bedouin** [bed′ ü ən] or "people of the tent." They herded camels, sheep, and goats. They lived in tents made of camel hair or wool. Their clothes were also made of camel hair or wool. They wandered about Arabia looking for grass and

The Muslim World Today

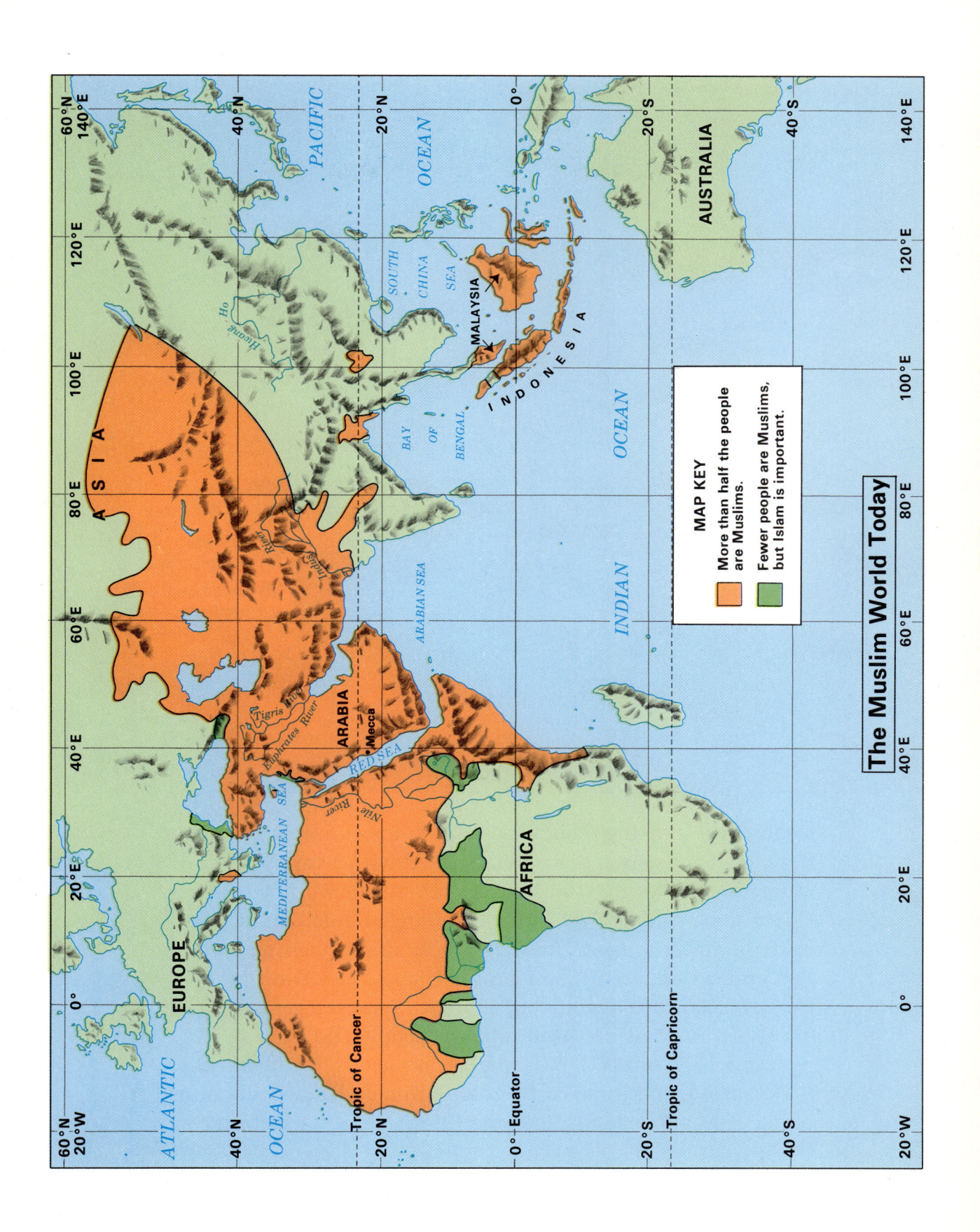

MAP KEY
- More than half the people are Muslims.
- Fewer people are Muslims, but Islam is important.

Annual Rainfall of the Arabian Peninsula

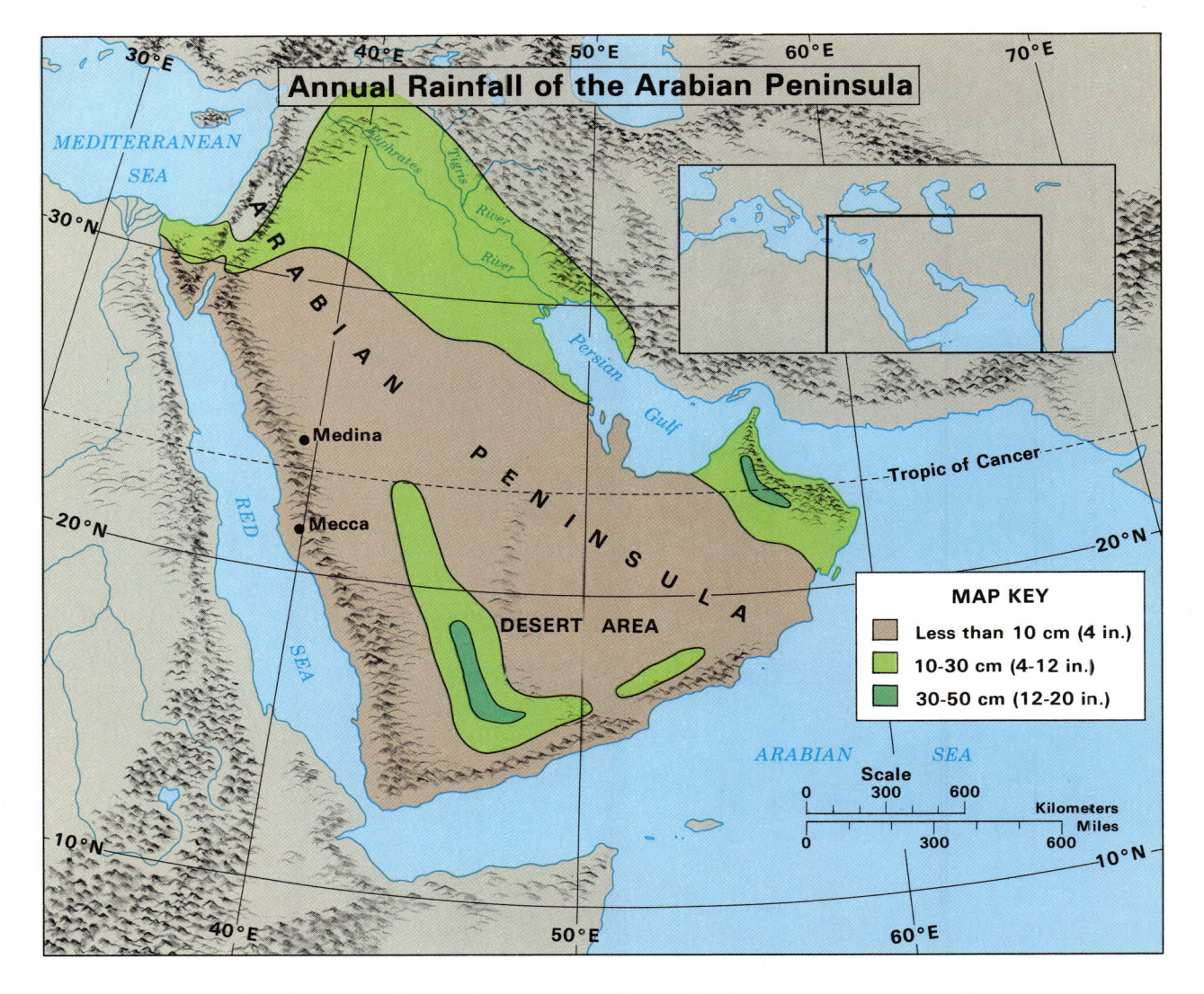

scrub, always taking their animals with them. Sometimes they stopped at an **oasis,** a place in the desert with a supply of fresh water. The water may be from a spring or a well.

In some parts of Arabia there is enough rainfall for farming. In these areas farmers grow grain and sweet-smelling spices. The farmers may send their products away by *caravan* [kar′ ə van]. A **caravan** is a group of people who travel together across the desert. Camels are used to carry people and their goods.

Around A.D. 600, caravans carried goods for merchants. They carried ivory from Africa, rubies from India, and silk from China. The merchants sold these things in Persia or Egypt or

274 THE GROWTH OF CIVILIZATION

Syria. When the caravans crossed the desert, they stopped at oases. That is how some oasis towns became rich. The most important of these towns was *Mecca*. Mecca was a town built at an oasis. Another town built at an oasis was *Medina*.

Before the time of Muhammad most Arabs were not civilized. Their societies were tribes that often fought with one another. Most of the people were animists in religion. They worshipped "spirits" in stones and trees. There were, however, some people in Arabia who followed Judaism and Christianity.

Muhammad the Prophet

Like Judaism and Christianity, Islam is a *revealed religion*.

A★ What is a *revealed religion*? How was God revealed to Jews and Christians?

The Muslims say that a dazzling light shone in the sky when Muhammad was born. They tell many stories about strange events in Muhammad's childhood. Let us read two of them.

A Visit from Two Angels

One day, when Muhammad was four years old, he was tending sheep. Suddenly two angels flew down. They grabbed the boy and laid him on the ground. Then they opened his stomach. From his heart they plucked out a black drop. Then they washed him with snow. All evil was thus washed away from Muhammad. From that time on, everyone knew that he would do great things.

A Monk Gives a Feast

When Muhammad was only 12 years old, he traveled to Syria with a caravan. For weeks the caravan had been moving over dusty desert trails. The animals, traders, and slaves were ready for a rest.

Soon the caravan was to pass the house of a Christian monk known for his wisdom. No one expected help from this holy monk. He had never before paid any attention to thirsty Arabs. As the caravan passed the monk's house, he called out to it. "Stop!" he said, "I want to entertain your caravan. Please be my guests at a great feast." He invited the slaves and children. Imagine the merchants' surprise!

Young Muhammad received a special invitation. The monk said that he had seen a strange thing as Muhammad rode by. A tree had lowered its branches! The monk wanted to question the boy.

The monk was amazed when Muhammad answered his questions correctly. Then he examined Muhammad's body. Between the boy's shoulders he found the mark of a prophet. The monk promised that the boy would do very special things.

Muhammad grew up in Mecca. He learned about Judaism and Christianity when he went with traders across the desert to Medina and to the Red Sea. He might even have traveled as far as Palestine.

When Muhammad was 40 years old, he came to believe that he was a prophet. He said that an angel came to him. The angel told him that there was one God, whose name was *Allah*. The angel also told Muhammad that he was God's prophet.

Muhammad set out to preach the message of God. He wanted the Arabs to end their worship of many gods. He hoped that Jews and Christians as well as Arabs would join him. Soon he found that people did not like his teaching. People preferred the old ways. In A.D. 622, Muhammad had to flee from Mecca. He went to Medina. There he found many followers.

Muslims kneel, facing toward Mecca, and pray to Allah. No matter where they may be, Muslims offer prayer five times a day.

Following his flight to Medina, Muhammad won success as a religious leader. From that time his teaching spread. That is why Muslims say that the flight from Mecca was the great moment in the history of Islam. The word for "flight" in Arabic is **Hegira** [hi jī′ rə]. Muslims begin counting the years of their calendar from the year of the *Hegira.* A.H. 1 is A.D. 622.

Muhammad was head of the Muslim community. He had to become a political leader as well as a religious leader. His followers agreed to live by the messages that he received from Allah. They agreed to follow laws that were based on these messages. The laws controlled every part of a Muslim's life. Muhammad told the Muslims when to pray and when to *fast* (not eat). He made rules for marriage. He made rules for carrying on business.

From Medina, Muhammad began to make war on people who refused to accept his message. He conquered Mecca, the city that had forced him to flee. When he died in A.D. 632 (A.H.11), he had united most of the tribes of Arabia.

The Controlling Ideas of Islam: Five Duties

Islam is the Arabic word for "submission" or "obedience." It means "submission to God, or Allah."

During his life Muhammad had many messages from God. After his death, the messages were collected. They became the Holy Scriptures of Islam, called the *Koran.* The **Koran** is the law for Muslims. According to the Koran there are five important duties for Muslims. They are called the Five Pillars of Islam.

The first duty is *faith.* Followers of Islam must believe in one God, Allah, and must accept Muhammad as God's prophet.

The second duty is *prayer.* Every Muslim must pray five times a day. Muslims do not have priests. They believe that God is very close to people. Each Muslim therefore prays directly to God, always facing Mecca. Muslims know when it is time to pray when they hear a man singing loudly, "God is most great" and "Muhammad is the prophet of God." The man sings this from a tower of a *mosque,* which is a Muslim place of worship.

ISLAM AND THE ARAB EMPIRE

Pages from a thirteenth-century handwritten copy of the Koran

A Muslim reads the Koran, the sacred writings of Islam.

Each year Mecca is visited by thousands of Muslim pilgrims from all over the world. One ritual is to circle the Kaaba (Black Stone) seven times.

The third duty is to *give to the poor and to be kind to others.*

The fourth is *fasting.* For one month each year, Muslims may not eat or drink from sunrise to sunset. This is the holy month of *Ramadan.* The month ends with a great party.

The fifth duty is a *pilgrimage.* Every Muslim must try to go to the holy city of Mecca at least once. The city is important to Muslims because of its association with Muhammad. It is also the home of a great black stone, the *Kaaba* [kä′ bə]. Muslims believe the Kaaba was given to Abraham by the Angel Gabriel.

Other Controlling Ideas of Islam

Before Muhammad, the Arabs were divided into many tribes. Muhammad said that all Muslims must join together. That, he said, was the will of Allah. Muhammad taught that all Muslims were brothers in faith.

ISLAM AND THE ARAB EMPIRE

Muhammad taught also that it was the duty of Muslims to fight the enemies of Allah. This is called a *holy war*.

Like Christianity, Islam teaches about heaven. God will reward faithful Muslims by taking them to heaven. Like Christianity, Islam also teaches that people are equal before God.

A▶ How did Muhammad unite the Arabs?
B● See if you can compare Islam and other world religions. Use the box "Questions about Controlling Ideas" (page 151).
   1. How would a Muslim answer these questions?
   2. Is Islam *monotheistic*? What other world views that you have studied are monotheistic?
   3. In what ways is Islam similar to Judaism and Christianity? Look at the five duties of Muslims. How close are they to Jewish and Christian ideas of duty? In what ways are they different?

The Spread of Islam

By the time Muhammad died, the Arabs had become united for the first time. They were full of faith. They had a duty to fight the enemies of Allah.

Muslims chose Abu Bekr to succeed Muhammad as their leader. He was called the *caliph* [kā′ lif], which means "successor." The Arabs now set out on a series of holy wars. Their targets were the empires in the Middle East and on the shores of the Mediterranean. Within a hundred years the Arabs had conquered a vast area. It was a new empire: the Arab Empire.

A▶ Why did the Muslims fight the enemies of Islam?
B● Look at the map "The Arab Empire, A.D. 632–732" (page 281).
   1. Had this area ever been in one empire before?
   2. Did the Muslims conquer the Persian Empire? Did they conquer the Byzantine Empire?
   3. What parts of Western Europe were in the Arab Empire?
C● Would you say that the Arab conquest was another case of barbarians attacking civilization?

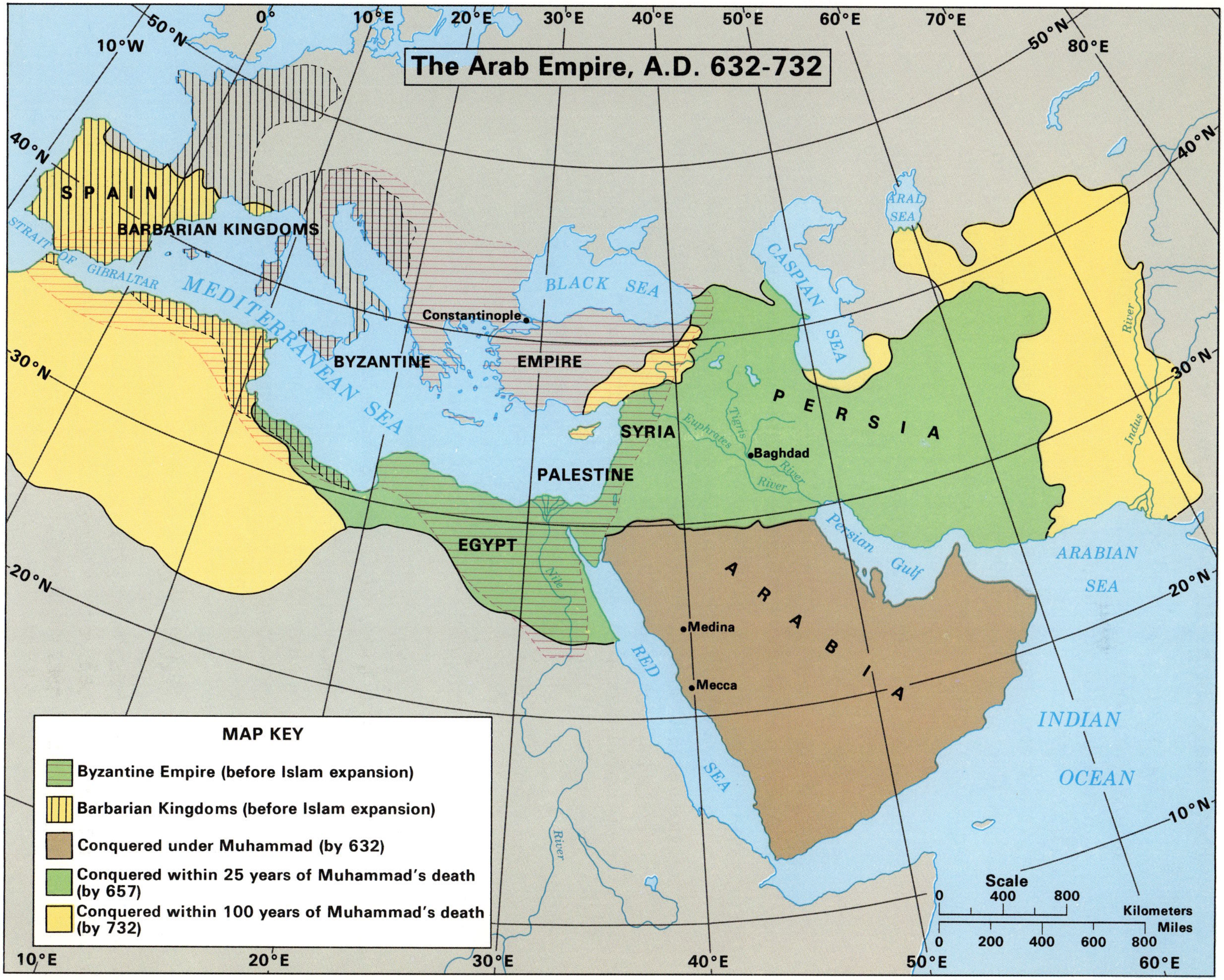
The Arab Empire, A.D. 632-732
MAP KEY
Byzantine Empire (before Islam expansion)
Barbarian Kingdoms (before Islam expansion)
Conquered under Muhammad (by 632)
Conquered within 25 years of Muhammad's death (by 657)
Conquered within 100 years of Muhammad's death (by 732)
SPAIN
BARBARIAN KINGDOMS
STRAIT OF GIBRALTAR
MEDITERRANEAN SEA
BYZANTINE
EMPIRE
Constantinople
BLACK SEA
CASPIAN SEA
ARAL SEA
PERSIA
SYRIA
PALESTINE
EGYPT
Nile
Baghdad
Euphrates River
Tigris River
Persian Gulf
ARABIA
Medina
Mecca
RED SEA
ARABIAN SEA
INDIAN OCEAN
Indus River
River
Scale
0 400 800 Kilometers
0 200 400 600 800 Miles
10°W
0°
10°E
20°E
30°E
40°E
50°E
60°E
70°E
80°E
50°N
40°N
30°N
20°N
10°N

How the Caliphs Ruled the Empire

The Muslims did not have an easy time choosing caliphs to follow Abu Bekr, the first caliph. Different groups wanted different men to be caliphs. Abu Bekr died of natural causes. Three of the next four caliphs were murdered!

The early caliphs were chosen for more than their leadership. They were chosen for their holiness, too. They were more concerned with religion than with politics. The second caliph, for example, was very strict. Many Muslims feared him. Muhammad himself had once told this man, "If the Devil himself saw you coming down the street, he would dodge into a side alley."

As time went on, the caliphs began to think more about politics and less about religion. They had to. They now had the problems of ruling an empire. Muslim law was still based on the Koran. It was still based on the example that had been set by Muhammad. Power, however, belonged to the caliph. Later caliphs became proud. They used power as they pleased. These caliphs believed they were more than Muhammad's successors. They believed that they were the "shadows of God on earth."

Here is a story about one caliph. It will give you an idea of how much power he had. Notice that he is called a king. This story is from *The Tales of the Thousand Nights and a Night.* This work is a famous collection of stories often called *The Arabian Nights.*

The Story of Queen Scheherezade

In the name of Allah, the Compassionate, the Merciful, Creator of the Universe, Who has raised the Earth without Pillars. . . .

Long, long ago there lived a king who was married to a queen as beautiful as the sunrise. The king and queen loved each other very much—or so the king thought. But one day he discovered that the queen's sweet smiles hid a heart full of poison. She was plotting to murder him and marry another man. When the king found out the truth, he was so angry that he killed the queen. Not only that, he took a vow to marry many times. And he vowed that, on the morning after each wedding, he would cut off the head of his new bride!

ISLAM AND THE ARAB EMPIRE

So it happened that many young girls lost their heads in this way. Finally, there were no pretty women left in the kingdom. All the pretty women who were left alive had been sent away to a healthier climate. The only ones left were the two daughters of the king's chief official, the Grand Vizier [vi zēr′]. The Grand Vizier had kept his daughters at home, for he could not bear to part with them.

One day the king called for his Grand Vizier. "I have decided to marry again," he said. "Find me a wife."

"But Master, all the young maidens have fled from your kingdom!" cried the Grand Vizier. "There are no wives to be found."

The king replied, "If I do not have a bride by nightfall—off with your head!"

What was the poor old man to do? Sadly, he walked home.

The Grand Vizier's older daughter was named Scheherezade [shə hār′ ə zäd′]. She was a girl as bright as she was beautiful. She had studied and thought very deeply. She knew a thousand different stories. When Scheherezade saw her father's long face, she guessed what the trouble was. "Do not worry, Father," she said. "I will marry the king. There is just one favor you can do. Early tomorrow morning, before the sun rises, send my sister to the palace. Tell her to bring us some sherbet cooled in snow. Then have her beg me to tell a story. Only make sure that she does not fail to come."

Scheherezade married the king. She was dressed in golden cloth scattered with jewels. A silken veil covered her hair. She looked lovelier than a garden in springtime. Everyone wept to think what would happen the following morning.

Early next day, Scheherezade's sister crept through the streets. She entered the palace and came to the royal chamber.

"I have brought you some refreshment, O King. But to help pass the time until sunrise, please have my sister tell us a story."

"That is a good idea," replied the king. "Will you entertain us, Scheherezade?" So Scheherezade began to tell a story. She finished it and was all ready to start on a new story, when the sun came up.

"O, my lord, I am sorry," she said. "This new story is even better than the first—but it is too late to begin it this morning."

The king answered, "Never mind. We will hear that story tomorrow."

That is how Scheherezade managed to live past the first night—and 999 nights after. Sometimes she would promise an even better

A Persian rug

An Arabian pitcher

Objects and buildings of great beauty — both in design and in decoration — were produced by the Arabs.

Detail from the interior of the Sheikh-lotfolah Mosque, Isfahan, Iran

story to come or would mix up two or three different stories—not finishing any of them.

On the thousand and first night, Scheherezade did something she had never done before. She did not leave enough time before sunrise to start a new story. Instead, she turned to the king:

"O King, for a thousand nights I have told stories to entertain you. Everyone knows that you reward even one simple joke with great treasures—yet I have never asked for any reward. Now I would like to claim mine. Allah does not ask you to fulfill an evil vow. Give up your wicked promise—and tell our poor father that both my sister and I will be safe."

"Scheherezade, my Queen," answered the king, "I have known for a long time now that I would never be able to fulfill my vow. I have seen how lucky I am to have such a good wife. And I have grown to love you very much. This day, everyone in my kingdom will know that, too."

So the king and queen lived happily together forever after.

A● What does this story tell you about the power of the Muslim rulers? About the place of women?

Arab Trade and Arab Civilization

The Arabs developed a new civilization very quickly. They were traders. Their ships sailed to the *Indies*. The **Indies** were what we call India, Southeast Asia, and Indonesia. Arab traders crossed the great desert of Central Asia to China. They brought spices, silk, cotton, and jewels from Asia. Arab traders crossed the Sahara, too. They traded for gold in West Africa. They sailed to East Africa for ivory, gold, and slaves.

Profits from trade gave the Arabs capital. With capital they built fine cities. They had irrigated farms and gardens. Their workers were skilled. They made weapons, carpets, leather goods, vases, metal goods, stone carvings.

A▶ Look at the pictures of Arab artifacts on page 285. These give you some ideas about the skill of Arab workers. Compare these artifacts with those from classical Greece and Rome. What big differences can you see? How do the differences tell us about the different world views of Greco-Roman and Islamic cultures?

THE GROWTH OF CIVILIZATION

B★ Why did Arab workers mainly use *geometrical* patterns?
C★ Look up the word *arabesque*. What does it mean?
D★ If you like stories about magic and adventures, read the "Voyages of Sinbad the Sailor" in *The Arabian Nights*. These stories were written down in Egypt in about the tenth century A.D. What do the stories tell you about the importance of trade in the Arab Empire?

With the growth of their power and wealth, the Arabs developed a class of learned persons and a high civilization. Learned Arabs took ideas, inventions, and technology from Greece, Persia, India, and even distant China.

Arab scholars translated many Greek and Indian writings into Arabic. By translating ancient books, the Arabs saved many of the great writings of the past from being lost. Soon the Arab scholars and inventors developed new ideas and technologies of their own. They learned about architecture from the Byzantines in Syria. They learned about paper-making from the Chinese. They also learned from the Chinese how to use *magnets* to make *compasses*. Soon the Arabs were developing their own styles in architecture, their own uses of paper, and their own skills in sailing the seas.

And the Arabs developed great things in mathematics. The Arab scholars learned that the Hindus of India had a special set of numerals. In the Middle East and in Greco-Roman civilization, mathematics always had been difficult. There had been no "place holder" or "zero."

E● Look at the chart "An Addition Problem in Roman Numerals" below. Why was arithmetic so difficult for the Romans?

An Addition Problem in Roman Numerals

M C L I V	(1154)
D	(500)
X C V I I I	(98)
M C M L X X	(1970)
X C	(90)
= M M M D C C X I I	(3812)

ISLAM AND THE ARAB EMPIRE 287

The Arabs adopted the Indian numerals. In Indian mathematics, there were nine numerals and a place holder called *sifr* [sif'ər]. *Sifr* means "empty." We get our word *cipher* (zero) from this circle or dot called *sifr*. The Arabs, too, used the *sifr* as a place holder.

- **F ▶** Look at the box "Hindu and Hindu-Arabic Numerals" (page 289). Why did *sifr* make arithmetic much easier? What number is shown on the right?
- **G ★** The Arabs also invented the mathematical science called *algebra*. What is algebra?

Learned Arabs also got many ideas from Greek philosophers. Arabs, too, looked for the "laws of nature." They had medicine based on scientific study. They began the science we call *chemistry*. The Arabs also knew about powerful *magnifying glasses*. They used these to study nature.

- **H ★** How do scientists use powerful magnifying glasses, or *microscopes*, to study nature? How do doctors use microscopes to find out about illnesses?

The Arabs also learned about **astronomy** [ə stron' ə mē], the study of the stars and planets. They built many buildings and instruments for looking at the stars. They knew how to measure the *angle* of the sun and the stars. From earlier thinkers, Arab scientists learned that the earth was round. This was 700 years before Columbus sailed west across the Atlantic.

In medicine, the Muslims knew about many things that we think are modern. They used surgery to fight diseases such as cancer. They had hospitals and even traveling clinics. Muslim doctors knew that disease was not the work of devils. They knew it had natural causes.

To choose the spot for a new hospital in Baghdad, one Muslim doctor had a good idea. He hung pieces of raw meat in different parts of the city. Then he watched to see in which place the meat rotted last of all. That is where he built his hospital.

- **I ●** Why did the Muslim doctor choose that place?

THE GROWTH OF CIVILIZATION

Hindu and Hindu-Arabic Numerals

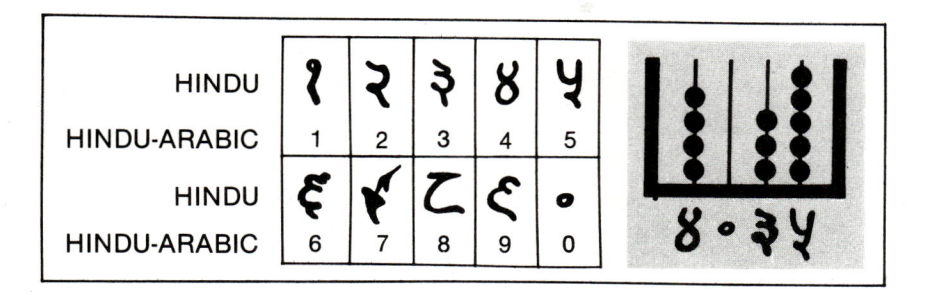

HINDU	۱	۲	۳	४	५
HINDU-ARABIC	1	2	3	4	5
HINDU	६	७	८	९	०
HINDU-ARABIC	6	7	8	9	0

Arab Culture Comes to Spain

Arab influence spread far beyond the Middle East. The Arabs ruled parts of Africa. They even ruled one part of Europe. That was Spain. The Muslims stayed in Spain for almost 800 years. In Spain, Islamic art and architecture are called *Moorish*—from the Muslim group known as Moors. Some Spanish Muslims studied and wrote about Greek philosophers. They tried to combine the Greek learning with their own faith in Allah.

The Arabs also helped Spain to become a great center of wealth. The Muslims brought orange trees and sugar cane to Spain. They taught the people new ways to irrigate the soil. They started some important industries. Among these were industries that produced steel, leather, paper, and cloth.

A● Were the changes just described economic or political? Do you think the Arab invaders helped Spain or hurt it? Explain.

B● What happened in Europe after the fall of the Roman Empire? Which do you think had the richer culture at this time—Muslim Spain or Christian Europe?

ISLAM AND THE ARAB EMPIRE

The Muslims brought many benefits to the Christians of Spain. Even so, the Spaniards hated the Muslim invaders and their religion. The Spaniards started a long fight to drive the Muslims out. In the end, the Spaniards won. Yet Muslim influence remained in Spain. From Spain, it passed to the rest of Europe. Because of the Arabs, Europe learned about many great ideas of the past.

C● Why might Spanish Christians have wanted to drive the Muslims out of Spain?

D● Is it true that the Arabs saved the great ideas of the Greeks for Europe? Explain your answer.

E★ Which of the following things or ideas reached Europe because of the Arabs? Which of these things were original inventions of the Arabs? Explain.

polytheism
chemical methods
Hindu-Arabic numerals
Christianity
the *sifr* (zero)
translations of Greek works
Roman books and poems

paper
Greek art
wares of skilled craftspeople
control of disease
the Old Testament
the idea that people should study the natural world

The Arab Empire Declines

We have seen that barbarians often copy civilization. No people, perhaps, ever built a great civilization so fast as the Arabs did. Yet the power of the Arab Empire did not last for long. By the eighth century A.D., Christian kingdoms were rising in Western Europe. Christians feared and hated Islam. The Arabs tried to conquer more of Western Europe, but they failed. In the end the Arabs were driven out of Spain.

It it interesting to know how Arab Muslims treated Christians and Jews in their empire. Arab Muslims tried to get Jews and Christians to become Muslims. But as long as Christians and Jews paid special taxes, they were allowed to keep their own religion. The Muslims thought that monotheistic religions were "on the same side" as Islam. Moreover, all three religions shared a respect for the Hebrew Scriptures.

The Court of the Lions in the palace of the Alhambra, located on a hillside at Granada, Spain. Note the lions guarding the fountain. This palace of Moorish kings and princes is a splendid example of medieval Islamic art in Europe.

A ● Is it wrong to force people to change their beliefs? Explain.

By the eleventh century, Arab civilization grew weak. This was only partly due to Christian attacks from Europe. One other cause of weakness was that the Arab Empire was governed by officials who would not, or could not, change the laws of Islam. (Those laws were meant for a simple desert society.) A more serious cause was a new wave of barbarians. These were *Seljuk* [sel jùk] *Turks* from Central Asia. The Turks had become Muslims. They had also become paid soldiers in the empire. In the end these soldiers took control of Arab civilization. The Islamic world was no longer mainly an Arab world. Islam continued to grow slowly, but the day of Arab leadership was over.

B ● Can you see any similarities between the fall of the Roman Empire and the fall of the Arab Empire? Explain.

ISLAM AND THE ARAB EMPIRE

Summary

About 100 years after the end of the Roman Empire in the West, a new religion began on the Arabian peninsula. For centuries, the Arabs had lived as nomads and believed in animism.

Then a caravan owner told of how an angel said that he, Muhammad, was a prophet and that he should preach the message of God. Muhammad hoped to get wide support for this message. In the beginning he had few followers. After the flight to Medina, however, the number of Muhammad's followers grew quickly.

Muhammad taught submission to the will of God. Every Muslim had to obey the Five Pillars of Islam and the laws of God contained in the Koran.

The Arabs went on to conquer a great empire in the Middle East. Wealth allowed for specialization. Islamic scholars made new discoveries in architecture, astronomy, and medicine. They also learned about other cultures and technologies. In this way, they found out about Greek writings and ideas, which they helped to preserve.

By the ninth century, the Arab domain was extended to North Africa and Spain. Learned Arabs brought to these areas the ideas of several civilizations.

In the eleventh century, Islamic civilization grew weak. Christian kings were reconquering parts of Spain. Islam was pushed out of Sicily. The Arab leaders of the Muslim empire would not change the laws set down in the Koran. Finally, a new wave of rough soldiers invaded the empire from Central Asia. These were the Turks. They later established a Muslim empire of their own.

Almost 300 years passed from the death of Muhammad until the end of the great Arab Empire.

Some Interesting Activities

1. Dramatization: One student can play the role of Muhammad preaching his message to the people of Mecca. Other students can argue against his ideas and against changing their religion.

2. Find out what the role of Muslim women in Arabia is today. Compare it with women's role in Muhammad's time.

3. Find as many pictures as you can of mosques in different sections of the Islamic world, such as Arabia, Morocco, Indonesia.

4. Read the tales of "Sinbad the Sailor" and "Ali Baba and the Forty Thieves."

5. Quite a number of words that we use in English are from Arabic. Many words begin with "al," the Arabic for "the." Look up these words in a dictionary or encyclopedia: *alcohol, alkali, algebra, algorism, alfalfa, alcove.* Which of these words are used in natural science or mathematics?

6. Some of the stars have Arabic names: *Betelgeuse* means "shoulder of the giant" (Orion). See if you can find out the meaning of *Aldebaran, Algol, Altair, Deneb, Rigel.* Can you find them on a star chart (map of the night sky)?

7. Islam is today divided into *Sunni* [sün′ ē] and *Shi'a* [shē′ə] Muslims. Look up these words. Are most Muslims *Sunni* or *Shi'a*? What kind of Muslims are most people in Iran? (Iranians are *not* Arabs.)

ISLAM AND THE ARAB EMPIRE

A bronze face mask from the kingdom of Benin. Bronze sculpture was a highly developed art among the people from the forest areas of West Africa.

CHAPTER 11

Civilizations of Africa

We have learned that Arab influence spread to Europe after spreading throughout North Africa. Arab influence also spread to other parts of Africa. It is mostly from Arab writings that we know about some civilizations of tropical Africa.

A▶ Where is tropical Africa?

Africa's Natural Environment

In land area, Africa is the second largest continent. Most of it lies between the Tropics of Cancer and Capricorn. Except on high mountains, Africa's weather is never cold. Yet Africa has many different kinds of natural environment. Some scientists think that the human race began in eastern Africa. As you read about some of Africa' environments, try to decide the one where the human race might have begun.

A▶ What is the meaning of *natural environment*?
B▶ What are the main parts of natural environment?

Most of Africa is a plateau (high plain) that ends in steep cliffs in many places. The eastern and southern parts of the plateau are higher than the rest. High mountains rise above the plateau in the east and in the northwest. The coastal lowlands are generally narrow plains. Most of Africa's rivers begin in the highlands.

C▶ On a map of Africa, find these physical features:
1. a high mountain near the equator
2. a mountain range in northwestern Africa
3. a large lake near the equator

D▶ Trace these rivers from source to mouth: Nile, Congo, Niger. Into what body of water does each river flow?

E● Why do you think that many of Africa's rivers have waterfalls?

The easiest way to get an idea of natural environment is to find out what plant life grows in a place *naturally.* This is the **natural vegetation.** Natural vegetation depends mainly on climate (temperature and precipitation).

Climate and plant life on the northern coast and on a small part of the southwestern coast of Africa are like those of Greece and Italy. Those coastal areas have a Mediterranean climate.

In western and central Africa, near the equator, is a tropical rain forest climate. Between the Mediterranean climate regions and the tropical rain forest region lie several different belts of climate and plant life. North and south of the tropical rain forest region are areas with a tropical savanna climate. Savanna is bordered by steppe, and steppe is bordered by desert.

F▶ Look at the map "Climate and Vegetation Regions of Africa" (page 297). Use the key to find each climate and plant life region. (Some regions are explained below.)

Tropical rain forest climate is hot and wet. The trees are tall. They are mostly broadleaf evergreens. The tall trees shut out sunlight. Few plants grow on the shady forest floor, but many vines grow and wind around the trees. Beautiful flowers, such as orchids, can also be found. Birds, monkeys, and snakes live in the forest. Crocodiles, hippopotamuses, and many kinds of fish live in the rivers.

Climate and Vegetation Regions of Africa

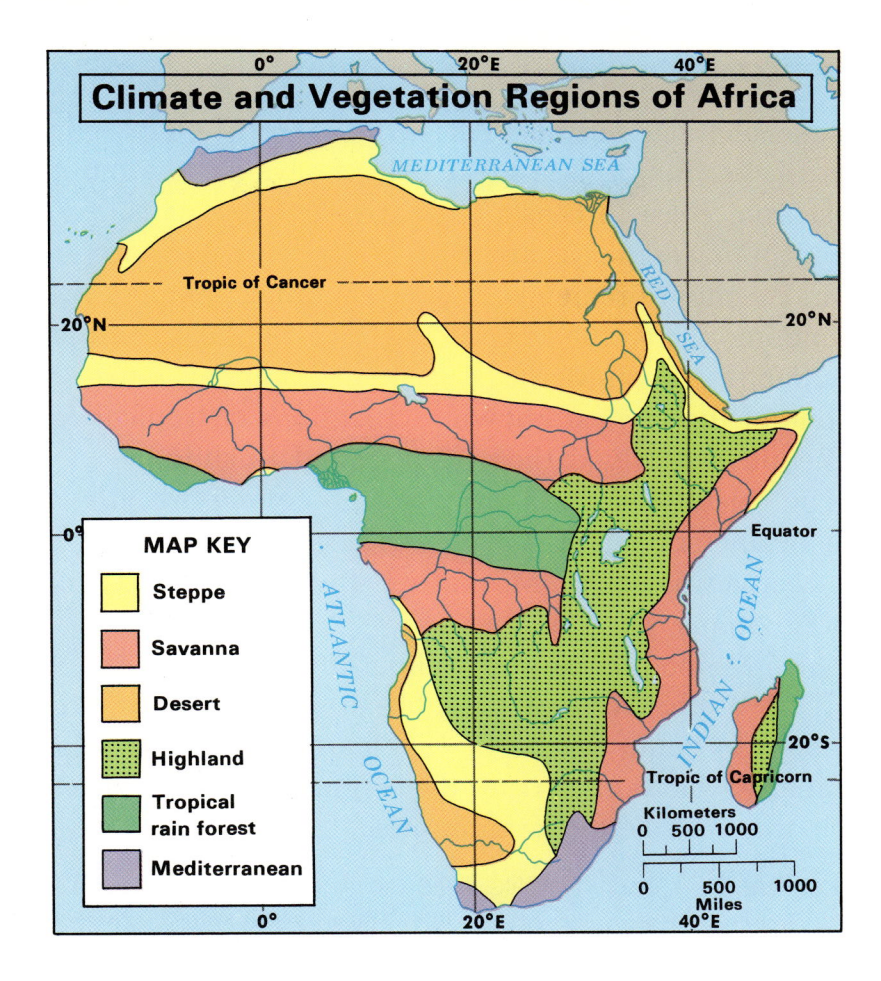

MAP KEY
- Steppe
- Savanna
- Desert
- Highland
- Tropical rain forest
- Mediterranean

Savanna is long grass, with small trees and bushes. The savanna climate is dry for part of the year. Many grass-eating animals, such as giraffes and zebras, live there.

Steppe is short grassland. The steppe climate is dry much of the year.

The *highland* region has Africa's highest mountains. It also has hills and plains. On the hills and plains, forests and grasslands are found. Grass-eating animals live there in herds. They are hunted by meat-eating animals, such as lions and leopards.

G • In what region do you think the first humans might have lived? Why?

H • In what regions do you think human societies might grow into civilizations? Why?

CIVILIZATIONS OF AFRICA

A Civilization in the Eastern Sudan

The Sahara, in northern Africa, is the world's largest desert. South of the Sahara is a great belt of savanna that stretches almost from coast to coast. This grassland area is called "the Sudan." Today at the eastern end of this area is a country called Sudan. We should remember that "the Sudan" and the *country* Sudan do not mean the same thing. It was in the eastern part of the Sudan that Kush-Meroë [kush mer′ ō ē′] began. Kush-Meroë was one of the earliest known civilizations of tropical Africa. The people who lived there were called Kushites.

The Kushites built their civilization along the Nile River, south of ancient Egypt. Egypt was a great civilization when Kush-Meroë was young. Most of what we know about it comes from Egyptians.

Kush-Meroë reached from about the Third Cataract (large waterfall) of the Nile to the present-day city of Khartoum. Khartoum is south of the Sixth Cataract. Kush-Meroë's first capital city was Napata. Later the capital was moved to Meroë, which was in a better farming area.

A ● Look at the map "The Nile Valley in Ancient Times" (page 299).
1. Find the cataracts of the Nile River. How many are there?
2. How would the cataracts affect travel on the Nile?
3. Find the area of Kush-Meroë and the cities of Napata and Meroë.
4. What present-day country includes the area of ancient Kush-Meroë?

The Egyptians called the lands south of the First Cataract of the Nile *Nubia*. Kush was part of Nubia. Meroë was the name of an area south of Kush as well as the name of a city in that area.

Nubia was rich in gold, ivory, and ebony. Egyptian writings tell us that a man in the service of the pharaoh traveled south in 2275 B.C. He brought back 300 donkeys carrying incense, ivory, ebony, gold, and hides. In raids on Nubia, Egyptians took people to use as slaves in Egypt. Later, from 1500 to 1000 B.C., Egyptian pharaohs conquered lands as far south as the Fourth Cataract of the Nile.

THE GROWTH OF CIVILIZATION

B ▶ What was an Egyptian pharaoh?
C ★ Find out what *ebony* is and how it is used.

After they were conquered by the Egyptians, the peoples of Kush began to follow many Egyptian customs. The Egyptian

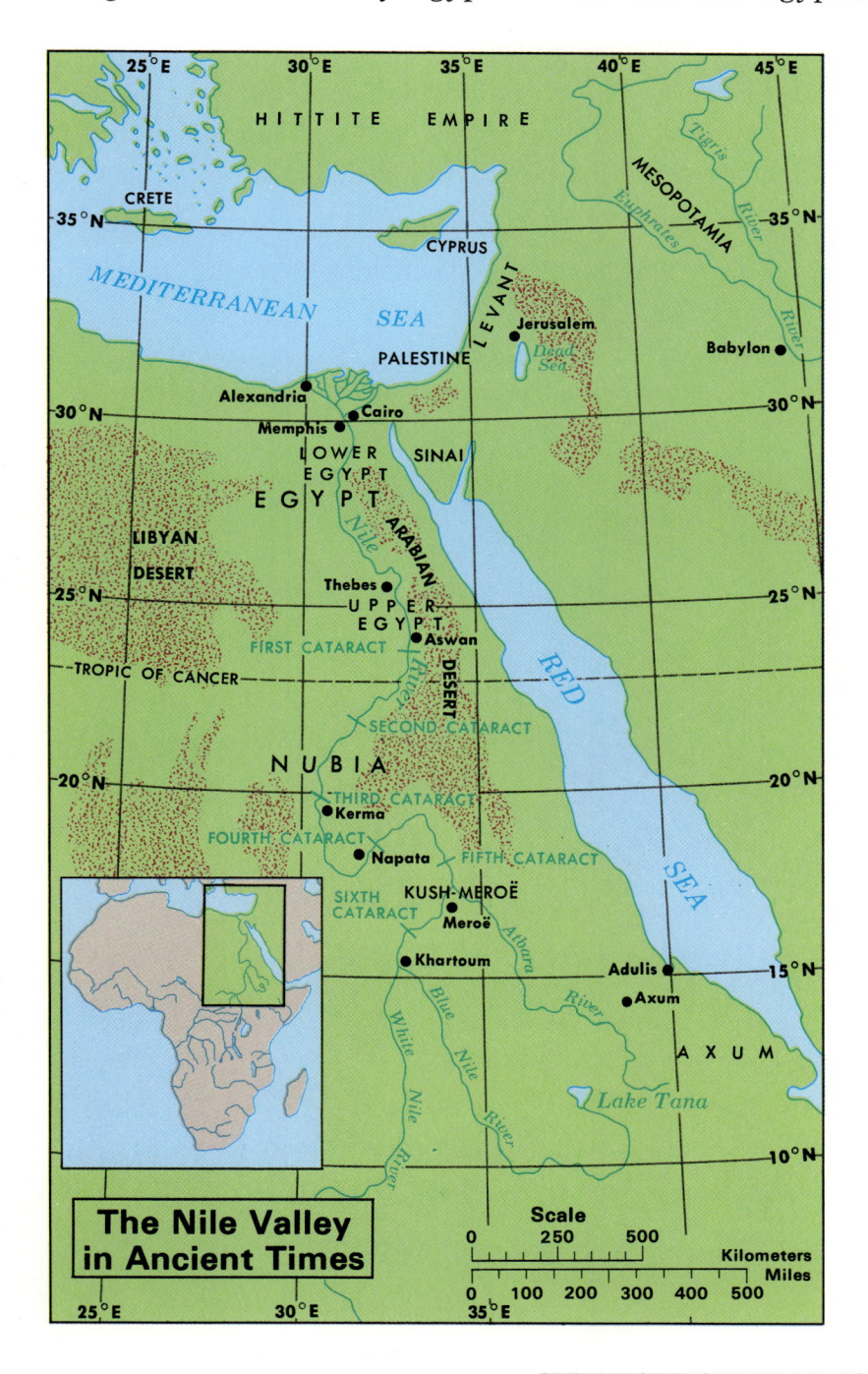

The Nile Valley in Ancient Times

CIVILIZATIONS OF AFRICA **299**

god Amon became one of the chief gods of Kush. The Kushites built great temples to Amon. They brought priests from Egypt to serve in them. They began to build great monuments to their dead, just like Egyptian pyramids. Like the Egyptians, the Kushites believed in *divine monarchy.* **Divine monarchy** is the belief that rulers are gods and so have divine powers. Divine monarchs were worshipped and feared by their people. The people believed that their rulers' actions decided such things as whether there would be a good harvest or whether it would rain.

D● How might the idea of divine monarchy help a civilization to grow?

Hatshepsut Temple at Dayr al-Bahri, Egypt, is a monument to Queen Hatshepsut. The queen held the title of pharaoh and ruled Egypt very effectively for 22 years — from 1503 to 1482 B.C.

After about 800 B.C., the great civilization of Egypt began to decline. Fighting between different groups in the society weakened Egypt from within. Foreign invasions weakened it from without. Egyptian civilization grew so weak that Kush was able to conquer Egypt. For about 100 years the kings of Kush ruled as pharaohs of Egypt. Then the Assyrians drove them out.

About a century later, the center of Kushite power moved south, to Meroë. One reason for this was that Meroë had iron ore and trees to use for fuel in smelting iron. Skill in ironworking was an important reason for Meroë's power. Even today visitors to Meroë can see big mounds of slag, the material left over from iron smelting.

From the third century B.C. to the first century A.D., Meroë was an important center of trade. It linked the Nile Valley and the Red Sea. Traders of Meroë traded the goods of the Sudan for goods from Arabia, India, and the Mediterranean area. Archaeologists have even discovered pieces of Chinese pottery in Meroë.

Meroë turned away from Egyptian culture. It developed its own forms of art, religious ideas, and writing. As Meroë began to develop its own writing, Meroitic writing began to replace Egyptian writing on public buildings. Scholars have not yet been able to read Meroitic writing. When they do, we will know a great deal more about Meroitic civilization.

In the first century A.D., Meroë's power began to decline. Another power had grown up in what is now Ethiopia. The name of the kingdom was Axum. Axum also knew how to work with iron. In about A.D. 350, Meroë fell to Axum's armies. Yet Meroë had lasting importance in African history. It was probably a link between the civilization of Egypt and the cultures in other parts of tropical Africa. From Meroë, the rest of Africa may have learned the valuable skill of ironworking.

E● The history of Egypt, Kush, and Meroë between c. 2000 B.C. and A.D. 350 are examples of culture contact. What were some results of this culture contact?

F● How does the history of these societies show the ebb and flow of civilization?

CIVILIZATIONS OF AFRICA

Kush-Meroë was a civilization of ancient history. Now we are going to look at some African civilizations that belong to a different period of history. We will learn about some African kingdoms of the *Middle Ages.*

The Middle Ages and Other Periods of History

The period from about A.D. 500 to 1500 is often called the **Middle Ages,** or the *medieval* [mē′ dē ē′ vl] *period. Medieval* is from Latin words meaning "middle age." The name *Middle Ages* was given to the period by European historians centuries ago. They thought that there had been only two great civilized periods. The first was Greco-Roman civilization, about 600 B.C. to A.D. 500. The second was Modern European civilization, from about A.D. 1500. These historians thought that time between these two great civilizations was uncivilized. It was in the middle. So they called it "the Middle Ages."

Those historians were wrong. In the first place, there have been many great civilizations. In the second place, Europe was *not* "uncivilized" from A.D. 500 to 1500. However, we still find it helpful to use the old name for the period.

A ▶ Why is the time from A.D. 500 to 1500 called the Middle Ages?
B ● Why might European historians three or four centuries ago make the mistake of thinking there were no civilized societies during the Middle Ages?
C ● Did the people in A.D. 501 *know* that they were starting a new period of history? Explain.

We must remember that periods of history are simply helpful ways of thinking about the past. They are not "real facts." If everyone agrees to use the same periods of history, much time and trouble can be saved. Periods of history are like weights and measures. It does not matter whether we use kilograms and grams or pounds and ounces. It *does* matter whether we agree on the *same* weights and measures.

302 THE GROWTH OF CIVILIZATION

The Main Periods of History

Name	Dates
Prehistory	c. 50,000 B.C.–c. 3500 B.C.
Ancient Civilization (or Ancient History)	c. 3500 B.C.–c. 600 or 500 B.C.
Classical Civilization (or Classical History)	c. 600 B.C.–c. A.D. 500
Middle Ages (or Medieval History)	c. A.D. 500–c. A.D. 1500
Modern Age (or Modern History)	c. A.D. 1500–the present*

*Note: Some historians think that another period should begin somewhere in the twentieth century. They call it the "Post-Modern" period.

D ● What would happen if we did not agree on weights and measures?

E ● Look at the box "The Main Periods of History" above, and answer these questions:
1. What big things do you remember about prehistory? What was the Neolithic revolution?
2. Why do we start ancient civilization about 3500 B.C.? What big change happened in Mesopotamia about that time?
3. What civilized societies can you name in the period of ancient civilization? What was the difference between a river valley civilization and a civilization in rain-watered lands?
4. What was the first (Western) classical civilization in the Mediterranean area? What civilized society in the Mediterranean area came to an end about A.D. 476?
5. During what period did the great Arab civilization develop? Do you think Arab historians would call this period the Middle Ages? Why or why not?

We will learn something about the Modern Age later in this book. But for now, we should remember that historians use the word *modern* in a special way. They do not mean "up-to-date"

CIVILIZATIONS OF AFRICA

when they say "modern." They mean "in the period since about A.D. 1500." For things that happened in the past 50 years or so, it is best to use the words **recent history.** If we want to speak about the present time, we can say "current events" or "in our own time."

F▶ What period of history are we living in today? How do you know?
G▶ When did the Modern Age begin? (When did the Middle Ages end?)

African Kingdoms of the Western Sudan

Long after the decline of Kush-Meroë in the eastern part of the Sudan, civilizations grew in the western part of the Sudan. In the Western Sudan, civilized kingdoms began in the Middle Ages.

There were three great kingdoms in the Western Sudan, from about A.D. 700 to 1600. These kingdoms rose one after the other. They were called Ghana [gä′ nə], Mali [mä′ lē], and Songhai [song′ hī].

Ghana, Mali, and Songhai were rich and powerful trading centers. What produced them and their high level of civilization? The answer has many parts. Part of the answer is natural environment. Part of it is trade and wealth. Strong political organization also played an important part. So did the spread of Islam. Let us see how the different parts of the answer fit together.

A▶ Look at the map "African Kingdoms, A.D. 700–1600" (page 305).
1. Find the Niger River and the Senegal River.
2. What were the three kingdoms of the Western Sudan?

B★ Today there are three African countries named Ghana, Mali, and Sudan. Find them in an atlas. Are any of them where the three medieval kingdoms were?

The natural environment of the Sudan helped civilization to grow. During the short rainy season, the savanna is green. At this time, grain and peanuts will grow. Most of the year, however, the savanna is dry and brown. Herds of cattle can feed on the savanna.

African Kingdoms, A.D. 700-1600

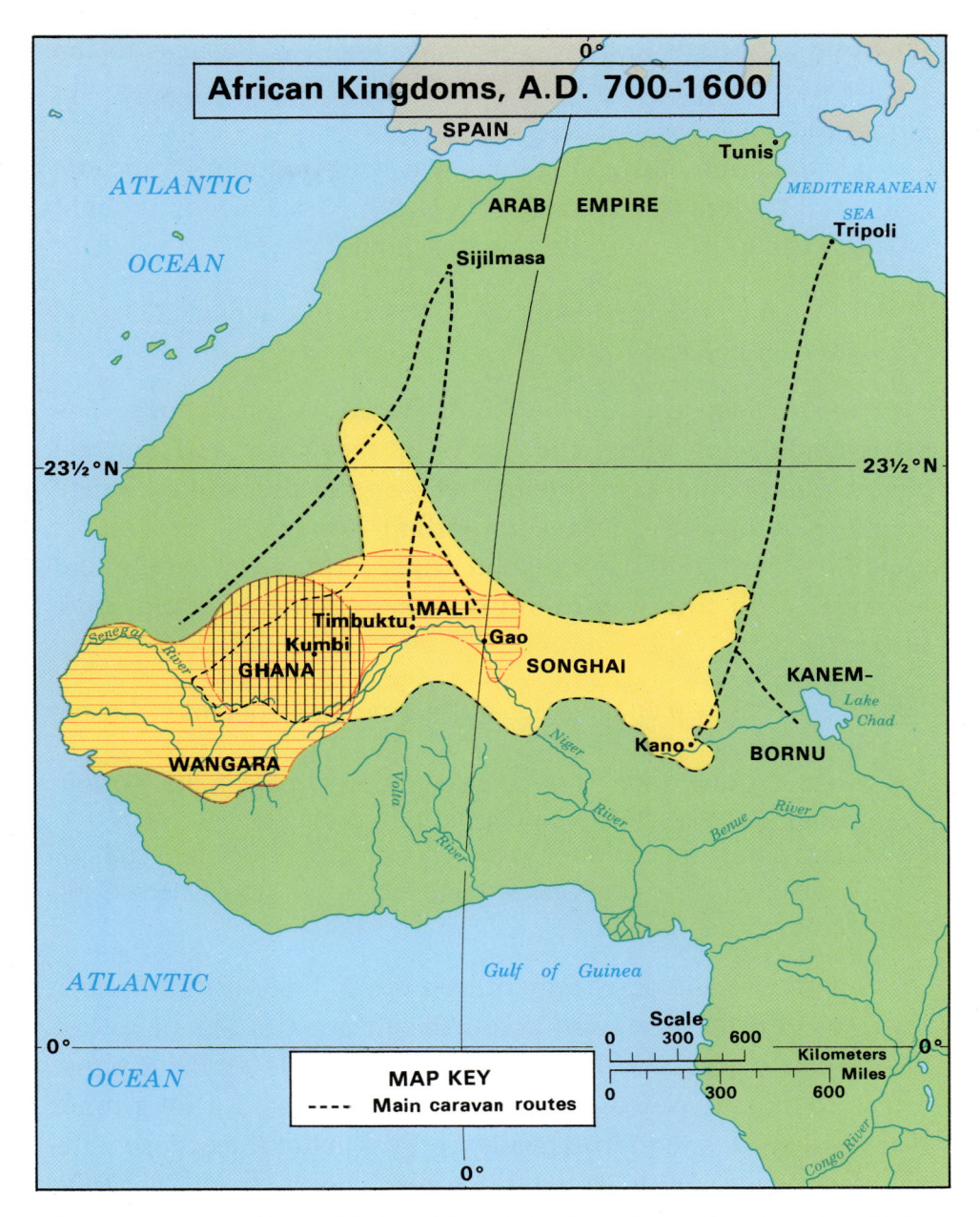

The kingdoms of Ghana, Mali, and Songhai followed one after the other. Mali was larger than Ghana. Songhai was larger than Mali. We do not know their exact boundaries.

The natural environment helped in other ways. To the north of the Sudan, the desert was a defense against enemies. To

CIVILIZATIONS OF AFRICA 305

the south, the rain forest was another defense. Because of the desert and the rain forest, the kingdoms of the Sudan were not easy to attack.

The location of the kingdoms was very important for trade. The chief traders were Arabs from North Africa. Trade brought wealth. Let us see how this came about.

C▶ On the map "African Kingdoms, A.D. 700–1600" (page 305), find the main caravan routes.

The African trading kingdoms began as settlements. The settlements were along the banks of the Niger and Senegal rivers. The people were able to travel on the rivers to exchange goods. There was another important advantage in a river location. The rivers were a good water supply for people and animals. With this water supply, the settlements could grow into cities. Slowly a trading economy developed.

D▶ Look at the map on page 305 again. Find the kingdoms of Ghana, Mali, and Songhai.
E▶ What physical feature lies between the kingdoms in the Western Sudan and the Islamic Empire in the north?
F▶ What rivers were important to the kingdoms of the Western Sudan?
G▶ About how far is it from Ghana to the Nile River? From Ghana to the Mediterranean Sea?

There was a good supply of iron ore in the Western Sudan. Iron was in use by the third or fourth century A.D. The people of the Sudan were able to make iron farm tools and weapons. These tools and weapons were strong and lasted a long time. Hoes and spades with iron heads were far better than those with wooden heads. With iron farm tools, people could produce more than enough food. They could farm more land. Then the land could support more people. The population could grow. Civilization could develop.

With iron weapons, the people of the Sudan were better able to defend themselves. A warrior with an iron spear could usually beat a warrior with a wooden spear. A group that knew how to make iron weapons could have iron spears and swords

THE GROWTH OF CIVILIZATION

for every warrior. Then powerful groups could fight and beat the weaker groups. More people and more land could be brought under the rule of a single group. Then strong central government could begin.

Using long poles, these men pry loose slabs of salt from a drying lake bed. In the Sudan, salt was so scarce that it was as precious as gold.

North African traders in search of ivory looked to tropical Africa, still one of the world's few sources of ivory. These ivory horns (from elephant tusks) were carved by artisans from a district in tropical Africa. The carvings represent scenes from everyday life.

Slabs of salt are for sale at a market in Mali. In olden times caravans of as many as 25,000 camels carried salt across the Sahara to the Sudan. Caravans are still used to transport salt.

Ghana and the Trade in Gold and Salt

Ghana probably started to develop in the second or third century A.D. At that time, nomads probably invaded the area and conquered the local people. About A.D. 700, the local people rebelled. They overthrew their nomadic rulers and were in power when the Arabs first appeared in the Sudan.

Arab merchants set up trading settlements in Ghana. Even before the Arabs came, there had been an important trade in salt and gold passing through Ghana. The gold came from Wangara, a region in the south of Ghana. The kings of Ghana controlled Wangara. The people of Ghana and Wangara needed salt. There was no natural source of salt nearby. Salt had to be brought across the Sahara all the way from North Africa. Gold from Wangara was used to buy this imported salt.

The exact location of Wangara was kept secret. Today scholars believe that it was near the Senegal River. The people of Wangara mined their gold to trade for salt. But the Wangara were shy about meeting outsiders. They traded for salt in an interesting way. We call it *silent barter.* This is how it worked.

First the Arab merchants would come to Wangara. They were led there by guides from Ghana. The Arabs would leave supplies of salt, cloth, and other goods on the riverbanks. They would beat a drum to signal the people of Wangara. Then the Arabs would go back a short way into Ghana.

After the Arabs were gone, the Wangara people would cross the river. Next to each pile of goods, they would leave a pile of gold. Then they would go back across the river, and the Arabs would return.

If the Arabs were satisfied with the amount of gold that had been left, they would beat the drum again. That showed that the trading was closed. If the Arabs were not satisfied, they would not beat the drum. They would not touch the piles of gold. Then the people of Wangara would have to leave more gold. All trading was done in this way. One side never met the other.

In this trading, salt and gold were of equal importance. Salt was mined by slaves in the North African region now called

CIVILIZATIONS OF AFRICA

Algeria. Salt was so valuable south of the Sahara that slabs of it were used as money.

A▶ On the map "African Kingdoms, A.D. 700–1600" (page 305), find the area where the Wangara people lived.

B▶ Why did the people of Ghana and Wangara trade gold for salt?

C● To us, salt is one of the cheapest goods, and gold is one of the most costly goods. Do you think the people of Ghana and Wangara in the Middle Ages had the same values? Why or why not? Why did salt matter so much to them?

The kingdom of Ghana itself did not contain either gold fields or salt mines. The kings of Ghana, however, controlled the caravan routes. All these routes went through Ghana. They connected with river routes in Wangara. The rulers of Ghana taxed all the gold and salt that passed through their land. Soon the rulers were very rich.

The kings of Ghana were powerful because of the people's religious beliefs. In Ghana, the people believed that the king was a god. They thought that they would suffer when the king was sick. They believed they would suffer if the king's power grew weak. Their religious belief helped the kings to keep their power strong. The powerful kings taxed the gold and salt carried through their land by traders. Money from these taxes was used to support large armies. With many soldiers at their command, the kings of Ghana could get even more power.

Ghana's capital was the city of Kumbi [kùm' bē]. Kumbi was really two cities. That is, it was both a royal city and a Muslim trading settlement. In the royal city was the king's palace—a fortress and several huts with rounded roofs, all enclosed by a wall.

About nine or ten kilometers (six miles) from the royal city was the Muslim trading settlement. It was a large city for its time. About 30,000 Arabs lived there in low stone houses. The Arabs built twelve mosques. The kings of Ghana allowed the Arabs to practice their religion freely.

Kumbi was the trading center of the empire. The market was crowded with cattle and sheep. Arabian horses were bought for use in Ghana's army. Sacks of grain and dried fruit

Arabs trading sheep and goats at a market

were sold, and so were pots of honey. Rolls of colorful cloth lay on the counters. Leather goods, ivory, copper, and pearls were offered for sale. Skilled workers made jewelry, weapons, pottery, and clothing. Everything was paid for with gold dust.

Kumbi also supplied slaves to Arabs and Europeans. Ghana made rich profits from the slave trade. In Africa, slavery was common. African slavery resulted mostly from tribal warfare. When strong tribes conquered weaker ones, captives were often used as slave laborers.

D▶ How did the people pay for goods?
E★ How was the slavery of black Africans in the New World different from early African slavery?

CIVILIZATIONS OF AFRICA   **311**

Muslim Influence and the Downfall of Ghana

The Arabs brought to Ghana the culture and ideas of Islam. The Arabs also brought learning and education. From the Arabs the people of Ghana learned writing, the use of money and credit, and Muslim laws. The people of Ghana were friendly with the Muslims, but they did not adopt the Muslim religion. Later African kingdoms did adopt Islam. After several centuries the ideas of Islam spread deeply into African culture.

The kingdom of Ghana lasted for almost a thousand years. Its downfall came in the eleventh century A.D. At that time it was attacked by nomads from the Sahara. These nomads were Berbers—poor but proud Muslims. The Berbers wanted a share in Ghana's wealth. Ghana held out against them for ten years. During those years there was fierce fighting. Finally Ghana was defeated. The kingdom was weakened, and many of the people were killed.

The Berbers did not stay in Ghana. Many small states then tried to gain control of Ghana. In the late twelfth century, law and order ended for a time in the Western Sudan. The caravan routes broke down. Trade became unsafe. The struggle for power lasted more than 100 years.

A ▶ Were the Berbers barbarians from Ghana's point of view? Explain.
B ● Do you think it likely that Ghana had been growing weak *before* the Berber invasion? Why or why not?

The winner of this struggle for power was the small state of Mali. Building on the ruins of Ghana, Mali created a kingdom that was even richer and more powerful. Mali's rise to power is the story of two great leaders—Sundiata [sun dē a′ tə] and Mansa Musa [mä′ sə mü′ sə].

Sundiata—the Founder of Mali's Empire

Toward the end of the twelfth century, a cruel and ruthless leader had arisen in the Western Sudan. He was Sumanguru [sü′ man gü′ rü], king of the Sosso people. Sumanguru wanted to gain the power that Ghana had lost. He began by capturing the city of Kumbi. He made slaves of many of its people and made them pay heavy taxes. Sumanguru's rule was so harsh that one group of Mali revolted against him. Led by Sundiata, this group defeated the armies of Sumanguru.

Sundiata became the first king of Mali. He is still honored as Mali's greatest national hero. After Sundiata defeated Sumanguru, he took over Ghana. New lands came under the rule of the kingdom of Mali. Under Sundiata, agriculture improved. The land once again began to yield many crops.

In many ways, the kingdom of Mali was like the kingdom of Ghana. Mali took Ghana's place in the gold and salt trade. Mali, too, gained wealth and power in this way. However, there was one important difference between the two empires. Soon after the Berber invasion, the people of Mali gave up their old religion. They became strong Muslims.

This is part of an old map showing Western Europe and North Africa. An Arab merchant is coming to trade with Mansa Musa.

CIVILIZATIONS OF AFRICA 313

A▶ What is the name of the Muslim religion?
B● For what reasons might the people of Mali have become Muslims?
C● How might the controlling ideas of Islam affect the lives of the people of Mali?

Under Sundiata, Mali rapidly became the most powerful empire in the Western Sudan. Still, it did not have a truly strong government and a system of law. It could not control the disorder and unrest in the Western Sudan. The golden age of Mali did not come until the rule of Mansa Musa, early in the fourteenth century.

The Reign of Mansa Musa

The high point of Mali's power came during the reign (rule) of Mansa Musa. He became *mansa* (king) of Mali in about 1307. During Mansa Musa's 25-year rule, the power of Mali spread to the Atlantic Ocean in the west and as far east as the city of Gao on the Niger River. It spread far into the Sahara in the north, and south to the edge of the rain forest.

A▶ Look at the map of African kingdoms on page 305. Find the kingdom of Mali.

Under Mansa Musa's rule, Mali's trade grew, especially the trade in gold and copper. Mali controlled gold-rich Wangara, as had Ghana. Mansa Musa also gained control of lands that were rich in copper. He opened up a major new trade route to Cairo in Egypt. He brought important trading cities into the empire. He set up a system of government and brought back law and order to the Western Sudan. He also brought back the system of taxes that Ghana had developed. The smaller states under the control of Mali paid taxes to Mali.

Mansa Musa was well known in Europe. In an atlas made in France, Mansa Musa is pictured holding a scepter and a gold nugget in his hand. On the map is written, "This Negro lord is called [Musa of Mali], Lord of the Negroes.... So abundant is the gold which is found in his country that he is the richest and most noble lord of all the land."

314 THE GROWTH OF CIVILIZATION

Mansa Musa was a great warrior and leader. He was interested in the arts and in learning. Mansa Musa's capital, Timbuktu, was famous for its wealth, its learning, and its university. There were also universities in Gao and in other cities. At these universities, Arab and Sudanese scholars wrote the *Tarikhs,* records of the events of the empire. They were written in Arabic, the language of Islam.

B▶ Why were Mali's records written in Arabic?

An Arab traveler who had lived in Mali described Timbuktu as follows:

Here are many shops of . . . merchants, and especially of such as weave linen and cotton cloth. And hither do the Barbary (North African) merchants bring cloth of Europe. . . . The inhabitants, and especially strangers there residing, are exceeding rich. . . . Here are many wells containing most sweet water; and so often as the river Niger overfloweth, they convey the water thereof by certain sluices [channels] into the

A fourteenth-century mosque at Timbuktu, Mali, built during the reign of Mansa Musa

The flute player — a bronze sculpture from Benin. Benin is also famous for its *terra cotta* (baked clay) sculptures.

town. Corn, cattle, milk, and butter this region [has] in great abundance: but salt is very scarce here; for it is brought hither by land from Taghaza which is 500 miles distant. . . . Here are [many] doctors, judges, priests, and other learned men, that are bountifully maintained at the king's cost and charges, and hither are brought [various] manuscripts or written books out of Barbary, which are sold for more money than any other merchandise.†

C ● What was the most costly merchandise (goods)? What does this tell you about the civilization of Mali?

†From Leo Africanus, *The History and Description of Africa Done into English* by John Pory (London: Hakluyt Society, 1896), as quoted in Roland Oliver and Caroline Oliver (eds.), *Africa in the Days of Exploration* (Englewood Cliffs, N.J.: Prentice-Hall, Inc., 1965).

Mansa Musa was a strong Muslim. He brought an architect from Egypt to design great mosques for the cities. Some of these mosques can be seen today. During Mansa Musa's reign, Islamic culture mixed with the native African culture. The result was a civilization marked by a strong feeling of law and justice. An Arab traveler told of his surprise at the absence of crimes in Mali. He said that travelers were as safe from bandits and thieves as people who stayed at home. He noted, too, that the Muslims of Mali paid close attention to their religious duties.

D▶ What are some duties of Islam?

More and more Africans made pilgrimages from Mali to Mecca. In 1324, Mansa Musa himself set out on a pilgrimage. It was a spectacular journey. In front of the king marched 500 slaves. Each carried a bar of gold. The royal company numbered 60,000 people. In the caravan, a hundred camels carried sacks of gold dust. That was money to be spent along the way. Mansa Musa's pilgrimage gave many people their first look at Mali's wealth and power. Mali was recognized as a great power.

E★ On a map of Africa and the Middle East, trace Mansa Musa's pilgrimage. From Timbuktu the caravan went to an oasis about 200 kilometers (124 miles) south of Tripoli, then east to Cairo. From Cairo the caravan went east and then south through Medina to Mecca. About how far is this route?

Other African Kingdoms

No civilized society lasts forever. Mansa Musa died in 1337. After that, the kingdom of Mali began to break up. It had become an empire as well as a kingdom. Perhaps Mali had grown too big for anyone but a very strong king like Mansa Musa to hold together. Peoples who belonged to the empire of Mali began to revolt, and nomadic peoples attacked the empire from the outside.

By the middle of the fifteenth century, a new power arose in the Western Sudan. It was the empire of Songhai, with its

A bronze head from Benin

capital at Gao. Timbuktu remained important in the Songhai empire. The power of Songhai reached as far as Lake Chad. Yet Songhai, too, fell apart. In 1591, barbarian invaders ruined Songhai. After that there came no more empires in the Western Sudan. Another kingdom in the Western Sudan, however, lasted until after the year 1800. It was Kanem-Bornu.

There were other African centers of civilization, farther south, on the Atlantic coast. These were in the tropical rain forest region of West Africa. They were called "forest kingdoms." Among them were Oyo, Ashanti, Dahomey, and Ife. Ife was the capital of the Yoruba people. Another was the kingdom of Benin, which lasted until late in the nineteenth century. Both Ife and Benin had great skill in bronze sculpture.

A ▶ Look at the map on page 305. Find Kanem-Bornu, Lake Chad, and the Gulf of Guinea.

B ★ Historians are still finding out more about medieval African civilizations. See what you can find out about one of the following kingdoms: Kanem-Bornu, Ashanti, Dahomey, Ife, Abyssinia (now Ethiopia).

An African Forest Kingdom

Benin probably began about A.D. 1300. It reached the height of its power in the fifteenth and sixteenth centuries. The Edo, as the people of Benin are called, have a myth about how Benin came to be:

A long time ago, Osanobua, the highest of the gods, decided to send his sons into the world. Osanobua said to his sons: "Each of you may take anything you desire into the world with you." Some of Osanobua's sons took gold and other material possessions. One took magical skills. But Osanobua's youngest son could not decide what to take. He thought and thought. Then a bird came and sat on his shoulder. The bird instructed him to take a snail shell with him into the world.

When Osanobua's sons arrived in the world, they found everything covered with water! The bird instructed the youngest son to shake his snail shell. When he did, sand fell out and spread out to form the land! Thus Osanobua's youngest son became the owner of the land. His older brothers had to come to him and barter their possessions in return for a place to settle. Osanobua's youngest son became the first *oba,* or king, of Benin. His brothers became the rulers of Ife and other forest kingdoms.‡

A▶ On the map of African kingdoms (page 305), find Benin.

Most people of Benin were farmers. They grew yams, rice, groundnuts, and peppers. It was trade, however, that made the kingdom of Benin grow and become rich. Benin traded with people who lived in what is now northern and central Nigeria. Benin supplied slaves, leopard skins, pepper, coral, and cotton cloth in exchange for copper and other goods. Beginning in the fifteenth century, Benin also opened up trade with Europeans on the Gulf of Guinea. Benin got firearms and other goods from Europeans in return for slaves, pepper, and palm oil.

B★ What is palm oil? How is it used?

‡Adapted from R. E. Bradbury, *The Benin Kingdom and the Edo-Speaking Peoples of Southwestern Nigeria* (New York: International Publications, Service, 1964), p. 19.

CIVILIZATIONS OF AFRICA

There were many crafts and industries in Benin. There were wood carving, ivory carving, leatherworking, weaving, and ironworking. Benin bronze casting and *terra cotta* (baked clay) sculpture were especially famous. Artisans could sell nothing without the permission of the *oba* (king). So most of the bronze and ivory sculpture became property of the royal court.

The oba was both the political and the religious head of the people. Like other African monarchs, the oba claimed divine powers. And like other African peoples, the people of Benin thought their own happiness and success depended on the monarch's health. The oba appeared in public only on the most important occasions. The rest of the time he lived in secrecy in his palace. It was forbidden under punishment of death to say that the oba ate, washed, slept, or died.

C ● Why do you think it was forbidden to say that the oba ate or slept or died?

The oba controlled nearly all trade and industry. He was the legislative, the judicial, and the executive branches of government. He decided whether there would be war or peace. All local officials or rulers had to be approved or appointed by him. He kept a large army. One visitor to Benin reported that the oba could call up 20,000 warriors in a day—and 80,000 in emergencies.

However, there were some checks on the oba's power. If the oba tried to take traditional rights or powers away from the rulers under his control, these rulers could fight him. Rulers would be more likely to fight if the oba was weak or if things were going badly.

Like other civilizations we have studied, Benin went into decline. There were some weak obas. There were civil wars in Benin over who would become the oba. Moreover, in the seventeenth century, the forest kingdom of Oyo began to grow.

The decline of Benin was also linked with the growth of the trade in slaves and firearms on the coast. Europeans began to want more and more slaves for their colonies in the New World. Many of the coastal peoples wanted to share in the profits from

This bronze sculpture from Benin shows an *oba* (king) and his attendants. It is about 50 centimeters (20 inches) high.

the slave trade. They fought the oba's control of trade. At one point the oba tried to cut off trade with the Europeans altogether. As the coastal peoples got firearms, they found it easier to fight Benin's armies.

During the late eighteenth century, Benin went through a period of new growth. But in the middle of the nineteenth century, Benin again declined. European visitors to Benin City at that time reported that it appeared orderly and lively. But the kingdom had become very small.

D★ Review the African cultures of Kush-Meroë, Ghana, Mali, and Benin. Why could these societies be called civilizations?

E● How did contact with Europeans affect the civilizations and cultures of West Africa?

Summary

Africa is the second largest continent. It has many natural environments. Most of Africa is a plateau. High mountains rise above the plateau in the east and in the northwest. Great rivers begin on the plateau and flow into the seas. Where the rivers flow down from the plateau, there are high waterfalls.

Most of Africa is between the Tropics of Cancer and Capricorn, so except on high mountains, its weather is never cold. Africa has many natural vegetation regions. Natural vegetation depends mainly on climate. In western and central Africa there is a tropical rain forest region along the equator. This is a region of much precipitation. Next to the rain forest is the savanna, an area of tall grass. Here the precipitation is lighter. Next to the savanna is the steppe, a region of short grass. The steppe has very light rain. Bordering the steppe regions are the deserts, which are very dry all year. Africa also has some coastal areas with a Mediterranean climate.

Some scientists think that the human race began in eastern Africa. Through Arab writings we know that there were early civilizations in tropical Africa. The earliest known civilization in tropical Africa was that of Kush-Meroë. Kush-Meroë was in the Nile Valley in the Eastern Sudan. (The Sudan is a great belt of grassland south of the Sahara.)

Kush-Meroë was conquered by the Egyptians. As a result of this culture contact, Kush-Meroë's culture changed. It took on Egyptian customs and beliefs. Later Kush-Meroë grew more powerful than Egypt. Then Kush-Meroë conquered Egypt and developed its own culture. The Kushites learned to mine and smelt iron ore and to make iron tools and weapons. Knowledge of ironworking spread from Kush-Meroë to other peoples of Africa.

Kush-Meroë was a civilization of the ancient history period. Dividing history into periods helps us to understand the past. It helps us to keep events in order. Even though we know that the term *Middle Ages* is not correct, we find it helpful to use the term. By "Middle Ages" we mean the period from about A.D. 500 to A.D. 1500. This is a period of a thousand years, from the end of the Roman Empire to the Modern period.

During the Middle Ages there were many civilizations in the world. Several of these were in the western part of tropical Africa.

Ghana, Mali, and Songhai were kingdoms of the Western Sudan. Benin was a kingdom of the rain forest region south of the Sudan.

Ghana, Mali, and Songhai were wealthy trading societies. They made great profits out of trade between Arabs in the north and the peoples of the rain forest region. Gold and salt were among the most important goods exchanged. Powerful kings, who claimed to be divine monarchs, controlled the trade. Mansa Musa was a great king in Mali. His wealth and power were known in Europe.

Benin, a forest kingdom, was also ruled by a divine monarch. Most people of Benin were farmers. However, Benin grew wealthy from its trade. Benin exchanged slaves, pepper, hides, and cotton cloth for copper and manufactured goods. The people of Benin were skilled in many crafts. Their bronze sculpture is especially famous.

Like all civilized societies we have studied, Kush-Meroë, Ghana, Mali, Songhai, and Benin had periods of great power. Then they grew weak and declined. In the course of time, Arabs conquered the kingdoms of the Western Sudan. Islam became their main religion. Islamic culture gave them learning and laws.

Some Interesting Activities

1. Make a list of the main climate and natural vegetation regions of Africa. In the left-hand column, write the name of the region. In the right-hand column, describe the region's climate and natural plant life. The map and map key on page 297 will help you. You should also look for more information in an encyclopedia.

2. Make a map showing Mansa Musa's pilgrimage from Timbuktu to Mecca. The route is described on page 317.

3. Pretend you are a camel driver who went along with Mansa Musa on the pilgrimage to Mecca. Write a story telling how you felt during the trip and how you felt about Mansa Musa. Tell about the things you saw and did. Tell about strangers you met.

4. Write a story about an Arab trader's caravan trip from somewhere in present-day Algeria to ancient Mali. What goods did he take along to trade? What did he hope to get in return for his goods? What hardships might he have suffered? Why did he think the long hard trip was worth the trouble?

Machu Pichu, an ancient fortress city in the Andes of Peru. Called the "lost city" of the Incas, it was unknown to the outside world until 1911.

CHAPTER 12

Civilizations in the New World

Europeans began to trade and settle in the Americas at the end of the fifteenth century A.D. They called the Americas the *New World*. The *Old World* was Europe, Asia, and Africa. The terms *New World* and *Old World* are useful. But we should remember that there were many millions of people already living in the Americas when the Europeans first arrived. Many native Americans were civilized. For these people, of course, the New World was the world they had always known.

In this chapter we will find out about some of the civilizations that arose in the New World. Most of the New World civilizations were in what is now Mexico and Central America. We call them *Mesoamerican* (middle American) civilizations.

How Did Mesoamerican Civilizations Begin?

Civilizations began in Mesoamerica more than 3,000 years ago. Historians do not agree about how these civilizations began. They have several different ideas. After civilization began in Mesopotamia, it kept spreading. It spread because noncivilized societies *learned from* civilized ones. Different cultures added new ideas, but the main pattern of civilization was copied again and again. However, there is so far no *proof* that Mesoamerican civilization was copied from the Old World. Many historians therefore say that the Mesoamerican people "invented" civilization for themselves.

A ● Explain how these "inventions" led to civilization in the Old World: agriculture and tame animals, irrigation, extra food, capital, division of labor, trade, towns and cities.

Other historians have a different idea. They think that a long time ago sailors may have drifted from the Old World to the New World. These unknown sailors may have carried the ideas that started civilization in the Americas. Let us see how these sailors might have drifted (or even might have sailed on purpose) to the New World. First we need to learn some facts about the oceans and the air.

Movement of Air and Water

The earth's air and oceans are never still. The earth and the air around it rotate together toward the east. Rotation and wind currents set the ocean currents in motion. The movement of the air and of ocean currents usually follow a *pattern.* One thing that affects this pattern is *air pressure.* **Air pressure** is the weight of the air on the earth's surface. Another thing that affects the pattern is rotation.

Let us see how air pressure affects wind patterns. Warm air is lighter than cold air. So warm air has less pressure than cold air. An area of warm air is a *low pressure area.* An area of cold air is a *high pressure area.* Winds blow from high pressure areas to low pressure areas.

326 THE GROWTH OF CIVILIZATION

A ● Look at the diagram "High Pressure, Low Pressure, and Winds" below. Explain what is happening to the air.

There are areas of high pressure and of low pressure in the Northern Hemisphere and in the Southern Hemisphere. The greatest low pressure area is at the equator. The low pressure area at the equator is called the *equatorial low.* There are high pressure areas at the poles. These are called *polar highs.* Between these areas are other areas of high pressure and low pressure. Air is always moving from high to low pressure areas. If the earth did not rotate, wind would always blow in a north or south direction. But winds do not always blow in a north or south direction. Because of rotation, air moving toward the equator moves in a generally westerly direction. Air moving away from the equator moves in an easterly direction. The earth's rotation causes winds in the Northern Hemisphere to blow in the opposite directions from winds in the Southern Hemisphere.

The diagram "Wind Patterns of the Earth" (page 328) shows the main winds on the earth's surface. The pattern is not really quite so neat, because the landmasses and the oceans change it. The pattern moves north and south as the sun's vertical rays move north and south between the Tropics of Cancer and Capricorn. We describe winds by the direction *from* which they blow.

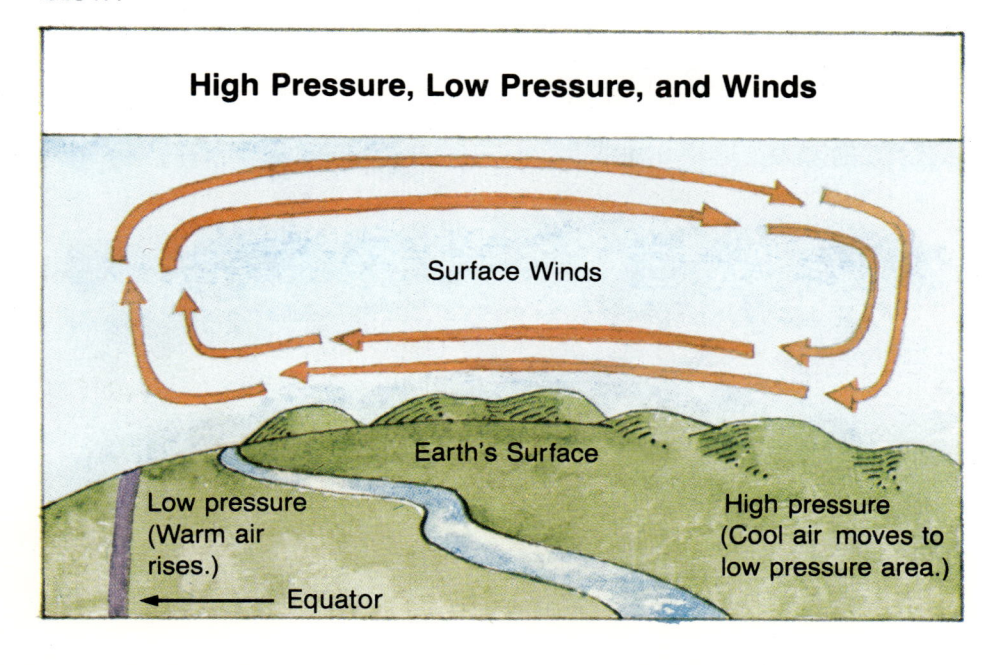

High Pressure, Low Pressure, and Winds

Surface Winds

Earth's Surface

Low pressure
(Warm air rises.)

High pressure
(Cool air moves to low pressure area.)

← Equator

327

Wind Patterns of the Earth

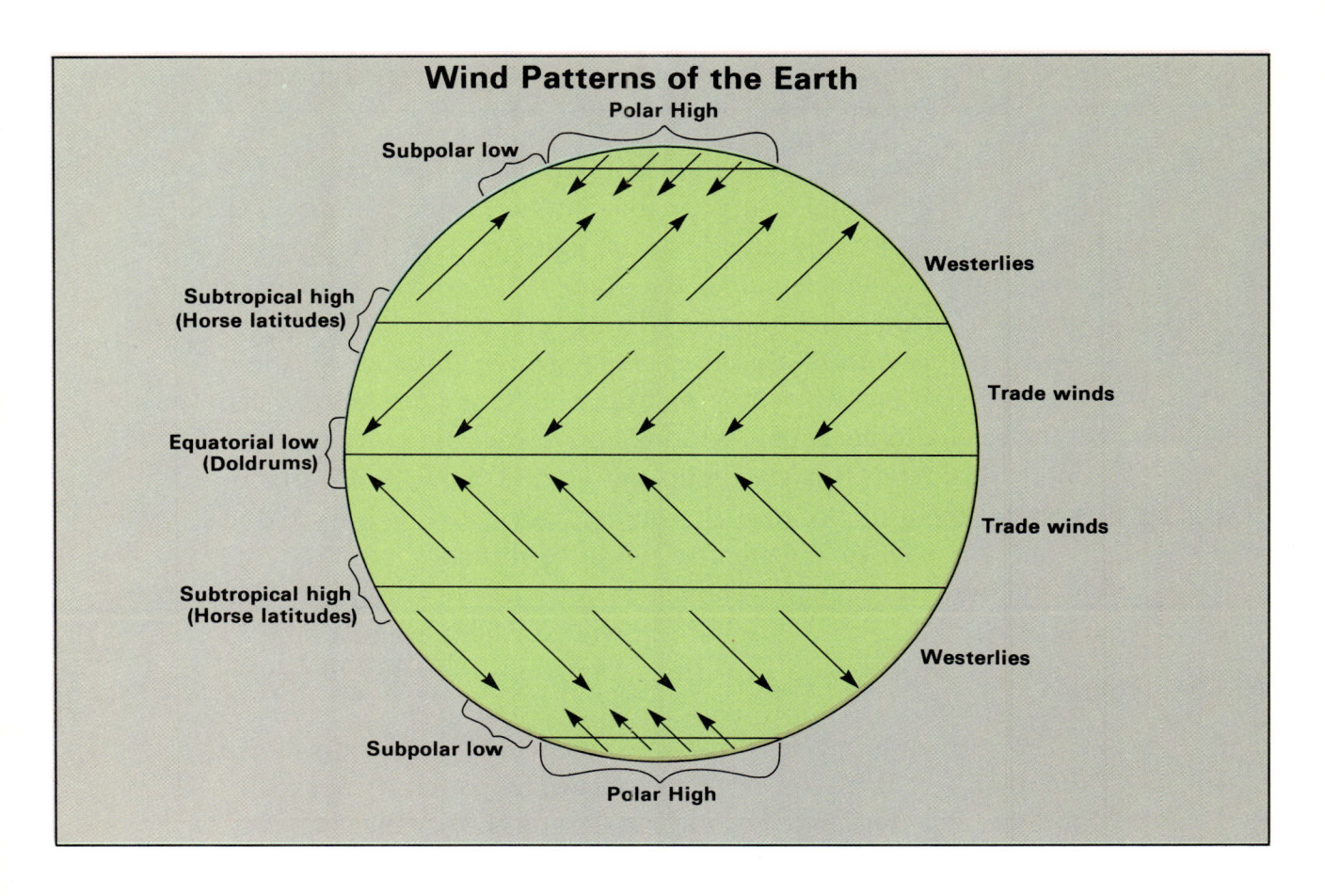

(Diagram showing wind patterns on Earth with labels: Polar High, Subpolar low, Westerlies, Subtropical high (Horse latitudes), Trade winds, Equatorial low (Doldrums), Trade winds, Subtropical high (Horse latitudes), Westerlies, Subpolar low, Polar High)

B▶ Use the wind pattern diagram to answer these questions:
1. Where are the high pressure areas on the earth? Where are the low pressure areas?
2. From which direction do the *trade winds* blow in the Northern Hemisphere? In the Southern Hemisphere?
3. From which direction do the *westerlies* blow in the Northern Hemisphere? In the Southern Hemisphere?

C★ The scientific name for the swing of winds to the right or to the left is the *Coriolis force* or *Coriolis effect.* You may want to find out about this in an encyclopedia. Why is the Coriolis effect important when we send space *satellites* round the earth?

D● Now look at the map "The Main Ocean Currents" (page 329).
1. Notice how the currents go in the Northern and the Southern Hemisphere.
2. Find the currents that might carry sailors from eastern Asia to the Americas.

328 THE GROWTH OF CIVILIZATION

3. Find the currents that might carry people from the Americas to islands in the Pacific Ocean.
4. Find the current that might carry sailors from Europe or the Mediterranean to the Americas.

E▶ Look again at the diagram "Wind Patterns of the Earth" (page 328). Notice that we describe a wind by the *direction from which it blows.*
1. What are the four main belts of winds?
2. What are the three main belts of calm?

F● Winds blow from areas of *high pressure* to areas of *low pressure*. Why do the trade winds *not* blow from north to south or from south to north?

The winds over the oceans were very important in the days of sailing ships. Sailors tried to find the best winds for their ships.

G● If you were on a sailing ship from Europe to North or Central America, which winds would be better for you?

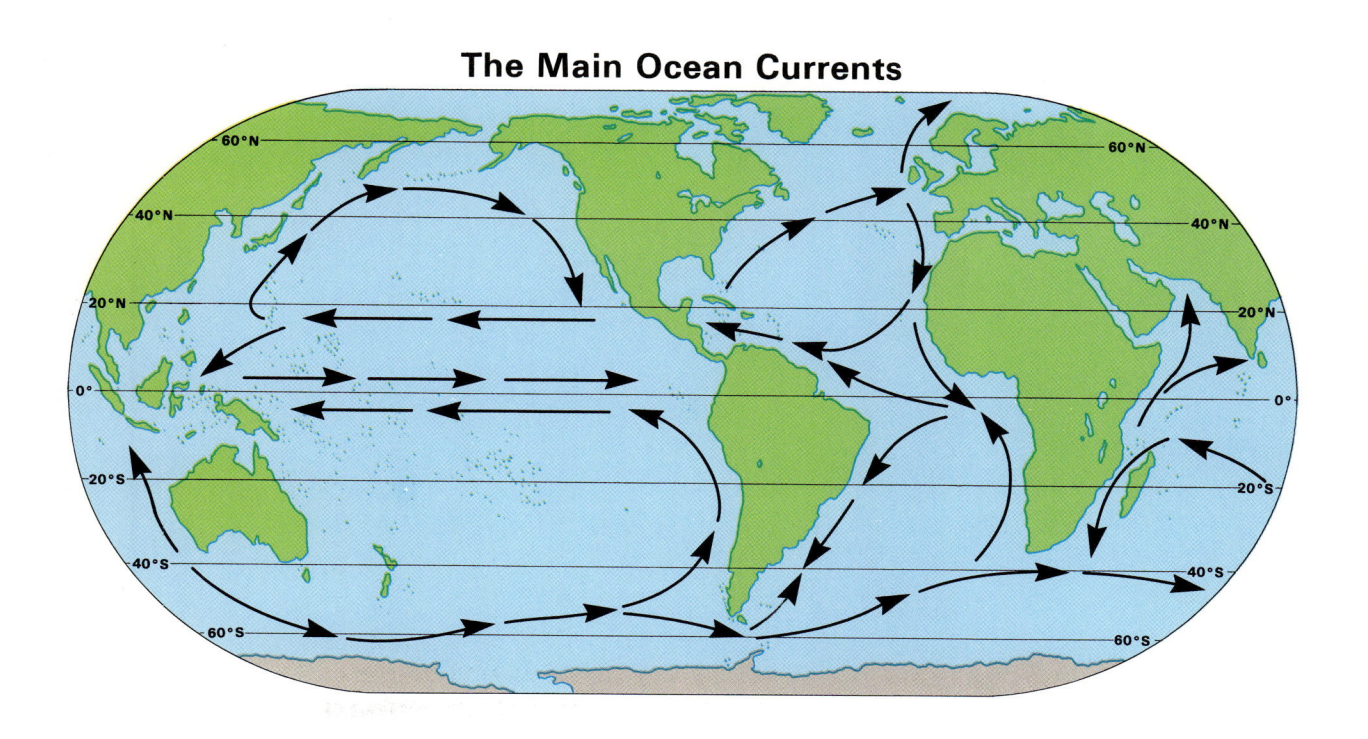

The Main Ocean Currents

CIVILIZATIONS IN THE NEW WORLD

- **H●** If you were sailing from North America to Europe, which winds would be better? Explain.
- **I★** Why did sailors call the belt of calm near the equator the *doldrums*?
- **J★** Why were *trade winds* called by that name?

It seems almost certain that sailors long ago were carried by currents and winds to the Americas. But we do not know if they brought the ideas of agriculture and civilization to the New World.

Recently a group of scholars built boats like those made 3,000 or 4,000 years ago. By sailing them across the Pacific and Atlantic oceans, they proved that these boats could cross the oceans. Some scholars claim to have found early writing on rocks in North America. They claim that this shows that people came across the Atlantic Ocean from Western Europe and Egypt long ago. We cannot be sure. If these scholars are right, then agriculture and civilization probably were *not* invented separately in the New World.

- **K★** Read about Thor Heyerdahl and his trips in the *Kon-Tiki* (a raft of balsa wood) and in the *Ra-2* (a ship of reeds, such as ancient Egyptians made). How do these ocean trips help to prove the idea that civilization spread from the Old World to the New World?

The *Ra-2*

Early American Cultures

Humans came to the Americas from Asia before the end of the Ice Age. Many historians think that they came when the ocean bed between Siberia and Alaska was dry land. This movement of people took place before the icecap melted, about 15,000 B.C.–10,000 B.C. The people who came to the Americas had a paleolithic culture. They used rough stone tools. They were hunters and gatherers. It took several thousand years for their descendants to spread throughout North and South America.

A ▶ Look at the map on page 49 showing how the races of the human species came to be in different parts of the world.

By 2500 B.C. agriculture had begun in Central America. Agriculture had also spread to most of North and South America. However, the people in the far north and far south went on living by hunting and gathering. Even in the middle latitudes, not all people grew crops. But some people both grew crops and hunted. Thus hundreds of culture groups grew up in the Americas. They were the ancestors of the native Americans. These native Americans were mistakenly called "Indians" by Europeans at the end of the fifteenth century.

B ★ What native American (Indian) culture groups or peoples can you name? In what parts of the Americas did they live 500 years ago?

The Civilized Society of the Maya

Civilization began in the New World about 3,500 years later than it began in Mesopotamia. The earlier civilized societies of the Americas grew up in Mexico and Central America. Later there came civilization along the west coast and in the mountains of South America.

By about 100 A.D., people were building big stone temples in Central America. Around those temples were towns. There were a great many villages. For these early agricultural Americans, the main food crop was maize (corn). Later the people grew beans, squash, and other crops.

CIVILIZATIONS IN THE NEW WORLD

One of these early civilizations was made by the Maya people. Archaeologists still are exploring the ruined cities of the Maya.

A ▶ Look at the map "Mayan and Aztec Lands" below.
1. Find Copan in what is now Honduras. This was the early center of Mayan civilization.
2. Find Chichen Itza [chē chen' ēt sä'] in the Yucatan Peninsula. Later this place became the center of Mayan culture.

Mayan and Aztec Lands

MAP KEY
- Aztec Lands c. 1500
- Mayan Lands c. 800
- Present-day international boundaries
- ( ) Names of present-day countries are in parentheses

332 THE GROWTH OF CIVILIZATION

The environment of these Mesoamerican cultures was very different from the environment of ancient Mesopotamia. In Central America, the natural environment was tropical rain forest. In Mesopotamia, the natural environment was dry, with few trees. Agriculture was difficult in Mesopotamia because there was not much water. Agriculture was difficult in Central America because there was too much water. The people of Mesopotamia built canals to bring water to their fields. The people of Central America built canals to drain water away from their fields.

In Yucatan, the land of the Maya, plants grew rapidly in the wet soil and the warm air. But often the soil was poor and soon wore out.

The farming technology of the Maya was like that of Neolithic farmers in the Old World. The slash-and-burn method was used to clear the land. The Maya used digging sticks to dig and plant. But unlike Neolithic farmers, the Maya had no cattle, no plows, and no wheeled carts. Nor did the Maya or other American Indians know about hard metals such as bronze and iron. They used silver and gold for jewelry, but all their tools and weapons were of wood or stone.

All Mayan culture was based upon the worship of many gods. For those gods the Maya built great temples of stone. These temples were pyramids with steps. The stepped pyramids look somewhat like the Mesopotamian ziggurats. (The stone of these temples was cut without metal tools and was moved without carts or draft animals.) The rich art of the Maya was made for religious purposes. And their mathematics and astronomy were bound up with their religious knowledge.

B ● Look at the picture of a Mayan temple on page 335. Does it remind you of early temples in Mesopotamia? Does it remind you of any buildings in ancient Egypt? Explain.

There were learned priests in the Mayan civilization. These learned men understood the science of astronomy. They worked out a calendar. The Mayan priests measured the length of a year. They said it was 365.2420 days. Today scientists say the year is

365.2422 days long. Since 0.2500 is one-fourth, 0.2420 of a day is almost one-fourth of a day. This means that the Maya priests differed from scientists today by only about 17 seconds!

> C● What do we mean when we say that a year (*a solar year*) is 365.2422 days long? What movement of the earth gives us a year? Would you say that the Maya priests were good at astronomy? Explain.

The priests also kept records. When they wrote their records, the priests used pictures instead of letters. We still do not know how to read these old books. There are very few of the books left. The Spanish conquerors burned most of them.

> D● Why do you think the Spanish conquerors burned the writings of the civilized societies they conquered?

Like the early people of Sumer, the Maya lived in a number of city-states. Probably most of the people lived in huts in the fields around their city. The society of each city-state had its own government and temples. However, the different city-states shared the same culture. The societies traded with one another and with other cultures.

> E● Look at the pictures of Mayan artifacts on pages 336–337. What feeling do you get about Mayan culture from the artifacts? Do you think that religion played a big part in Mayan life?
>
> F● Compare these artifacts with those of other cultures on earlier pages. Is the art of any of these cultures similar to the Mayan art? Explain.

The Toltecs and the Aztecs

The Maya seem to have been a peaceful people. Other peoples copied their civilization, but were warlike. The civilized society of the Maya began to fall apart in the tenth century A.D. We do not know how or why this culture was ruined. Copan and other cities became empty. We do know that Chichen Itza was conquered by a people called the Toltecs, from northern Mexico.

The ruins of a Mayan pyramid, Chichén Itzá, Yucatan, Mexico.
The Mayans built their pyramids as temples to their gods.

A Mayan stele. Most steles had carved portraits of priest-rulers and included astronomical information.

A Mayan priest. The priest was one of two rulers that each Mayan city-state had. He devoted all his time to priestly and astrological duties. Observe the priest's high headdress.

336 THE GROWTH OF CIVILIZATION

A Mayan ceremonial procession. Processions like this one often passed through the streets and public squares of Mayan cities on their way to the ceremonial courts in front of the pyramids.

After the Toltecs, in the fourteenth century, another barbarian people came from the north of Mexico. These were the Aztecs, fierce conquerors. They settled in central Mexico. They made subjects and slaves of the people already living in Mexico. The capital city of the Aztec Empire was Tenochtitlan [te nôch′ tē tlän′]. Today Mexico City stands where Tenochtitlan was 500 years ago.

The Aztec culture took many ideas from the earlier cultures. The same calendar and the same writing were used. For temples to their gods, the Aztecs built the same kind of pyramids. Their cities and towns were beautiful with many gardens. They had good agriculture and seem to have been prosperous.

But the Aztecs were almost always making war. Their polytheistic religion called for human sacrifices. They made war in order to take prisoners. Then they sacrificed those prisoners to the gods.

Scholars are not sure why the Aztecs sacrificed human beings. One explanation is that an important Aztec god was their god of war and of the sun. The Aztecs believed that this god had led the Aztecs to Tenochtitlan and had made them a great people. They thought they must show this war god that they were grateful by killing men on his altar.

An Aztec legend said that when the sun set, the sun god entered a dark underworld. He had to fight his way through the

CIVILIZATIONS IN THE NEW WORLD

(above) A reproduction of an Aztec calendar stone. The calendar year of the Aztecs contained 18 months of 20 days each. At the end of this period they added five extra days. *(below)* Head of Aztec goddess Coyalxauhqui. The head is made of jadeite.

darkness. Only if he won the fight, could he rise again the next morning. The Aztec priests tried to keep the sun god well fed for his nightly struggle. This god of war and sun did not eat ordinary food. He fed on human hearts. The human sacrifices at the tops of temples would give the god human hearts. If the sun god were to lose his fight in the darkness, the earth would be destroyed by earthquakes. So the Aztecs gave him their help. To the Aztecs, human sacrifice was a necessary part of daily living.

When the Spaniards landed in Mexico early in the sixteenth century, they were horrified by these human sacrifices. That was one reason why the Spaniards completely destroyed Aztec civilization.

A ▶ Why did the Aztecs sacrifice human beings?

The End of Mesoamerican Civilizations

There were two powerful civilizations in the New World at the beginning of the sixteenth century A.D. One was the Aztec Empire in Mexico. The other was the Inca Empire along the northwestern coast of South America.

Suddenly both these empires were smashed by a small number of conquerors from Spain. How could a few European soldiers wipe out two great empires?

Historians think that they know why these societies fell so easily. One reason was *technology*. The Europeans had firearms and horse soldiers; the American Indians did not. Another reason was *disease*. The native Americans had been free of the diseases suffered by people in the Old World. When Europeans arrived, smallpox, measles, and other illnesses came with them. American Indians had no *resistance* to these diseases. Possibly nine out of every ten native Americans died from these diseases. It was easier for the Europeans to conquer peoples who had been weakened by sicknesses.

A ★ What do we mean by *resistance to disease*? Why might culture contact between societies that had never met before bring deadly *epidemics* of disease?

CIVILIZATIONS IN THE NEW WORLD

Summary

In Mesoamerica, civilization existed more than 3,000 years ago. Did the Mesoamericans "invent" civilization for themselves? Or did they "copy" it from the Old World? Nobody can say for sure. The winds and ocean currents of the world could have brought sailors from the Old World to the New World long ago. If so, it must have been very long ago, because various inventions of the Old World were not known in the Americas until the Spaniards arrived at the end of the fifteenth century and the beginning of the sixteenth century. In the Mesoamerican civilization there were no plows, no carts with wheels, and no iron or bronze tools or weapons.

One of the great Mesoamerican civilized societies was that of the Maya. This culture was based on agriculture in tropical rain forests. Among other societies of the New World was the powerful and warlike Aztec civilization. Both the Mayan culture in Yucatan and the Aztec culture in central Mexico had writing, mathematics, a calendar, and great architecture and art.

At the beginning of the sixteenth century A.D., Spanish conquerors overthrew both the Aztec Empire in Mexico and the Inca Empire in northwestern South America. The Spanish military technology was more advanced than were Mesoamerican weapons. Also diseases that came with the European conquerors weakened the American Indians.

So the history of Mesoamerican civilization breaks off suddenly, just a few years after A.D. 1500. A quite different Western civilization took the place of the American Indian civilized societies.

Some Interesting Activities

1. Make a simple time line of the history of peoples in the New World up to A.D. 1532. Include the dates and historical happenings listed below. Find others to include.
    a. c. 30,000–15,000 B.C.: People came from the Old World to the New World by a "land bridge."

    b. c. 2500 B.C.: Maize agriculture began in Mesoamerica. (Some historians say that agriculture came later.)

c. c. A.D. 100–1000: The Mayan civilization flourished.

d. c. A.D. 1000: Warrior invasions began; Toltec culture appeared.

e. c. A.D. 1300–1521: The Aztec civilization ruled Mexico.

f. c. A.D. 1200–1532: The Inca Empire ruled Peru and other South American lands.

You can make another time line on the same sheet of paper showing events that happened in the Old World about the same times shown above.

2. Use an encyclopedia to find out more about one of the following: the Maya, the Toltecs, the Incas, the Aztecs.

3. Copy pictures of a Mesoamerican pyramid, an Egyptian pyramid, and a Sumerian ziggurat. What was each building used for?

4. Form a committee with a few of your classmates to find out about diseases that have caused great loss of human life. *Measles* and *smallpox* came with Europeans to the New World. Europeans suffered from a New World disease called *yellow fever.* In the fourteenth century A.D. a disease spread from Asia through Europe. It was called the *Black Death,* or the *plague* or *bubonic plague.* Discuss whether such terrible *epidemics* can happen in our time.

5. Make a copy of the diagram on page 328 that shows the pattern of the earth's winds. You should remember that this is only a *pattern.* The patterns of actual winds are not so neat, because the earth's landmasses cause the winds to vary near or over land areas. You may find more detailed maps of the earth's winds in an atlas or encyclopedia. Compare these with the diagram.

A city scene from medieval Japan

CHAPTER 13

Civilizations and Barbarians in Asia in the Middle Ages

What was happening in Europe and Asia during the Middle Ages? In southeastern Europe the Byzantine Empire lived on but grew weaker. In Western Europe a new civilization grew. We shall read about Western European civilizations in the next chapter. In Asia there were civilizations in the Middle East, in India, in Southeast Asia, in China, and in Japan. Three of these civilizations were shaken or shattered by barbarian invasions.

Let us look first at a civilization that was saved from the barbarians. This was an island civilization: Japan. The Mongol barbarians conquered China and Korea. They twice tried to invade Japan by sea—in 1274 and 1281. Both these invasions failed.

The Islands of Japan

In the Pacific Ocean, not far from the mainland of Asia, lie the islands of Japan. The islands are lovely but mountainous. They rise from the deepest parts of the ocean. The Japanese islands were formed long ago by earthquakes and volcanoes. There are 200 volcanoes in Japan today, and 60 of them are active (still dangerous). Earthquakes also still happen in Japan.

A ▶ Look at the map "Physical Features of Japan" (page 345).
   1. Between what latitudes does Japan lie?
   2. How far is Japan from the Korean peninsula?
   3. What are the four largest islands of Japan?
   4. What is the capital of Japan?

The whole of Japan is about the size of California. Because of mountains and volcanoes, there is not much land in Japan that can be used for farming. So Japanese farmers have always tried to use every bit of land wisely. To get more flat land for growing crops, they cut steps (called terraces) into the sides of hills and mountains.

Japan's climate is good for agriculture. Most of northern Japan has an *east maritime climate.* This means cold winters, warm summers, and plenty of precipitation. New England, in the United States, has the same kind of climate as northern Japan. The climate of southern Japan is like the climate of the states of Georgia and Florida. This is a *humid* (wet) *subtropical climate,* with warm, wet winters and hot, wet summers.

Now that we know something about Japan's natural environment, let us see how Japan's civilization grew.

The Rise of Civilization in Japan

About 250 B.C., some newcomers arrived in southern Japan. They came from Korea, which was then under Chinese control. The Koreans brought something new to Japan. It was rice. Before the Koreans arrived, the Japanese got most of their food by hunting and gathering. The Koreans taught people in Japan how to grow rice.

Physical Features of Japan

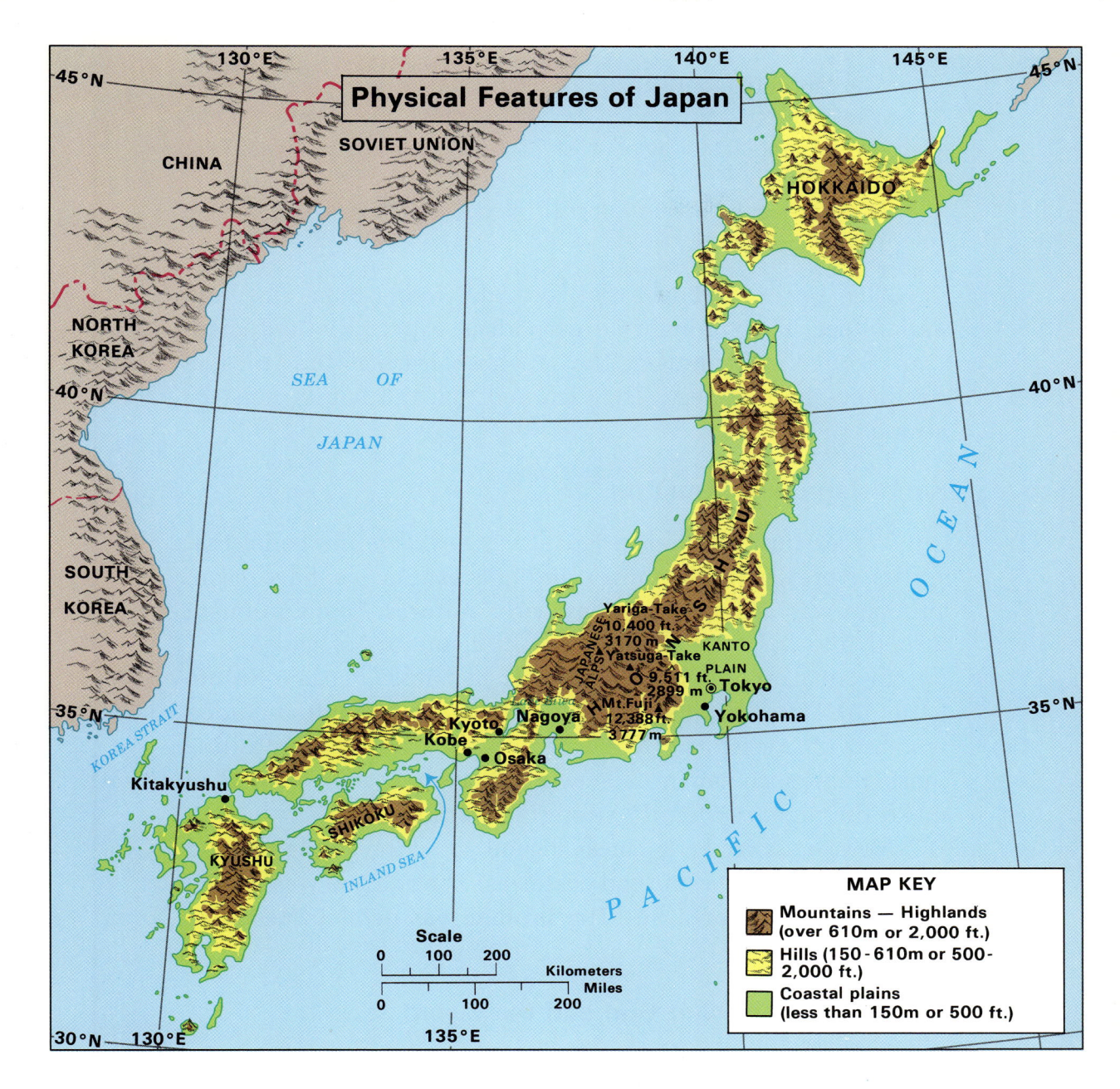

Large amounts of rice can be grown in a small area. Yet rice needs a special kind of agriculture. The fields in which it is grown need to be flooded. Therefore the fields must be flat. Moreover, the rice must be tended very carefully. Farmers must work hard at weeding and transplanting. Since they work so hard, they want to be sure of a good harvest. Farmers need a government to keep order and to defend their land and crops.

CIVILIZATIONS AND BARBARIANS IN ASIA IN THE MIDDLE AGES

A ▶ Who taught the Japanese how to grow rice?
B ● Why would rice be a good crop in Japan? (Clue: What have you learned about the amount of flat land available in Japan for farming?)
C ● Why can't people who get their food by hunting and gathering make a civilization?

The settlers from Korea brought more than rice and agriculture. They brought Chinese ideas, especially Confucianism. From Confucianism, the Japanese learned the rules of obedience and respect. They learned that the family must be strong.

Early Japanese Religion

The earliest religion in Japan was *animism,* the belief that spirits were in many things and places. As we have seen, animism was common in many early cultures. Often animism turned into *polytheism,* the belief in a number of gods.

In Japan, the worship of spirits in nature became **Shinto** [shin′ tō]. *Shinto* means "the way of the gods." Shinto included worship of ancestors. Here we see how Chinese controlling ideas influenced Japan. The worship of ancestors helped to make the Japanese family strong and united.

Now let us read a Japanese legend about the gentle sun god and her wild brother, the god of storms. The sun god was named Amaterasu [ä′ mä tə rä′ sü]. Her brother was named Susanowo [sü′ sä nō′ wō].

The Sun God and the Sword

Everyone in heaven and on earth knew that Susanowo was a terrible troublemaker. He especially loved to tease his beautiful sister, Amaterasu. One day he went just a little too far. First he trampled through her fresh garden. Then he tore down the walls between her rice fields. When Amaterasu heard what he had done, she was very sad. She crept into the deepest cave she could find. She said she would never come out.

When the sun was hidden inside a cave, the earth grew very dark. Soon everything on earth began to die. All the other gods began to worry. They gathered outside Amaterasu's cave. They begged and begged, but she refused to come out. Then they had an idea.

The gods set a huge mirror outside the cave. All over the mirror they hung jewels. Then one of the gods began to do a funny dance. It made the other gods laugh.

Amaterasu heard all the laughing. "What's going on?" she wondered. Poking her head out of the cave, she saw her reflection in the mirror. "Who is this beautiful creature?" she wondered. When she stepped out to see, one of the gods quickly rolled a stone over the cave. Amaterasu could not get back in. Never again could the sun disappear from heaven.

CIVILIZATIONS AND BARBARIANS IN ASIA IN THE MIDDLE AGES

To punish Susanowo for his mischief, the gods sent him away from heaven. He went to the earth, to the Japanese islands. One day he came upon a farmer's cottage. Inside were the farmer, his wife, and his beautiful young daughter. They were all sitting on the floor, weeping. "What's the trouble?" asked Susanowo.

They began to cry all the harder. "Tonight the eight-headed dragon is going to eat our daughter," said the old man.

Susanowo promised to kill the horrible monster. "Just fill eight bowls with rice wine, and leave the rest up to me," he said.

That night, the dragon came roaring out of the forest. He saw the bowls of rice wine. Using every one of his eight heads, he began sucking up the wine. Then he fell over—drunk. Susanowo ran out and chopped off the dragon's eight heads. When he slit open the dragon's tail, he found a great jeweled sword inside.

A long time later, Amaterasu sent her grandson down to rule Japan. She gave him three things—the mirror the gods had put outside her cave, one of the jewels that had hung over the mirror, and the jeweled sword that Susanowo had won.

- A● Do you think such legends as this would help to strengthen a ruler's control over the people? Explain.
- B▶ What is *polytheism*? Was Shinto polytheistic?
- C▶ In earlier parts of *The Growth of Civilization,* we read about other cultures in which nature gods were worshipped. Give some examples of these cultures.

The legend about Amaterasu and Susanowo tells us something about Japan's early culture. For example, it tells us that the early Japanese must have had bronze or iron. They made mirrors of polished metal. They also made swords. Swords became the sign of power and authority in Japan. Beautiful swords were handed down from father to son. Even today, the mirror, the jewel, and the sword are the signs of Japan's royal family. Only in 1945 did the emperor of Japan give up his claim to be descended from the god of the sun.

- D● Shinto and Confucianism taught the worship of ancestors. How would this worship make ancient customs strong in Japan?

Monks from China and Korea brought another religion to Japan in the sixth century A.D. This religion was Buddhism. At first, the Japanese were eager to learn all they could about Buddhism. You will remember that this "new" religion had started in India in the sixth century B.C. This was more than a thousand years before it reached Japan. Buddhism was much changed by the time it came to Japan. Some Japanese thought that the Lord Buddha had power to control the destructive forces of nature. Some thought Buddhism would help to unite the people.

Buddhism became Japan's second major religion. Then the emperors began to worry. Maybe the Buddhist priests had too much power. Maybe they were getting dangerous. The emperors made the priests move their temples away from towns and cities. They forced the Buddhists to build their temples deep in the forests or on the mountain tops. Gradually, a mixture of Shinto and Buddhism became the main religion of Japan.

The Great Buddha of Kamakura, one of Japan's treasures, was cast in 1252 during the period when the shogun's headquarters were at Kamakura.

Feudal Society in Japan

Emperor (figurehead)

Shogun (most powerful daimyo)

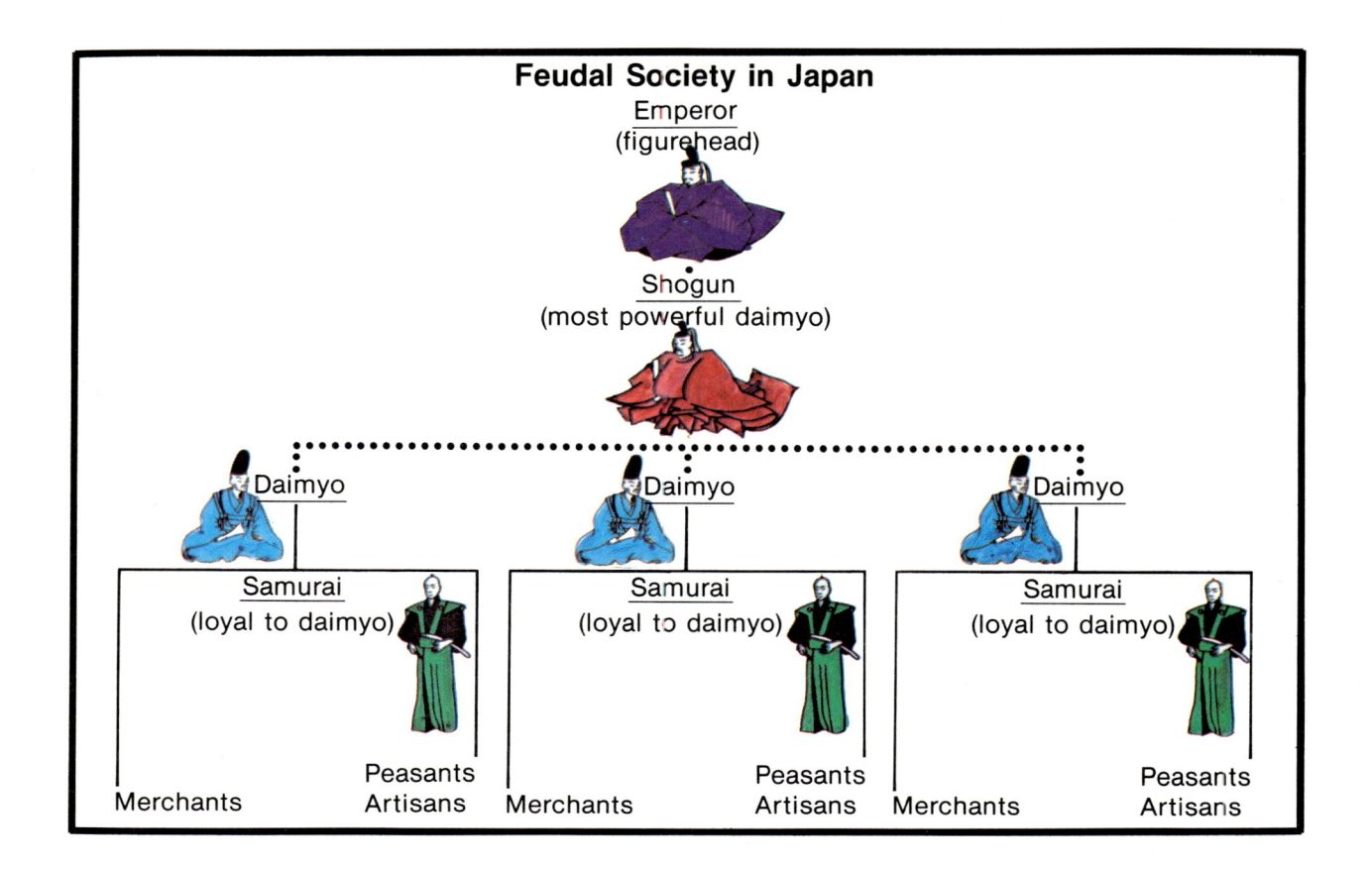

Daimyo — Daimyo — Daimyo

Samurai (loyal to daimyo) — Samurai (loyal to daimyo) — Samurai (loyal to daimyo)

Merchants — Peasants Artisans — Merchants — Peasants Artisans — Merchants — Peasants Artisans

Feudalism in Japan

The Japanese worshipped the emperor as a god. From the time of the first emperor there was always one of his descendants on the throne. Yet the emperor did not have great power. Why was this so?

The reason is that Japan had a system of *feudalism.* **Feudalism** was a way of organizing and defending societies that had no strong central government. Under feudalism, the real power was divided among the noble families. Japanese nobles owned the land. The farmers worked for the nobles. Each noble had his army of warriors, or soldiers. The Japanese name for "noble" was **daimyo** [dīm′ yō]. The warriors were the **samurai** [sam′ ə rī]. Under feudalism the warriors were loyal to their noble leader. In return, the leader gave the warriors land and money. As the power of the daimyos increased, the emperors lost power.

At times the daimyos made war on one another. Throughout these times of civil war, the emperor remained in his palace at Kyoto. The aim of the most powerful *daimyo* was to rule in the emperor's name. The most powerful *daimyo* was usually a great general. The Japanese word for great general is **shogun** [shō′ gun]. The *shogun* had real power. The emperor was a figurehead.

Sometimes Japan had a strong *shogun.* It was then that the country enjoyed law and order. Sometimes the *shogun* was weak and ineffective.

A ▶ Look at the box "Feudal Society in Japan" (page 350). It shows how society was organized. Who had the most power in Japanese society?

The Samurai and Their Code

The *samurai* were the key to power. They were great fighters. They wore heavy armor and were able to fight on foot and on horseback.

A ● Look at the picture of a *samurai* dressed for battle on page 355. Notice the heavy armor. The armor and weapons probably weighed 40 kilograms (more than 80 pounds). Notice that the *samurai* carried a bow and arrows as well as a lance and a sword.

The *samurai* were fiercely loyal to their *daimyo.* They had a *code* (a set of rules) of loyalty. It was called *bushido* [bü shē′ dō], or the code of the warrior. They were ready to die at any time for their *daimyo* and his family. *Bushido* left a deep mark on Japanese culture.

We can learn more about the *samurai* from a famous story entitled "The Story of the Forty-seven Ronin." The *Ronin* [rō′ nin] are *samurai* who have lost their master.

The Story of the Forty-seven Ronin

Every spring the emperor used to send a message of peace to the *shogun*. The *shogun* would choose two lords, or *daimyo,* to greet the emperor's messengers. Neither lord knew how to greet the messengers. Both lords had to be taught by the *shogun's* secretary. This secretary was named Kira. He was a greedy, jealous man. He did not give lessons for nothing. He expected the two lords to give him rich gifts in return. One of the lords knew what Kira expected, so he gave him some gold. But the other lord did not know what Kira expected. He did not offer him anything at all. This lord's name was Asano.

Furious with Asano, Kira vowed he would not teach him anything. He took every opportunity to insult Asano. One day the ribbon on Kira's shoe came untied. "Get down and tie that ribbon," Kira ordered. Asano was angry, but he got down and tied it. Then Kira turned to the other nobles with a laugh. "Look at that! This peasant can't even tie a shoe properly." At that Asano lost his self-control. He drew out his sword and struck at Kira. The blow just scratched Kira's arm. But Asano had committed two crimes. He had drawn his sword in the *shogun's* palace, and he had wounded the *shogun's* high official. For those crimes, Asano knew he must die. That night, in a cool moonlit garden, he killed himself.

Asano had had many *samurai.* Now they were *ronin.* These *ronin* thought that Kira was guilty, too. He had murdered their lord just as surely as if he had stabbed him. Now 47 of the *ronin* decided to seek revenge. Of course, Kira was on his guard. Since he was so suspicious, they had to throw him off guard. So for almost two years, they lived a wild, drunken life. They seemed to have forgotten their dead lord.

At last, Kira began to relax. Then the *ronin* struck! Dressed in black silk, they slipped over the walls of Kira's palace. After a short battle, they killed all the guards. Then they found Kira himself. He was hiding in a shack behind some bags of charcoal. Quickly they cut off Kira's head and placed it on Asano's tomb. Asano had been avenged!
Then all the *ronin* killed themselves.

B● 1. What does the story tell about *samurai* loyalty?
2. Why did Asano kill himself?
3. Why did the *ronin* kill themselves?
4. Does the story seem to teach *treachery* and *violence* as well as loyalty? Explain.

Zen Buddhism and the Tea Ceremony

To be a good *samurai* was hard. A *samurai* should never think of himself first. He must be ready to give up his life to defend his lord. He should not try to get money or property for himself. The *samurai* found help in a special kind of Buddhism. This was **Zen Buddhism.** *Zen* means meditation, or very deep thought. As we know, Buddhism taught that life was unreal. For

CIVILIZATIONS AND BARBARIANS IN ASIA IN THE MIDDLE AGES

the Zen Buddhists, death was therefore unimportant. The aim of the Zen Buddhist was to know oneself. By meditation a person could find truth and simplicity. Zen Buddhists learned to be calm and brave no matter what happened to them.

There were others in Japan who became Zen Buddhists, but for the *samurai,* this religion was especially important. It was, they thought, a soldier's religion. It gave courage and calmness in the face of suffering and death. The *samurai* liked the simplicity of the religion, too. Zen Buddhism called for deep, inner feeling about truth. A Zen teacher summed this up when he said: "Those who know do not speak; those who speak do not know."

A ▶ Why did Zen Buddhism take away the fear of death?
B ● What values were "left out" of the *samurai's* code and Zen Buddhism? Might Zen Buddhism, as used by the *samurai,* make people unmerciful? Explain.

Zen Buddhist priests would spend hours every day sitting and thinking. To keep awake, they would drink cups of a strange liquid. It was hot and bitter. This strange liquid was tea. Tea was first brought to Japan from China by a Zen priest.

Drinking tea became an important ceremony in Japan. Every large house had a special building where friends met to drink tea. In this small building were two or three beautiful and simple things. A simple painting or vase of flowers might decorate the room. The tea kettle and the tea cups were special. They might be very costly, yet they would look plain.

There was a reason for the simplicity of these objects. The tea ceremony was supposed to free people from worries. In this way the ceremony was like Zen. The Zen teachers taught that the simplest things are the most beautiful things. One famous Japanese tea master (Zen teacher) said: "In earthly life, easy living and good food are supposed to mean happiness. But if people have shelter to protect them from the rain and enough food to keep them from being hungry, that is all they need. This is the heart of the tea ceremony, as well as of Buddha's teaching."

Peasants and Merchants

Japanese society, like most civilized societies, was divided into different classes, or levels of society. At the top were the *daimyo*. Next came the *samurai*. Then came the peasants (farmers), artisans (skilled workers), and merchants.

The lives of the common people were usually hard. Most of them were peasants, working on land owned by someone else. Every year they tended their rice plants, hoping that their crop would not be ruined. Often they were disappointed. Their villages might be destroyed by war among the *daimyo*. People might be killed or robbed by bands of outlaw soldiers. Sometimes it seemed that only good luck and the merciful Buddha saved them from starvation. Getting enough to eat was always a worry.

While the peasants were often miserable, another group of people were growing rich. These were the merchants. The *daimyo* and *samurai* wanted tea and silk and porcelain from China. Japanese merchants imported those goods and exported lumber, pearls, and gold. Port cities like Osaka [ō sä′ kə] grew rich.

Although the merchants became rich, they had little power. They wanted peace. They wanted strong rulers to keep peace in the land. At last such rulers came to power as *shoguns*.

A samurai dressed in armor. The word *samurai* means "one who serves." The samurai served the shogun and the daimyo. They were bound by a code of loyalty *(bushido)* to their superiors.

CIVILIZATIONS AND BARBARIANS IN ASIA IN THE MIDDLE AGES   355

Japan and the "Outside" World

Up to the sixteenth century A.D., Japan's only contact with other cultures had been with China. Even in dealing with China the Japanese had been careful. They wanted to keep their own culture. Before the sixteenth century, Japanese culture had changed little. However, in the sixteenth century a new thing came to Japan.

In 1543 traders from the faraway country of Portugal reached Japan. European sailors were exploring the oceans of the world. Now they arrived at Japan.

The Japanese had never seen people like these strangers from Europe. The Europeans brought many new things to Japan. The Japanese were especially interested in the guns that the Europeans had. Japan had many skilled workers. Within a few months the Japanese were able to make guns of their own.

Soon the Japanese learned other things from this new *culture contact.* Christian *missionaries* came to Japan. Many Japanese became Christians. At this point the leaders of Japan began to worry. They saw that their culture would change.

Beginning in 1550, new strong *shoguns* came to power. They united Japan. Each had a strong army.

The new *shoguns* also decided to get rid of foreign priests. They forbade Christianity in Japan. Japanese Christians who would not give up their religion were killed. Foreign traders could use only one port, Nagasaki. From 1639 Japan was cut off from the rest of the world. Not until 1854 did Japan again have culture contact with other countries. In that year an American, Commodore Matthew C. Perry, got the Japanese to sign a treaty that opened trade between the United States and Japan.

The *shoguns* who ruled Japan from 1603 were the Tokugawa *shoguns.* When the Tokugawa *shoguns* lost power in 1867, the emperor once again ruled Japan. At that time Japan began to develop into the great industrial society that we know today.

A ▶ Why did the *shoguns* forbid contact with foreign cultures?
B ● Review the story of Japanese culture. What controlling ideas might have helped to make Japan a strong industrial nation today?

Tokugawa Ieyasu. In 1603 the emperor of Japan appointed Ieyasu shogun. Sixty-one years of age at the time, Ieyasu was the first shogun of the Tokugawa shogunate that was to rule Japan for 264 years — until 1867.

The Turks and the Mongols

What was happening in the Middle Ages to the oldest areas of civilization? In the eleventh century, Islamic civilization in the Middle East was controlled by the *Seljuk Turks,* who had become civilized. At about the same time, India was divided into a number of *Hindu kingdoms.* China was ruled by the *Sung* emperors. The Chinese Empire was strong and prosperous, with many artists and learned persons. Into these three areas of civilization came great waves of barbarians.

Millions of people were killed during the invasions of the barbarians. Agriculture was upset. Many cities were looted and destroyed. For most civilized peoples of Asia the Middle Ages were times of great trouble.

Two groups of barbarians came from Central Asia. The Turks came from the lands east of the Caspian Sea. The Mongols came from Mongolia, to the north of the Chinese Empire.

Across the continent of Asia lie steppes that stretch for hundreds upon hundreds of kilometers. The poorest part of this vast area is Mongolia. Two-thirds of Mongolia is steppe with a

CIVILIZATIONS AND BARBARIANS IN ASIA IN THE MIDDLE AGES

few mountain ranges. The other third is the great Gobi Desert. This desert is a rocky area. It has little vegetation. Few people live on it.

Mongolia is a very dry land. It gets little rain. Moist air coming from the Indian Ocean is blocked by high mountains to the south of Mongolia. Temperatures in Mongolia change greatly from season to season. Summers are short and very hot. Winters are long and bitterly cold. There are few trees and valleys to give shelter from winter storms.

A▶ What is a *steppe*?

B● Look at the map "The Steppes of Asia" (page 359).
1. Find the Gobi Desert.
2. How would you describe the natural environment of the Turks and the Mongols?
3. Can steppes be used for agriculture? How? (Look at Mesopotamia and at north China at the big bend of the Hwang Ho.)

The Turks and the Mongols were nomadic. They had herds of horses and camels and sheep. They lived in small groups that moved from place to place.

They also made their living in another way. They led traders in caravans across the deserts and steppes. Nearly all trade between China and Europe or the Middle East went through the lands of the Turks and the Mongols. In this way the nomadic peoples learned much about civilized societies.

You will remember that when barbarians learn about civilization, they want to share the wealth of civilized societies. Often they choose to do this by making war. That is what the Turks and the Mongols did.

Invasions and Conquest of India

The Turks lived on the steppe east of the Caspian Sea. They had become Muslims. Many of them took Muhammad's idea of a holy war very seriously. They especially hated polytheists who had *idols*, or images of the gods. The Hindus of India had many images.

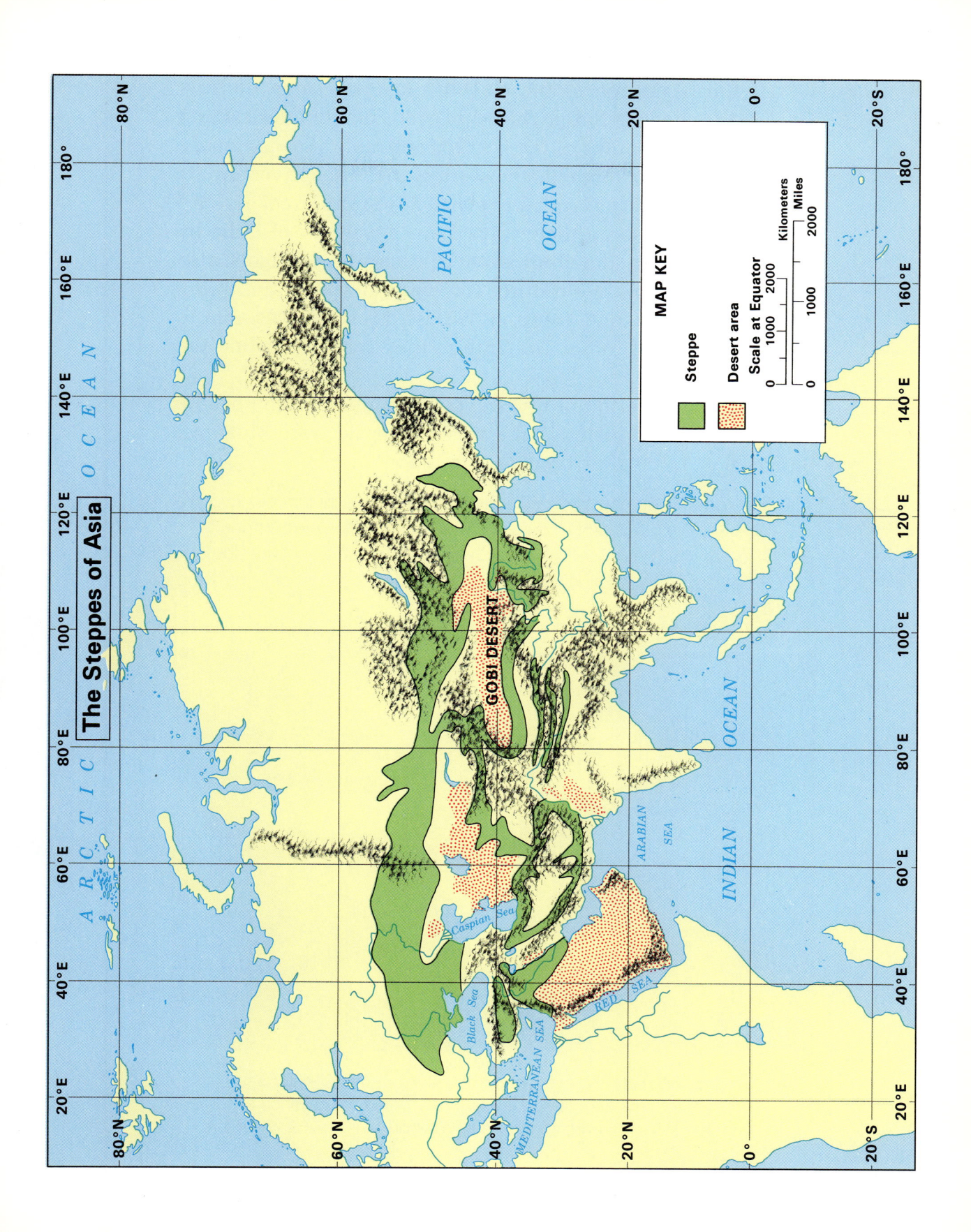

The Steppes of Asia

MAP KEY
- Steppe
- Desert area

Scale at Equator: 0–2000 Kilometers / 0–2000 Miles

Labels: ARCTIC OCEAN, PACIFIC OCEAN, INDIAN OCEAN, Arabian Sea, Red Sea, Mediterranean Sea, Black Sea, Caspian Sea, GOBI DESERT

At the beginning of the eleventh century came the first Turkish invasions of India. These invasions brought destruction to the Hindu kingdoms of the *Punjab* [pun jäb']. (*Punjab* means "five rivers.") The **Punjab** is the plain of the Indus River and its *tributaries.* **Tributaries** are rivers that flow into larger rivers.

From this time on there were many invasions of India by Muslim Turks. In the fourteenth century the Mongols also invaded India, but they did not stay very long. Finally, in the sixteenth century, one group of Turkish Muslims was able to take control of all India. The empire they set up is called the *Mughal Empire.*

During this period of invasion and conquest, many people in India became Muslims. The rulers of India were Muslims. But most Hindus kept their own religion.

A★ The Indian peninsula today is divided into three countries. Two are Muslim; one is mainly Hindu. What are the three countries?

B● Look at the pictures "The Two Cultural Traditions of India" below. What do the two buildings tell you about the religions, or controlling ideas, of Hinduism and Islam?

These buildings illustrate the two cultural traditions of India: Hindu and Islamic. *(left)* A ninth-century temple in the richly ornamented Hindu style. *(right)* A tomb featuring the dome and rounded arch of Islamic architecture.

THE GROWTH OF CIVILIZATION

More Turkish Invasions

The Turks who first took over the Islamic empire in the Middle East were the Seljuk Turks. For a time they were content to rule in Mesopotamia with their capital at Baghdad. They then decided to make their empire larger. So they conquered Asia Minor. The defeated Byzantine Empire was now pushed out of Asia Minor and was left with control only of the Balkan Peninsula.

The Seljuk Empire soon broke up. In the fourteenth century A.D., a new group of Turks began raiding and conquering. These were the *Ottoman Turks,* who became very powerful. They took all Asia Minor, replacing the Seljuks. Then they invaded the Balkans. In 1453 the Ottomans took Constantinople. The Byzantine Empire came to an end. It had lasted nearly a thousand years after the fall of the Roman Empire in the west.

For centuries the Ottoman Empire ruled the Middle East and the eastern Mediterranean. The Ottomans made Constantinople the capital of their new empire. The Ottoman Empire came to an end in 1918.

A★ Constantinople is today called Istanbul. In what country is Istanbul? What does the name of the country tell you about its history?

Genghis Khan and the Mongol Conquests

In central Asia the Mongols had for centuries been divided into tribes. In the thirteenth century A.D., however, they became united under a great war leader known as Genghis Khan [jeng′ iz kän′]. *Khan* means "ruler." *Genghis* means "perfect warrior."

When he was young, Genghis Khan was named Temujin. He was the son of the chief of a Mongol tribe. Even as a boy, Temujin was a great fighter. He was the best wrestler in the tribe. Every day he practiced with his father's heavy bow and arrows.

When Temujin was 13 years old, his father died. He was probably poisoned by members of another tribe. Temujin was

CIVILIZATIONS AND BARBARIANS IN ASIA IN THE MIDDLE AGES

too young to become chief. The members of the tribe decided to break up. Every family tried to join another tribe that already had a strong chief. Temujin, his mother, and his six brothers and sisters were forced to live alone.

As Temujin grew older, he had the idea of uniting all the Mongols. He slowly built up a band of loyal followers. More and more people flocked to him for protection against enemy tribes. Soon they began to seize the riches of enemy tribes.

By the year 1200, Temujin had a following of 100,000 Mongols. Within a few years, he was able to unite all of Mongolia. As chief of all the Mongols, Temujin was given the name Genghis Khan. Genghis made himself supreme leader of all Mongol armies. No one disobeyed his commands. The armies were organized to travel fast and far. They began to attack civilized societies.

When the Mongols attacked civilized societies, they had two advantages. They were horse riders. Most of their enemies' warriors fought on foot. The Mongols had learned how to "live off the land." Unlike other armies, Mongol warriors did not have to carry supplies from home. They simply took what they wanted from the people they conquered.

Genghis Khan conquered more land than Alexander the Great. In addition to central Asia, his armies took Mesopotamia, Persia, and China. After Genghis Khan's death, Mongol armies took what is now the Soviet Union to the banks of the Dnieper River and invaded eastern Europe. Wherever they went, the Mongols spread terror. At first they were interested only in looting. Then they made their conquests into a steady source of wealth. They first discovered how to do this in China.

The Mongols Rule China

There had been civilization in China for about 2,500 years. From the beginning the Chinese had to defend themselves against barbarians from the north. Indeed, in the third century B.C., the Chinese built a great wall to stop barbarian raids. This **Great Wall of China** was made stronger in the sixth century A.D.

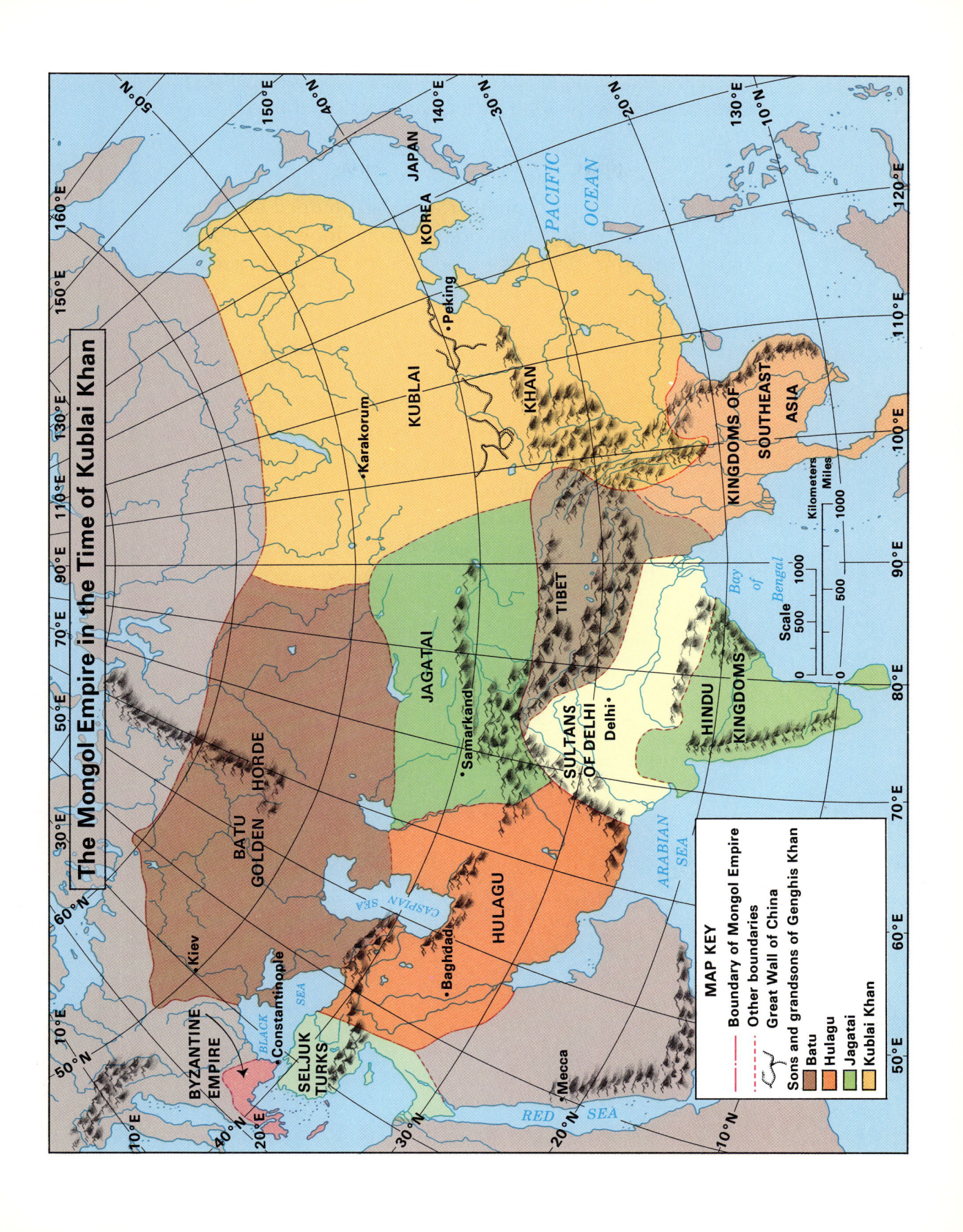

The Mongol Empire in the Time of Kublai Khan

MAP KEY
- — · — Boundary of Mongol Empire
- — — — Other boundaries
- ⛰ Great Wall of China

Sons and grandsons of Genghis Khan:
- Batu
- Hulagu
- Jagatai
- Kublai Khan

A ▶ Look at the map "The Mongol Empire in the Time of Kublai Khan (1259–1294)" (page 363). Find the Great Wall of China.

In the thirteenth century A.D., there were 50 Chinese people for every Mongol. But few Chinese were soldiers. Genghis Khan's troops moved fast. Genghis Khan also planned his attack on China well. One part of the Mongol army drew the Chinese army in one direction. The rest of the Mongol army attacked the Great Wall far from the main Chinese army. The Mongols poured into China. One by one the cities of China were conquered until Genghis Khan controlled all of China north of the Hwang Ho.

For a time the Mongols were interested only in looting, burning, and killing. Then a Chinese scholar gave Genghis Khan a better idea. Why not make the Chinese work for the Mongols? Why not make them pay **tribute,** or taxes, every year? Genghis Khan agreed. He himself did not like civilized ways, but he was happy to take the riches of a civilized society.

Genghis Khan died in 1227. Genghis's sons and later his grandsons ruled the lands he had conquered. The Mongols added conquests in Europe and in Russia.

(right) Genghis Kahn (1167–1227) addresses some followers.
(below) Kublai Kahn (1216–1294)

Kublai Khan, Genghis's most famous grandson, completed the conquest of China. He also tried to conquer Japan but failed.

B● Look again at the map "The Mongol Empire in the Time of Kublai Khan (1259–1294)." It shows areas ruled at that time by one of Genghis Khan's sons (Jagatai) and by three of his grandsons (Batu, Hulagu, and Kublai).
1. Find the four main divisions of the empire.
2. Which part was ruled by *Kublai Khan*?
3. Find Kiev. This was the main city of the Russian states.
4. Under whose rule were the Russians?
5. Find the area ruled by the Turkish sultans of Delhi.
6. Find Peking. This is the capital of China today. It was called "city of the Khan" (*Khanbalik* or *Cambaluc*).

Chinese Civilization Recovers

Chinese culture had been badly damaged by the Mongols. But Kublai Khan admired Chinese civilization. Kublai made his capital at the city that we call Peking today. Under his rule, China was peaceful. Learning and art made progress again in the lands ruled by Kublai Khan.

In western Asia, however, civilization suffered terribly from the Mongols. Another of Genghis Khan's descendants, named Timur (or Tamerlane), made smashing raids into Persia, Mesopotamia, and northern India.

A★ People in Western Europe learned about Kublai Khan from a book written by Marco Polo in 1298. Most people did not believe what Marco Polo wrote. Find out about Marco Polo's travels and adventures.

The Mongols controlled China until 1368, 74 years after Kublai Khan's death. Then a new family of emperors, called the Mings, came to power in China. The Ming emperors drove the Mongols back into Central Asia. Once more the Chinese Empire was independent and powerful.

B● The Chinese said that the Ming emperors had "the will of Heaven." What did that mean?

CIVILIZATIONS AND BARBARIANS IN ASIA IN THE MIDDLE AGES

Summary

One of the leading civilizations of Asia during the Middle Ages was found on the mountainous islands of Japan. Japan had borrowed important ideas from Korea and China in the third century A.D. One of those ideas was growing rice. The climate of Japan is good for agriculture, but there is not much level land in Japan. Since large amounts of rice can be grown in a small area, rice became Japan's main crop. Once they had a steady food supply, the Japanese no longer had to be hunters and gatherers. They could settle down and build a civilization.

Other borrowed ideas that helped form Japanese culture came from Confucianism—rules of obedience and respect, the importance of strong united families, and the worship of ancestors. Ancestor worship became part of the Japanese religion called Shinto. About the sixth century A.D., Buddhism was introduced in Japan, and gradually a mixture of Shinto and Buddhism became the main religion in Japan.

Japan had a feudal society. Feudalism was a way of organizing and defending societies that had no strong central government. Japan's society was divided into classes made up of the emperor, *shogun*, *daimyo*, *samurai*, merchants, artisans, and peasants who farmed for the noble *(daimyo)* families. The emperor was worshipped as a god, but he did not have much power. The strongest *daimyo* became the *shogun*, who ruled in the emperor's name.

Every *daimyo* had a group of *samurai* (warriors). The *samurai* lived by the code of loyalty called *bushido.* Under this code the *samurai* were ready to die for the *daimyo* and his family.

Japanese culture changed very little until the sixteenth century, when Portuguese traders came. The Portuguese introduced guns and, later, Christianity to the Japanese.

Beginning in the eleventh century India suffered many invasions by nomadic barbarians who were Muslim Turks. During the time of the invasions, many people in India became Muslims. Most Hindus, however, kept their own religion.

In the fourteenth century the Ottoman Turks became powerful in southeastern Europe and took Asia Minor from the Seljuk Turks. Constantinople fell in 1453. This ended the Byzantine Empire, which has lasted nearly a thousand years after the fall of the Roman Empire in the west.

China and other parts of Asia were troubled by barbarian invasions from Mongolia in the thirteenth century. The nomadic Mongols had been united by Genghis Khan. Genghis Khan's armies of horse soldiers lived off the land, taking what they wanted from the peoples they conquered. Genghis conquered northern China. Later his grandson Kublai Khan conquered the rest of China.

China was ruled by the Mongols from the time of Genghis Khan's conquest until 1368. At that time the Ming emperors came to power in China and drove the Mongols back into Central Asia.

Some Interesting Activities

1. Imagine that you are a *samurai*. Write a story about what *bushido* and *Zen Buddhism* mean to you.

2. Make a map of Asia and the Middle East showing how the Turks and the Mongols invaded and conquered civilizations in the Middle Ages. Use the maps in this chapter to help you.

3. Pretend you and your friends are Chinese generals. You learn that Genghis Khan's armies are advancing on China. These horsemen move much faster than any armies ever moved before. Discuss your problems of defense. What can they do to prepare for, or to stop, the invasion?

4. Research topics:
    a. Marco Polo and his visit to the court of Kublai Khan
    b. Francis Xavier and Christians in Asia
    c. Timur (Tamerlane) and his conquests
    d. Iyeyasu, founder of the Tokugawa *shoguns*
    e. Lady Murasaki and her book *Tale of Genji*
    f. Kublai Khan (1216–1294)
    g. Ivan the Great and the growth of Moscow's power
    h. Genghis Khan (1162?–1227) and his conquests

This illuminated manuscript page from a twelfth-century French Bible introduces the Gospel of Saint Matthew.

CHAPTER 14

The Rise of Latin Christendom

In the chapters about Africa, the New World, and Asia, we covered the whole period of the Middle Ages up to the beginning of the Modern Age in the sixteenth century A.D. Now we must turn back to the time when the Roman Empire in the West came to an end, in the fifth century A.D.

After the breakup of the Roman Empire, great changes took place in Western Europe. From the fifth century to the ninth century, Western Europe suffered from many waves of barbarian invasions. Yet a different civilized society would come out of this fierce time. One name for that society is *Christendom.* **Christendom** means "the world of Christ" or "the world of Christians."

Latin Christendom and Greek Christendom

Christendom in the Middle Ages was divided between two churches. One was the *Catholic church.* The other was the *Orthodox church.*

The Catholic church had its center in Rome. The bishop of Rome was head of the Catholic church. He was the *pope,* or Holy Father. The church services were said in the old language of Rome: *Latin.* The Catholic part of Christendom was called **Latin Christendom.**

The center of the Orthodox church was Constantinople, in eastern Europe. The head of the Orthodox church was the patriarch of Constantinople. Until the fall of Constantinople in 1453, the Byzantine emperor had much power in this church. Orthodox services were said in the Greek language. The Orthodox part of Christendom was called **Greek Christendom.**

A★ Look at the map "Christendom and Islam c. A.D. 1200" (page 371).
1. The following are some present-day countries: Spain, Greece, the Soviet Union, France, England, Ireland, Bulgaria, Italy, Germany, Poland, Romania, Sweden, Hungary. Which were *Catholic* in the Middle Ages? Which were *Orthodox?*
2. Find the cities in which the heads of the Catholic church and the Orthodox church lived.
3. From what direction did Islam at first threaten Latin Christendom? (See page 280.)
4. What part of Christendom was conquered by Ottoman Turks in the fourteenth and fifteenth centuries? (See page 361.)

The "Dark Ages" in Western Europe

During the time of the Roman Empire, civilization had spread across much of Western Europe. The Roman Empire had sent its armies and laws to many lands as far north as Scotland. But by the fifth century A.D., the Roman armies could no longer protect Western Europe from invasion. From the sixth to the ninth century, barbarians pushed into Western Europe from the

THE GROWTH OF CIVILIZATION

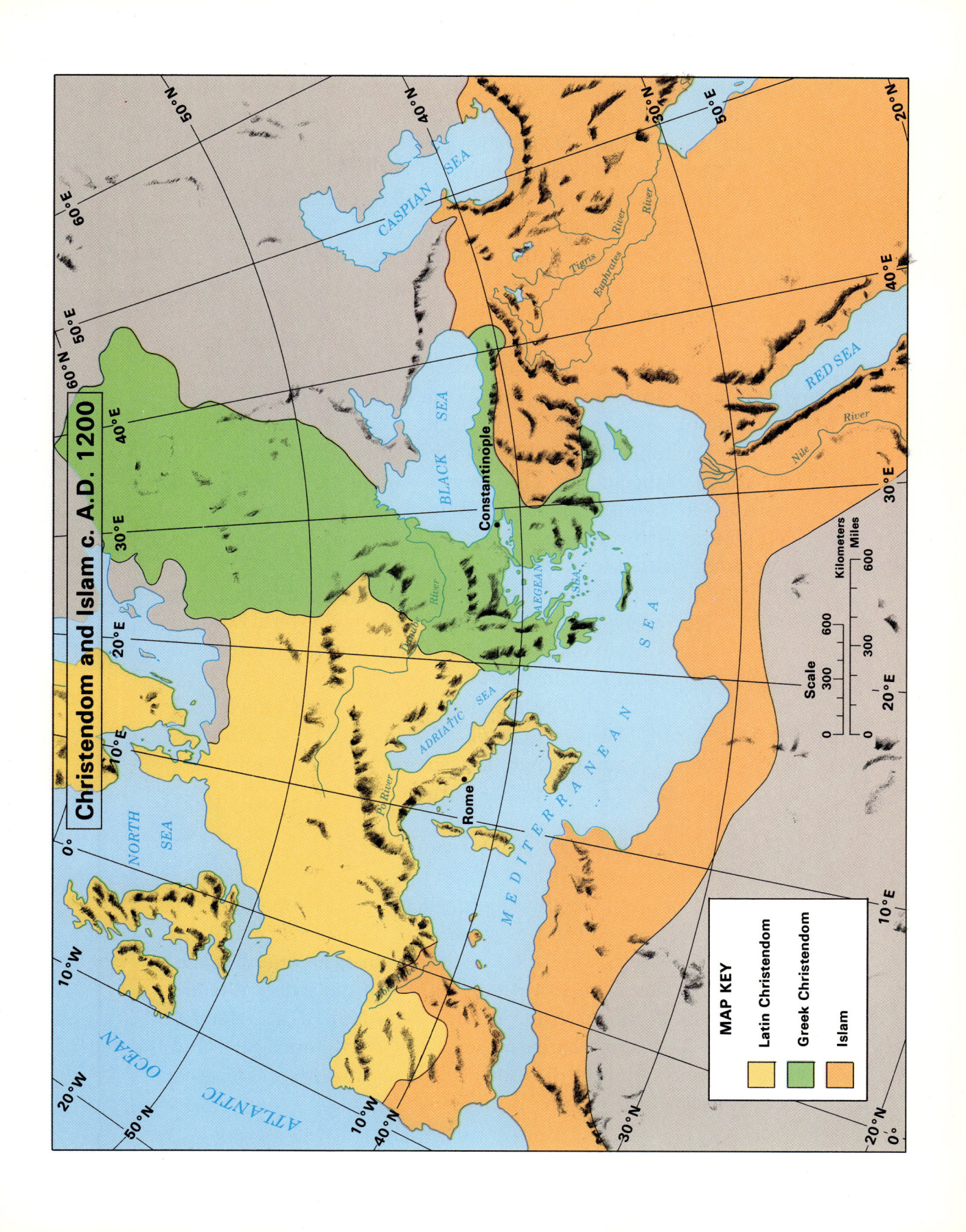

Christendom and Islam c. A.D. 1200

MAP KEY
- Latin Christendom
- Greek Christendom
- Islam

north and the east. This period of time, the early part of the Middle Ages, is called the **Dark Ages.**

During the time of the barbarian invasions, there was almost no order in Western Europe. No strong governments remained. Starvation, disease, and war nearly wiped out the population in some regions. Many cities and towns fell into ruin. There was little trade. Roman roads and harbors were abandoned. It looked at times as if the light of civilization would go out in Western Europe.

During the Dark Ages, nevertheless, the light did not quite go out. Always, in some part of Western Europe, agriculture, government, and even learning were still carried on.

The strongest force for civilization in Latin Christendom was the Catholic church. The church had no armies, yet the barbarians respected it. The church taught faith, hope, and charity. It helped the poor. It had schools to keep learning alive. The church also carried on many Roman ideas about law and government and literature.

After the barbarians invaded Western Europe, they began to settle down. They set up new kingdoms in Western Europe. They became Christians. The barbarians looked to Rome, not to the Byzantine Empire, for leadership.

A pattern for Latin Christendom began to take shape during the Dark Ages. There would be one church with great authority. There would be many kingdoms, some of which would later become the nations of modern Europe.

A ▶ Why did the barbarians respect the church?

At the end of the eighth century A.D., a new emperor of the West was crowned. He was *Charlemagne* [shär′ lə mān′], or Charles the Great. He ruled the area that is now France, Germany, Austria, and northern Italy. He defended Western Europe against the Arab Empire in Spain and Africa. He also defended it against barbarians in the north and east. But Charlemagne's empire did not last long. After his death (A.D. 814) it broke into separate kingdoms.

In the ninth century A.D., there began new waves of invasions. Western Europe was attacked from all sides. Barbarian horsemen attacked Europe from the east. From the south came Muslims and pirates. And from the north came the Norsemen (or Vikings).

Defending Latin Christendom

The people of Latin Christendom had to deal with the new invasions. Charlemagne's empire had collapsed. There were several kingdoms, but they were not able to protect the people. Kings could not pay and feed the large armies that were needed to defend their lands. Peasants were at the mercy of raiders. Until people could be safe, there would be little trade. Until there was trade, there could be little saving and capital.

A ● Could civilization grow without defense, safety, and capital?

How could the people of Western Europe get defense against the raiders? We have seen that there were different ways of fighting battles at different times. In the ancient world, often *horse-chariots* won battles. At other times, *trained foot soldiers* marching close together could sweep the battlefield. Foot soldiers won the Battle of Marathon. Foot soldiers made the

Charlemagne, or Charles the Great (742–814). Crowned emperor of the West in 800 by Pope Leo III, he successfully governed his large empire for 14 years. He was interested in the arts and encouraged learning through the establishment of schools.

empire of Rome. By the ninth century A.D. in Western Europe, battles were won by horse soldiers.

During the Dark Ages, two inventions reached Western Europe that made horse soldiers much better fighters than they had been in classical times. The first invention was the *stirrup*. Stirrups are fastened to the saddle. The rider's feet are in the stirrups. With the stirrups the rider can sit firmly. He can charge against a strong line of foot soldiers. It is not easy to knock the rider off the horse.

The second invention was the *horseshoe*. Horseshoes are pieces of iron nailed to a horse's hoofs. Before horseshoes, horses' feet were hurt by hard ground and rocks, so horses could not travel fast. They could not carry heavy loads without damaging their feet.

Western Europeans used stirrups and horseshoes to invent a new way of fighting. Now horse soldiers lined up and charged. Their long *lances* pointed forward as their horses galloped toward the enemy. The soldiers and their horses wore *armor*.

Two Inventions and the Knight-in-Armor

Horseshoe

Stirrup

THE GROWTH OF CIVILIZATION

Arrows bounced off the armor. For hundreds of years horse soldiers controlled the battlefield. During the Middle Ages, these armored soldiers on horseback were called *knights.*

Early in the Middle Ages, every knight-in-armor wore a coat made of heavy links of iron. Later, knights wore iron or steel plates that protected the shoulders, chest, arms, and legs. A knight's head was covered by an iron or steel helmet. The helmet had a movable facepiece. Even the knight's hands were protected. He wore iron gloves. When a knight put on all of his armor, it was hard to tell who he was. But he carried a shield. His "coat-of-arms" was painted on this shield. The coat-of-arms told what family he came from.

B▶ Why were the horseshoe and the stirrup important inventions?

C● Look at the picture "Two Inventions and the Knight-in-Armor" (page 374).
1. Notice the knight's lance and shield.
2. How much might the knight's armor and weapons weigh?
3. What would happen to a horse without horseshoes carrying such weight?
4. How would the horseshoes help the horse to keep steady over soft, slippery ground?

D▶ Look at the pictures of shields on page 376. Each shield has a knight's coat-of-arms. Why were coats-of-arms needed?

It was very costly to supply a knight with armor. The peasants of Europe could not afford to buy armor and big horses. Yet without knights there could be no good defense. Let us see how Europe in the Middle Ages supported thousands of knights.

The Feudal System in Europe

Invasions from the east, the south, and the north during the ninth century broke up what was left of Charlemagne's empire. Because there was no central government to protect people, local leaders began to set up their own systems of defense. Some of these leaders were great landowners. Others were royal officers called *counts.*

In feudal times each knight had a "coat of arms," or design, for his shield.

These local leaders offered to protect people in their neighborhoods. In return, some of those neighboring people were expected to help the local leaders by serving as soldiers on horseback. This was the beginning of what is called the *feudal system.* By the early years of the tenth century A.D., the feudal system, or *feudalism,* had become the way of organizing society in France and in some other parts of Europe. Eventually the feudal system spread to most of Europe.

Feudalism was a way to organize and defend a country that had no strong central government. The feudal system was based on two things. The first of these was ownership of the land. The second was the loyalty of the knight to his lord.

Look at the chart "Feudal Society" (page 379). This will give you some idea of how the feudal system in Europe worked. At the top of the society was a king. Next stood the greater and lesser lords and their ladies. Below the lords were the knights. At the bottom of the society, producing the food to support everybody, were the peasants.

A ▶ What other feudal system have you read about? (Look at pages 350–351).

In the beginning of the feudal system, the lords were the great landholders or royal officials who offered protection to lesser people. The armed horsemen who fought for a lord were called knights. The lord promised to protect the land held by his knights. In return, every knight swore to be loyal to his lord and to help him in war.

Knights and other free people whose land was protected by a lord were called **vassals** [vas′ əlz]. (The word *vassal* comes from an old word meaning "servant.") Every vassal had to swear an **oath of fealty** [fē′ əl tē]. (*Fealty* means "being faithful.") The land held by a vassal and protected by the vassal's lord was called a **fief** [fēf]. Another word for fief was "fee," or "feu," from which comes the word feudal.

Not all vassals had to serve as soldiers for their lord, but most of them did. During the Middle Ages there was little money. Most people paid for the things they wanted by providing services instead of money. In payment for protection of their lands, vassals provided military services. For each fief, a vassal had to provide a certain number of knights on horseback for the lord—often for 40 days out of the year if the lord needed armed men.

The feudal system, you can see, was a military and political system for defending a country or a region. People who did not have weapons and did not serve in war were outside the feudal "contract," or oath of fealty, even though they might be controlled by the lords and the knights.

The vast majority of people during the Middle Ages were peasants, who grew crops and raised animals. Peasants could not be lords or knights, although sometimes peasant men would serve as foot soldiers. The peasants had no political or military power.

The peasants who lived on a fief were ruled by the lord or knight who held the fief. They were not free to move away from that fief unless the lord or knight gave them permission. Many peasants were *serfs*. Although they were different from slaves, **serfs** were not free persons, because they were bound to work on the land where they were born.

By this feudal system, the peoples of Europe got protection from invaders, robbers, and other armed bands. The king of a country was the greatest of the lords. The lords and knights were prepared to fight at any time. Because those lords and knights owned the land, they were able to keep horses and armor. The peasants who farmed the land were governed and protected by the lords and knights.

- **B** ▶ What was a *vassal*? Could a peasant be a vassal?
- **C** ▶ What did a knight owe to his lord in return for a fief?
- **D** ● Look at the chart "Feudal Society" (page 379). Can you see a weakness in the feudal system? (Remember what happened in feudal Japan. Suppose a great lord decided to disobey his king. Suppose two great lords fought each other. To whom would the lords' vassals be loyal?)

From the tenth century to the fifteenth or the sixteenth century A.D., feudal lords were powerful throughout Western Europe. Sometimes a great lord would be more powerful than his king. The greater lords were also called nobles or barons. In most European countries, they were governors and judges as well as military leaders.

- **E** ● Can you think of some countries where there are still lords and ladies today?

The Manor

Along with the feudal system, there grew up in the early Middle Ages the economic unit and social community that we call the *manor* [man′ ər]. A small fief usually was a manor, and manors usually were held by knights. (Many manors, though, belonged to the church.) The **manor** was an area of land and the *unit of agricultural production.* Most manors had one or more villages where peasant families lived. Usually there was a church with a priest. The lord of the manor—the baron or knight who held the fief—lived in a manor house, or small castle.

The lord of the manor protected the villagers. Usually he owned the mill and perhaps the blacksmith shop. He was judge over all the people who lived on the manor.

Ordinarily a peasant family did not have its own farm. Instead, the lands of the manor were divided into strips. Every

Feudal Society

KING (or QUEEN)

Lords and Ladies — Lords and Ladies

Knights — Knights — Knights — Knights

Peasants — Peasants — Peasants — Peasants

year these strips were assigned to someone. Some strips were the lord's. Others were the priest's. The remaining strips were divided among the peasants. The peasants worked on their own strips and also on the strips of the lord and the priest. The plan of work was made up by the whole community.

During the early Middle Ages, every manor produced and consumed nearly all its own goods. As time passed, however, agriculture became more **efficient** (very productive). This meant

THE RISE OF LATIN CHRISTENDOM

that part of the crops could be traded for goods made in other communities. When this happened, towns with merchants and skilled workers began to grow.

A ▶ Look at the picture "A Medieval Manor" (page 381). Notice how the land is divided into a pasture (shared by the whole village) and three big fields. The three fields are laid out in strips. Every peasant family had some strips for growing crops.

New Agricultural Inventions

Before Western Europe could have wealth and civilization, efficient agriculture was needed. Farmers in northwestern Europe had a special problem. The best soil was in the valleys and the plains, but this soil was wet, heavy, and often *swampy*. The cause of this was the heavy precipitation from the *westerly* winds.

At first, the peasants in northwestern Europe used a light plow. It was like the plow used by the Greeks and Romans. This kind of plow was fine for turning the dry, light soil of the Mediterranean region. It was pulled by only one or two oxen. In northwestern Europe, however, this plow was not strong enough. It could not break up the wet, heavy soil of the valleys and plains. People were forced to farm the poorer soil on the hills. Then a new plow was invented. It was the *heavy, wheeled plow.*

A ● Look at the pictures "The Light Plow and the Heavy, Wheeled Plow" (page 382).
1. Notice that the light plow was not much more than a digging-stick pulled by animals. Why did the light plow not need wheels?
2. On the heavy plow, find the iron *blade,* or *colter.* This cuts the soil.
3. Find the *plowshare.* This iron plate digs sideways into the soil.

With the heavy plow, the heavy, wet soils could be plowed. The furrows helped to drain water away when rains were heavy.

A Medieval Manor

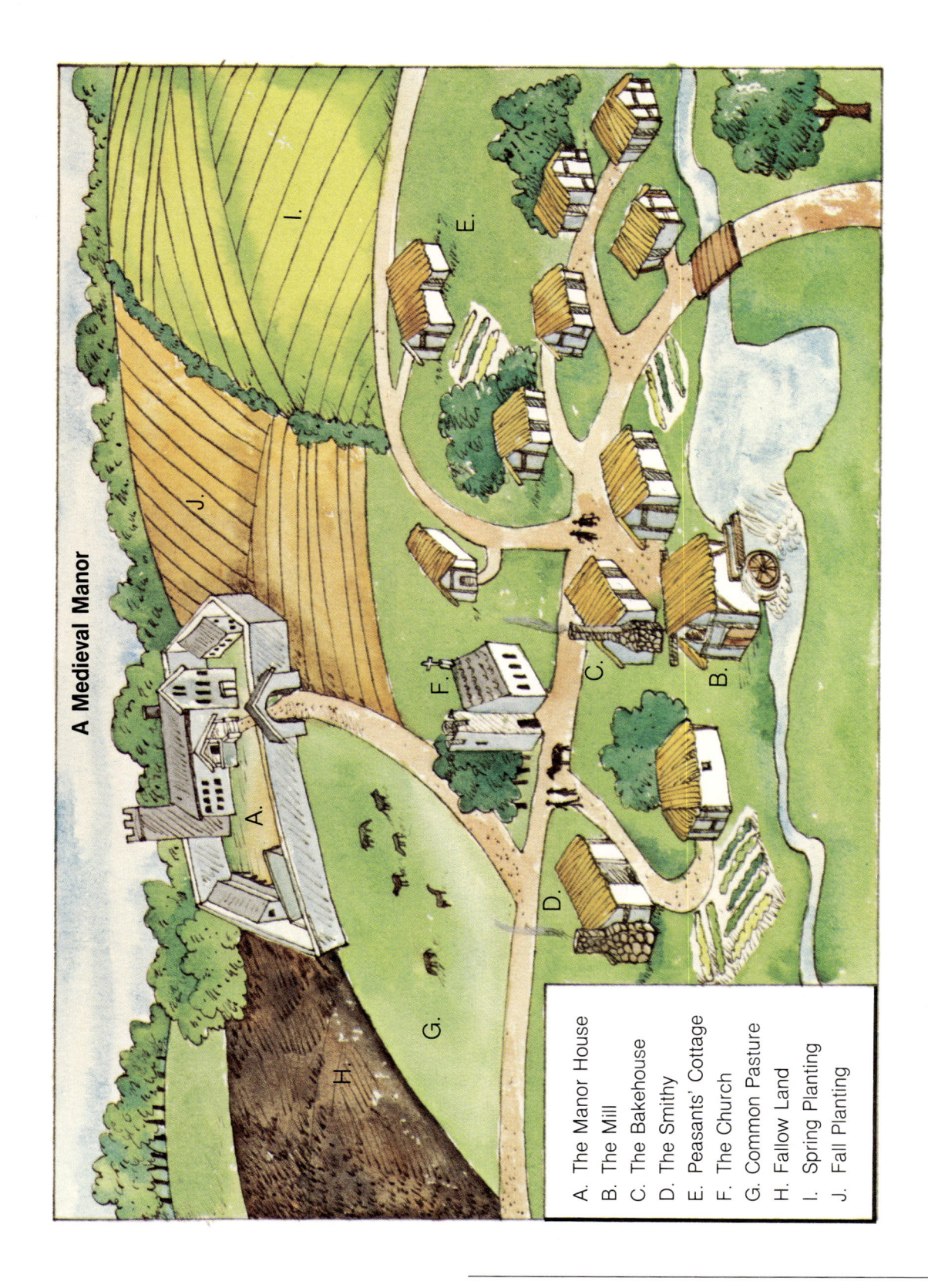

A. The Manor House
B. The Mill
C. The Bakehouse
D. The Smithy
E. Peasants' Cottage
F. The Church
G. Common Pasture
H. Fallow Land
I. Spring Planting
J. Fall Planting

THE RISE OF LATIN CHRISTENDOM

The Light Plow and the Heavy, Wheeled Plow

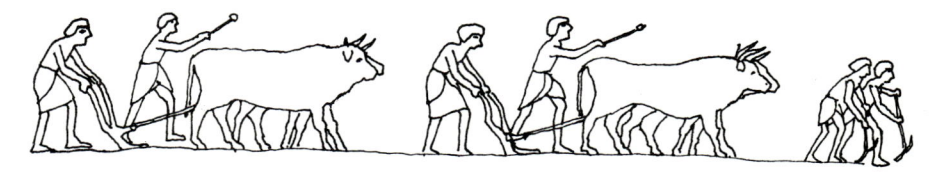

This Egyptian picture from 1900 B.C. shows the light plow and people hoeing.

This drawing shows the heavy, wheeled plow pulled by four oxen. Often eight oxen were used.

The people of northwestern Europe learned several other things that helped them grow more crops. They learned how to build ditches and drains to carry away floodwater and to get rid of swamps. They learned to leave part of their land unused during a growing season. One field was planted with seeds; another was not. In the next growing season, the "rested" land was planted with seeds, and it yielded a larger crop. This is called the *two-field system.* Later the people divided the land into three fields. By using two of the fields each year, they increased production even more.

B ● Was the water problem in northwestern Europe the opposite of the water problem in Mesopotamia and Egypt? Explain.

The Great Castles

When you visit Europe you will see many stone castles. Some castles are still kept as they were long ago. Other castles are in ruins. These castles remind us of feudal times.

Most often the lords and ladies built their castles for defense. Many of the knights lived at the castle and helped to defend it. Within the castle, the people had to be able to protect themselves against attacks from the enemies. That is why the castle was built with towers and thick stone walls. Sometimes the walls were as thick as three or four meters (10 or 13 feet).

A *moat* surrounded the walls of the castle. The **moat** was a ditch filled with water. This provided more protection for the castle. A *drawbridge* from the entrance of the castle across the moat could be raised or lowered. The peasants lived outside the castle walls. If enemies approached, all the people outside the castle went inside the castle walls. Animals and food were brought inside the castle walls. The drawbridge was raised. Sometimes fighting with the enemy could last for weeks, months, or even years.

How did the people in the castles live when the land was at peace? On the walls of the smaller rooms in the castle were *tapestries* (heavy cloth woven with pictures in it). The tapestries helped to keep the rooms warm and comfortable. The largest room was the great hall. All people living in the castle had their meals together in the great hall. The lord and lady and other important persons ate at a high table at one end of the room. Often there was a great fire of wood to give warmth. The stone floor was spread with *rushes*.

People living in the castle usually were well fed. There were bread, cheese, poultry, meat, and fish. For drink there were water, milk, and wine. There were no forks and spoons. People ate with their fingers and used their own knives. Sometimes they had bowls made of wood, but often the food was served on pieces of bread. Cups were made of horn or metal.

During meals and after meals there was often entertainment. There were singers and harpists. Storytellers recited tales.

THE RISE OF LATIN CHRISTENDOM

(below) Fenis, an Italian castle built in 1340

(left) This fifteenth-century illustration shows that castles in the High Middle Ages were much more elaborate. Observe, too, the contrast in the life style of the nobility and the peasants.

Most lords and ladies had *jesters* whose job was to make people laugh. Jesters were allowed to make fun even of the lords and ladies.

Lords and ladies spent much of their free time out of doors. Hunting was the great sport. The lords, ladies, and knights hunted deer and wild boar in the forests. They chased smaller animals such as hares. They hunted birds by flying trained hawks.

Of course, there were more serious things to do. The lord's steward had to watch over the land, the peasants, the crops, and the herds. Food had to be stored for winter and spring. The knights had to practice riding and using their weapons. The women of the castle made cloth and clothing. Young people were educated in the castle. Few learned to read and write

384 THE GROWTH OF CIVILIZATION

unless they were going to be priests. Young men learned how to become knights. Young women learned how to run a large household.

Such was the way of life of the castle in the Middle Ages. It suited the rough and dangerous times before civilization grew strong again.

A● Look at the pictures "Medieval Castles" on page 384. Each lord had a strong fortress. How did these fortresses reduce the power of a monarch? How would they encourage civil wars?

The Economic Base for Civilization in Western Europe

Feudalism was a *political* base on which civilization could be built. The feudal system gave law and order, although sometimes it also led to civil wars.

The new agriculture gave an *economic* base for civilization. Agriculture was efficient. The peasants produced enough food for themselves and for the other groups in society. The rulers, soldiers, and priests could do their own special work. As time went on, more men and women could be spared to produce cloth, tools, and buildings. There was enough production to support schools and hospitals. Money came into use. Trade grew. Towns became centers of trade. People were able to save. There was more capital to help production. Civilization grew once more in Western Europe.

A▶ How did efficient agriculture give a base for civilization in Western Europe?
B● How did efficient agriculture give a base for the first civilization in Sumer?
C● Why is trade with *money* easier than trade by *barter*?
D● Why does money make saving easier?

By the twelfth century in western Europe, the civilization of Latin Christendom was taking shape. In spite of troubled times, this civilization went on growing. In the next chapter we shall study the civilization of Latin Christendom in the **High Middle Ages** (the thirteenth through the fifteenth centuries).

Summary

By the fifth century A.D., Christianity was the main religion of the Roman Empire. In that century the Roman Empire in Western Europe came to an end, and barbarians took over. In eastern Europe the Roman Empire lived on until A.D. 1453. As a result, Europe was divided into two main culture regions. Eastern Europe had the Orthodox church, centered in Constantinople. Western Europe had the Catholic church, centered in Rome. Eastern Europe we call Greek Christendom, and Western Europe we call Latin Christendom.

For a time in Latin Christendom, it seemed as if civilization might die out as a result of wave after wave of invasions. The people of Western Europe had to find a way of organizing local defense against raiders and invaders. An answer was found in the feudal system. Knights-in-armor became the most important force on the battlefield.

In the feudal system, great lords owned large areas of land. The great lords gave land to their *vassals,* who were lesser lords. These vassals had knights as their own vassals. The peasants worked the land for the lords and knights. Land held by a vassal was a fief, or feu, and each vassal swore fealty (loyalty) to his lord. In time, kings and queens gained more power. However, in a feudal monarchy the great lords could, and often did, disobey the monarch. Lords with their stone castles and bands of knights might defy kings and queens.

During this time agriculture became more efficient. The manor, with its two or three large fields divided into strips, was the unit of production. The new, heavy plow, drawn by a team of oxen, could till and drain the rich, wet soil of Western Europe. Food production grew better. Workers could be spared to make goods such as cloth and tools. The division of labor led to trade, towns, the use of money, and savings for capital goods.

Some Interesting Activities

1. Find pictures of medieval castles. See if you can also find a *plan* of a castle. Draw a sketch of a castle, and label some of its parts. You may use a dictionary to help. Here are some names that you

may use: *courtyard, great hall, keep, turret, curtain wall, moat, drawbridge, portcullis, battlements, loopholes.*

Some castles had a barbican. Some had two or more circles of curtain walls and turrets.

2. Draw a knight-in-armor. Label his armor and weapons. Use a dictionary to make sure you know the following words:
    a. helmet
    b. visor
    c. breastplate
    d. greaves
    e. gauntlets
    f. chain armor
    g. lance
    h. shield
    i. dagger
    j. battle-axe
    k. mace
    l. two-handed sword

3. Use an encyclopedia to report on one of the following:
    a. The Emperor Charlemagne (742–814)
    b. Pope Gregory I (the Great) (540?–604)
    c. Pope Gregory VII (Hildebrand) (1020?–1085)
    d. William I (the Conqueror) (1027–1087)
    e. Matilda (or Maud), empress and queen of England (1102–1167)
    f. Eleanor of Aquitaine (1122?–1204)
    g. The Cid (Rodrigo Diaz de Bivar) (1040?–1099)
    h. Alcuin of York (735?–804)

4. With members of the class, role-play characters in a feudal monarchy. You can have a king and a queen, a great lord and a lady, a knight and a lady, a bishop, a priest, a nun, a blacksmith, and peasants or serfs. Each character tells about his or her duties and fealty and work and play. You may wish to add merchants, crafts workers, and housewives from a city such as Rome, London, or Paris. Remember that townspeople were mainly "outside" the feudal system; they did not usually owe fealty to a lord.

5. Use a historical atlas to find out about invasions of Western Europe from the fourth to the ninth century. Here are the names of some invading peoples: (in the earlier centuries) Goths, Huns, Vandals, Angles, Saxons, and Franks; (in the ninth century) Vikings (Norsemen), Magyars, and Saracens (Muslims).

Sainte-Chapelle, Louis IX's palace chapel, Paris (1248). A magnificent example of classic Gothic architecture, it is famous for its stained glass windows.

CHAPTER 15

Latin Christendom in the High Middle Ages

Civilization grew rapidly in Latin Christendom after the eleventh century. In this chapter we shall look at the culture of Latin Christendom in the *High Middle Ages,* that is, in the thirteenth, fourteenth, and fifteenth centuries. We shall see that many of the controlling ideas of Latin Christendom passed on into modern times.

The Controlling Ideas of Chivalry

One important set of ideas in Latin Christendom was the code of behavior of the knights. The *samurai* of Japan had a code called *bushido.* The knights of Christendom had a code known as "chivalry." The word *chivalry* is from the French word for knight, or horseman: *chevalier* [shə val′ yā]. **Chivalry** was the way of life of a knight. It was a mixture of soldiers' duties and Christian ideas. Many of our ideas about good manners today come from chivalry.

To become a knight, a boy usually had to be from a noble family—a family of lords and ladies. As a rule, a boy began his training for knighthood when he was about seven. First he became a *page* and helped the ladies of a lord's castle. As a page, he served at the feasts held for the knights. Next he became a *squire* and learned to fight and hunt. When he was about 20, he became a knight. As a knight, he was ready to fight whenever there was need for him. A knight had to be tough. He had to know all the skills of battle. One way of practicing these skills was by mock battles called *tournaments* [tėr′ nə mənts].

As time went on, this rough soldier's code developed into something different. It was the beginning of our own Western ideas of good manners. How did this happen? As Latin Christendom grew more civilized, the meaning of chivalry changed. A good knight had to be more than a brave fighter. He had to be polite as well. He had to show the highest loyalty to the persons he served. He could never break a promise. He could never shrink from his duty—even if it meant giving up his life!

A good knight was loyal to the church. He was kind and gentle to the weak and the wounded. It was his duty to protect any lady from danger. Of course, few knights lived up to all these ideals. Still, the pattern was set. To this day, a "gentleman" is judged, in part, by standards of chivalry.

Christianity was also a great influence in changing manners. Jesus had taught that people should be loving. In the eyes of God, he said, women are equal to men. The Catholic church taught people to love and honor Mary, the mother of Jesus. Lessons such as these helped to bring new respect for women. It was different from the codes of most earlier cultures.

The change in behavior did not take place quickly. It did not affect everyone. Not all knights kept their promises. Nor were most women treated as equals with men. Still, a new set of ideas did come into being. The ideas are still with us.

A ● Look at the box "The Code of Chivalry" (page 391). Which ideas seem feudal? Which are Christian? Which ideas do we still use?

The Code of Chivalry

Chivalry required a knight to be —

1. loyal to his lord

2. faithful to the lady he loved

3. loyal to the church

4. a protector of the weak, the poor, the helpless, and all women and children

5. a brave and well-trained fighter who could bear great suffering and hardship

6. fair, just, kind, and truthful

The Stories of Chivalry

In the High Middle Ages, the lords and ladies held great feasts in their castle halls. Often these feasts were to honor their knights. During the feasts, they would listen to stories about famous battles and heroes. Some of these heroes were real people in history. Yet most of the stories about the heroes were made up by the storytellers. Even so, these stories tell us much about medieval people and their culture. They tell us what people liked to hear. They describe the deeds that people most admired.

Let us read a story about Roland, a famous hero of the age of chivalry.

A twelfth-century relief showing Roland in combat with a Muslim

The Song of Roland

Charlemagne brought the peoples of Western Europe together. His twelve best knights were the *Twelve Peers of Charlemagne. (Peer* meant "companion.")

The finest knight of all was young *Lord Roland*. Roland was a perfect example of chivalry. He was brave, faithful, kind, and gentle.

Charlemagne took his army into Spain to fight the Muslims there. The Twelve Peers went with Charlemagne. Together they defeated the Muslims. Charlemagne said that the Muslims must give up much treasure. Then he would take his army back to France.

Charlemagne sent a lord named Ganelon [gan′ ə lon] to collect the treasure from the Muslims' camp. Ganelon, however, was a traitor. He was Roland's stepfather, and he hated Roland. Charlemagne did not know that Ganelon was a traitor. This mistake led to a terrible loss. Ganelon told the Muslim king how to trap Lord Roland and the other peers and their soldiers.

"Tomorrow," said Ganelon, "Charlemagne's army will go back to France. The army will go through a pass in the Pyrenees [pir′ ə nēz] Mountains. The army will be stretched out in a long narrow line. Charlemagne will lead the army. He will leave the Twelve Peers and their soldiers at the rear of the army. The Twelve Peers will defend the pass until the rest of the army is safely through."

Ganelon gave a cruel laugh. "I will show you how to attack Roland and the other Peers with your whole army. You can kill them all before

392 THE GROWTH OF CIVILIZATION

Charlemagne can turn back to help them. Charlemagne's heart will be broken. He will never come back to fight you again."

The Muslim king was delighted with this plan. He gave Ganelon many gifts, and Ganelon went back to Charlemagne.

Everything happened as Ganelon planned. Most of Charlemagne's army went through the pass. When the main army was miles ahead, thousands of Muslims attacked Roland and the other Peers from all sides.

The Peers knew that Ganelon had betrayed them. They asked Roland to blow his magic horn. They said: "Charlemagne will hear the horn and come back to help us."

Roland would not blow the horn. "We shall fight alone," he said. "Our faith and honor are at stake."

So the Twelve Peers and their soldiers fought for hours. They killed many enemies, but at last all the Christians were dead or wounded. Roland himself was badly hurt. He decided to blow his horn, so that Charlemagne would come back and punish the Muslims.

Far away Charlemagne heard the sad notes of the magic horn. "Roland is in trouble," said Charlemagne.

"How can that be?" said traitor Ganelon. "The Muslims want peace."

Again the horn sounded over the mountains. Charlemagne knew now that Ganelon was a traitor. He arrested Ganelon, and turned back with his army.

It was too late. When Charlemagne reached the pass all the knights and soldiers were dead. Roland was lying on his great sword. He had hidden the sword with his body so that the enemy would not take the sword.

The Muslims had fled. Charlemagne was indeed heartbroken. But Ganelon was wrong when he thought Charlemagne would be too sad to fight any more.

Charlemagne led his army against the Muslims. He chased and killed many enemies. He destroyed their towns. Ganelon was tried and executed. Thus Charlemagne took revenge for the deaths of the noblest knights of France.

A● Compare the story of Roland with the story of the 47 Ronin on page 352. What controlling ideas seem to be shared by the two stories? Do both stories tell about cultures in which soldiers were very important? Explain.

LATIN CHRISTENDOM IN THE HIGH MIDDLE AGES

B ▶ What kinds of stories do you like to read or to see in movies or on television? Do these stories tell you about *your* culture and its controlling ideas? Discuss.

C ★ Other famous stories of chivalry are the stories about *King Arthur and the Knights of the Round Table.* Find out about these stories.

The Work of the Catholic Church

The main controlling ideas of Christendom were Judeo-Christian ideas. These were taught throughout Western Europe by the Catholic church. During the Middle Ages, it was the only church in Western Europe.

People of the Middle Ages believed that the church was like an army. They thought that it must fight to save the souls of men and women. They felt this way because of their belief in God and in the devil.

People feared and hated the devil. They felt that the church must fight a never-ending war against the devil and against their own temptations to do evil. Church services were daily battles against sin and evil. Church buildings protected the towns and villages where Christians lived. They protected the fields where Christians worked. They protected the churchyards where Christians were buried.

The Middle Ages in Europe has been called the "Age of Faith." This is a good description. People knew they were caught in a battle between good and evil. To help them win the battle, they wanted a strong church. The church was organized in a way that reminds us of the Roman Empire. At the head of the church was the bishop of Rome, called the *pope,* or Holy Father. The pope was chosen by the *cardinals.* All the lands of Latin Christendom were divided into *bishoprics* and *archbishoprics,* with *bishops* or *archbishops* as their heads. The *bishoprics* were divided into *parishes.* Each parish had its church, with a *priest* and, often, assistant priests.

There were also a number of *religious orders,* each made up of *monks, nuns,* or *friars.* These religious orders did many services for the people. Some looked after the poor. Some took care of children whose parents were dead. Some ran hospitals.

Some taught in schools and universities. Some copied books. (There were *no printed books* until late in the fifteenth century.)

A ● Today churches still provide some of these services, but other organizations provide most services. What organizations today provide for poor people and orphans? Provide health care and education?

We can see how important the church was in the lives of the people. The church was very powerful. It had its own laws and law courts. The clergy (priests, monks, and nuns) could be tried only in church courts. Church courts also dealt with marriages and matters of religious belief.

The church was wealthy as well as powerful. Lords and rich merchants gave land and money to the church.

At times, kings and great lords tried to interfere with the church. However, the popes and bishops usually were able to block these attempts for several centuries. For example, a strong king of England, Henry II, thought that a priest who was accused of a crime should be tried in the king's law courts. He also tried to control the choice of bishops in England. In the struggle over these matters, some of Henry's knights murdered the archbishop, *Thomas Becket.* This act shocked everyone. Henry II had to give in. He knelt at Becket's tomb and was whipped for the evil deed that his knights had done.

For centuries the church kept its independence. Even strong monarchs had little control over the church. But this changed at the end of the Middle Ages. At that time many governments took control of religion in their nations. Today this has changed once more. In most Western nations today, governments do not try to control religious beliefs and worship.

This illuminated manuscript illustration shows the murder of Archbishop Thomas Becket in Canterbury Cathedral.

Notre Dame Cathedral, Paris, completed in 1245. Its classic Gothic features include pointed arches, buttresses, and stained glass windows.

The Church Buildings

The most beautiful and costly buildings of the Middle Ages were churches and cathedrals. People spent a great deal of time and money to make beautiful buildings in which they could worship. They designed the churches so as to help worshippers to think of heaven and of the power and glory of God.

The people of the High Middle Ages built their churches in a style that is called **Gothic architecture.** This style was different from any architecture that had come before. In earlier times, the roofs of the churches had been held up by thick, strong walls. The church builders had put few windows in the walls. They knew that the walls would be stronger without windows. Then French builders learned to hold up the roof of a cathedral in a new way. They found that they could use pointed arches. To support these arches, they used strong stone props. These props were called *buttresses*.

With pointed arches and buttresses, the French builders could build tall cathedrals. The cathedrals seemed to reach straight up to heaven. The walls could have huge windows. Workers made these windows out of bits of brightly colored glass. We call it *stained glass*. As the light came through the windows from the outside, they seemed to be made of bright jewels. Most of the windows showed pictures that told Bible stories. In those days most people could not read. The pictures in these stained-glass windows helped them remember the teachings of their Christian faith.

- A● Use the "Questions about Controlling Ideas" on page 151 to review the controlling ideas of Christianity. How would a strong church with learned priests strengthen these ideas? What did *chivalry* add to them?
- B● Look at the pictures of Gothic church architecture (pages 388 and 396). How do they help you to understand how people felt about religion?

Troubles in Latin Christendom

With civilization, people's lives were better in many ways. Barbarian invasions were stopped. Food supplies were greater. There was more wealth. Yet Latin Christendom, like other civilizations, had troubles and problems. Feudalism caused many civil wars. There were also many wars among monarchs. These wars were usually for land and power. England and France, for example, fought wars in every century from the twelfth to the fifteenth century. One of these wars lasted on and off from 1337 to 1453. It is known as the *Hundred Years' War*.

- A● Suppose you are a historian studying old writings. You find a letter written in 1338. The writer of the letter says: "The Hundred Years' War began last year." Do you think that the letter was *really* written in 1338? Why or why not?

One of the most exciting true stories of the Hundred Years' War is the story of *Joan of Arc*. It tells how the French learned to *unite* against the English. The English kept winning battles because France was *divided*. Feudal loyalties were strong in France. Joan of Arc showed French people how to be loyal to their king.

The story of Joan of Arc is a story of deep religious faith. It is a story, too, of **patriotism** (love of one's country). Joan was a simple peasant girl. All through her childhood she saw around her the effects of war and of the English invaders.

When Joan was 13, she had a *vision*. While she was looking after her father's sheep, she heard saints from heaven. The saints told her to go and lead the French to drive out the English. For three years Joan could not believe that this vision was true, but the voices kept on telling her to go. At last she went to a knight who lived near her village. She told the knight that he must give her a horse and armor and some soldiers.

The knight at first thought that Joan was crazy. What could a 17-year-old girl do in a bitter war? He said that he would send her home. But Joan's faith won the knight to her side. Soon she was riding, with six soldiers, to see the king of France.

The king, too, could not help believing in Joan. He gave her a small army. Joan led her army to the city of Orléans [ōr' lā on']. She drove away the English who had been trying to take Orléans. This was the turning point of the war. The French became full of hope and patriotism.

An equestrian statue of Joan of Arc in the Square of the Pyramids (Place des Pyramides), Paris

Soon after this, Joan was captured in a battle. The English thought that they could put an end to her influence. They asked a court made up of French bishops and priests to bring Joan to trial. The court said that she had been led by the devil and that she was a witch. The English burned Joan to death in 1431. She was not more than 20 years of age at the time of her execution.

Joan's trial was unfair. Her punishment was cruel and wrong. Joan's death did not help the English. It only made the French more determined. The French went on to fight better and better. About 20 years after Joan's death, the English had lost all land in France except one town on the northern coast. The Hundred Years' War was over. Many years later the Catholic church announced that Joan was a saint.

A ● How does the story of Joan of Arc help to show good and bad sides of the civilization of Latin Christendom?
B ● Does the story show that the people in Western Europe were turning from *feudal* loyalty to *national* loyalty? Explain.
C ▶ What city in the United States is named for the city that Joan saved from the English?

Religious Persecution

The story of Joan of Arc reminds us of the two sides of an age of great religious faith. Joan's faith gave her great courage. It made the French people brave and united. Yet the English used religion as an excuse for burning her to death.

In an age of great religious faith, people can become *intolerant*. **Intolerance** is an unwillingness to respect the rights of others to have beliefs different from one's own. People who have great faith may think that they have a duty to *force* other people to share their faith. They may think that in this way they will save other people's souls as well as their own. Muslims were at times intolerant toward polytheistic religions. Christians were often intolerant toward all religions except their own.

In Latin Christendom, people who disagreed with the church were punished. Sometimes those who preached other beliefs were killed. Often, like Joan, they were burned to death. This kind of intolerance is called *persecution*.

A ▶ What examples of *religious persecution* can you remember from the history you have read?

B ● Why do most people in free countries today believe that religious intolerance and religious persecution are wrong?

The only people who were allowed to have a religion other than Catholic Christianity were the Jews. Jews and Christians believed in the Old Testament, or Jewish Scriptures. But Jews did not believe that Jesus was the Son of God.

Even though the church tolerated the Jews, the Jews were never quite safe. Jews were not allowed to own land. Often they had to live in one part of a city called a *ghetto.* Sometimes intolerant mobs attacked the Jews. Sometimes the Jews were forced to leave a country.

The worst attacks on the Jews began at the same time as the religious wars known as the **Crusades.** *Crusade* comes from a Latin word that means "to mark with a cross." Most of the Crusades were against the Muslims. But they led to hatred of all who were not Christians and even of those who were not Catholics.

The Crusades

The Crusades were wars that Western European Christians fought against Muslim Turks. Let us see why the Crusades came about.

Wars with the Muslims started when the Arab Empire took over Spain. The Muslims invaded France in the eighth century A.D. But they were driven back over the Pyrenees into Spain.

In the eleventh century, a large army of Seljuk Turks invaded the eastern part of the Byzantine Empire. They conquered Palestine, which the Christians called the *Holy Land.* The Turks were Muslims.

Stories came to Europe of how Muslim Turkish soldiers were damaging or destroying Christian holy places in Palestine. The Turks also interfered with Christian pilgrims to Palestine. The pope decided that Christians should unite to drive the Turks out of the Holy Land.

A group of Crusaders on their long march to the Holy Land. The Crusades took place between the eleventh and the thirteenth centuries.

At this time the people of Western Europe were beginning to have wealth and power. They had stopped the barbarian invasions. Kings, lords, and knights were ready to carry out invasions themselves.

We can see that one big cause of the Crusades was religious. Christians wanted to free the Holy Land from the Muslims. Another big cause was that leaders in Western Europe wanted more wealth and power.

In 1095 the pope, Urban II, called for a holy war against the Muslims in Palestine. This led to the *First Crusade,* which began in 1096. French lords and knights joined the Crusade. They were called *Crusaders.* They wore the cross as their symbol.

The First Crusade was successful. For nearly 100 years after that Crusade, there were *Western feudal governments* in Palestine and in the lands near Palestine. In the end, however, Muslim Turks drove the Christian lords and knights out of these lands. There were seven more Crusades after the First Crusade. These wars for religion and power went on for about 180 years.

The Crusades are interesting and puzzling. They show us the power of religious faith in Latin Christendom. Yet they show us a strange mixture of violence and religion. Many Crusaders seemed more interested in loot and adventures than in religion. The Crusaders claimed that they were helping the Byzantine Empire to drive back the Muslims. Yet in the Fourth Crusade (1202–04), the soldiers of the cross took the Christian city of Constantinople. They looted the city and killed thousands of people. The emperor in Constantinople found himself fighting against *two* invasions. The Turks came from the east. The Crusaders came from the west. It was hard to say which invaders were worse.

A★ Find out more about the Crusades. A hero of the Third Crusade was *Richard the Lion-Hearted,* king of England. Yet he was captured by a Christian ruler on his way back through Europe. He had to pay a ransom in order to get back to England. A king of France, Louis IX, or *Saint Louis,* led the Seventh and Eighth Crusades.

B● Look at a map of the Middle East. Find Syria, Israel, and Lebanon. This is where many of the Crusaders' battles took place.

Other Troubles: Famine and Disease

The people of Latin Christendom were troubled by many wars. There were wars between nations, holy wars, and feudal civil wars. There were other troubles, too: famine and disease.

Agriculture in Western Europe depended on rain. Farmers did not have irrigation. Bad weather often spoiled the crops. In years with little precipitation, crops withered and died. In years with too much precipitation, crops were flooded and drowned. Such things caused *famines.* Many people starved.

A● Would better transportation and wider trade make famines less terrible? Explain.

Another trouble came from disease. Sometimes a disease would break out and kill many people. *Cholera* was one such disease. Today doctors can give "shots" to prevent cholera, but in the Middle Ages no one knew about such cures.

THE GROWTH OF CIVILIZATION

A dreadful disease came from Asia in the fourteenth century. It was the *plague.* Fleas that lived on rats carried the plague. About this disease doctors knew very little. The people called the plague the *Black Death.* Historians tell us that the Black Death killed about one-third of the people in northwestern Europe in the fourteenth century.

B ● How would you feel if over a period of a few months one-third of the people in your community died of a strange disease? How would you feel if no one knew what caused the disease or how people caught the disease?

C ● What would be the *economic* effects of the deaths of one-third of the population? (Think about the work force, production of food and other goods, and prices of food and of labor.)

The Rise of Towns

The trade that grew with civilization brought bad things as well as good things. As you know, civilization brought towns and cities. But the Black Death was made worse by the growth of towns and cities.

The dreadful disease came to Europe on ships trading between the Middle East and France and Italy. Sick rats came on

A medieval Dutch marketplace that is a beehive of activity. See how many activities you can find and name.

the ships at Middle East ports and then went ashore at European ports. The Black Death might have been less harmful if towns had been fewer and less crowded. Yet towns were necessary if people were to have the good things of civilization.

> A● Why are towns necessary if people are to have the following things: (a) much division of labor; (b) capital goods; (c) many different consumer goods; (d) centers for trade; (e) higher culture (learning, art, fine buildings, and so on)?

As trade grew, so did towns. At first, food from the manors was exchanged for goods made by town workers. Farmers produced wool, which was made into cloth and clothing in the towns. Some parts of Europe *specialized* in certain goods. England and The Netherlands were great producers of woolen cloth. France was a center for wine. Furs came from Norway and Sweden. Metals were mined in many parts of Europe and turned into goods. Iron was plentiful. Tin, lead, copper, silver, and gold were much used.

Shipping became a big business. Ships and barges carried goods on the rivers. Ships sailed back and forth along the coasts of Europe. By the twelfth century, merchants from Italy and southern France were trading with the Middle East. Merchants in the Middle East brought goods from faraway China and India and the Spice Islands (now Indonesia). Gold and ivory from Africa also found their way to Europe.

> B★ Goods from Asia and the Middle East were *luxury goods*. Only rich people could afford them. These luxuries were jewels, silk, perfume, and spices. Some spices are pepper, cloves, cinnamon, and nutmeg. What are these spices used for?
>
> C★ What famous traveler from Italy visited China and lived there from 1275 to 1292?

The towns of Latin Christendom were *outside* the feudal system. Many townspeople were descended from peasants who had left their manors. These people became *free* workers and merchants. They traded with money. Some were able to save money and so build up capital goods. The great cathedrals were built with the aid of gifts from rich merchants as well as with gifts from feudal lords.

In the towns, *free societies* grew. The townspeople set up their own governments. Representatives of business groups ran the town government. These business groups were called **guilds.** Most were *craft guilds,* made up of skilled workers who owned their own business. Among the craft guilds were the clothmakers' guild, the goldsmiths' guild, the glassblowers' guild, and many others. There were *merchant guilds* also, made up of persons who made profits by trading and who owned ships and warehouses.

D ● How would the rise of towns help to weaken the feudal system?
E ● If you were a merchant, would you want the feudal lords to be strong? Explain.

During the High Middle Ages the towns became larger and wealthier. More people lived in the towns. These people were not like the serfs on manors. They did not have to work for their

Carcassonne in southern France, a medieval walled city. Built in the thirteenth century, it was restored in the nineteenth century.

LATIN CHRISTENDOM IN THE HIGH MIDDLE AGES

lord. They could choose their jobs. They could change their *employer.* They could often save money or borrow money to start a business of their own. In this way a **market economy** slowly took the place of the feudal economy. At the same time more people learned to read, write, and keep accounts. Merchants and shopkeepers had to know these things. Priests were no longer the only persons who could read and write.

Learning and Science in Latin Christendom

With civilization came the growth of *higher culture.* At first, learning was kept up by priests and monks and nuns. Later, the townspeople shared in learning. Then the people of Western Europe began to learn ideas from other cultures.

When people from different cultures meet, they are likely to get new ideas. Then their own culture changes and grows. This is what happened in Western Europe. Crusaders brought ideas from the Middle East. Traders brought ideas from the Middle East and from faraway parts of Asia. Traders also exchanged ideas with people from different parts of Europe. Some ideas came from Jewish scholars. Many ideas came from the Muslims in Spain.

A▶ What were some of the things that Latin Christendom learned from Islam? (Look at pages 286–290).

For centuries most of the learned persons in Western Europe were priests. As civilization grew, more people learned to read and write. The church had schools. Rich merchants and landlords gave money to help these schools.

By the twelfth century, *universities* had begun in Latin Christendom. In some ways they were copied from Muslim universities. Some of the subjects they taught came from classical Greek and Roman schools. Universities were also modeled on the *town guilds,* the organizations of skilled crafts workers and merchants. In a guild a worker learned skills under a master worker. In a university young men learned to become scholars from master teachers.

B● Look at the box "What Students Learned in Medieval Universities" below.
1. Make sure you understand what each subject deals with.
2. Name some things you can learn in universities today that are not in this list.
3. *Theology* is the study of religion. Why was this combined with philosophy in Latin Christendom?

C● Our word *trivial* comes from *trivium*. The three subjects in the trivium were *elementary* subjects—things students had to learn before they could do harder studies. How did our word *trivial* get its modern meaning?

D● Natural science, or the study of the laws of nature, did not advance in medieval Europe. The Muslim Arabs were far ahead in this field. Why did scholars in Europe not pay much attention to science? (Think: In the Middle Ages, which controlling ideas were stronger—Greco-Roman ideas or Judeo-Christian?)

As we shall see, Europeans made great advances in technology and science at the end of the Middle Ages. They also became interested in social studies. People became more interested in nature and in human nature.

What Students Learned in Medieval Universities

1. "The Seven Liberal Arts"
    a. The Trivium ("Three Roads")
       Grammar
       Rhetoric (writing and public speaking)
       Logic (clear reasoning and arguing)
    b. The Quadrivium ("Four Roads")
       Geometry
       Astronomy
       Arithmetic
       Music

2. Special Subjects (Usually one of these would be chosen.)
    a. Medicine
    b. Theology (including philosophy)
    c. Law (church law and civil law)

Language in Medieval Europe

For many centuries all learned people of Latin Christendom used the same language: Latin, the language of the church. It was the only language used for writing. Learned persons from any part of Latin Christendom could communicate with learned persons from any other part.

Most of the people in Latin Christendom, however, did not use Latin. They spoke many languages. Different languages were used in various parts of Western Europe. During the Middle Ages these languages became the languages we know today. Most people could speak only their own language. They were not able to write it.

The different languages of Western Europe belong to three main *language families*. A **language family** is a group of languages that came from one older language. Two Western language families came from barbarian invaders. One language family came from the Roman Empire.

**Language Families
and Languages of Latin Christendom**

Romance Languages (from Latin)
Spanish, Portuguese, French, Italian (Romanian is also a Romance Language, but Romania was part of Greek Christendom.)

Germanic Languages (from Old German)
German, Dutch, Norwegian, Swedish, Danish, Icelandic, English (English also has many words from French.)

Slavic Languages (from the barbarians who settled in Eastern Europe)
Polish, Czech, Slovak (Russian and Ukrainian are also Slavic, but Russia and the Ukraine were part of Greek Christendom.)

A ▶ Look at the box "Language Families and Languages of Latin Christendom" (page 408). What are the three big "families" of language in western and northeastern Europe?

As time went by, people began to write these languages as well as to speak them. This happened as the *nations* of Europe came into being. Today we use the word **nation** for a group of people under one government. In Western Europe, most nations were made up of people with the same language and traditions. Let us see how these nations grew and how they were governed.

Monarchic Governments in Latin Christendom

The governments and laws of Latin Christendom were at first those of feudalism. In nearly all of Western Europe, there were kings. But real power was in the hands of feudal lords.

A ▶ Look at the box "Using the Social Sciences To Study a Culture" (page 91). How many of these topics have we studied in Latin Christendom?

During the High Middle Ages, civilization grew. There were more towns and increased trade. There was more capital. There was more money. There were many rich merchants. More and more people wanted a strong government to keep order. In those times people thought that the strongest government was a monarchy. If one person were head of the government, everyone could be loyal to that person. The civil wars of feudalism would end.

Early in the Middle Ages, monarchs were *elected* by the lords. This was not satisfactory. For one thing, the lords did not want a strong monarch. For another thing, elections led to quarrels: two kings might claim the throne. That meant another civil war. So most countries chose to have *hereditary monarchs.* A **hereditary monarch** is a member of the *royal family*. When a king or queen dies, the next person in line for the throne becomes the new king or queen. This person is usually the son or daughter of the dead monarch. Everyone is expected to be loyal to the hereditary monarch.

LATIN CHRISTENDOM IN THE HIGH MIDDLE AGES

Isabella of Castile. Queen Isabella (1451–1501) ruled Castile. Her marriage with Ferdinand of Aragon brought national unity to Spain.

William I of England, better known as William the Conqueror. He set up a strong monarchy in England after he conquered the land in 1066.

- **B** What good points can you see in hereditary monarchy, especially as a way out of feudalism? What may be some bad results of hereditary monarchy?
- **C** Why would many people want a strong monarch? (Would such a government help trade and production? Would it be good to have one set of laws and courts of law in a country instead of dozens of feudal laws and feudal courts? Explain.)
- **D** How would monarchies help nations, each with a national language, to come into being? How would a national language help a monarch to be powerful?

During most of the Middle Ages, governments in Western Europe seesawed between feudalism and strong monarchies. Different groups of people in society wanted different kinds of government. There were many civil wars. In the end, however, most European countries became nations, with strong hereditary monarchs.

- **E** Below are listed some classes of society in the Middle Ages:
  - serfs
  - knights
  - feudal lords
  - bishops and priests
  - free farmers
  - merchants and townspeople

  Which classes might favor a strong monarch? Which might favor a weak monarch? Why?

410 THE GROWTH OF CIVILIZATION

Philip II of France, also known as Philip Augustus. He was a strong and effective king of France for 44 years (1180–1223).

Margaret of Denmark. Queen Margaret united the Scandinavian kingdoms of Denmark, Sweden, and Norway in 1397.

There were several areas of Western Europe that did not have hereditary monarchs. The biggest areas were the lands now called Germany and Italy. Here feudal nobles and city-states divided the land and the power. Most of Germany and northern Italy made up the **Holy Roman Empire.** The emperor was elected by feudal nobles and had little power.

In countries such as France and England, monarchy, feudalism, and the church shared the power of government. In the long run, however, the monarch took more and more power.

In a feudal kingdom, the king needed the support of great lords. There were *some* knights who were loyal to the king, but most knights were loyal to their own lords. The king could get *some* taxes from the royal lands. But if the king or queen needed extra money for a war, that money had to come from the great lords. The king could not collect taxes from all the people.

These things changed as time went by. First in England and then in France, the king had an army of many knights and foot soldiers who were loyal first of all to the monarch. The monarch began to collect taxes from free farmers and from townspeople, not just from great lords.

F ▶ Remember how Joan of Arc taught French people to be loyal to the king and to France. How did this make the monarch stronger and the feudal lords weaker?

G ● Look at the box "A Strong Monarchy in the Late Middle Ages" (page 413).

1. Why did the monarch need officials and an army?

2. How were the officials and army paid for? How did this differ from feudalism?

3. Might the bishops and priests be torn between loyalty to the pope and loyalty to the monarch? Explain.

Constitutional and Representative Government

One very important thing came out of the struggles for power in the Middle Ages. It was *constitutional, representative government.* A **constitutional government** is a government under law. In a constitutionally governed country, people have rights that the government may not take away. In the Middle Ages, many of these rights were written down in long letters called *charters.* The charters were written by a lord or a king. A **representative government** is a government in which the people have persons to speak for them (to *represent* them) when laws are made or taxes are raised.

In order to get the power they wanted, monarchs had to agree to rule according to law. Monarchs also had to agree that groups in society could have representatives. In the late Middle Ages most monarchs in Latin Christendom had some kind of constitutional, representative government. But, in the sixteenth and seventeenth centuries, most monarchies became **absolute monarchies.** This meant that the monarch claimed complete power. The monarch did not allow representative government.

The big exception was England. For a time, monarchs in England were very strong. But in 1215, an important event happened. It is still important to everyone who wants freedom and rights and the rule of law.

A ● What is the opposite of the rule of law?

THE GROWTH OF CIVILIZATION

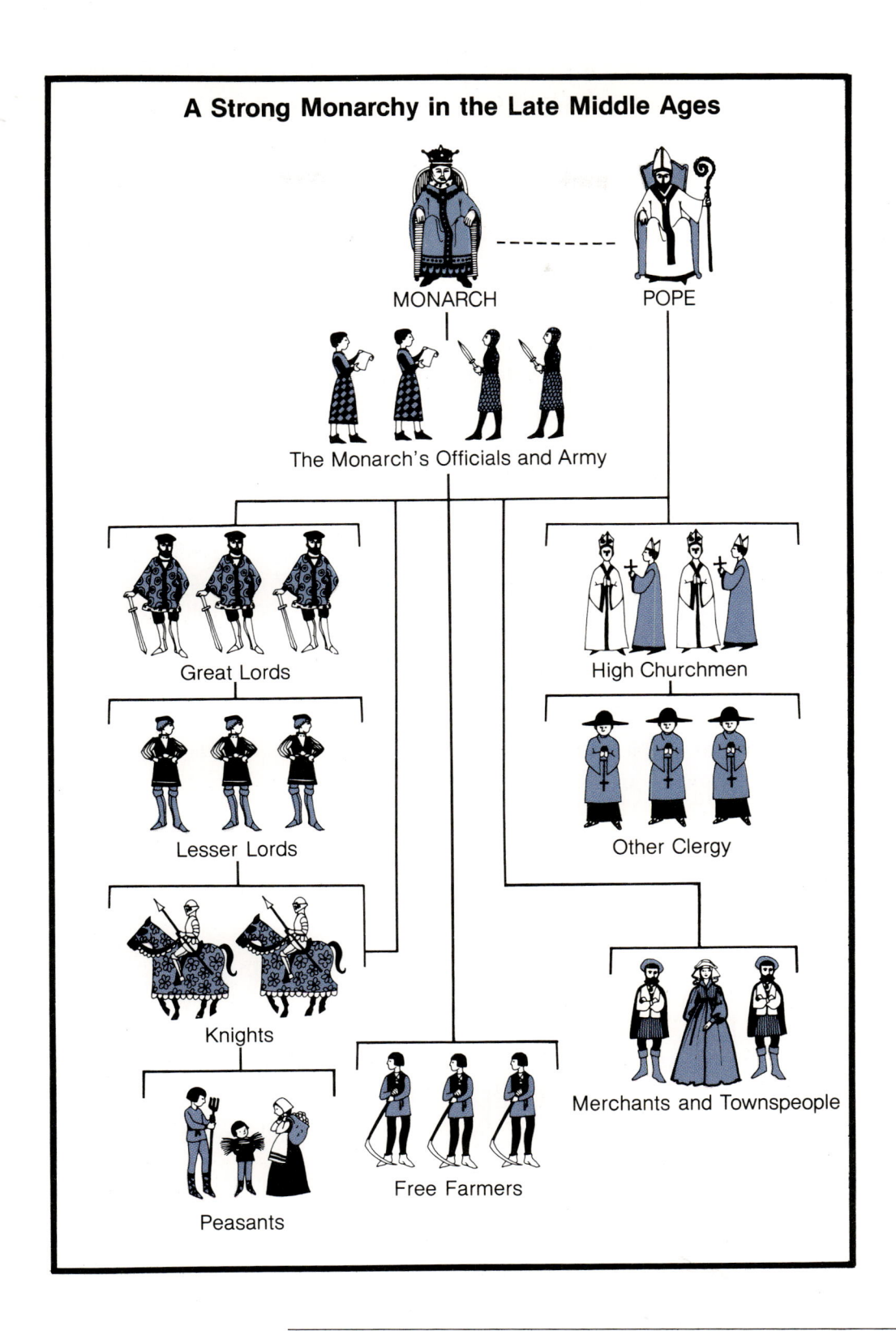

A Strong Monarchy in the Late Middle Ages

MONARCH — — — — POPE

The Monarch's Officials and Army

Great Lords

Lesser Lords

Knights

Peasants

Free Farmers

High Churchmen

Other Clergy

Merchants and Townspeople

LATIN CHRISTENDOM IN THE HIGH MIDDLE AGES

King John of England was a bad king. He lost wars with France. He attacked the church. He raised taxes whenever he felt like it. He used the law courts, through fines, to get money. Such actions by the king led the powerful groups in society to join against him. In 1215, the great nobles and the churchmen forced John to sign a charter, promising rights and good government. This is called the *Great Charter,* or, in Latin, **Magna Carta.**

The Magna Carta had 63 paragraphs. Here are some of the rights that King John swore to respect:

The Church of England should have its rights. It could choose its own bishops.

The great nobles should have their rights. They would not be asked to pay more taxes to the king than they had paid in the past.

If special taxes were needed, a council must vote. The council would be made up of the great nobles and clergy.

The city of London should have its rights. So should other towns and cities.

For a free man to be put in jail or fined, two things were necessary. He must have broken the law. He must have been tried by a jury.

B● How do these rights show that England was a *feudal society?*

The Magna Carta speaks of a council to agree to taxes. This council became the **Parliament** of England. *Parliament* is from a French word meaning "talking meeting." In it the representatives of groups in society could talk about their problems and their wants.

In the Middle Ages, after the reign of King John, Parliament was made up of two *houses.* In the **House of Lords** were the great nobles and the bishops. In the **House of Commons** were representatives of the towns, of the knights, and of the free farmers. Today the House of Lords has little power. The House of Commons is the more important part of British government.

C★ What two *houses* does the American Congress have? Do you think the idea came from England as well as from the Roman Republic?

D▶ Look at pages 238–240. Was the government of England in the Middle Ages a *mixed government?* Explain.

414 THE GROWTH OF CIVILIZATION

English Parliament in session (1295). On the throne is King Edward I. On one side of him is the king of Scotland. Other members are lords and bishops.

LATIN CHRISTENDOM IN THE HIGH MIDDLE AGES

Summary

In this chapter we have seen how Western cultures were formed in the Middle Ages. We have seen how many controlling ideas Western cultures owe to the cultures of Latin Christendom. The story we have read is a record of great changes. We have seen how the end of the Roman Empire in the west left civilization in ruins. We have seen how, over a thousand years, civilization grew again.

By 1100, civilization was growing in Western Europe. Feudal lords and ladies were the ruling class. The code of the knights, or chivalry, was one of the main sets of controlling ideas in this culture. Chivalry was a mixture of soldiers' duties and some ideas of love and kindness that came from Christianity.

The other main controlling ideas were the teachings of the Catholic church. For centuries the only learned persons in Latin Christendom were priests. The priests taught the people to obey the church. People thought that the church was like an army fighting the devil. The Middle Ages was an age of faith. The great Gothic cathedrals show how deeply people felt about their religions.

The people of Latin Christendom had troubles. Feudalism caused civil wars. There were also many wars between monarchs. One such war was the Hundred Years' War between England and France. Another group of wars was the Crusades. Although many Crusaders set out on a Crusade because of religious faith, many others were driven by a desire for power and land. After eight Crusades over a period of 180 years, the Muslims kept control of the Holy Land.

In spite of disease and famine, European civilization went on developing. Towns grew. Trade increased. In the towns the classes of free persons—merchants and workers—increased. More people were educated. Universities grew up.

Gradually the languages of Europe took form. People learned to write and read, as well as to speak, their language. The main languages of Europe are in three language families: Romance, Germanic, and Slavic.

As nations grew, the feudal system became weaker. People, especially townspeople, began to be loyal to kings instead of to feudal lords.

The kings were expected to obey the laws. They had to have the consent of important classes in the nation if they wanted to change the laws and raise taxes. The kings also had to recognize the rights of different classes in society. In this way constitutional, representative government came into being in Latin Christendom. England was a good example of medieval constitutional government. Magna Carta (1215) listed the rights of different classes. The representative body was Parliament. Parliament had two houses: the House of Lords and the House of Commons.

As we look over the history of Latin Christendom in the High Middle Ages, we can see that many of today's controlling ideas of Western cultures took shape in medieval times.

Some Interesting Activities

1. Find in your school or public library a book about medieval chivalry. Look especially for the games the knights used to play. What is a *joust,* for example?

2. Dramatizations:
    a. Marco Polo returns from China and tells his relatives in Venice what he saw.
    b. Act a play about Joan of Arc. The knight who gave her a horse and armor and six soldiers was called *Baudricourt* [bō′ drē koor′]. The king of France was *Charles VII.* The English general was the *Duke of Bedford.* The chief judge at her trial was the French *Bishop of Beauvais* [bō′ vay]. You can have many other characters: French and English nobles, judges, soldiers. (A famous play about Joan is *Saint Joan* by George Bernard Shaw.)

3. Prepare a map of Europe. Use one color to indicate areas that were predominantly Greek Orthodox. Use another color to indicate areas that were Roman Catholic.

4. Pretend you are a knight setting out on a Crusade. Write a story telling why you are going, what equipment you will take, and how you will travel.

5. You read about Saint Joan of Arc in this chapter. Find out about another famous saint of the Middle Ages—St. Francis of Assisi.

6. Use an encyclopedia to find out about *the Black Death* and the two main kinds of *plague*—*bubonic* and *pneumonic.*

Exploration was one of the things that marked the beginning of the Modern Age.

CHAPTER 16

The Modern Age Begins

Historians generally call the period that starts about the end of the fifteenth century the *Modern Age*. During the Modern Age, change became more rapid. There were great advances in science and technology. There were many changes in government. The population of the world grew much faster than it had ever done. The whole world was explored. The peoples of the whole world came to know one another. Trade became worldwide.

These big changes began in Western Europe. Let us see why and how the civilization of Western Europe took the lead over other civilizations in the Modern Age.

The Four Areas of Civilization in the Old World

About the beginning of the Modern Age there were four main *areas of civilization* in the Old World. Each area had its own *cultural tradition.* Those civilization-cultural areas were as follows:

1. Christendom, centered in Western Europe
2. Islam, centered in the Middle East
3. India, whose Hindu culture was at this time ruled by Muslim conquerors
4. China, whose rulers at times controlled Tibet and Southeast Asia

There were other civilization-cultural areas, such as Russia, the African kingdoms south of the Sahara, Japan, and Indonesia. However, these branches of civilization were not as powerful as the four main areas of civilization. In addition, there were civilization areas in the Americas, but these had been cut off from the rest of the world for thousands of years.

Suppose a person in the fifteenth century were asked this question: *What one of the four main branches of civilization was likely to become the most powerful after 1500?* The person might begin by thinking about *geography. Which branch of civilization was at the center of the known Old World?* The answer would be *Islam.* The other branches of civilization were all on the outer edges of the Old World. Surely, then, Islam had the best chance of expanding and taking over other areas.

Then the person might think of *economics. What branch of civilization had the best trade? What branch was the richest?* Again, the answers seem to be Islam, which was the center of trade among the peoples of Europe, Africa, and Asia. Islam had ships and caravans that traveled east, west, south, and north. Islam had great prosperous cities that produced cloth, carpets, and metal goods. Islam had some of the best agricultural land in the world. Its universities and its scientists were ahead of those of other civilizations. So economics also pointed to Islam as the most powerful branch of civilization.

Islam was a great center of learning. Shown here is the Courtyard of Midrassa (College of Islamic Studies) of Fez, Morocco, founded in the twelfth century.

The person might then ask: *What does history tell us about the future?* For about 800 years Islam had been expanding. It controlled North Africa and the coasts of East Africa. It had conquered the Byzantine Empire. It controlled northern India and the lands now called Iran and Afghanistan. Why should Islam not go on expanding?

Finally, our thinker might ask: *What branch of civilization had the strongest government? What civilization was the most united?* Here the answers would be fairly clear. Western Europe was divided into quarrelsome nation-states. Northern India was ruled by Muslim emperors, but central India and southern India were divided among Muslim and Hindu kingdoms. In China the power of the emperor was weak, and the Mongols often attacked from the north. The Islamic area was also divided politically. Persia (Iran) and Afghanistan were independent states. North Africa was divided among several Muslim kingdoms. But the Ottoman Empire was very powerful. It controlled much of southeastern Europe and all Asia Minor, Mesopotamia, Egypt, and Arabia. The rulers of North African kingdoms took orders from the Ottoman Empire. Thus Islam seemed almost sure to be the most powerful branch of civilization.

THE MODERN AGE BEGINS

Yet this answer proved wrong. By the sixteenth century, things had changed. Europeans discovered the New World. Suddenly Europe, not Islam, was the "center" of the known world. Trade routes changed, as ships from Europe began to sail the oceans. World trade no longer had to go through the Middle East. Islam did not go on expanding. The Ottoman Turks were stopped in eastern Europe and in the Mediterranean by European armies and fleets. Europe was still divided into nations that fought with one another, but these nations sent ships, traders, and settlers to many parts of the world.

A ▶ Look at a globe. Show how the Middle East was the "center" of the known world until Columbus sailed to the New World in 1492. Show how Western Europe became the "center" when the New World was discovered and ships sailed across the oceans.

Ideas: Culture Contact and Interaction of Cultures

Ideas are most important in human societies. This is because ideas show us how to behave. They help us to think and to find *new* ideas. The use of new ideas was one reason that big changes began in Western Europe.

A ● How does *culture contact* help to spread ideas? How may culture contact lead to *new* ideas?

Culture contact may be *destructive* as well as *creative.* The civilizations of Islam, of India, and of the Byzantine Empire had a great deal of contact with other cultures in the Middle Ages. Barbarians from central Asia had raided and conquered in these civilized areas for centuries. Sometimes the effects had been to *weaken* civilization.

China, too, had been overrun by the Mongols. China recovered under the Ming emperors. China was on one edge of the Old World civilizations. Both China and Japan had little contact with other cultures in the early Modern period.

After the fall of the Byzantine Empire, part of the culture of Greek Christendom lived on in Russia. But Russia, too, was set

422   THE GROWTH OF CIVILIZATION

back by a long period of Mongol conquest. Feudalism lasted in Russia longer than in Western Europe. Not until the late fifteenth century did a strong government rise in Russia. Even after that there were troubles that made it difficult for Russia to keep in contact with other cultures. Serfdom went on in Russia until the middle of the nineteenth century.

Western Europe had a different history from all these civilizations. Civilization rose again in Latin Christendom. The peoples of Western Europe, like the peoples of China and Japan, defeated the barbarians from central Asia. Unlike China and Japan, however, Western Europe went on getting ideas from other cultures. The Crusades, trade, and the curiosity of learned persons all helped Western Europe to get ideas from other cultures.

Many ideas came through contact with the culture of Islam. Some of these ideas had to do with technology. Here are some of them: the number system, printing, paper, gunpowder, and the compass and other aids to navigation.

B▶ What does technology mean?
C● Why are the technological ideas listed above important?

Arab astronomer Tagi el-Din at the observatory at Istanbul

THE MODERN AGE BEGINS **423**

Another Cultural Interaction: Greco-Roman Ideas and Judeo-Christian Ideas

During the fourteenth and fifteenth centuries Western Europe found another set of ideas. They came from history.

As we know, the Catholic church carried over some ideas from the Roman Empire. Yet throughout the Middle Ages the main controlling ideas of Latin Christendom were Judeo-Christian.

A ▶ Look at the picture "Two World Views of Western Culture" on page 266. What were the main interests of Judeo-Christian ideas?

Some Greek ideas came to Western Europe when Arab scholars found the writings of the philosopher Aristotle. From the thirteenth century, learned persons in Latin Christendom studied Aristotle's ideas.

In the fifteenth century, however, Western scholars became interested in the whole of Greco-Roman culture. They discovered other Greek philosophers, especially Plato. They dug up Greek and Roman statues and vases. In this way they learned about Greco-Roman *humanism.* They began to think about human life in a more *earthly* way. They began to study natural science and social science as the Greeks had done.

A Greek statue of a woman (in marble)

(left) A statue of Charles the Wise, Rome. *(right)* Statue of David by the famous Italian sculptor Bernini — from the Renaissance period. Renaissance artists learned from Greek and Roman sculptors to be interested in the beauty of the human body.

To many scholars the civilization of Greece and Rome seemed much better than the culture of Latin Christendom. The Roman Empire had given people peace and the rule of law in all the lands around the Mediterranean. The art of Greece and Rome seemed fresh and "natural" compared with medieval art, and the buildings of Greece and Rome seemed simple and airy compared with Gothic cathedrals. Scholars who loved the civilization of Greece and Rome even thought that Latin Christendom was not really civilized. They began to talk about the "Middle Ages," by which they meant a period *between* two

THE MODERN AGE BEGINS 425

civilizations. They called the period and its art "Gothic." The Goths were referred to as "barbarians." So *Gothic* means "barbarian," or "noncivilized."

> B● Do you think that the scholars were correct when they said that Latin Christendom was not a civilization? Explain.

The Renaissance

The discovery of Greco-Roman culture in the fifteenth century is called the *Renaissance*. **Renaissance** means "rebirth." People used the word to mean the "rebirth of learning." There had been much learning in the Middle Ages, but Renaissance meant the rebirth of *classical* learning.

Why did this *Renaissance* happen? It began in Italy, where there were many artifacts of Roman civilization. It was speeded up by the fall of Constantinople in 1453. When the Ottomans took Constantinople, Byzantine scholars fled to Italy. They brought with them knowledge of the Greek language and classical Greek writings.

At first the Renaissance was very unsettling. Many scholars in Italy seemed ready to *replace* Judeo-Christian ideas with Greco-Roman humanism. Even some leaders of the church in Italy were *more humanists than Christians*.

Most people kept their belief in Christian teaching. But interest in science and in earthly things spread. So did Greco-Roman ideas about government and politics. In time, many Western Europeans learned to live with two world views. This was not easy.

> A● Can you see how these two world views would make people *restless*? Would they have to find new ideas to hold the two world views together? Explain.

Some historians say that the problem of living with two different world views made Europeans adventurous and inventive. That may be true. Certainly from the time of the Renaissance, Europeans *were* inventive and adventurous.

426 THE GROWTH OF CIVILIZATION

Geography and the Rise of Western Europe

The "causes" of big changes in history are seldom simple. Many things came together to help Western Europe take the lead. One thing that helped was geography. Western Europe was in the northwestern corner of the civilizations of the Old World. This gave it some protection from the barbarians of Central Asia.

Waterways, Mountains, and Some Trading Cities of Western Europe

MAP KEY
- High mountains
- River
- Trading city

THE MODERN AGE BEGINS 427

The *natural environment* of Western Europe was also important. Agriculture based on the heavy wheeled plow helped Europeans to produce good supplies of food. The physical features of Western Europe helped in another way.

A ▶ Look at the map "Waterways, Mountains, and Some Trading Cities of Western Europe" (page 427).
   1. The only big mountains in Western Europe are the Pyrennees (between France and Spain) and the Alps (between Germany and Italy). Find these mountain barriers. There are a number of passes through these mountains.
   2. Notice the large number of big rivers in Western Europe. How did these help trade in the Middle Ages?
   3. Notice the number of seaports and river ports. There were many more than are shown on the map.

B ● How was trade encouraged by the physical features of Europe (including the long seacoast)?

Like the Greeks, Europeans were sailors. There was a difference, however, between the Atlantic Ocean and the Mediterranean. The Atlantic was rough and stormy. Its waves were big. Only strong ships and fine sailors could sail the Atlantic.

C ● The main natural vegetation of Western Europe was forest. Until about 1800 the most important material for technology and fuel was *wood*. How did geography give Western Europe a technological advantage over Islam? How did it help shipbuilding? What *ecological* problems would the using up of the natural forests bring? Might there be a *shortage of energy*? Explain.

Geography, Exploration, Expansion

As early as A.D. 1000, Vikings from Norway had crossed the Atlantic to Iceland, Greenland, and the coast of North America. But these voyages did not lead to trade or colonies in America.

In the fifteenth century, explorers began to search for *ocean trade routes* to the Indies. The Ottoman Turks controlled the eastern Mediterranean. Trade between Europe and the Indies was difficult and expensive. Portuguese sailors were the first to look for new trade routes. They explored the west coast of Africa. These explorations were started by *Prince Henry the Navigator* of Portugal. Spain also began to send out explorers.

A ▶ Look at the map "Some Early European Explorations" (page 431) and the box "Dates of Early Explorations" below.
1. When did Portuguese sailors begin to sail to and trade with northwest Africa?
2. When did Bartolomeu Dias sail round the Cape of Good Hope?
3. When did Columbus first sail to the New World?
4. When did Vasco da Gama reach India?
5. What voyage gave England its claim to North America? When?
6. Who was leader of the expedition that first sailed all round the world? When?
7. When did Portuguese merchants reach Japan?

Dates of Early Explorations

1433	The Portuguese reach northwest coast of Africa. Trade in slaves and gold begins.
1445–57	The Portuguese reach Senegal and Gambia on the West Coast of Africa.
1487	Bartolomeu Dias (Portuguese) rounds the Cape of Good Hope, the southernmost tip of Africa.
1492–93	Christopher Columbus (Italian) makes two voyages to the New World for the monarchs of Spain.
1497	John Cabot (Italian) sails to North America for the king of England.
1498	Vasco da Gama (Portuguese) reaches India after sailing around Africa.
1513	The Portuguese sail to China.
1519–21	Ferdinand Magellan (Portuguese) is employed by Spain. His expedition sails around the world.
1542	The Portuguese sail to Japan.

THE MODERN AGE BEGINS

B ▶ What happened after the Portuguese reached Japan? (Look at page 356.)

C ▶ What happened to the Aztec and Inca civilizations about 30 years after Columbus reached America? What caused this disaster? (Look at page 339.)

D ● Look again at the map "Some Early European Explorations." Before the explorations Western Europe was on the far western edge of the land known to the civilizations of the Old World. What was the position of Western Europe *after* the explorations?

We can see how geography helped Western European civilization. Nearness to the seas encouraged many Europeans to become sailors. It encouraged them to explore the oceans. Their explorations made Western Europe the center of the known world. The discoveries led to European *colonization* in the Americas and other parts of the world. **Colonization** means sending people from a country to found a *colony*—that is, to settle permanently as a community in a different country. This colonization led to worldwide trade. The ideas of Western civilization spread farther than any world view had ever done before.

The Importance of Technology in Exploration

The explorations could not have happened without better technology. Early European trading ships were not built to explore unknown waters. The ships were made of wood. Both ends of a ship were shaped almost exactly alike. Each ship had only one mast that held up one square sail. This kind of ship could sail only in the direction the wind was blowing.

Gradually, European shipbuilders improved their ships. They changed the wooden body, making it narrower in the front and wider in the back. This new shape made it easier for the boat to move through the water. The shipbuilders made the lines of their ships longer and lower. Then the ships could not be tossed around so easily by the high waves.

The European shipbuilders borrowed an important idea from the Muslims. They used sails that were shaped like

Some Early European Explorations

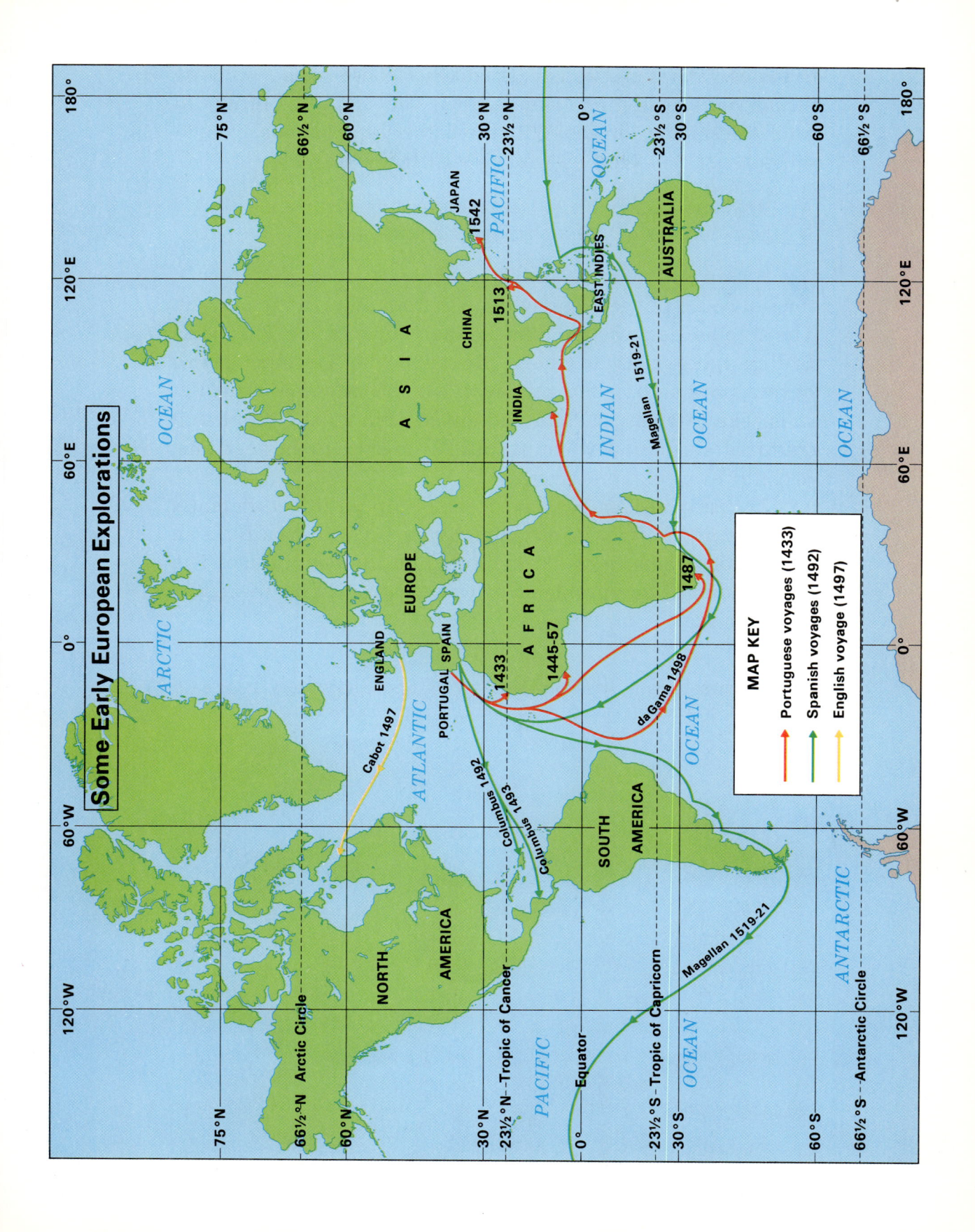

MAP KEY
- Portuguese voyages (1433)
- Spanish voyages (1492)
- English voyage (1497)

triangles. The Europeans learned that these sails could be turned more easily than square sails. They could be turned to catch the smallest breeze. With them, the ship could be made to sail *against* the wind as well as *with* the wind.

A● Why was it important to be able to sail *against* the wind?
B★ Find out how a sailing ship *tacks* against the wind.

A ship with only one sail could not be very large. If it were, the sail could not gain enough power from the wind to move it. The shipbuilders wanted to make their ships larger. They tried adding more sails to them. By 1450 the Portuguese had developed a ship called a caravel, which had three triangular sails. The caravel was light and quick, with a flat bottom so it could sail in shallow water. It could keep close to the coastline. It could even explore rivers.

The shipbuilders designed each ship a little differently from the one before. Prince Henry sent each new ship on an expedition. Then its captain reported on the new design. The captain told of any problems or weaknesses. He made suggestions for improving the ship.

The Portuguese caravel was strong and fast. Its *square-rigged* and *lateen* sails and its rudder enabled it to sail a zigzag course against the wind.

Sailors suggested using square sails together with triangular sails. By changing the combinations of sails, a ship could sail in almost any weather. The sailors learned that the caravel was too light for the rough Atlantic. So the Portuguese began to make some of their ships heavier.

Along with the better ships, sailors needed better ways of *navigating* (finding one's way) the oceans. On a clear night, navigators north of the equator could always find north. They had only to look for the polestar, or North Star. Its position in the sky was always north. On a cloudy night, they could use a compass. Its needle always pointed north. Either way, navigators could tell the direction they were going. However, they could not tell where they *were.* They needed an instrument that would do this. The instrument had to be accurate and simple enough for any sailor to use.

Portuguese scholars learned that there already was such an instrument. The Arabs used it in sailing on the Indian Ocean. The instrument was called an **astrolabe** (as′ trō lāb). This instrument was marked off in degrees. It helped sailors find their north-south location at night.

(left) A magnetic compass. This instrument always pointed to *magnetic north.* Sailors could thus know the direction of the ship. *(right)* An astrolabe. One of the world's oldest scientific instruments, it was used by navigators to determine the position of the sun or of the stars.

433

C★ Find out more about the astrolabe and how it works.
D● We still mark north-south position in degrees. What do we call these degrees? Find the north-south position of the city in which you live.
E▶ What are the degrees that mark east-west positions on maps?
F★ Does a compass needle usually point to *true north*? Where does it point? Why is it important to know the difference between *true north* and *magnetic north*?

It was more difficult for navigators to find their east-west position. They had to know two things. First, they had to know how long the ship had been sailing. Second, they had to know how fast it was going. Suppose the navigators knew they had left port 10 hours ago. They were sailing west at 6 kilometers (4 miles) an hour. Then they knew they were 65 kilometers (40 miles) west of the port.

Telling time on a ship was done with a sandglass. It took a certain amount of time for the sand to run from the top of the glass to the bottom. Each time all the sand had gone to the bottom of the glass, that amount of time had passed. By watching the sand and counting the times it went to the bottom of the glass, the sailors could tell how long the ship had been sailing.

It was a little harder to tell how fast the ship was going. A sailor would throw a log overboard from the front of the ship. Then the navigator would find out how long it took the ship to sail past the log. This gave the ship's speed. The daily record of a ship's voyage became known as a **logbook.**

G▶ If a ship 30 meters (100 feet) long took 20 seconds to sail past the log, how far would the ship go in 20 seconds? How many meters (or how many feet) would it go in one minute? One hour? How many kilometers (or how many miles) would it go in one hour?
H● This method was not very accurate. Name some things that could go wrong and make the navigator's calculations incorrect.
I★ Find out about the *chronometer*, which was used to find longitude after about 1762.

The Use of Gunpowder

(left) An early cannon. Cannon and mines could smash castle walls. *(right)* In this picture from a fifteenth century manuscript a cavalryman is using an *arquebus*. [är′kə bəs]. Small guns such as the arquebus could send bullets through armor.

Another Technological Change: Gunpowder

Gunpowder was invented in China. The Chinese used gunpowder for fireworks, but Europeans used it to change ways of war. First they used *cannon* to fire heavy stone balls. They also used big packages of gunpowder to blow holes in the stone walls of castles or of cities. Then they invented smaller guns. A soldier could carry the small gun and shoot enemy soldiers. Gunpowder changed ways of fighting. No army could hope to win without cannon and foot-soldiers with small guns.

- A. Look at the pictures "Use of Gunpowder" above. Gunpowder helped to bring an end to feudalism and to knights-in-armor. Can you explain why?
- B. An army with cannon, small guns, and supplies of powder and shot was very expensive. Only strong rulers could have such armies. How did this fact help the change from feudalism to strong monarchies?

THE MODERN AGE BEGINS

The New Technology of Printing with Movable Type

In classical and medieval times people made books by copying them by hand. Yet there were other ways of copying. The Sumerians knew how to copy by pressing designs on soft clay tablets. In the eighth century A.D., the Chinese learned how

Development of Printing

Cylinder-seal printing

Wood-block printing

Movable type

436   THE GROWTH OF CIVILIZATION

to carve characters (Chinese words) and pictures on blocks of wood. They spread ink on the blocks. Then they pressed sheets of paper on the blocks. This was **wood-block printing.**

The Chinese also invented **movable type.** This means having a separate little block for each character. Each block was a piece of type. The pieces of type could be put together to make different pages. There was no need to carve a whole big block of wood for each new page.

A● Why was *printing with movable type* better than *wood-block printing?*

The Chinese also invented paper made from rags. This was much cheaper than the sheepskins (parchment) that were used for books in medieval Europe.

These Chinese inventions came to Europe. As in the case of gunpowder, Europeans made more use of them than the Chinese had done. A number of Europeans worked at printing with movable type. The most successful was a German, John Gutenberg. Gutenberg used movable *metal* type. He printed the Bible in Latin. Soon there were many **printing presses** turning out thousands of books each year in Europe. By 1500 more than 15 million books had been printed in Western Europe.

B● Look at the pictures "Development of Printing" (pages 436 and 438). What were the three early stages of printing?

C● Why was the printing machine called a *press?*

D● Look at the box "Supply, Demand, and Price: Some Economic Laws" (page 439).
  1. What happened to the price of books after the invention of the printing press?
  2. What would happen to the demand for books?
  3. Would many more books be made and sold as a result of the printing press? Explain.

E● The printing press led to many changes in Western Europe. See how many you can think of. Here are some ideas: number of persons who could read; schools and education; spread of ideas; the Bible; national languages; new books; speed of change; demand for reading glasses (Europeans had learned about magnifying glasses from the Arabs).

THE MODERN AGE BEGINS

Development of Printing (continued)

Part of a page printed by hand

Part of a page printed with movable type

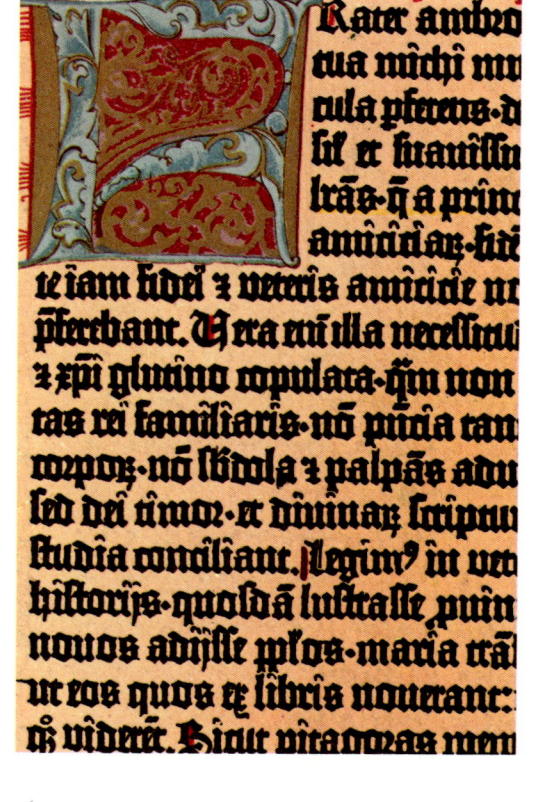

438 THE GROWTH OF CIVILIZATION

> **Supply, Demand, and Price:
> Some Economic Laws**
>
> 1. When supply goes up and demand stays the same, prices fall.
> 2. When prices fall, demand goes up.
> 3. When demand goes up, prices rise again.
> 4. When prices rise, supply goes up and demand levels off.

Political Changes: Nations and Nationalism

The changes we have been looking at happened at the same time as political changes took place.

A ● What kind of government was taking the place of weak, feudal monarchies in most parts of Western Europe at the end of the Middle Ages? What happened to representative government (parliaments) in most countries? (Look at pages 412–414.)

In most countries of Western Europe the power of feudal nobles grew weak. At the same time monarchs grew stronger. In the Middle Ages, most monarchs were *constitutional monarchs.* They obeyed the old laws and charters of the country. If they wanted to change laws or increase taxes, they had to get *representative bodies* (such as Parliament) to agree. However, by the sixteenth century, monarchs began to act more like *dictators.* (A **dictator** is a ruler who has great power over the lives of all the people in a country.) The monarchs claimed to rule by **divine right,** that is, because God had chosen them to rule. The mass of the people were at first happy to have strong rulers. A strong ruler brought an end to feudalism and civil wars.

The strong monarchs united their peoples. As a result, *nations* came into being. The word *nation* has two meanings. Nation means, first, a group of people living in an area governed by one government. This is also known as a **nation-state.** Its

THE MODERN AGE BEGINS

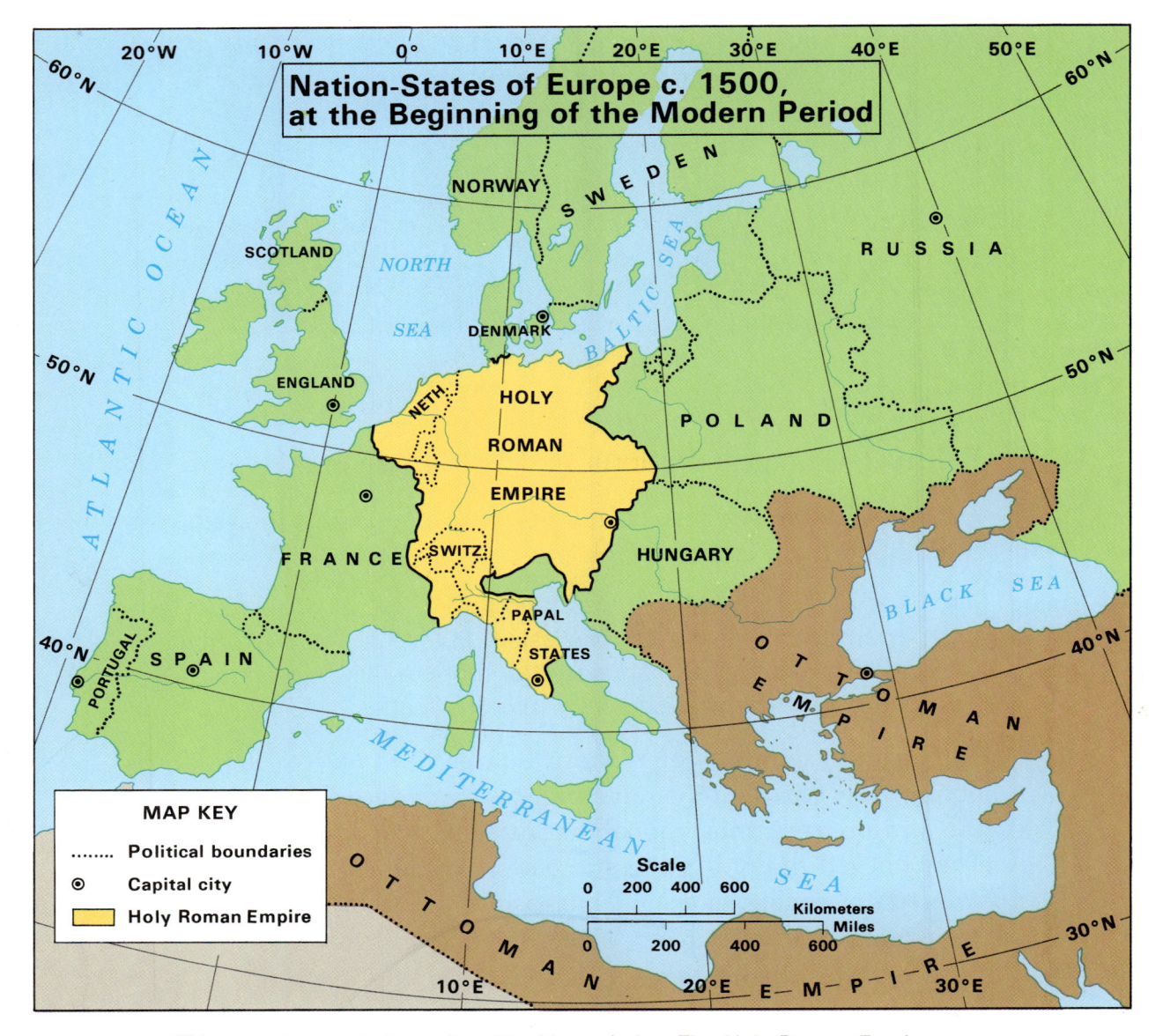

Nation-States of Europe c. 1500, at the Beginning of the Modern Period

MAP KEY
- .... Political boundaries
- ⊙ Capital city
- ▇ Holy Roman Empire

This map does not show all political boundaries. The Holy Roman Empire was split into many small monarchic-feudal states. Italy was divided between the Papal States (ruled by the pope) and the states of Milan, Venice, Florence, Naples, and others. Switzerland was a group of small city-states. The Netherlands was ruled by foreign powers until the end of the sixteenth century.

440 THE GROWTH OF CIVILIZATION

second meaning is a group of people *sharing the same culture,* especially language. This is a **nationality,** or **nationality group.**

Most nation-states had a large nationality group. There were often smaller nationality groups as well as the larger one, but in most nation-states one national language came to be used. The British Isles, for example, had Irish and Welsh people (speaking Gaelic) as well as English people, but the English language came to be used. France had different language groups, but nearly everyone began to speak and write French. One national language came to be used even in nations that were not united under a monarch, such as Germany and Italy.

B● Look at the map "Nation-States of Europe c. 1500, at the Beginning of the Modern Period" (page 440).
   1. Find these monarchic nation-states: Norway, Sweden, Denmark, Scotland, England, France, Spain, Portugal.
   2. Find these capital cities: London (England); Paris (France); Madrid (Spain); Lisbon (Portugal); Copenhagen (Denmark); Vienna (Holy Roman Empire); Rome (Papal States).
   3. What four big countries were in Eastern Europe?

C● Italy and Germany did not become nation-states until the nineteenth century. Find them. How were they governed in the sixteenth century?

D★ Compare this with a map of Europe today. What changes can you see? What nationalities are there in Eastern Europe? In Western Europe?

E★ Most Americans are descended from European nationalities. Others are from other continents. Find out the national origins of the members of your class.

At the beginning of the Modern period, most Europeans became aware of the nationality group to which they belonged. In many cases national monarchies helped to make people feel strongly about their nation. The feeling of strong loyalty to a nation is **nationalism.**

Another thing that helped the feeling of nationalism was **national literature** (poems, books, and plays written in the national language). In each nation great writers wrote about their country and its traditions and heroes.

THE MODERN AGE BEGINS

F● How did nationalism help to get rid of feudalism?

G★ You may want to find out about some early national writers: Geoffrey Chaucer (English); William Shakespeare (English); François Rabelais (French); Michel de Montaigne (French); Dante Alighieri (Italian); Francesco Petrarch (Italian); Luis de Camoëns (Portuguese); Miguel de Cervantes (Spanish).

Those parts of Europe that were not united under a monarch often suffered. Italy, for example, was invaded and fought over many times between 1494 and 1556. Germany, or the Holy Roman Empire, was fought over from 1618 to 1648. This long and bloody struggle was called the *Thirty Years' War*.

Nation-states and nationalism led to competition among nations. The monarchs fought for power and wealth in Europe. Often several states would join together against another group of states. This became known as **balance-of power politics.** Generally, *balance-of-power politics* in Europe stopped one nation from conquering large areas outside its boundaries.

H● Look at the box "How the Balance of Power Works" (page 443).
1. Do you think C and D are right to help B? What might happen to C and D if they do *not* help B?
2. How did balance-of-power politics help to keep Europe a continent of nation-states instead of becoming a big empire? Would Europe have been better off with one government and one empire?
3. Did the Greek city-states have a similar idea of balance of power? (Think about the Persian Wars and the Peloponnesian War.)

Overseas Empires and Colonies

Competition among European nations spread far beyond Europe. The exploration of European sailors led to colonization.

A▶ What is colonization?

Spain claimed the New World of the Americas. Portugal set up colonies and trading posts in Africa, India, and East Asia. Portugal also gained control of Brazil. Later other European

How the Balance of Power Works

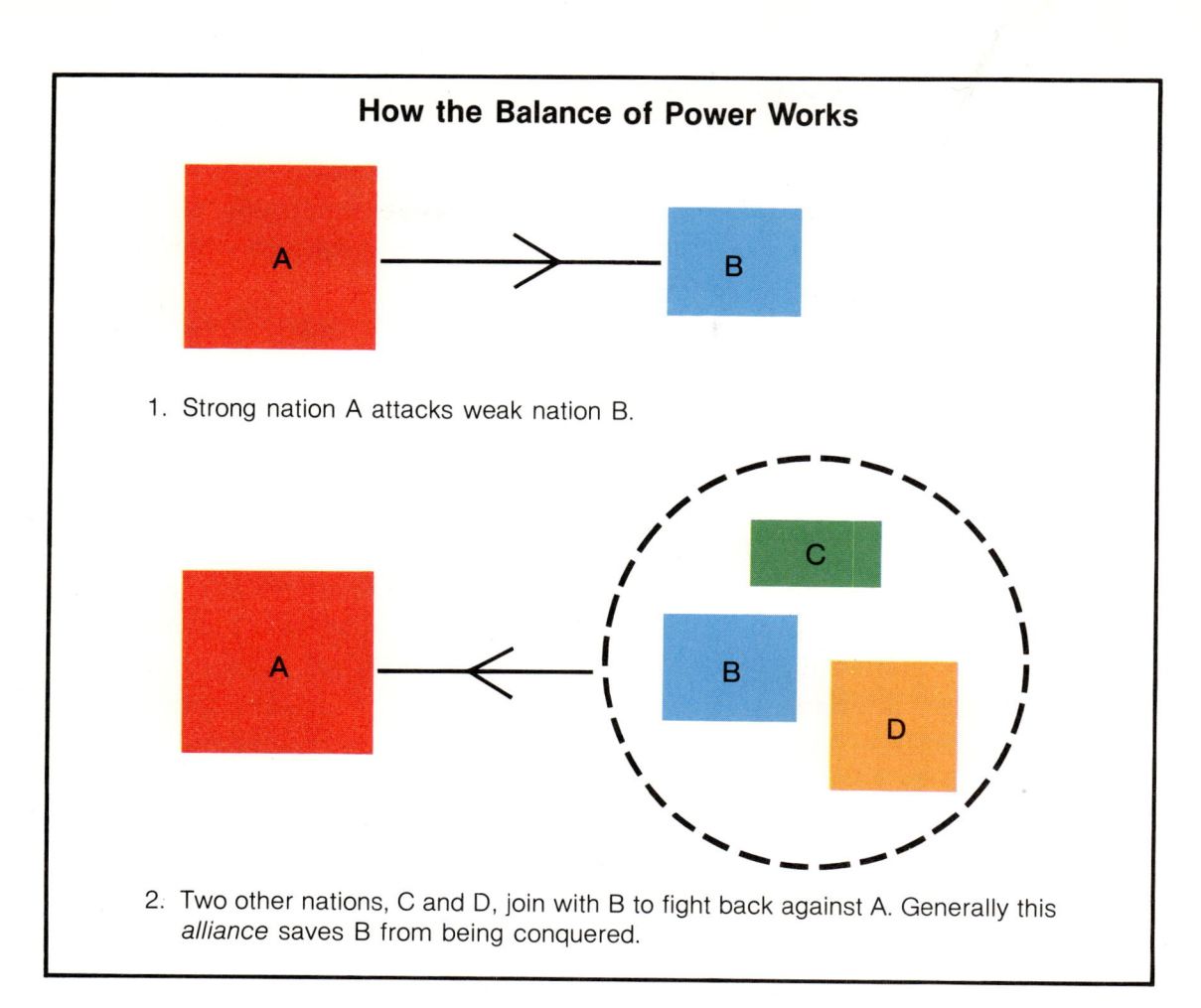

1. Strong nation A attacks weak nation B.

2. Two other nations, C and D, join with B to fight back against A. Generally this *alliance* saves B from being conquered.

countries joined the struggle for colonies. England founded colonies in North America. So did France, in what is now Canada. For a time the Dutch and Swedes had colonies in North America. The Dutch also founded colonies in the East Indies and the West Indies.

B● Look at the map "Important European Colonies and Trading Posts Set Up between 1470 and 1652" (page 445). This map does not show *all* colonies and trading posts in this period.
   1. What does the map tell about the *adventurousness* and *competitiveness* of Western Europeans at that time?
   2. What two governments divided what is now Latin America? What nation settled Brazil?

C● Why was it easier for Europeans to colonize (send settlers to) the New World than places in Asia? (Look at page 430.)

THE MODERN AGE BEGINS   **443**

D★ On the map find French, English, Dutch, Swedish, and Spanish settlements in what are now the United States and Canada. What happened later to these settlements (date of founding is given)? Quebec (1608); Virginia (1607); New England (1620–36); New Amsterdam (1613–26); New Sweden (1638); St. Augustine (1565); Santa Fe (1609).

E● Why do you think Western Europeans were eager to have settlements and trading posts in so many parts of the world?

Colonies, Trade, and Mercantilism

The last question leads us into *economics*. The Western European nations wanted trade, because trade brings wealth. As we know, people trade, or exchange, goods because each person in an exchange will be more satisfied, or better off, when the exchange is made. One person may produce apples *more efficiently* than the other persons. Another person may be more efficient at producing shoes. Yet another may be better at growing wheat. These persons *divide the labor* and then *trade their goods.* They are all better off than if each of them tried to produce all the goods he or she wanted.

This rule about trade is also true of cities, countries, and regions of the world. When colonies were set up, each colony was efficient at producing certain goods. These colonial goods were usually crops, lumber, fish, furs, and minerals such as gold and silver. The nations of Europe were more efficient at producing *manufactured* goods such as cloth, hats, china, and metal products. The nations of Europe could also provide defense, sailing ships, and savings for capital. If colonies and home countries traded these goods, everyone would be better off.

But the governments of European nations seemed to misunderstand the rule about trade. Maybe they were just greedy. Instead of free trade among nations and colonies, the home country governments set up *monopolies.* A **monopoly** is the control of a supply of goods by one group of persons. Only merchants of the nation that owned the colony were allowed to

444 THE GROWTH OF CIVILIZATION

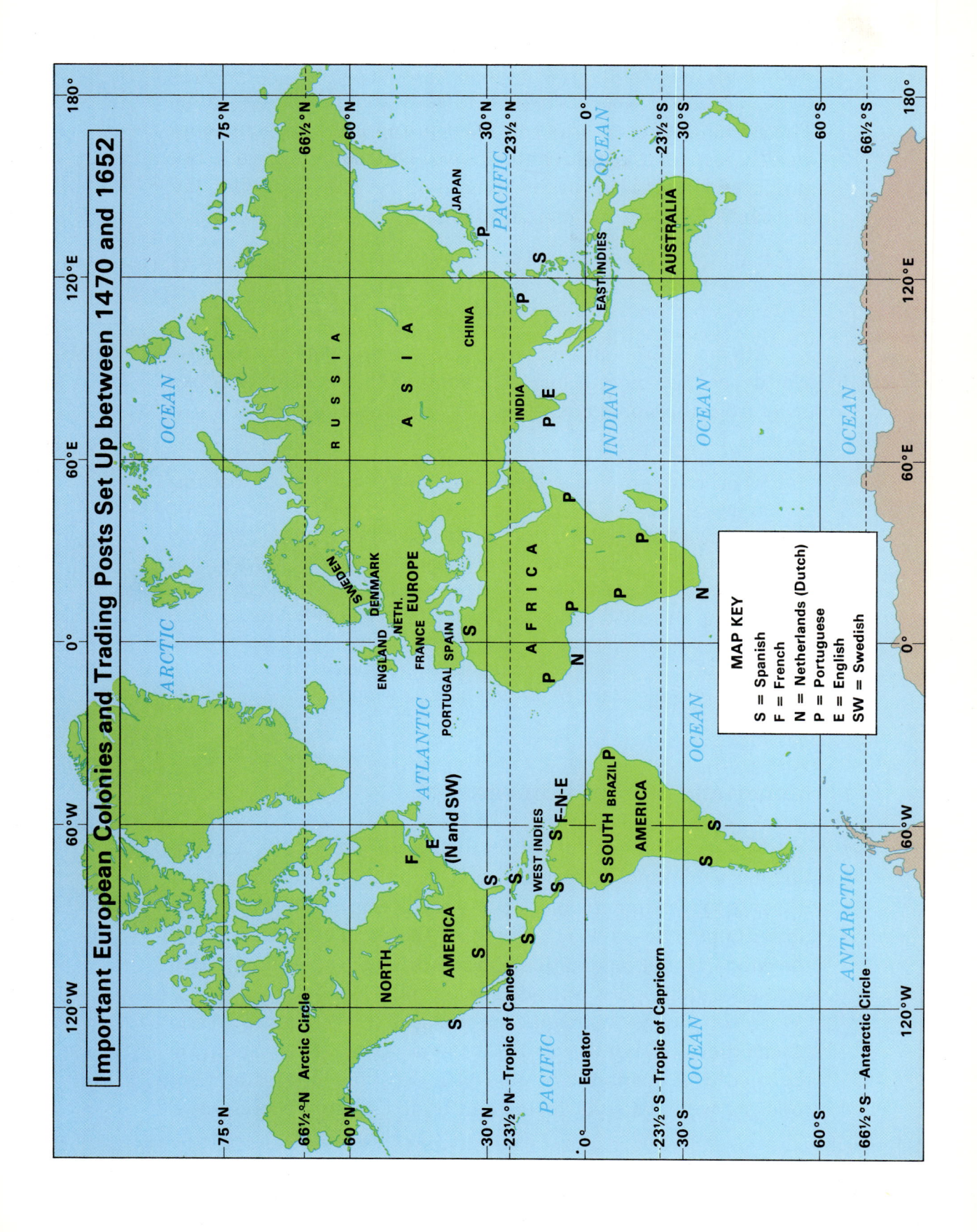

Important European Colonies and Trading Posts Set Up between 1470 and 1652

MAP KEY

S = Spanish
F = French
N = Netherlands (Dutch)
P = Portuguese
E = English
SW = Swedish

trade with that colony. Often only one company was allowed to trade. Colonists were forbidden to start manufacturing goods. The home country wanted to keep piling up more and more wealth, especially gold and silver. The colonies were not supposed to get as rich as the home country. This was called the **mercantile system,** or **mercantilism.**

- A● Explain how the *mercantile* system went against the economic rule about trade.
- B● How would colonists feel about the mercantile system?

After centuries of mercantilism, the colonists in the New World became angry. One after another these colonies broke away from the home countries. The nations of the New World became independent.

- C▶ What colonies in the New World were the first to become independent?
- D★ Do any governments today have things similar to the mercantile system? (Think of monopolies and special favors, fixing prices and wages, government control of trade.)
- E★ Among the "goods" traded under the mercantile system were slaves from Africa, sent to work on plantations in the New World. Later on, the nations of Europe agreed to abolish the *slave trade.* Why were the slave trade and slavery wrong?

Money-and-Market Economy

Mercantilism was based on the idea of *monopoly.* A group that has a monopoly of certain goods can set the price as high as it wants to. Customers have to buy the goods at the price set or do without. There is no *competition,* that is, no other source of the goods. Under mercantilism each European government tried to keep a monopoly of trade for its own merchants.

In some ways, mercantilism was like the economic system of a medieval manor. It was a *closed, noncompetitive* system. Yet the medieval economic system was decaying in Western Europe. As we have seen, towns and trade had grown in Europe.

London at the beginning of the Modern Age

Trade brought much wealth. *Money* came into use. People could save. They had *capital.* They had *division of labor.*

More and more goods were traded in the open market. Sellers and buyers competed for goods. *Prices* were set by *supply* and *demand.* Even so, governments often tried to *set* prices and wages at home just as they tried to have monopolies of foreign trade.

With money and new wealth, the manor economy broke down. Peasants paid *money rents* to the landlords instead of services or other goods. Many peasants left farming. They went to the towns to become skilled workers or managers or merchants. The system that was taking the place of the feudal economic system was a *money-and-market economy.* A **money-and-market economy** is an economic system with capital investment, division of labor, wages, and profits. With a money-and-market economy, people were free to use their

THE MODERN AGE BEGINS

savings (capital) to make a profit. They could open a business. They could buy more land. They were free to sell their labor to get better wages. These changes came slowly. Many people had a hard time during the changes. But the wealth of each nation grew under the new system.

A ▶ How did governments try to control trade inside their countries?

B ● Make sure you know the meaning of *monopoly, competition, goods, capital, profit, money, market, supply, demand, price.*

C ● Profits from trade and manufacture were often bigger and faster than profits from agriculture. How would this change the power of merchants and townspeople compared to the power of the nobles who owned land?

Banking and Joint-Stock Companies

Some rich merchants became bankers. They were able to lend money at *interest*. **Interest** is the price people pay for borrowing money. Banks made it easier for people to get capital for their businesses. Banks also made trade easier. A merchant need not carry gold or silver coins to pay for goods. Instead merchants had *letters of credit* (rather like checks) from a bank in one city to a bank in another city.

A ● What services do banks offer today? How do banks help people to save? How do they help people to get loans? Are checks a form of money? Explain.

In the sixteenth century a new kind of business started. It was called a **joint-stock company.** A number of merchants and bankers would put their money together to start a business that one person alone could not afford. The owners would share the profits as well as the costs of the company. In England and the Netherlands, joint-stock companies did much of the early trading and colonizing overseas.

B ★ What part did the *London Virginia Company* and the *Plymouth Company* play in early settlements in North America? Find out about the *English East India Company* and the *Dutch East India Company.*

C Why were the joint-stock companies important to *economic growth*?

D Companies and corporations today are descended from joint-stock companies. However, there is an important difference between a corporation today and the old joint-stock companies. Today corporations are based on *limited liability*. What does that mean? How does limited liability help people who are not very rich to invest in business?

The economic changes we have been looking at led to the system of *private capitalism*. Under this system, in the eighteenth and nineteenth centuries, the *Industrial Revolution* started. That revolution made the *developed nations* of today.

Religious Changes: Reformation and Counter Reformation

We have seen that a large number of changes and "causes" led to the spread of Western European culture across the world. There is one other big change to think about.

Martin Luther spoke out against some practices and teachings of the Catholic Church. Here he witnesses the burning of a papal document condemning his views.

THE MODERN AGE BEGINS 449

During the Middle Ages there was one church in Western Europe. It was the Roman Catholic Church. Its head was the pope. In the sixteenth century, however, western Christendom came to be divided. The movement that made this division is called the **Reformation.** The name tells us that the leaders of the movement wanted to *reform* (to make better) the Catholic church.

The Catholic church had become very rich. In Italy its leaders had also become *worldly.* Many people were troubled about this. Many did not like sending money from their countries to Rome. Many persons could now read the Bible for themselves. In 1517 a German priest, Martin Luther, spoke up against some teachings of the church because they were not in the Bible. He suddenly found that many Germans—rulers, nobles, and townspeople—agreed with him.

A● How did the Renaissance help make church leaders worldly?
B★ The thing that Luther first objected to was Indulgences. Find out about these in an encyclopedia.

The Reformation began when Luther spoke up against some of the church's teachings. Soon Luther, and others in Germany, began to question the *authority* of the Catholic church. In northern Germany, separate churches called **Protestant** churches, were started.

In those days, the rulers believed that every Christian should belong to the same church as the ruler of the country. They believed, too, that there could be only one true set of Christian beliefs. These ideas led to terrible religious wars in Western Europe between Catholics and Protestants. In every country, these ideas also led to torturing and killing those who disagreed with the ruling church.

C● Religious wars and persecutions lasted for 200 years. Then at last people learned to be *tolerant* of religious differences. What does *religious toleration* mean? Why did people take so long to learn to be tolerant?

Saint Ignatius Loyola (1491–1556) founded the religious order known as the Society of Jesus (Jesuits).

D★ Look up the Constitution of the United States, Amendment I (1791). What does it say about a state church and about religious beliefs? Is religious toleration an important part of American law? Explain. Why did Americans insist on this?

The Reformation spread to other parts of Europe. John Calvin started different Protestant churches in Switzerland. Calvin's teachings spread to France, Scotland, the Netherlands, England, and New England. In England, the rulers set up the Church of England. In this church they combined some Catholic and some Protestant teachings. However, English monarchs would not have the pope as head of the church.

Meanwhile, the Catholic church started its own "reformation." This is called the **Counter Reformation.** It took many years, but in the end, the abuses Martin Luther had complained about were stopped.

E★ Find out about the work of *Ignatius Loyola* and the *Jesuits.*
F★ Find out more about John Calvin and the English Calvinists called *Puritans.* What part did Puritans play in colonizing New England?
G● Look at the map "Religion in Europe after the Reformation (c. 1648)" (page 452).
  1. What countries were Catholic? What were Protestant? What big country was Protestant in the north and Catholic in the south?
  2. Find the Greek Orthodox area. Did the Ottoman Empire tolerate Christianity?

THE MODERN AGE BEGINS

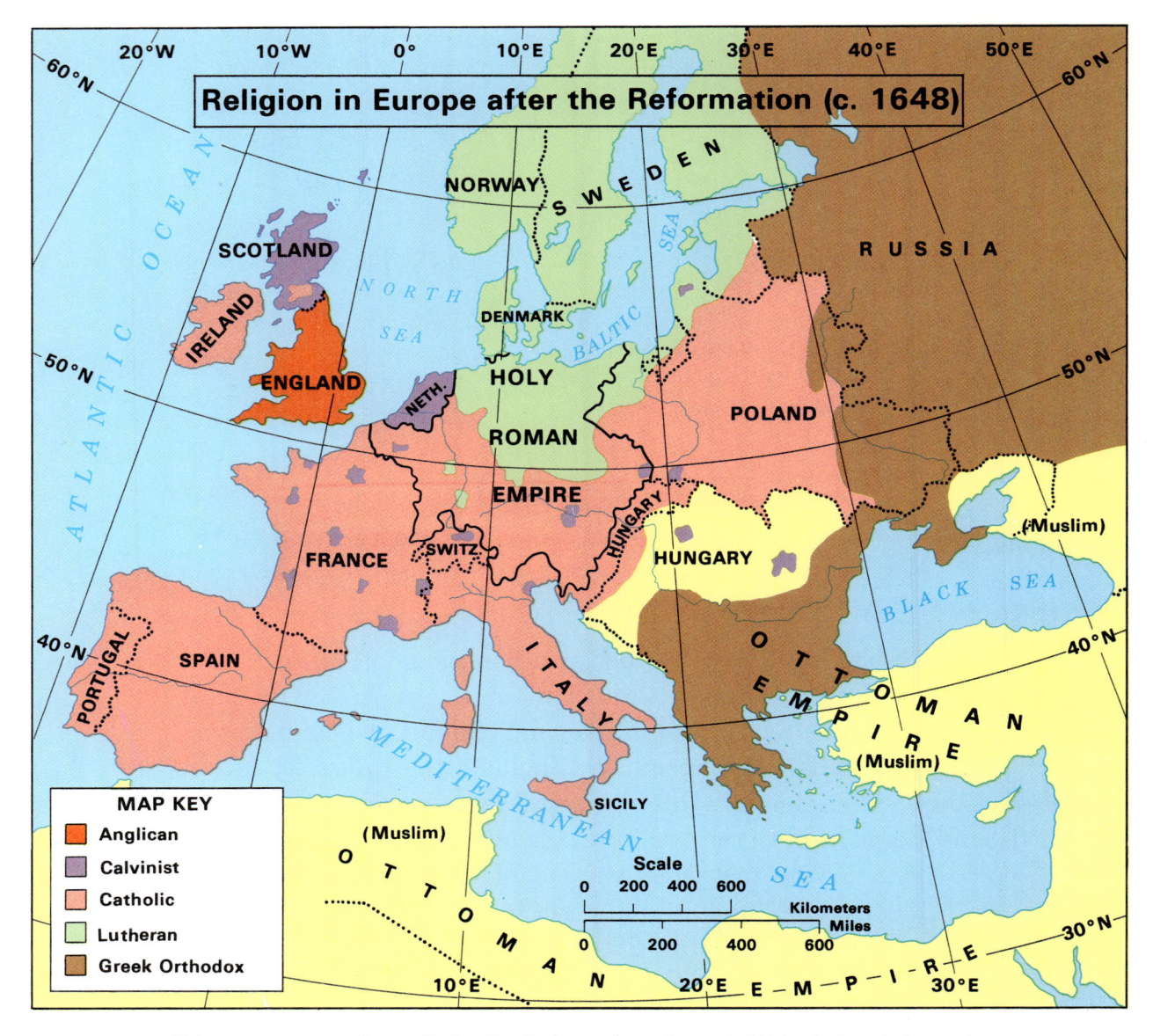

Religion in Europe after the Reformation (c. 1648)

MAP KEY
- Anglican
- Calvinist
- Catholic
- Lutheran
- Greek Orthodox

This map cannot show all details. It does show the *established* church in each area, except Ireland. In Ireland the established church was the Church of England (Anglican), but most of the population was Catholic. In the Balkans, the Ottoman Empire allowed the Greek Orthodox church and the Catholic church to continue. In most parts of northern Europe there were small groups with churches different from the established church in the area.

The Reformation and Counter Reformation showed that the Renaissance of Greco-Roman humanism had not replaced Judeo-Christian beliefs in Europe. After the Reformation, Europeans took their religion—Protestant or Catholic—with them wherever they settled. Missionaries taught Christianity to people of many cultures. Christianity was an important part of Western culture wherever Europeans colonized and traded.

Today few Christians wish to fight about religion. Yet the religious ideas of the sixteenth and seventeenth centuries are still very strong. The Reformation and Counter Reformation are important in understanding the Modern period of history.

H● How did the following help to bring about the Reformation: the Renaissance, printing, translations of the Bible, the rise of towns, nation-states and national monarchies?

The Population of the World

During the Modern Age a very big change happened in the population of the world. Until the Modern Age, population grew very slowly. Sometime after the fifteenth century, it began to grow faster.

A● Look at the box "World Population" below.
1. About how much did world population grow in the 500 years from 1300 to 1800?
2. About how much did it grow in the 180 years from 1800 to 1980?

World Population

The earlier figures are based on careful guesses. Reliable *censuses* of population came in the last two centuries.

Year	Population
1300	350 million
1680	500 million
1800	850 million
1980	4,000 million

THE MODERN AGE BEGINS

Why did this change happen? There are many possible causes. The key fact is that in the Modern Age people began to have longer lives.

It is hard for us to imagine how hard life was before the nineteenth century. Even in civilized societies most people were poor. Famine, disease, and war killed many people. The **expectation of life,** or **life expectancy,** was low. Few people lived to old age. Babies often died soon after they were born. In fact, if a family had six babies, only two or three were likely to live to be adults. For thousands of years the human population grew very slowly. This began to change about 200 years ago.

B● Look at the box "Why Life Expectancy Grew and, with It, Population" (page 455).
   1. Why might these things give people longer life expectancy?
   2. Notice number 4. Why would worldwide trade help to lessen sudden outbreaks of strange diseases? (You might expect just the opposite!)
   3. There may have been other causes. For example, people had cleaner, cheaper clothes. They learned more about how diseases are caused by dirty water and bad sanitation. Can you think of others?

The Modern Period and Rapid Change

We have studied some of the things that happened in Western Europe at the start of the Modern Age. There were other civilizations and many other cultures in the world. Western civilization, however, took the lead. Under Western leadership, the peoples of the whole world came to know about one another. The peoples of the Americas and of Australia had been cut off from the rest of the world for millennia. The peoples of central Africa had also been cut off from most other peoples. During the Modern Age all this changed.

A● Look back over this chapter. See if you can sum up some of the things that led to the spread of Western culture. (Think of ideas—culture contact—geography—technology—economics—government—anything else.)

> **Why Life Expectancy Grew and, with It, Population**
>
> Changes during the eighteenth and nineteenth centuries caused people to live longer. As a result, the population of the world grew fast. Here are some of the possible "causes":
>
> 1. Trade and better transportation made famines fewer and less harmful.
> 2. Industry brought better production of goods (including food).
> 3. Science and medicine improved.
> 4. Worldwide trade made most people better able to resist diseases.
> 5. People opened up new lands all over the world so that there was more agriculture and more food.
> 6. There *may* have been a change in climate that made more land usable for agriculture.
> 7. There have been no great *barbarian invasions*. There have been great movements of people, but these movements did not lead to the *breakdown of food production* as the great barbarian invasions of the past did.

We do not have the time or space to study all of the Modern Age in this book. Nor can we study recent times. Some historians call recent history the Post-Modern period. For example, Western Europe no longer leads the world. There will be time to study these things later on.

One of the most interesting things about the Modern period is the *speed of culture change.* From the fifteenth century the speed of change has grown faster and faster. This speeding up makes living exciting. It also makes thinking about human problems more difficult than ever. That is why history is so important to us. History is the best clue we have to human behavior.

In the Conclusion we shall try to find some useful lessons from the things we have studied in this book.

THE MODERN AGE BEGINS

Summary

The Modern Age is the period of history that begins about A.D. 1500. Under Western leadership the peoples of the world had much culture contact. They exchanged goods and ideas. As a result, the Modern Age was a time of rapid change.

One reason for big changes in Western Europe was the rediscovery of the ideas of Greco-Roman civilization. Greco-Roman ideas made people interested in worldly things such as human cleverness and human beauty and better government and laws. These Greco-Roman ideas were in old writings of Greeks and Romans. They were shown in statues and in the ruins of classical buildings. The rediscovery of Greco-Roman ideas is called the Renaissance, or rebirth of learning.

Europeans had to learn to live with two very different sets of controlling ideas, or values. This problem made Europeans restless and adventurous.

Another thing made Western Europe more important in the world. In 1492 Columbus discovered the New World (the Americas.) From that date Western Europe became the center of the known world.

In addition, there were many technological changes. Western Europeans began to build ocean-going sailing ships. They had new tools to help them navigate far from land. Such tools were the magnetic compass, the log, and tools for finding latitude. Gunpowder came into use. It changed the whole art of war. John Gutenberg invented printing with metal movable type. Books became more plentiful. More and more persons learned to read.

A change in governments also happened. The power of feudal lords died away. People joined in nations. They learned the controlling idea of nationalism: loyalty to a nation sharing a national culture (including a national language). In most countries the monarch of each nation became very powerful. However, in England constitutional government lived on.

Nation-states often fought one another. Countries used balance-of-power politics. The countries of Western Europe also competed for settlements and trade across the oceans. Colonies were set up in the New World, on the coasts of Africa and of Asia, and on islands in many parts of the world.

The main reason for empires and colonies was the desire for wealth through trade. The governments of European nations did not allow free trade with their colonies. Under the mercantile system the colonies were kept poorer than the home countries. After two or three centuries of mercantilism the colonies won independence.

While the mercantile system was in use, a very different system grew up inside some nation-states of Europe. This system was the money-and-market economy. This system encouraged competition. It helped people to start new businesses, to make profits, and to save more capital.

The growth of capital helped banks and joint-stock companies and was, in turn, helped by them. These things brought more economic growth and more wealth.

In addition to the above changes, there was a great change in religion in Western Europe. The Reformation, begun by Martin Luther, divided Europe into Catholic and Protestant churches. Monarchs persecuted people who would not join their church. Cruel religious wars were fought.

A major change in the Modern Age was the rapid growth of population in much of the world. The expectation of life grew longer in most countries.

Some Interesting Activities

1. Collect pictures from magazines and make a display of the art of Western Europe in the Middle Ages and in the Renaissance. Show paintings, statues, and buildings. Show how Greco-Roman ideas about art were added to Judeo-Christian ideas.

2. Use an encyclopedia or a book from the library to make a report on *one* of the following:
   a. Christopher Columbus
   b. Ferdinand Magellan
   c. John Gutenberg
   d. Martin Luther
   e. Ignatius Loyola
   f. Michelangelo
   g. Philip II of Spain
   h. Louis XIV of France
   i. Leonardo da Vinci
   j. Henry VIII of England

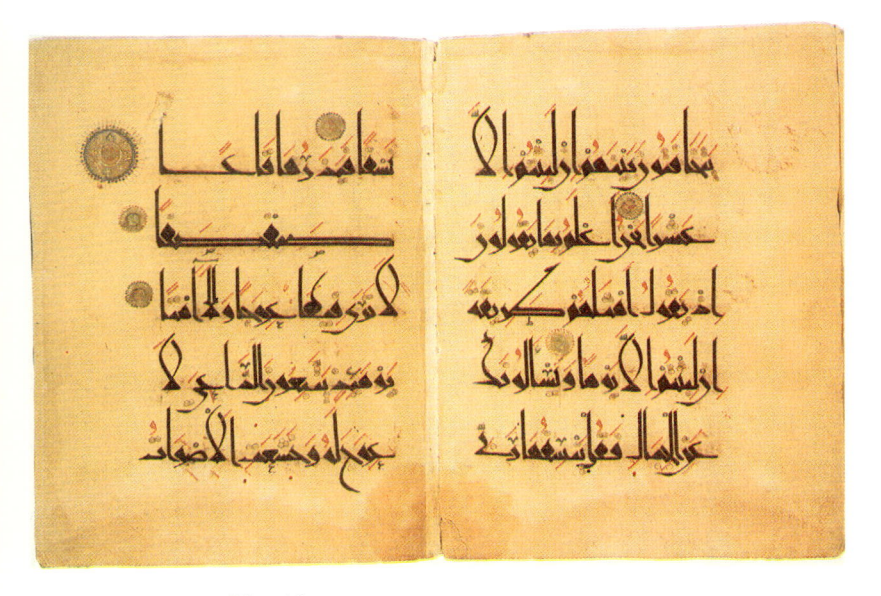

The Koran

An illuminated MS page from the Bible

Controlling Ideas in History

Confucius

Buddha

CONCLUSION

Lessons of History

Homo sapiens has been clever at learning and inventing. Perhaps the greatest invention was language. Language makes possible the passing on of ideas and wisdom. Because of this invention, human knowledge has kept growing.

Yet human beings have much to learn. As we look back over history, we can see how often *Homo sapiens* has failed. We can see the same mistakes and the same problems coming up again and again.

A● Think about the things you have studied in this book. What are some problems that keep coming up in human history? (Think of the following: civilization, barbarians, culture conflicts, wars, using the environment, freedom and slavery, changes in government.)

B● Think about some of the world views you have studied. What is the aim of *philosophy* and of the great religions? Have human beings found the answers to their problems in these ideas? (Think carefully.)

There is still much to learn. Human beings are clever, but they are not perfect. As we look back on the history of civilizations, we see that humans have learned a great deal since the times when a few thousand people kept alive by hunting and gathering.

The first problem of a human society has always been how people can best use their environment.

Human Ecology

The study of how creatures live in their environment is **ecology**. Much of this book is about *human* ecology. How humans use their environment depends on two things: *technology* and *social organization*. Technology is ways of doing things. It includes tools and machines. Social organization enables people to divide the work in an *efficient* way.

A● Look at the box "Human Ecology and Technology" (pages 462–463). The story is simplified, but it helps you to remember some of the changes you have studied.
1. What is *slash-and-burn* agriculture?
2. Why did irrigated river-valley agriculture lead to *civilization*?
3. Why did civilized societies have social classes?
4. *Feudalism* is not mentioned in the box. What was feudalism, and how did it arise?
5. Why could industrial societies get rid of slavery or serfdom?

When humans use their environment, they change it in some way. Sometimes they damage the environment. Sometimes they use it up so that it can no longer support human life. Early hunters sometimes did great damage. They would set grasslands or woods on fire in order to drive animals into traps.

B● What did thousands of years of irrigation do to the soil of Mesopotamia? (Look at pages 121–122.)

Civilization may bring *ecological problems*. Diseases spread rapidly in crowded cities. Sometimes civilization leads to *overpopulation*. Then people become weak, or they may starve because there is not enough food.

Sometimes the environment is damaged by war. The Romans destroyed Carthage and the agricultural lands around it after the Third Punic War. The Mongols caused fearful destruction in the Middle East.

C● Is there a danger of *overpopulation* in the world today? Explain. (Look at pages 453–455.)

D● Industrial civilization may be destroying our environments today. How? What can be done about this problem?

E★ In the Modern Age the people of Western Europe used up their main supply of fuel—the forests. What fuel did they find to cure this *energy crisis?* Do we have an energy crisis today? Explain.

Weaknesses of Civilization

There have been many civilized societies since Sumer. Sooner or later every civilized society became weak. Sooner or later it fell and gave place to some different culture. Will human beings ever learn to stop this rise and fall of civilization? We do not know the answer to that question.

An industrial area in Sheffield, England, experiencing heavy pollution from the factories. Steps are being taken in many communities to control the use of the environment in order to avoid such pollution.

Human Ecology and Technology

TECHNOLOGY	TOOLS, OR CAPITAL GOODS	SOCIAL ORGANIZATION
Hunting and gathering	Stone axes Spears Digging sticks Nets Traps	Small nomadic group
Early slash-and-burn agriculture (Neolithic revolution)	Stone tools Hoes and spades Baskets Pots Bows and arrows Storehouses Looms for cloth	Small villages
Domesticated animals: goats, sheep, cattle; (later) horses and camels	Similar to Neolithic agriculture	Nomadic herding groups
Irrigated, river-valley agriculture	Hoes Plows Irrigation ditches Brick or stone buildings Domestic animals Use of metals	Towns Civilization begins Division of labor
Irrigated agriculture and agriculture in rain-watered lands	Same as for irrigated agriculture Bronze and (later) iron weapons and tools Chariots Ships Architecture	Towns Civilization Social classes Slavery Large empires Trade with distant lands Writing and learning

THE GROWTH OF CIVILIZATION

Human Ecology and Technology (continued)

TECHNOLOGY	TOOLS, OR CAPITAL GOODS	SOCIAL ORGANIZATION

After the breakthrough to civilization, we find civilizations organized as empires and also (as in Greece) as city-states. Many improvements in science and technology come slowly: astronomy, mathematics, the heavy plow, stirrups, horseshoes, armor, steel, water wheels, windmills, gunpowder, clocks, the magnetic compass, the magnifying glass, printing, and the manufacture of many goods. These changes in technology lead to exploration, trade, and more capital goods, which bring in the eighteenth and nineteenth centuries:

Industry and improved agriculture (developed economies)	Machines of iron and steel Factories New sources of energy, such as coal and steam Steamships Railroads, etc.	Cities and nation-states Monarchies and (later) representative government End of slavery in most developed countries Scientists, managers, inventors

A● What are some possible causes of the fall of civilizations? (If you need help, look back at page 145.) Might some of these causes be important in one civilization but not in others? Explain.

Historians have found other possible causes of the weakness of civilization. Sometimes conflict between social classes weakens a civilized society. Sometimes civilized people grow lazy and selfish. They stop being loyal to their society. Then the society cannot defend itself against enemies. Or perhaps people stop working hard. Then the economic system runs down. The society becomes poor. Without goods and capital it cannot keep up its defenses.

B● Do you think it is important to try to understand this problem? Why or why not?

Cultures and World Views

Another of the lessons we learn from history is about *cultures*. The lesson is this: every human society builds up a way of life.

- **A** ● Look at the box "Some Parts of a Culture" (page 41). What are the main parts of a culture? How does environment affect a culture? Does environment *determine* (or decide) what a culture will be? Explain.
- **B** ▶ What do we mean by *controlling ideas,* or *world views*? What world views have you studied in this book? (Look at pages 151 and 152–153.)
- **C** ▶ What do we mean by Western cultures, Eastern cultures, and "other" cultures? Give examples. (Look at page 190.)

The culture of a society is its way of life. The culture tells people how to make a living. It tells them how to behave. Culture also brings problems.

- **D** ● What problems does *culture contact* bring?

People of different cultures often fought one another in the past. They did not understand one another. However, as time went by, *culture groups* became larger. A civilized society often had many cultures living peacefully under one government. Such civilized societies were **culturally pluralistic.** As a result, people learned to respect different cultures. At the same time, a *common culture* came into being. Having a **common culture** means sharing some of the same ways of life. This common culture of the civilized society grew up to include many smaller local cultures. This can be seen in most of the civilizations we have studied.

- **E** ● Did Western Europe in the Modern Age have a common culture? (Did it have one government? One religion? One language? A common world view?)
- **F** ● Is the United States today *culturally pluralistic*? Does it have a *common culture*? Explain.

A Common Culture for the World?

During the Modern Age, all the different cultures of the world came into contact with one another. There were many conflicts, but there were also many new mixtures of ideas. There was, too, a great increase in life expectancy and food supply. Perhaps the world today is moving toward a *common world culture.*

In the big cities of most countries today we can see parts of a common culture.

Differences in technology among cultures may be growing fewer. But there are many differences in *religion* and *politics* and *values.* Will this change? Will all human beings learn to agree on some **moral values** (values of right and wrong)?

> **A●** Would *agreement on moral values* help to keep peace between societies? Why or why not? Are wars always caused by different moral values?

If people agreed on moral values, they would have a better chance of settling quarrels peacefully. For example, if all nations agreed that promises should be kept, it would be easier to have laws for all nations **(international law).** At least 2,000 years ago some philosophers and religious leaders argued that if humans used their *reason,* they would agree on some *moral values.*

> **B●** Look at the idea of naturalism in classical Greece on page 201. Look at the box "Questions the Greeks Tried To Answer" (page 204). How do these Greek ideas lead to the idea of values on which reasonable people might agree?

The idea of moral values found by reason is called **natural law.** It is possible for humans in all cultures to use reason. Therefore, natural law will be the same all over the world. It would be possible for two very different cultures to have the same moral values. For this reason, natural law values are sometimes called **universal values.**

> **Natural Law, or Universal Values**
>
> Philosophers who believe in natural law have suggested values such as the following:
>
> 1. All humans are equal in the sight of God.
>
> 2. All humans should be free. (No one should be a slave.)
>
> 3. All humans should have certain rights.
>
> 4. People should keep their promises.
>
> 5. Governments should respect human dignity.

- C● Look at the box "Natural Law, or Universal Values" above. Does reason lead us to these values? Explain.
- D★ What *rights* does the American Declaration of Independence say every human being should have?
- E● Many people think that the idea of natural law is good. Yet it is difficult to put the idea into practice. What difficulties can you think of? Does history suggest some difficulties? Explain.

The Value of Freedom

Philosophers and religious leaders have tried to lead human beings toward moral values similar to those of natural law. However, humans do not always follow reason. They are sometimes selfish.

- A● If we were all reasonable and unselfish all the time, would we need laws and government? Explain.

It seems that human societies generally have to allow for the fact that humans are not perfect. Let us look at a value that most people would agree on: the value of *freedom*.

Freedom, or *liberty,* means being able to think and act as one wishes. It means the opposite of being forced to behave in a certain way. It means being able to choose for oneself.

B ▶ What did *freedom* mean to the Greeks? (Look at page 205.)

When we think about freedom, we can see that there are all sorts of checks on human freedom. There are *natural* checks. We cannot choose to be ten feet tall. We cannot choose to live for 150 years. There are also natural checks that we can learn to overcome. We cannot choose to jump into deep water without drowning—unless we learn to swim. We cannot fly, unless we learn to make airplanes. We cannot understand great ideas unless we learn to read, to study, and to think.

C ● Think about natural checks on freedom. Give some examples. How does knowledge or education help us to have more freedom?

D ● Was there more or less freedom for humans after the invention of agriculture? After the beginning of civilization? Explain.

There are *social* checks on freedom, too. Humans must live in groups. A member of a group cannot behave as if nobody else matters. A member of a group must fit into the group and must obey its rules. Thus persons lose some freedom when they obey the rules of their group. However, they would have *no* freedom and *no* safety if *nobody* obeyed the rules.

E ● There are other problems about freedom. These problems have troubled great thinkers and religious leaders. For example: how would a Buddhist find freedom? What does freedom mean in Judeo-Christian religions?

Let us think about freedom as simply as we can. Most of us want freedom to choose. We know, however, that we cannot have complete freedom. The question is: How can we have as much freedom as possible?

Freedom, Civilization, and Government

In a traditional agricultural village group, people had little freedom to choose. They had to live and work in, and for, the group. The group was a **closed society.** New ideas were not allowed. Ideas from other culture groups were thought to be wrong and dangerous.

With the growth of civilization things changed. There were different jobs to be done in society. A few people had freedom to learn about the stars and about mathematics. They learned to write and read. Some were rulers, who made laws. Some were merchants, who could travel and make profits. Some were farmers, who could sell their goods in the marketplace. Most of the people, however, had to obey orders. Many were slaves. Yet new ideas did come into civilized societies. Early civilized societies were a bit more *open* to new things than were traditional small societies. This was partly the result of overseas trade and travel. It was also, in part, the result of war and conquest.

A● Civilization led to a new threat to freedom. Can you think what it was? (Think of the power of government. Think of the priest rulers of Sumer. Think of the great empires of the ancient Middle East. Think of the Aztec Empire.)

In traditional, closed societies freedom was blocked by the traditions of the group. In a civilized society, freedom was often blocked by the great power of the government. The rulers had great freedom, but the people were at the mercy of a ruler's army.

The Greeks and the Jews, in their different ways, saw that the great civilized empires were empires of slaves. They began to see that the enemy of freedom in civilized societies was often the government. Yet government and laws were necessary.

B● Why are government and laws necessary? (Think of the need to keep order inside society. Think of the defense of society against enemies.)

C● What can be done to stop governments from crushing freedom?

Checks on Government

Since the period of ancient civilization, there have been many experiments in civilization. There have been many attempts to set up societies with freedom as well as with strong government. The governments of the Jews were based on the laws revealed to Moses. In Islam, governments were powerful, but they were expected to obey the laws laid down in the Koran. In this way people discovered the idea that governments must be guided by a higher law.

The Greeks had a different idea. They believed that citizens should share in the government. In city-states such as Athens all the men (except slaves) shared in government. This was *democracy*. In other city-states, such as Sparta, a small number of persons shared in government. This was *aristocracy* or *oligarchy*.

The Greeks and Romans also learned how to divide the work of government.

A● Look at the charts "The Government of Athens" and "The Government of the United States" (page 214). How does the government of the United States compare with the government of Athens? What is *direct democracy?* What is *representative democracy?* What is a *constitution?*

B● What is a *republic?* Why do we call the government of the Roman Republic a *mixed government?* Did Rome have the *rule of law?* Explain. (Look at pages 238–241.)

In the end the Greek and Roman experiments in government and freedom broke down. The Greek city-states fought among themselves. Then they were conquered, first by Macedon, then by Rome. The Roman Republic ended in a *military dictatorship* after a century of class conflict.

Freedom Today

In Western Europe, civilization grew slowly after the Roman Empire in the West came to an end. Out of feudalism came representative institutions such as the English Parliament. Feudalism also gave the idea that different groups in society must have rights. *Magna Carta* in England listed those rights.

In Western Europe another interesting thing happened. The Catholic church lived on when the Roman Empire ended in the

West. The barbarian monarchs of Europe had great respect for the church. They could not control the church. Thus it happened that religion and government were not controlled by the same persons in Western Europe. This **separation of church and state** helped freedom in Europe. In the Modern period, the Reformation led to greater freedom. By the eighteenth century, most people were learning about *religious freedom.* Governments no longer tried to force people to belong to one *established* church.

> A● Did the Reformation at first lead to government control of religion in Europe? How did religious toleration and religious freedom begin? (Look at pages 449–453.)

At the same time, Europeans also gained *economic freedom.* For a time the strong national monarchies that came into being in the sixteenth and seventeenth centuries tried to control economic affairs.

> B▶ What was the *mercantile system,* or *mercantilism?*

Alongside mercantilism, however, was the system of *private capitalism.* This system brought the end of feudalism and serfdom. It also helped bring about great technological changes. Much capital was invested in trade and production of goods. There were more goods. People were better off than they had ever been before.

Finally, one nation after another in Western Europe began to have *representative, democratic government.* The United States became independent in 1776–82. The Constitution of the United States set up a *federal republican* government in 1789.

For a time it seemed as if people all over the world would copy these Western ideas of freedom. Today, however, things have changed. In many countries the governments are dictatorships. In some, the governments are similar to those of the ancient empires or the Roman Empire. Human beings still have some lessons to learn from history.

470 THE *GROWTH OF CIVILIZATION*

Some Interesting Activities

1. Make a chart similar to the one on pages 462–463 showing the history of human ecology and technology. Use pictures to show tools and social organization at each stage. The pictures may be cutouts from magazines or your own drawings.

2. Make a chart to show how people learned ways of having freedom at different stages of history. Use the summary at the end of the chapter.

3. Set up committees. Each committee should report on *one* of the world views and religions you have studied (Confucianism, Buddhism, Judaism, Greek naturalism, Christianity, and Islam). Then discuss the following questions together. (a) What *moral values* (controlling ideas) are similar in all these world views? (b) What *values* or *beliefs* make each view different from the others? (c) Could people belonging to these different religions or philosophies live together peacefully in one society? Discuss carefully.

4. Make a display of pictures (cutouts or drawings) showing the buildings of the cultures and civilizations you have studied in this book. Start with a Neolithic (early agricultural) village. Then go on to Sumer, Egypt, Mohenjo-Daro, China, Greece, Rome, Islam, Timbuktu, the Maya and Aztec, the Mongols, Japan, Latin Christendom, and the European Renaissance. The last scenes could be big city buildings of our time.

5. Have a pageant of world history. Students may dress up as people from different cultures and civilizations. Each student may tell something about his or her culture, or way of life.

6. Write a story about any society that you have studied. Choose the society and culture that is the most interesting to you.

7. On an outline map of the world, label the places where the civilizations you have studied grew up. If you can do so, write in the centuries of each civilization.

8. Something that you have learned in this book must have been exciting! Write a poem or a paragraph about your idea or your feelings.

Glossary

Some words have many meanings. This list gives the meanings of words as they are used in this book. You will find other meanings of these words in a dictionary.

absolute monarchy: a form of government in which one person rules (for example, a king or a queen) and in which the ruler's power is not limited in any way.

A.D.: abbreviation of the Latin words *anno Domini*, meaning "in the year of the Lord"; used to date events that took place after the birth of Jesus (Christ).

Age of Pericles: period from 461 B.C. to 429 B.C., when Pericles was chief political leader in Athens; the high point of Athenian power and culture.

agricultural revolution: the change in methods of food production from hunting and gathering to agriculture—in the Old World c. 8000–6500 B.C.; also called the Neolithic revolution. In the Americas, agriculture began c. 1000 B.C.

agriculture: the growing and harvesting of crops and the raising of livestock.

air pressure: the weight of the air on the earth's surface.

ancient history: the period of civilizations c. 3500–500 B.C.

animism: worship of spirits believed to inhabit nature or natural objects.

archaeologists: scientists who learn about the past by digging up and studying objects that ancient peoples made and used.

archipelago: a large group of islands

aristocracy: government by a small group (of nobles or members of the upper class); from the Greek *aristos*, meaning "best," and *kratos*, meaning "strength" or "power." In the strict sense, *aristocracy* means "government by the best people."

artifacts: objects produced or shaped by humans, such as tools, weapons, pottery, glass, and ornaments.

assembly: a number of persons gathered together to take part in government.

astrolabe: an instrument used to determine the position of the sun and of other heavenly bodies.

astronomy: the study of the stars and of the planets.

authority: the right to give orders or commands.

autumn equinox: one of the two times of a year when the sun is directly overhead at the equator and when all places on the earth have exactly equal lengths of day and night (about September 22).

axis: an imaginary line through the center of the earth from the North Pole to the South Pole.

balance-of-power politics: actions taken by governments to keep any one nation or group of nations from controlling other nations: for example, a group of weak states may join together to stop a strong state from conquering them.

barbarians: noncivilized peoples who live on the edges of civilization.

barter: a simple form of trading through the exchange of goods.

B.C.: abbreviation of *before Christ*; used to date events that took place in the years before the birth of Jesus (Christ).

Bedouin: "people of the tent"; Arab nomads.

Brahmanism: an early East Indian religion. Two of its teachings were polytheism and reincarnation.

Buddha: "enlightened one"; a great Indian teacher who lived in India in the sixth century B.C.

Buddhism: the teachings of Buddha about life.

bushido: the code of the *samurai*, the Japanese military class.
Byzantine Empire: the Roman Empire in the East, which lasted until 1453, with its capital at Byzantium (Constantinople).

calendar: a system of arranging time into days, weeks, months, and years.
capital goods: goods (such as machines, tools, and buildings) that are used to produce other goods.
caravan: a group of people traveling together, using camels to carry them and their goods.
caste: in Brahmanism and Hinduism, a social class into which a person is born and in which he or she stays until death.
Catholic church: the church of Latin Christendom in the Middle Ages that had its center in Rome and was headed by the pope.
C.E.: abbreviation for "Christian Era" or "Common Era"; used instead of A.D. by some people.
century: 100 years.
chariots: lightweight, two-wheeled carts (as used by the barbarians).
chivalry: the way of life of medieval knights. Chivalry was the beginning of our ideas of good manners.
Christ: from the Greek word for "Messiah"; the title of Jesus, founder and focus of Christianity.
Christendom: the area from the Byzantine Empire to the Atlantic Ocean, in which Christianity was practiced; Europe in the Middle Ages.
city-state: a city that has its own independent government.
civilization: a stage of human society marked by the following: efficient food production, much division of labor, learned persons, many capital goods, and towns or cities.
classical civilization: Greek and Roman cultures during the period c. 500 B.C. to A.D. 500.
classics: ancient Greek and Roman literature and art.
closed society: a society that allows only one culture.
colonization: the setting up of a community of people in a new land. The people live in a new place but keep their ties with the mother country.
comedies: plays that poke fun at human foolishness.
common culture: ways of life shared by a group of people.
community: a group of people living or working together.
competition: in industry, trying to win the same customers or markets.
Confucianism: the teachings of Confucius; a most important controlling idea in China.
constitution: the basic law of a government, sometimes in the form of a single written document as in the United States.
constitutional government: a system in which the power of government is limited by law. In a country that has a constitutional government, people have rights that the government cannot take away.
consuls: the executive branch of the Roman government.
consumer goods: goods that people use to satisfy their wants, such as food, clothing, furniture.
controlling ideas: ideas that control or direct the way a person acts. Each culture has its own set of controlling ideas.
cooperating: working together.
Counter Reformation: the movement in the Catholic church to reform itself and to halt the spread of Protestant ideas.
Crusades: religious wars fought by West European Christians against Muslim Turks, A.D. 1096–1274. The movement began in France.
culturally pluralistic: a term describing a society that is made up of different culture groups living together peacefully. Each group keeps its own identity and many of its old ways of doing things.
culture: the traditions and customs of a people; a people's way of life and thought.
cuneiform: wedge-shaped marks; writing invented by the Sumerians.
cylinder seal: a picture or design carved on a piece of stone or pottery that could be rolled across soft clay; used by ancient peoples to sign their names.

daimyo: Japanese nobles who owned land and led small armies of *samurai* soldiers. The *daimyo* were vassals of the *shogun*.
Dark Ages: the early part of the Middle Ages, c. A.D. 500–1000.
decade: ten years.
decline: to grow weak.
democracy: rule by the people; a form of government in which the people are the government or elect the government.
dictator: a ruler who has great power over the lives of all the people in a country.
direct democracy: government by the people themselves as opposed to government by elected representatives.
discipline: training or teaching oneself or others to act in certain ways.
divine monarchy: the belief that rulers are gods and have divine powers.
divine right: belief that rulers receive their power from God and are responsible only to God.
division of labor: a separation of workers into different jobs so that more and better goods can be produced. Another name for division of labor is *specialization*.
domesticating: taming of wild living things by humans.
draft animals: animals that pull things such as plows and carts.

Eastern cultures: cultures that began in Asia—for example, China, India, and Japan.
ecology: the study of how creatures live in their environment.
economic changes: changes in the ways in which goods are produced and consumed.
economic classes: divisions within a society based on income or standard of living.
edubbas: the Sumerian word for "schools."
educate: to teach.
efficient: productive, with as little waste and effort as possible.
emperor: the ruler of an empire.
empire: the rule of one government over a number of different societies.
enlightening: Gautama's discovery of the light of truth. Gautama became known as Buddha, the "enlightened one."

equator: the latitude line that goes around the middle of the globe; it is half way between the North Pole and the South Pole.
equinox: time of year when the sun is directly overhead at the equator and when all places on earth have exactly equal lengths of day and night; spring, or vernal, equinox, about March 21; autumn equinox, about September 22.
era: a period of time.
Exodus: the journey of the Hebrews out of Egypt.
expectation of life, or **life expectancy:** in general, the number of years people born at a certain time in a society can expect to live.
export: (n.) merchandise sent out of a country for sale or trade; (v.) to send goods to other countries for sale or for trade.
extended family: a family consisting of parents and their children together with such family members as grandparents, aunts, uncles, and cousins.

Fall of Man: the act of disobedience to God of Adam and Eve.
feudalism: a way of organizing and defending societies that had no strong central government. Power was divided among many noble landowners.
feudal monarchy: the rule of a king or a queen at the head of a feudal system.
feudal system: social, political, and economic system of Western Europe in the Middle Ages, based on ownership of land. In return for land, knights paid military service to their lords.
fief: under the feudal system, a piece of land granted by a lord to a knight.

gladiators: in Rome, armed persons who fought (often to the death) for the entertainment of the people.
global grid: the pattern on a globe of intersecting lines formed by meridians of longitude (north-south lines) and parallels of latitude (west-east lines).
globe: a model of the earth.
Gothic architecture: a medieval style of architecture whose features are buttresses

474 THE GROWTH OF CIVILIZATION

(stone props), pointed arches, and stained glass windows.

Greco-Roman culture: the mixture of early Greek culture and Roman culture.

Great Wall of China: a wall (about 2,400 kilometers, or 1,500 miles, long) built by the Chinese to keep barbarians out of China.

Greek Christendom: Eastern Europe in the Middle Ages; the Orthodox part of the Christian world in the Middle Ages.

grid: a checkerboard pattern of east-west and north-south lines.

guilds: groups formed by merchants or by various types of skilled workers who owned their own businesses. Representatives of guilds ran town governments.

Hegira: the flight of Muhammad and Abu Bekr from Mecca to Medina.

Hellenes: the ancient Greeks' name for themselves.

Hellenism: the culture of ancient Greece (especially Athens in Pericles' time).

Hellenistic: modeled after, or imitating, Greek art and customs. The Hellenistic Age and culture started after the conquests of Alexander, c. 323 B.C.

hereditary monarch: a ruler, such as a king or a queen, who inherits his or her authority.

hieroglyphics: Egyptian picture writing.

High Middle Ages: the thirteenth through the fifteenth centuries.

historians: scholars who learn about the past by studying written records.

history: the study of the past.

Holy Roman Empire: a weak, loosely connected group of states in west central Europe from 962 to 1806.

House of Commons: the part of British Parliament made up of representatives elected by the people.

House of Lords: the part of British Parliament made up of bishops and nobles.

humanism: studying human beings to find the meaning and purpose of human life—a part of the Greek world view.

Ice Age: a period from about 1,500,000 B.C. to 8000 B.C., during which much of the earth was covered periodically by glaciers.

icecap: a cap of ice over an area, sloping in all directions from the center.

import: (n.) goods brought from other countries for sale or trade; (v.) to buy goods from other countries.

Indies: India, Southeast Asia, and Indonesia.

Industrial Revolution: a period of great changes in industry as people began to use power-driven machines to make things in factories. The First Industrial Revolution began in England in the eighteenth century.

interest: money paid for the use of a loan; money paid on savings accounts by banks.

international law: rules that all nations are supposed to follow in dealing with one another.

intolerance: an unwillingness to respect the rights of others to have beliefs different from one's own.

irrigation: method of supplying the land with water by artificial means, such as ditches, channels, canals.

Islam: the Muslim religion based upon belief in one God and the teachings of Muhammad.

joint-stock company: a company formed by a number of persons who agree to share the costs and the profits of a business venture.

Judaism: the religion of the Hebrews based upon belief in one God and obedience to His laws.

Koran: the holy book of Islam. It contains Muhammad's teachings—the law of Allah as given to Muhammad by the Angel Gabriel.

language family: a group of languages that come from one older language.

Latin Christendom: in the Middle Ages, Western Europe; the Catholic part of the Christian world in the Middle Ages.

legends: stories handed down from early times and often accepted as truth.

levees: walls of earth that prevent flooding from rivers.

liberty: freedom.

lines of longitude: imaginary lines on the earth's surface, running from the North to South poles; also called *meridians of longitude*.

logbook: the daily record of a ship's voyage.

lot: picking names at random.

Magna Carta: the charter of the rights of English people, signed by King John in 1215. Magna Carta means "Great Charter."

majority: the greater number or a number that is more than half of the total number.

manor: the smallest division of land under the feudal system and also the unit of agricultural production; it consisted of one or more villages inhabited by peasant (farmer) families, a manor house or small castle where the lord of the manor lived, a church and a priest.

map: a flat drawing of the earth's surface.

market: (1) the place where buyers and sellers meet to trade, or exchange, goods; (2) all the trade that goes on between buyers and sellers.

market economy: an economy, or part of an economy, based on producing and selling what people will buy.

Mediterranean climate: a climate consisting of mild, rainy winters and warm or hot, dry summers.

medium of exchange: money; anything generally accepted in exchange for other things.

mercantile system, or **mercantilism:** government control of an economy through regulation of manufacture, commerce, and trade.

meridian: a line of longitude; an imaginary line on the earth's surface running from North to South poles. Meridians are measured in degrees of longitude.

Mesoamerican: Middle American.

Messiah: God's chosen leader who would deliver the Jews and establish God's kingdom.

Middle Ages: the medieval period; the period of European history from c. A.D. 500 to 1500.

military dictators: rulers whose power is based on their armies.

military technology: a way of fighting, such as using chariots, horses, iron weapons and armor.

millennium: 1,000 years.

minority: a group of persons or things numbering less than half of a total.

mixed government: a government that combines several forms of rule. These may include ideas of democracy, monarchy, and aristocracy.

moat: a ditch filled with water, which surrounded the walls of a medieval castle.

Modern Age: the time beginning about A.D. 1500 to the present.

monarchy: rule by a single person—for example, a king.

money-and-market economy: an economic system with capital investment, division of labor, wages, and profits. Prices and products depend on demand and supply.

monopoly: the control of a supply of goods by one group of persons.

monotheism: belief in one God; from the Greek words *mono* (one) and *theos* (god).

monotheist: a person who believes in one God.

moral values: values of right and wrong.

movable type: separate pieces of type, each with a single character (letter, number, punctuation mark) that can be used over and over again for printing. Johann Gutenberg is generally considered the first European to print from movable type.

Muslims: the followers of Muhammad; people who practice the religion of Islam. *Muslim* (sometimes spelled *Moslem*) means "one who surrenders" his or her life and thoughts to the will of God.

myths: stories told by ancient peoples about the gods.

nation or **nation-state:** a group of people living in an area governed by one government.

nationalism: the feeling of strong loyalty to one's country.

nationality, or **nationality group:** the nation to which one belongs, or all the people belonging to a particular nation.

national literature: poems, books, and plays written in the national language.

naturalism: seeking truth in nature and natural causes—one definition of the Greek world view.

natural law: those laws, duties, and rights

---

476   THE GROWTH OF CIVILIZATION

that all human beings recognize and share; sometimes called *universal law*.

natural sciences: sciences based on knowledge of nature. Chemistry, biology, and physics are among the natural sciences.

natural vegetation: the plant life of an area that grows or grew without human interference; often connected with climate types.

Neolithic period: New Stone Age.

Neolithic revolution: the change in methods of food production from hunting and gathering to agriculture—c. 8000–6500 B.C.; also called *agricultural revolution*.

New Stone Age: the period during which people learned how to tame wild plants and wild animals; also known as the Neolithic period.

nirvana: in Buddhism, the state of freedom and peace that comes from knowing the truth and overcoming earthly desire; escape from "continual rebirth."

nomads: people who move from place to place and do not settle down.

nuclear family: one set of parents and their children.

oasis: a fertile spot in a desert.

oath of fealty: a solemn promise of loyalty.

Old Stone Age: the period when people lived by hunting and gathering food in their environment and made stone tools.

oligarchy: government in which the power is held by a small group of persons; from Greek words meaning "rule of the few."

Paleolithic period: Old Stone Age. *Paleolithic* is from Greek words meaning "Old Stone."

parallels of latitude: imaginary circles drawn east and west around the surface of the earth. The circles are the same distance from each other and grow smaller as they approach the poles.

Parliament: representative body in the government of England.

patricians: the highest class in Rome, members of the noble (the oldest and most important) families.

patriotism: love of one's country.

pharaohs: strong rulers of ancient Egypt.

philosopher: a lover of wisdom; one who thinks about the meaning of life and of being human.

philosophy: a love and pursuit of wisdom—from the Greek words *philos* (love) and *sophos* (wisdom); a system of thought about the meaning of life and the nature of humankind.

physical traits: things like skin color, kind of hair, shape of head, color of eyes, etc.

plagues: great evils that cause widespread disaster; sometimes an epidemic disease.

plebs: members of the lowest class of Roman citizens.

polar regions: the high latitudes; 66½° north and south.

political science: the scientific study of the principles and conduct of government.

polytheism: belief in many gods;—from the Greek words *poly* (many) and *theos* (god).

prehistoric times: the times before written records were kept.

prime meridian: the zero meridian (0°), from which longitude east and west is measured and which passes through Greenwich, England.

printing presses: machines for printing.

private capitalism: an economic system in which there is private ownership of the means of production; investments determined by private decision rather than by state control; and prices, production, and the distribution of goods determined mainly in a free market.

profit: the money left over from the sale of goods after production costs have been paid.

property: the goods that people own. Property may be owned by a person, a family or other group, or a government.

prophets: in religion, persons who speak with God and pass on God's word to others.

Protestant churches: groups that broke away from the Roman Catholic Church.

Punjab: the plain of the Indus River and its tributaries. Punjab means "five rivers."

race: a group of people with similar physical traits. The four main racial groups are Australoid, Mongoloid, Negroid, and Caucasoid.

rain-watered lands: lands that have enough rainfall to grow crops without irrigation.
recent history: history of the last 50 years.
Reformation: the sixteenth-century religious, social, and political movement that led to the division of Latin Christendom and the establishment of Protestant churches.
reincarnation: one of the controlling ideas of Buddhism and Hinduism. Souls are born and reborn (again and again) in different bodies.
Renaissance: the time in Europe (c. 1450–1600) of the "rebirth" of interest in the art and literature of classical Greece and Rome.
representative government: government in which people elect others to govern them.
republic: in Rome, the government for the benefit of all free citizens; today, government in which power is in the hands of representatives who rule for the common good.
revelation: direct contact of human beings with God.
revolution: in geography, the motion of the earth around the sun. One complete revolution is called a year.
Roman Empire: the Roman state after the overthrow of the Republic. It began in the reign of Augustus c. 27 B.C.; it was later divided into the eastern and western Roman empires. The Western Roman Empire ended A.D. 476. The Eastern Empire became the Byzantine Empire, which lasted until A.D. 1453.
rotation: in geography, the motion of the earth on its axis every 24 hours. A complete rotation takes 24 hours, or one day.

samurai: Japanese soldiers who fought for the *shogun* and the *daimyo*. The virtues of the samurai were loyalty and bravery.
saving: not consuming everything that is produced.
scholar: a learned person—especially one who knows a great deal about a certain subject.
scripture: writing.
scrub: low evergreen plants with a few trees.
Senate: (1) part of the legislative branch of the United States government; (2) in Rome, the most important and powerful body of the legislative branch, made up of 300 lifetime members.
separation of church and state: system in which religion is not controlled by the government.
serfs: persons who were bound to stay and work on the land where they were born. Serfs could not be sold off the land, and they passed with the land from one owner to another.
Shinto: Japanese religion of nature and ancestor worship. Shinto means "the way of the gods."
shogun: Japanese word meaning "great general." The *shoguns* were nobles who controlled weaker nobles and, in time, even the emperor.
silt: sand and soil carried along by river waters.
slave: a person who has to work for an owner.
social classes: ranks, or levels, of society.
social relationship: the way in which two or more persons get on together.
social sciences: the branches of science that deal with human beings in societies or as individuals, or with human societies and their history, functions, and customs. Sociology, anthropology, political science, history, economics, and geography are among the social sciences.
society: a group of humans living together.
solstice: from Latin words meaning "a standing still of the sun"; the date on which the sun is directly overhead on either the Tropic of Cancer (*summer solstice* in the Northern Hemisphere, about June 21) or the Tropic of Capricorn (*winter solstice* in the Northern Hemisphere, about December 22).
specialize: to do one special job.
species: a group of creatures who are alike.
spring equinox: also *vernal* equinox; time of year when the sun is directly overhead at the equator and all places on the earth have exactly equal lengths of day and night, about March 21.
steppe: grassy plains; prairie.
Sumer: the land of southern Mesopotamia

where the first civilization arose; now part of Iraq.
Sumerians: the people who lived in Sumer.

Talmud: collections of rabbis' writings put together after the Jews were driven from Jerusalem.
technology: a way of getting things done or of producing goods in a society.
tels: mounds made up of the remains of a settlement or city of one or more ancient civilizations.
Ten Commandments: laws which are most important controlling ideas in the lives of Hebrews.
terminator: the dividing line between light and darkness on the earth at any given time.
time zones: in geography, areas between lines of longitude that have the same time. When passing from one time zone to another, one must put one's watch forward or back one hour.
Torah: Hebrew word (meaning "law" or "teaching") for the Law of Moses. The Torah is also the first five books of the Christian Bible.
tragedies: serious plays with sad endings.
Tribunes of the People: Roman officials who represented the plebs.
tributaries: rivers that flow into larger rivers.
tribute: taxes paid to a foreign government.

tropics: the low latitudes; the region between the Tropics of Cancer and Capricorn.

universal values: See *natural law*.

values: beliefs that we think are important.
vassal: in medieval times, knights and other free people whose land was protected by their lord and who usually owed military service to their lord.

Way of Heaven: in Confucianism, the path to wisdom and goodness in human lives.
Western cultures: ways of life that started in Western Europe; found today in Europe, North America and South America, Australia, and South Africa.
Will of Heaven: in Confucianism, a great spirit of wisdom and goodness that helps a ruler to govern well.
wood-block printing: an early form of printing.
world view: a set of controlling ideas that tell us how to think and behave; a whole way of looking at the world and at our place in it.

Zen Buddhism: a form of Buddhism involving meditation, or very deep thought.
ziggurat: a Sumerian hill temple where the Sumerians worshipped their gods.

Index

Abraham, 74, 174, 186
absolute monarchy, 412
A.D. (anno Domini), 19, 22
Adam and Eve, 182
Africa
    Arabs in, 309–311, 313, 372
    kingdoms in, 304–321, 421
    natural environment of, 295–297, 304–306, 322
    religions in, 310, 312, 322
    trade, 306, 309–311, 313, 314
Age of Pericles, 213–218, 228
agricultural revolution, 52
agriculture
    discovery of, 51, 56–61
    efficient, 379–380, 385, 386
    inventions in, 380–382
    methods of, 382
air pressure, 326
Akkadian Empire, 126, 146
Alexander the Great, 224–227, 229
Allah, 276, 277, 279
Amaterasu and Susanowo, legend, 346
American cultures, 331
American Indians, 339, 340
ancestors, 156–157
ancient history, 141–143, 147
animism, 169, 186, 346
Arab Empire, 280–281
    caliphs in, 282–286
    decline of, 290–291
    religions of, 275
    in Spain, 289–290, 292, 372, 400
    trade, 286–288
Arabia, 272–275
Arabs, 279–280, 309–311
    Bedouins, 272–275
archaeologists, 71, 80, 86
archipelago, 192
aristocracy, 205, 469
Aristotle, 223, 424
arithmetic, 64, 102–105, 287
artifacts, 71, 77, 86
Aryans, 134, 138, 164
assemblies, 114–115, 123, 239–240, 244

Assyrian Empire, 74, 139, 146, 179, 301
astrolabe, 435
astronomy, 288
Athens, 208, 210, 219–220
    Age of Pericles, 213–218
    democracy in, 211–213, 224, 228–229, 238
    end of classicism, 223–224
Augustus (Octavian), 252–254, 260, 268
authority, 237
autumn equinox, 14
axis, 8, 13–14, 22, 27, 30
Axum, kingdom of, 301
Aztecs, 334–339, 340

Babylonian Empire, 73–75, 126, 146, 172, 179–181, 200
balance-of-power politics, 442–443
banking, 448–449
barbarians, 125, 290, 291
    and Africa, 318
    and China, 343, 357–365
    and India, 134
    and Roman Empire, 260, 262, 263
    and Sumer, 138, 146
    and Western Europe, 370–373
barter, 94, 309
B.C. (before Christ), 19, 22
Becket, Thomas, 395
Bedouins, 272–275
Benin, 318, 319–321, 323
Berbers, 312, 313
Bible, 74, 86, 173, 255
Black Death, 403–404
Brahmanism, 162–164, 168, 186
bronze, 85, 86, 139, 320
Brutus and His Sons, 243
Buddha, 154, 164–167, 168, 186
Buddhism, 153, 162–168, 182, 186
    spread of, 167–168, 349, 366
    Zen, 353–354
bushido, 351, 389
Byzantine Empire, 263, 268, 343, 361, 366, 370, 400, 402

Caesar, Julius, 251, 268
calendar, 19, 333–334

480   THE GROWTH OF CIVILIZATION

caliphs, 280, 282–286
canals, 61, 96, 333
capital goods, 64, 94, 96, 97
caravan, 274–275
Carthage, 245–248, 461
caste system, 163–164, 168
castles, 383–385
Catholic church, 263, 370, 386, 390, 469–470
  Counter Reformation, 451
  organization of, 394
  power of, 372, 395, 450
C.E. (Christian Era), 19
century, 10, 20–21, 22
Charlemagne, 372–373, 375, 392–393
Chinese Empire
  barbarian invasions of, 343, 357, 362, 367, 421–423
  culture of, 154–156, 160–161, 189, 190, 287, 356, 365, 436–437
  Mongol rule of, 362–365
  religions in, 160–162, 346
chivalry, 389–394, 416
Christendom, 367, 450
Christianity, 184, 255–262, 280
  Constantine and, 261–262
  rise of, 255–256, 268
  spread of, 356, 366
  See also Catholic church; Latin Christendom
Christian kingdoms, 290, 291, 292
churches, 256, 259–260, 394
  Gothic, 396–397
cities, 64, 102, 122, 131–134
city-states, 122–214
  Greek, 142, 192, 204–206, 219, 224, 228, 248, 469
  Mayan, 334
  Sumerian, 122–124, 146
civilization, 114, 116, 467–468
  areas of, 420–422
  characteristics of, 65
  ebb and flow of, 144, 147
  origins of, 65, 71, 80, 86, 89
  rise and fall of, 121–146
  spread of, 127–146, 152
  weaknesses in, 461–463
classes, 64, 112–114, 238–239, 355
classical civilization, 189, 426

classics, 189
closed society, 467
colonies, 320–321, 442–443, 444, 446
comedies, 216–217
common culture, 464–465
community, 150–152
competition, 442
Confucianism, 153, 154–161, 182, 186, 346, 366
  family in, 156–157, 167
  government in, 158–519
  social relationships, 158
Confucius, 154–161, 167
Constantine, 261–262, 268
Constantinople, 262, 263, 361, 370, 402
constitution, 206
constitutional government, 412–415
constitutional monarchs, 439
consuls, 239, 244
consumer goods, 64
controlling ideas, 152–153, 186
copper, 82, 85, 86, 314
Counter Reformation, 449–453
Crusades, 400–402, 406, 416
culturally pluralistic, 464
cultures, 40, 142–144
  change in, 455
  grouping, 190, 191
  interaction of, 422–426
  study of, 90, 91
  world view of, 149, 186, 464
culture contact, 356, 422, 456
cuneiform, 76–79, 86, 105–111, 118
cylinder seal, 106–107, 438

daimyo, 350–351, 352, 355
Darius the Great, 77–78, 207, 208
Dark Ages, 370–373
David, 179
decade, 10
Delian League, 219
Della Valle, Pietro, 75–76
democracy, 205, 211, 228, 269
  Athenian, 211–213, 224, 228–229, 238
  direct, 212
  representative, 212, 213, 239, 470
dictator, 439

INDEX   **481**

discipline, 237
disease, 122, 288, 339, 340, 402–403, 460
divine monarchy, 300
divine right, 320, 439
division of labor, 50, 63–64, 93, 118, 444
domestication, 50, 51, 56
draft animals, 62

earth
   axis of, 8, 13–14, 27, 30
   rotation and revolution, 8–12, 27, 326–327
   wind patterns of, 326–330
Eastern cultures, 190, 191
ecology, 460–463
economic changes, 63–64
economic classes, 112–114
efficient, 63, 92, 379–380, 385
Egypt
   civilization in, 172, 200, 298–301, 322
   Hebrews in, 174–179
   See also Nile River Valley
emperor, 124, 253, 260, 366
empires, 124, 146, 219, 457
   European, 442–443
   of the Middle East, 139–141
England, 397–399, 411–415, 443, 451
enlightening, 166
environment
   changes in, 121–122
   humans and, 39, 42, 460–461
epic poems, 199
equator, 27
equinox, 14, 15, 22, 33
era, 19
Esther, Queen, 181
Etruscans, 241–243
Europe
   balance-of-power, 442–443
   classical influence, 189, 231
   explorations, 339, 356, 428–430
   Muslim influence, 290
   trade, 422, 428, 444–448
Exodus, 175–178
explorations, 428–430, 442–443
   technology and, 430–434

export, 94–95
extended family, 157

Fall of Man, 182
family life, 73, 110, 156–157, 237
famine, 402–403
feudalism, 350–351, 366, 423
   in Europe, 375–378, 397, 416, 469
feudal system, 375–378, 379, 386, 409, 411
fief, 377
floods, 57, 60, 61, 98-99
foot soldiers, 373–374
forest kingdoms, 318, 319–321
France, 397–399, 411, 443
freedom, 466–470

Gautama, 164–167
Genghis Khan, 361–362, 364, 367
Ghana, 304, 309–313
Gilgamesh, 108–109
gladiators, 250
global grid, 27–28, 29
globe, 25
gods
   Greek, 199–201
   Mayan, 333
   myths of, 170–172, 199–200
   Roman, 238
gold, 85, 86, 309–311, 313, 314
Gordian knot, 224–225
Gothic architecture, 396–397, 426
government
   changes in, 456
   forms of, 205–206, 207, 211-213, 215, 240, 405, 412–415
   mixed, 240
   need for, 54, 468
   parts of, 206
   power of, 114, 116–117
   ways of controlling, 117, 468–469
great leap forward, 39, 68
   stages of, 49–52, 54, 56–65
Great Wall of China, 362, 364
Greco-Roman culture, 248, 263, 424–426, 453, 456
Greece
   Age of Pericles, 213–218
   art and athletics in, 203

482 THE GROWTH OF CIVILIZATION

culture of, 189, 289, 469
government in, 205–206, 211–213 215, 228
natural environment of, 192–198
in Persian wars, 207–211, 219, 228
religion in, 199–201, 238
See also city-states; Hellenism
Greek Christendom, 370, 386, 422
Greek myths, 170–171, 197–200, 224
grid, 26, 36
guilds, 405, 406
gunpowder, 435, 456

Hades and Persephone, 170–171
Harappa, 132, 134
Hebrews, 173–179, 186
Hegira, 277
Hellenes, 192
Hellenism, 192, 224–227, 248
Hellenistic, 224–226, 229
Henry the Navigator, 429, 432
hereditary monarch, 409–410
Herodotus, 73
hieroglyphics, 129
High Middle Ages, 385, 389
Hinduism, 164, 168
Hindus, 287, 357, 358, 360, 421
historians, 1, 71, 86
history, 1–3, 22, 41, 91, 455
ancient, 141–143
lessons from, 460, 470
measuring time in, 19–21
periods of, 141–143, 147, 302, 322
prehistory, 141
Holy Roman Empire, 411, 442
holy wars, 280, 400–402
Homo sapiens, 2, 459
Horatius at the Bridge, 241–243
horse-soldiers, 139, 373, 374
House of Commons, 414
House of Lords, 414
human ecology, 460, 462–463
humanism, 201, 267, 424, 426
humans, 39, 40–41, 295, 322, 460
Hundred Years' War, 397–399, 414
hunters and gatherers, 38, 42–45, 51

Ice Age, 45, 47–49, 68
icecap, 45

ideas, 149–152, 422–423, 467
controlling, 152–153
Iliad, 199
import, 95
Incas, 324, 339, 340
India, 162
civilization in, 189, 190, 226, 287–288, 421
invasion of, 358–360, 366
religion in, 349, 358–360
Indies, 286, 428
Indus River Valley, 129, 131–134, 146
Industrial Revolution, 449
interest, 448
international law, 465
intolerance, 399
inventions, 380–382, 437
iron, 139, 301, 306
irrigation, 61–62, 68, 96, 118, 121–122, 132, 135
Islam, 184, 271, 280, 291, 360, 469
in Africa, 312–313, 315, 317, 322
controlling ideas of, 277–280, 282, 292, 420–421, 423
history of, 276–277
in Spain, 289–292, 392, 393, 400
Israel, 179, 185
Italy
natural environment, 232
Rome conquers, 244–245
See also Rome; Roman Empire; Roman Republic

Japan
agriculture, 344–345, 366
civilization of, 190, 343–346
classes of society in, 351–352, 366
feudalism in, 350–351, 366
natural environment, 344
and other cultures, 356, 366
religions in, 346–349, 353–356, 366
Jesus, 255, 256–259, 268, 400
Jews, 179, 180–182, 186, 256, 260, 290, 400
Joan of Arc, 397–399
John, King of England, 414
joint-stock companies, 448–449
Judah, 179
Judaism, 153, 168–186, 190, 256, 468

history of the Hebrews, 174–179
spread of, 183–185, 255
Ten Commandments, 176–178
Judeo-Christian view, 266, 267, 394, 424–426, 453

knights-in-armor, 375–378, 383, 386, 411
chivalry of, 389–394, 416
Koran, 277
Korea, 343, 344
Kublai Khan, 365
Kumbi, 310–311, 313
Kush-Meroë, 298–301, 322

land bridges, 47–48, 68, 331
language, 2, 441, 459
language family, 408–409, 416
Latin Christendom, 423
defense of, 373–375
governments in, 409–413
in High Middle Ages, 385, 389–416
Jews in, 400
learning in, 406–407
in Middle Ages, 370–385, 386
troubles in, 397–400
Latins, 231, 232, 234
latitude, 27, 29, 32, 36
laws, 54, 244
written, 114–116, 118, 244
laws of nature, 201, 267
legends, 2
levees, 59–60
liberty, 466
life expectancy, 454, 455
lines of longitude, 15–16
longitude, 15, 22, 27, 29, 36
low pressure area, 326–327
Luther, Martin, 450, 451

Magna Carta, 414, 416, 469
majority, 205
Mali, 304, 312–317
manor, 378–380, 386, 446, 447
Mansa Musa, 312, 314–317
map grids, 25–26
maps, 25–26, 36
market, 64, 93
market economy, 406

Maya, 331–334, 340
Mecca, 275–277, 317
medieval period. See Middle Ages; High Middle Ages
Mediterranean climate, 193, 232
medium of exchange, 94
mercantilism, 446, 457, 470
meridian, 15–16, 22, 27
Meroë, 298, 301
Mesoamerica, 190, 325, 331–340
religion in, 337–339
Mesopotamia, 68, 73, 86, 89
first agriculture, 56–62, 333
later empires in, 126–127, 139–141
See also Sumer
Messiah, 255
Middle Ages, 302–304, 322, 370–385, 425–426
Middle East, 33–35, 190
empires of, 139–141
See also Judaism
military dictators, 122–124, 146, 251, 252, 254, 469
military technology, 136–139, 146, 373–375, 435
millennium, 10
minority, 205
mixed government, 240, 244
moat, 383
Modern Age, 303–304, 419, 456, 465
rapid change in, 454–455
Mohenjo-Daro, 132, 134
monarchy, 205
money-and-market economy, 446–448
Mongolia, 357–358, 362
Mongols, 357–358, 360–362, 461
rule of China, 362–365, 367, 422–423
monopoly, 444–446
monotheism, 173, 186, 201
monotheist, 173
moral values, 465–466
Moses, 176–178, 256–258
mosque, 277, 317
movable type, 437
Muhammad, 271, 275–280, 282, 292
Muslims, 271, 289, 292, 358–360. See also Turks, Muslim
myths, 170. See also Greek myths

nation, 409, 410, 439–442
nationalism, 439–442, 456
nationality group, 441
national literature, 441
nation-state, 439–441, 456
natural environment, 39, 44, 56–57, 272, 333, 428
  of Africa, 295–297, 304–306
  of Greece, 192–198
  of Italy, 232
  of Japan, 344
Naturalism, 153, 198–228
  art, 203
  controlling ideas, 198
  government, 204–206, 211–213
  humanism and, 201–202, 267
  philosophy, 201, 221–222
  political science, 204–205
  religion, 199–201
natural law, 465–466
natural sciences, 198
natural vegetation, 296, 322
navigation, 432–434, 456
Neolithic period, 50, 63, 68, 333
Neolithic revolution, 52–54, 68
New Stone Age, 41
New World, 325, 331, 456
Nile River Valley, 129–131, 146
nirvana, 167
nomads, 122, 176, 272
nuclear family, 157

oasis, 274
oath of fealty, 377, 386
ocean currents, 326, 330
Octavian (Augustus), 252–254, 260
Odyssey, 196–197, 199
Old Stone Age, 41
Old World, 325
oligarchy, 205, 469
Olympic Games, 203
Orthodox church, 263, 370, 386
Ottoman Turks, 263, 361, 366, 421, 422
outcastes, 163, 164

Paleolithic period, 42–45, 63, 64, 68
Palestine, 178–179, 255

parallels of latitude, 27–28, 30–33
Parliament, 414
patricians, 239
patriotism, 398
peasants, 355, 377–379, 383
Peloponnesian War, 220, 228
Pericles, 213, 215, 216, 220, 224
Persian Empire, 77–79, 139–141, 146–147, 181, 189, 224
  wars with Greece, 207–211, 219, 228
pharaohs, 131, 176, 298
Philistines, 179
philosophers, 155, 201, 221–222
philosophy, 201, 221–222
physical traits, 45–47
plagues, 176
Plato, 223, 424
plebs, 239
plow, 62, 380
polar regions, 27, 31
political science, 204, 206
polytheism, 169, 182, 186, 199, 201, 238, 346
pope, 262, 370, 394
population, 453–454, 460
Portuguese, 356, 366, 429, 442
prehistoric times, 41, 44, 68
prehistory, 141, 147
priests, 96, 114, 118, 123–124, 333
prime meridian, 15
printing, 436–438
private capitalism, 449, 470
production, 63, 96, 97, 118
profit, 104
Prometheus, myth, 197–198
property, 54
prophets, 173, 180–181, 275–277
Protestant churches, 450–451
Punic Wars, 245–248
Punjab, 360

races (human), 45–49
rain-watered lands, 135–137, 146
raw materials, 96, 97
recent history, 304, 455
Reformation, 449–453, 457
reincarnation, 162–163, 164
religion
  earliest, 169

INDEX   **485**

Reformation and Counter Reformation, 449–453, 457
See also Crusades; gods; names of religions; names of countries and empires
religious persecution, 399–400
Renaissance, 426, 456
representative democracy, 212, 213, 239–240, 470
representative government, 412–415
republic, 238
revelation, 173
revolution (change), 52
revolution (Earth's), 8, 22
rice, 344–346, 366
river valleys, 127–136, 146
Roman Empire, 231, 252–253, 370, 425
under Augustus, 252–254, 260
Christianity and, 184, 259–262
decline of, 260–261
fall of, 231, 262–263, 267, 361, 369
Jews in, 184
Roman Republic, 268
culture change and social problems, 248–250
end of, 251, 254, 469
government, 238–241, 244
Punic Wars, 245–248
war with Etruscans, 241–243
Rome, 226, 268
conquers Palestine, 255
culture of, 189, 231
early, 232–238
legends of, 234–236, 241–243
life in, 236–238
Romulus and Remus, legend, 234–236
ronin, 352
rotation, 8, 22, 326
rule of law, 244
Russia, 422–423

salt, 309–311, 313
samurai, 250–255, 366, 389
Sargon I, 126, 146, 179
savanna, 296, 297, 322
saving, 92
Scheherezade, Queen, 282–286
scholar, 1

scriptures, 173, 180–181, 183, 186, 277, 400
scrub, 195
Senate, 239, 244
separation of church and state, 470
serfs, 377
Shinto, 346, 349, 366
ships, 431–433, 456
shogun, 351, 352, 355, 356, 366
Shubad, Queen, 82–83
silt, 59
silver, 85, 86, 94
slaves
in Africa, 309–310, 311
in the colonies, 320–321
in Egypt, 176, 298
in Greece, 205
in Rome, 248–249
in Sumer, 114, 179
social classes, 112–114, 238–239
social organization, 460, 462–463
social relationship, 158, 159
social sciences, 90, 91, 198
society, 40, 64, 156
Socrates, 221–222, 223
Solomon, 179
solstice, 33, 36
Song of Roland, 392
Songhai, 304, 317–318
Spain
Arabs in, 289–290, 292, 392, 393, 400
explorations, 339, 340, 429, 442
Sparta, 208, 210, 219–220, 228–229
specialize, 52–53, 63, 206
species, 1–2
spirits, 169
spring equinox, 14
steppe, 297, 322
Sudan, civilizations in, 189
Eastern, 298–302, 322
Western, 304–321, 323
See also Africa
Sumer, 68, 71–86
agriculture in, 59–62
culture of, 89–118
economic life in, 90–95, 97
fall of, 121–126, 146
government and laws in, 114–116

486 THE GROWTH OF CIVILIZATION

learning, 64, 102–109, 118, 200
  rediscovery of, 72–86
  religion in, 96–102, 169
  society in, 64, 110, 112–114, 118
  tombs, 80–84
  writing, 64–65, 76–79, 105–111, 436
Sumerians, 59
summer solstice, 33
Sundiata, 312–314

tablets, 75–77, 86, 106–108, 111, 436
Talmud, 185
Tarquin the Proud, 239, 241
taxes, 116, 310, 314
technology, 90, 339, 460–463
  changes in, 435–438, 456
  in exploration, 430–434
  mixed, 52
tels, 75–77, 86
temples, 102, 111, 124, 331, 333, 349
Ten Commandments, 176–178, 180
terminator, 13–14
Timbuktu, 315–316, 318
time, 22
  earth's axis and, 13–14
  earth's rotation and revolution and, 8–12, 22
  longitude and, 15
  measuring, in history, 5, 19–23
time zones, 16–18
Toltecs, 334–339
tools
  agricultural, 62, 306
  Neolithic, 41, 50, 53
  Paleolithic, 41, 43, 46
Torah, 173, 174, 182, 255
towns, rise of, 403–406
trade
  African, 306, 309–311, 313, 314
  Arab, 274–275, 286–288
  European, 420, 422, 428, 444–448
  growth of towns and, 404
  Sumerian, 93–95, 118
tragedies (drama), 216–217
tribunes of the people, 240, 244
tributaries, 360
tribute, 364
tropical rain forest climate, 296, 322
tropics, 30, 36

Turks, 263, 291, 293, 357–361
  Muslim, 360, 366, 373, 400–402
  Ottoman, 263, 361, 366, 421, 422
  Seljuk, 357, 361, 400
universal values, 465–466
universities, 406–407
Ur, 80–84, 86

values, 152–153
vassals, 377, 386

wars
  role of, 136, 146
  within a society, 122–124
  with other societies, 125–126
  See also military technology
Way of Heaven, 156, 159
Western culture, 190, 226, 228, 266–267
Western Europe
  civilization in, 385, 419
  Dark Ages in, 370–373
  geography and, 427–428, 456
  natural environment, 428
  See also Latin Christendom
wheel, 62, 95
Will of Heaven, 159–160
wind patterns, 326–330
winter solstice, 33
wood-block printing, 437
Woolley, Lady Katherine, 81–82
Woolley, Sir Leonard, 81–84
work force, 96, 97
world view, 149, 153–154. *See also* Buddhism; Confucianism; Judaism; Naturalism
writing
  cuneiform, 76–79, 86, 105–111, 118
  earliest, 41, 64–65, 79
  hieroglyphics, 129, 301
  Meroitic, 301
written laws, 114–116, 118

Xerxes, 181, 207, 210

Zen Buddhism, 353–354
zero, 105, 287, 288
ziggurat, 102

INDEX **487**

Acknowledgments

Photographs: pp. viii—Allyn and Bacon/Talbot D. Lovering. 3—Woodfin Camp & Associates/Marc and Evelyne Berheim. 4—Stock, Boston, Inc./Peter Menzel. 7—John Tenniel. 24—Stock, Boston, Inc./Jean-Claude Lejeune. 42—Editorial Photocolor Archives, Inc. 43—L. K. Marshall. 46 and 47—Lee Boltin. 63 and 65—The British Museum, London. 70—Editorial Photocolor Archives, Inc. 72—Historical Pictures Service Inc., Chicago. 75—Allyn and Bacon/Talbot D. Lovering. 76—The British Museum, London. 78—Editorial Photocolor Archives, Inc. 81T—The British Museum, London. 81B, 84, and 85—Editorial Photocolor Archives, Inc. 88 and 92—The British Museum, London. 93 and 95L—Editorial Photocolor Archives, Inc. 95R—Directorate General of Antiquities, Baghdad, Iraq. 99—University Museum, University of Pennsylvania. 101—The British Museum, London. 106—Lee Boltin. 107T—Collection of the General Theological Seminary. 107B—Editions Arthaud. 109 and 110—Editorial Photocolor Archives, Inc. 112—Walter A. Fairservis, Jr., *Mesopotamia: The Civilization That Rose Out of Clay* (with permission of Macmillan Publishing Co.). 115—University Museum, University of Pennsylvania. 117—The British Museum, London. 120—State Museum, Berlin. 125—The British Museum, London. 130T—Lee Boltin. 130CL and 130CR—Metropolitan Museum of Art, New York. 130B—Editorial Photocolor Archives, Inc. 131—Frank Siteman. 133TL and 133BR—Woodfin Camp & Associates/Jehangir Gazdar. 133TR—Editorial Photocolor Archives, Inc. 133BL—Photo Researchers/Paolo Koch. 134—Allyn and Bacon/Talbot D. Lovering. 135—Giraudon. 138—Editorial Photocolor Archives, Inc. 141—Stock, Boston, Inc./George Bellerose. 148—Museum of Fine Arts, Boston. 157—Editorial Photocolor Archives, Inc./Jan Lukas. 161—Metropolitan Museum of Art, New York. 165—Marilyn Gartman Agency/Milt and Joan Mann. 169—Editorial Photocolor Archives, Inc. 172L—The Jewish Museum, New York. 172R—Woodfin Camp & Associates/Sepp Seitz. 178—Jewish Theological Seminary/Frank J. Darmstadter. 183—The Bettman Archive, Inc. 185—deWys, Inc./Vidler. 188—Editorial Photocolor Archives, Inc. 195—Philip Jon Bailey. 196—Lou Jones. 199 and 200—Editorial Photocolor Archives, Inc. 203—The Image Bank/Steve Niedorf. 210—The Bettmann Archive, Inc. 212—Woodfin Camp & Associates/William Hubbell. 214 and 217—Editorial Photocolor Archives, Inc. 218—Portfolio. 223—Metropolitan Museum of Art, New York. David, *The Death of Socrates.* Woolfe Fund 1931. 225—Naples Museum, Italy. 230—Frank Siteman. 235—The Bettmann Archive, Inc. 237—Musée Clavet. 242—The Cleveland Museum of Art. Giovanni Battista Tiepolo, *Horatius Cocles Defending Rome Against the Etruscans.* Purchased from the J. H. Wade Fund. 245 and 249—Frank Siteman. 250—Allyn and Bacon/Talbot D. Lovering. 252 and 259—Editorial Photocolor Archives, Inc. 261—Hirmer Fotoarchio, Munchen. 263T—Editorial Photocolor Archives, Inc. 263B—Marilyn Gartman Agency/Donald Smetzer. 270—Allyn & Bacon/Talbot D. Lovering. 276—Stock, Boston, Inc./Diane Lowe. 278T—Museum of Fine Arts, Boston. 278B—Stock, Boston, Inc./Owen Franken. 279—Woodfin Camp & Associates/Abu Hander. 285TL—Editorial Photocolor Archives, Inc. 285TR—Peabody Museum, Salem. 285B—Marilyn Gartman Agency/Donald Smetzer. 291—Editorial Photocolor Archives, Inc. 294—American Museum of Natural History. 300—The Image Bank/Luis Villota. 307—Photo Researchers/Dr. Georg Gerster. 308T—American Museum of Natural History. 308B—Philip Jon Bailey. 311—Afrique Photo. 313—The British Museum, London. 315—Shostal Associates/E. Streichen. 316—The Brooklyn Museum. Gift of The Guennol Collection. 318—Metropolitan Museum of Art, New York. 321—Museum of Primitive Art. 324—Stock, Boston, Inc./Jim Holland. 330—Norwegian Information Service. 335—The Image Bank/Gerald Brimacom. 336-7, 336L, and 336R—Lee Boltin. 338T—Rainbow/Christiana D. Hmann. 338B—Peabody Museum/Harvard Hillel Burger. 342—Gemini Smith. 349—Editorial Photocolor Archives, Inc./Martha Cooper Guthrie. 355—Metropolitan Museum of Art, New York. 357—Sekai Bunka. 360L and 360R—Marilyn Gartman Agency/Milt and Joan Mann. 364L—Historical Pictures Service Inc., Chicago. 364R—The British Museum, London. 368—Jewish Theological Seminary/Frank J. Darmstadter. 373—Allyn and Bacon. 384 and 388—Editorial Photocolor Archives, Inc. 392—MAS, Barcelona. 395—The Bettmann Archive, Inc. 396—Allyn and Bacon/Talbot D. Lovering. 398—Editorial Photocolor Archives, Inc. 401—Brown Brothers. 403—The Bettmann Archive, Inc. 405—French Government Tourist Office. 410L—The Bettman Archive, Inc. 410R—Allyn and Bacon. 411 and 415—The Bettmann Archive, Inc. 418—Library of Congress. 421—Editorial Photocolor Archives, Inc. 423—Topkapi Sary Museum. 424 and 425—Editorial Photocolor Archives, Inc. 432—National Maritime Museum, Greenwich, England. 433L—The Bettmann Archive, Inc. 433R—The British Museum. 435L—The Bettmann Archive, Inc. 435R—Historical Pictures Service Inc., Chicago. 438—Bodleian Library, Oxford. England. 447—Historical Pictures Service Inc., Chicago. 449—Editorial Photocolor Archives, Inc. 451—The Bettmann Archive, Inc. 459TL—Museum of Fine Arts, Boston. 459TR—Jewish Theological Seminary/Frank J. Darmstadter. 459BR—Editorial Photocolor Archives, Inc./Martha Cooper Guthrie. 459BL—Museum of Fine Arts, Boston. 461—The Bettmann Archive, Inc.

Title page: L—Editorial Photocolor Archives, Inc. C—Metropolitan Museum of Art, New York. R—The British Museum, London.

Maps: I² Geographics.